THE UNDERSIDE OF AMERICAN HISTORY
Other Readings

THE UNDERSIDE
OF AMERICAN HISTORY
Other Readings

VOLUME II: since 1865

Edited by
THOMAS R. FRAZIER
The Bernard M. Baruch College of The City University of New York

Under the General Editorship of
JOHN MORTON BLUM
Yale University

HARCOURT BRACE JOVANOVICH, INC.
New York   Chicago   San Francisco   Atlanta

To Myles Horton and the Highlander Idea

Preface

The United States was forged in the crucible of conflict—conflict of ideas, conflict of economic and political systems, conflict of peoples with different cultural backgrounds, different needs, and different ambitions. Indeed, our history is the story of many peoples and of unsteady progress. Yet traditional history textbooks often trace the development of this country as though it were the gradual, almost natural, growth of a single people into a unified nation. Historians have concentrated on what they considered the dominant themes in American life—themes that almost invariably centered on the dominant groups of Americans. In the process they have sometimes overlooked vital aspects of the American past, neglecting whole groups within the nation. Today, the part of the past that has remained hidden—the "underside" of American history—is forcing itself into the public consciousness, and historians have begun to reexamine the past in order better to understand and to deal with the conflicts and stresses of the present.

The Underside of American History, intended to supplement existing textbooks, presents a selection of *un*traditional readings in American history. These readings deal in various ways with a variety of oppressed groups in America. They do not attempt to give an exhaustive catalog of the prejudices and injustices that have plagued American life, but they do offer vivid testimony to the fact that much of today's unrest has its roots deep in the nation's past.

This collection is arranged roughly chronologically: Volume I begins with the colonial period and continues through Reconstruction, and Volume II covers the period from Reconstruction to the present. Each volume contains a general introduction presenting the major themes to be taken up in the readings. In addition, each selection is introduced by a brief headnote placing the selection in the appropriate historical context and explaining its significance. Annotated bibliographies, with books available in paperback marked by an asterisk, close each of the books' major sections.

I gratefully acknowledge the advice and assistance of the following historians: Barton J. Bernstein of Stanford University, Selma Cantor Berrol of the Bernard M. Baruch College of the City University of New York, Dan T. Carter of the University of Maryland, and James M. McPherson of Princeton University. I also want to thank Joanna Freda, who provided valuable assistance in the preparation of the manuscript.

THOMAS R. FRAZIER

Contents

Depression 151

The Second World War and After 197

Revolt of the Victims 259

Contents

THE UNDERSIDE OF AMERICAN HISTORY
Other Readings

Introduction

To introduce the following readings, it may be helpful to provide a brief
sketch of the aspects of post–Civil War American history with which
they deal. As in Volume I of *The Underside of American History*, we
wish to stress at the outset that these notes and readings, within the
context of this collection, may suggest a harsher view of American
history than is actually warranted. They do, however, present an essential
part of the whole, and a part too often neglected in the standard narrative histories of this country.

In the Northern view, the Civil War was a struggle not only to
secure the Union but also to abolish slavery permanently. With Northern
victory over the rebellious Southerners, the United States government
won an opportunity to reorganize American political and economic life
so that the egalitarian ideas expressed in the Declaration of Independence
would extend to the lives of blacks as well as whites. And, indeed, federal
legislation in the decade after 1865 held out considerable promise for the
future of the democracy: the Thirteenth Amendment ended slavery or
involuntary servitude within the United States; the Freedmen's Bureau
was created to provide Southern blacks with services of various types;
universal male suffrage was established; and federal authority was used
in attempts to nullify the various "black codes" by which Southern states
sought to restrict the lives of the freedmen as they had restricted the lives
of the slaves. However, federal concern for the civil rights of the freedmen soon gave way to growing public sentiment for conciliation of the
South. Reaction to the deprivation of the war years and to the unprecedented federal intervention in states' affairs during the Reconstruction
period worked again to deprive Southern blacks of federal protection,
leaving them at the mercy of political opportunists and deeply embittered
Southern whites. By 1877, when the last of the Reconstruction governments collapsed, control over the South had passed back into the hands of
local officials. National unity had been restored, but only at the cost of
forcing the freed blacks back into positions of political and economic
dependence. For the most part, sharecroppers replaced slaves, and owner-

1

ship of the large plantations shifted from the planters of the old aristocracy to the prospering businessmen in the cities and towns.

In the last quarter of the nineteenth century, the moral fiber of the
nation appeared to disintegrate completely. Fraud and corruption characterized the post-Reconstruction governments in the South, and the
politics of the boss-controlled Northern cities were no better. The nation
as a whole embarked on a course of unabashed materialism that was to
earn the postwar decades the label "the Gilded Age," a term supplied
by Mark Twain. As industrial capitalism took root in the United States,
the world of business defined a new elite and a new ethic, and private
interests assumed a large measure of control over public policy. "Laissez
faire," or "let alone"—the very opposite of the philosophy that had prevailed during the brief Reconstruction period—became the watchword
of the age, with disastrous results for the traditionally oppressed groups
of Americans—the freedmen, Indians, laborers, and immigrants—for the
sprawling cities, and for the land itself, which was heedlessly exploited.
Laissez faire philosophy was written into new state constitutions, reviving
the doctrine of states' rights. And rigid segregation as well as systematic
disfranchisement proceeded apace in the South. The convict-lease system,
by which law enforcement authorities hired out prisoners to plantation
owners, and laws governing contract labor and "vagrancy" operated in
the interest of the powerful Southern whites, with the result that most
blacks were reduced to virtual serfdom by the end of the century.

In the postwar years, the theory of social Darwinism, an application
of the theory of evolution to society, provided a new rationale for the
idea of white supremacy. Adherents to this philosophy held that certain
natural laws operated to destroy the elements of society that were least
fit for survival. Thus, in the view of the social Darwinists, the best means
of improving society was to let nature take its course—to allow competitive struggle to purify civilization in the slow process of social evolution.
Running parallel to social Darwinism and based on equally dubious historical and scientific research were new racial theories asserting the
superiority of the Anglo-Saxon and his institutions. The term "Anglo-
Saxon" replaced the term "Protestant English" as the designation of the
self-conscious racial elite in the United States, and a cult of Anglo-Saxon
(or Teutonic, or Aryan, or Nordic) supremacy developed among the
upper classes of the East as well as among whites of the South. Antiblack
racism, which had existed for centuries in the New World (as well as in
the Old World), was now provided with "scientific" underpinnings, as
was prejudice against the Irish, Central and Southern Europeans (who
were mostly Catholics or Jews), East Asians, and all other ethnic, racial,
or religious groups who could not easily be assimilated into white Protestant culture.

Late in the nineteenth century, the new racism was put to the service
of imperialism. The "white man's burden" was seen as the need to extend
his civilization over all the world, and the old doctrine of Manifest
Destiny was revived to justify the new interest in extraterritorial expansion. "Scientific" racism increased sentiment for the restriction of immi-

gration until, in the first decade of the twentieth century, Congress effectively ended Chinese and Japanese immigration to this country. Furthermore, the racist ideology fueled antiblack feeling to the point that both rural and urban blacks across the country faced the constant threat of personal violence. As racist concepts fermented in both the North and the South, the first years of the twentieth century were perhaps the worst since the Civil War for American blacks. Between 1889 and 1918, more than two thousand blacks were murdered by white lynch mobs. So pervasive was the climate of violence in those years that white mobs lynched over seven hundred whites as well.

The Gilded Age was also a dark period in the history of American labor. The last two decades of the nineteenth century brought rapid economic expansion and increasing mechanization. Yet as industrialization progressed, the plight of urban laborers worsened. Child and convict labor were exploited, employers commonly used wage cuts and layoffs to increase profits, working weeks grew longer, and working conditions became ever harsher and more dangerous. The few national trade unions that had existed since the Civil War largely excluded blacks and immigrants; in any case, they protected only skilled craftsmen. Moreover, there was no federal legislation to protect factory workers. When in desperation these workers attempted to organize to improve their position, they met concerted resistance from factory owners, who sometimes hired private armies to thwart attempts at unionization. Especially during depressions, disputes between labor and capital tended to erupt into violence, and the number of strikes and lockouts soared. By the end of the century, the American Federation of Labor, stressing practical, economic goals rather than the moral or political aims of its predecessors, had successfully united the more conservative craft unions in a national body. Industrial unionism, however, was not really successful until the late 1930's, when a concerted campaign for organization in the mass-production industries finally won management recognition of the unions' right to bargain on behalf of their members.

Throughout the Gilded Age, powerful forces—including Protestantism and capital—fought to maintain the status quo. Yet there were strong dissident elements in American society, continuing the domestic tradition of social and political radicalism first expressed by the authors of the Declaration of Independence. As refugees from the failed republican and socialist revolutions of mid-nineteenth-century Europe came to the United States in search of a more receptive climate for their doctrines of social change, they reinforced the ranks of dissidents. Toward the end of the nineteenth century, socialists, communists, anarchists, and radicals of various convictions played leading roles in a variety of new movements and political parties that challenged the ideas and policies of the dominant groups in American life. Indeed, from colonial times to the present, radical ideas have given many Americans a vision of a more humane world than that produced by the uncontrolled competition of capitalism.

Populism, one protest movement of the turbulent 1890's, marked an important attempt to draw the groups most urgently in need of social and governmental reform—especially black and white farm laborers and industrial workers—into a single movement. Though the movement in itself made no significant gains, it paved the way for a new era of reform that opened with the twentieth century.

Progressivism, the new reform movement, grew out of a widespread recognition of the need to reassess and adjust American economic and political institutions. Spearheaded by President Theodore Roosevelt, the new movement reflected the energy of renewed prosperity and apparent stability. Generally, the Progressives' goal in politics was to return the government at its various levels to the people. This called for breaking up the political machines that dominated municipal, state, and national government. In economics, the Progressives called for breaking up the large industrial and financial combines—trusts, cartels, and other business coalitions—that had a stranglehold on the American economy and virtually owned the United States Senate.

Though in theory this movement was a reassertion of traditional democratic principles, it failed to take any real steps toward bringing the ethnic and religious minorities in America into the mainstream of American life. Indeed, the progressive movement was based squarely on America's comfortable and growing white urban middle class, and progressive ideas reflected the self-interest and the biases of this acknowledged elite. The white middle class tended to link the corruption of the cities with blacks and immigrants, especially after the large movement of Catholic and Jewish immigrants into Northern cities in the first decade of the twentieth century. Not incidentally, some of the political machines attacked by the Progressives were made up of immigrant groups that had formed voting blocs in an attempt to secure a voice in American government after normal routes to political power were closed to them.

In fact, the years in which Progressive ideas met their greatest triumphs were also years of some of the most violent social disruptions and the most oppressive governmental activity of this century. The administration of President Woodrow Wilson reversed a long-standing national policy against racial segregation of federal office workers. The Ku Klux Klan, which had originated in the South immediately after the Civil War, was revived in 1915 and was active for over a decade not only in the South but in Northern cities, where it attacked blacks, Catholics, Jews, and "aliens" generally. Violent race riots exploded in the North and the South, culminating in the bloody summer of 1919. Both laborers and immigrants were increasingly suspected of radicalism, and radicalism was increasingly associated with the "red menace." Government suppression of assumed radicals reached mammoth proportions at the end of the First World War, when, during the Red Scare of 1919 and 1920, thousands of people were arrested on dubious charges of subversion and sedition and many innocent immigrants were deported. Fear and resentment of immigrants reached such heights that in the 1920's Congress halted virtually all immigration from countries outside Western Europe. The much contested, unenforceable Prohibition Amendment of 1919 was perhaps indicative of the Progressives' rather naive faith in moral legislation as the solution to social ills.

On the positive side, the Progressives undertook several significant and useful reforms that moved state and city governments closer to the ideal of representative government. Also, they generally supported the goals of organized labor, thereby bringing about industrial labor reforms that were long overdue.

Perhaps more dramatically, the Progressives provided influential support for the women's suffrage movement, which had made little headway since the first women's rights convention in 1848. Ironically, by the time the feminists won the vote with the Nineteenth Amendment of 1920, the women's movement had split into so many factions that the new vote had little effect on existing social, economic, or political policy. Rather, most of the feminists came from the white middle class and voted in the interest of that group, reflecting the bias of the Progressives in general.

The 1920's were years of regression, as Americans, wearied by the First World War and disappointed with the results of the reform efforts of the preceding two decades, focused again on private interests. The government went a step beyond laissez faire to adopt a protective attitude toward business, and there was a resurgence of elitism among white Protestant Americans. Continued prosperity seemed to confirm the conviction of middle-class America that business was an agent of the general good. Yet the 1920's rivaled the Gilded Age as a period of corrupt political and financial operations. During these years, even the gains made by labor since the beginning of the century were all but nullified, as public opinion, political power, and even the United States courts sided with management in labor disputes arising from the disparity between wage increases and rising profits and the rising cost of living.

Two slogans that epitomized the attitudes of the dominant groups of Americans during the 1920's were voiced by Presidents: Harding called for a return to "normalcy"—which seems to have resembled the status quo of the 1880's—and Coolidge proclaimed that "the business of America is business." The pervasive materialism of this era of abandoned ideals alienated large numbers of Americans, particularly among the young and in the middle and upper classes. Often they responded by denying all interest in politics and all responsibility for public well-being. Thus rebellion took the form of pursuing private pleasures, winning the period such names as "the roaring 20's" and "the Jazz Age" and contributing to the post-urbanization breakdown of the traditional social structures without providing any viable alternatives.

During the reign of "normalcy" in American life, most of the structural problems of society were either ignored or expected to disappear with increasing affluence. What went largely unnoticed beyond the nation's farms was the fact that a serious agricultural depression was in progress, and that the slogans of good health and prosperity would mean nothing when the bubble of economic stability burst. Burst it did. With the crash of 1929, not only the United States but the entire Western world was plunged into the deepest and most far-reaching depression of modern times.

The Depression affected almost everyone in the country. Despite federal attempts to protect banks and industry, the bottom fell out of the

American stock market. Thousands fell from prosperity as a result of their own financial speculations. As investment and private spending dropped, many businesses were forced to shut down, causing widespread unemployment among both white-collar and industrial workers. Urban America was hard hit, but the nation's agricultural workers, whose position in the economy had been declining since the early twenties, suffered most from the economic collapse.

In the South most farm laborers, black and white, still worked as tenant farmers or sharecroppers, and foreclosures began adding to the numbers of tenants and migrants. These workers had virtually no economic or political power, though they often constituted a majority in their political jurisdictions. As farm prices went down and the federal government launched no positive program for control, agricultural laborers found themselves increasingly helpless, and violence flared up in rural America. Desperate workers attempted to organize to force aid from the landlords and the local political establishments, who were usually the same people. On the West Coast, migrant workers, many of foreign origin, also sought to protect themselves by banding together. However, most attempts at organization faltered before the joint opposition of landowners and law enforcement authorities. To this day, farm laborers—largely unorganized—remain one of the most depressed segments of the American working class. And, since the closing years of the Depression, federal attempts to aid agriculture have consisted primarily in granting government subsidies to the landlords without requiring that a just portion be passed along to the workers—a pattern that only reinforces the existing inequities.

The coming of the Second World War finally enabled the United States to recover from the Depression. The decision of the Roosevelt administration to supply war materiel for the Allies gave a spurt to American industry, and, with America's entry into the war in 1941, most of the nation's unemployment problems temporarily disappeared because of the demands of a wartime economy.

At the same time, the coming of war led to one of the most repressive acts in the history of American government—the arbitrary arrest and imprisonment of over 100,000 resident aliens and American citizens of Japanese ancestry. For several years these prisoners were kept in concentration camps in the nation's interior, while their property was confiscated without due process of law. The fact that German-Americans were not subjected to the same kind of treatment, even though many of them had openly supported the Nazi regime during the early years of the European war, testifies to the continued tendency of the dominant powers in America to discriminate against nonwhite minorities.

Probably never before or never since have the American people been as unified as they were during the Second World War. The pressures of the war economy brought industrial unions increased recognition and bargaining power, yet labor-management conflicts were few. Once the war was well under way, most Americans closed ranks in order to win it. In 1945, the atom bomb finally brought the war to a close, and those who had supported the Allied struggle for freedom abroad expected to share in the fruits of victory at home. Members of all minority groups had participated in the war, many nonwhites in segregated military units. Back in civilian life, they were unwilling to settle again for the second-class citizenship that had been forced upon them before the war. Especially in Northern cities, renewed racial unrest began to signal the presence of the volcano that was to erupt so visibly in the 1960's.

During and after the Second World War, American blacks won a series of minor victories in the area of civil rights. Under President Roosevelt, racial discrimination in the civil service and in the defense industry was curtailed somewhat, and in 1948 President Truman issued an executive order that officially ended segregation in the armed forces. Action in federal courts brought gains in the areas of voting rights and property ownership. With respect to public facilities, federal courts still upheld the "separate but equal" principle enunciated by the Supreme Court in 1896, but they at last seemed determined to see that separate facilities were truly equal. The Eisenhower administration continued the process of desegregating the civil service and the military.

Finally, in 1954, the civil rights movement won a major victory with a Supreme Court decision reversing the "separate but equal" doctrine by declaring segregated public schools inherently unequal. Although the federal government did little to implement the ruling—indeed, President Eisenhower opposed forced desegregation—minority groups in America began to feel renewed confidence in the regular political processes of the nation. Blacks of North and South as well as liberal whites joined in direct-action campaigns aimed at securing full citizenship rights for the minority populations of America, and leaders such as Martin Luther King emerged to champion nonviolent resistance to discrimination of all types.

The optimism of the late 1950's and early 1960's was shortlived, however, and by 1964 most nonwhite groups in America had ceased looking to Washington, to the courts, or even to sympathetic whites for assistance in their struggle. Legal victories had proved hollow for the masses of nonwhites, who were still virtually powerless economically and politically, and racism still pervaded white society. Now new leaders such as Malcolm X urged nonwhites to free themselves from white domination by any means possible—by revolution, if necessary. Oppressed groups of Americans increasingly repudiated the philosophy of nonviolent coercion, and a new string of uprisings exploded in urban ghettos. In a literal sense, the decade of the 1960's was marked by the revolt of the victims of American history.

Borrowing the metaphors of colonialism and stressing unity with the colonized peoples around the world who were seeking to throw off foreign domination, America's nonwhite minorities began to explore ways to achieve some degree of power and the right to self-determination in American society. The watchword of the revolution of the 1960's was "Black Power," a slogan first injected into the public consciousness in 1966 by young blacks of the Student Nonviolent Coordinating Committee (since renamed the Student "National" Coordinating Committee in keeping with its newly militant commitment). Other groups seeking similar freedoms adapted the slogan to their own use and took its lesson to heart. And so the cries of "Brown Power" were raised by Mexican-Americans, "Red Power" by American Indians, and "Woman Power" by militant feminists.

The programs of these various movements are often indefinite and shifting, but one thing is clear: the opportunity for self-determination and control over the institutions that govern their lives are basic demands of all groups. If the United States is to achieve a truly cohesive national identity, it must accept a changed one; it must become a genuinely pluralistic nation, able to acknowledge and accept the rights of different racial, ethnic, religious, and sex groups within its boundaries.

The
Gilded Age

Industrial Workers
Struggle for Power

HERBERT G. GUTMAN

Too often the history of the workingman in the United States has been depicted as the slow, inexorable growth of the craft union and, until the Second World War, the spectacular failures of industrial unionism. This is only a partial view of the American worker, however, for at no time in the history of our country have a majority of the workers been enrolled in unions.

Labor organizations were not widespread before the end of the Civil War, and with the possible exception of the labor movement during the Jacksonian period, they rarely had either a consistent program or sufficient power to carry out any projects they began. Even the Jacksonian labor movement died in the Panic of 1837 and the ensuing waves of unemployment, which—along with an influx of poor white immigrants—placed power in the hands of the owners of industry. Craft workers, since they remained in relatively short supply, were able to sell their skills individually and had little to gain from collective bargaining. The unskilled and semiskilled workers of factories and mines, however, were put at a great disadvantage by increased competition for jobs, for their work required little training and they were easily replaceable. Ironically, it was the craft unions that attained the earliest successes, and the skilled workers were those protected by the first permanent national labor organization, the American Federation of Labor (the AFL), which was founded in 1881.

After the Civil War, industrial development in the United States took place at a rate perhaps unprecedented in the history of the world. The great wealth of natural resources, the abundant—indeed, superabundant—supply of labor, and fifty years of peace (the ten-week Spanish-American War of 1898 being only a minor diversion in American life) favored the United States in its competition with European industrial powers.

During this period of rapid industrial advance, each new wave of immigrants, chiefly from Eastern and Southern Europe, stiffened the competition for unskilled jobs. Profiting from the oversupply of labor, the owners of many industries drove wages down and thus increased profits at the expense of the workers. In the contest for jobs and profits, various groups of workers were often pitted against one another, thus exacerbating existing hostilities among different religious and ethnic groups. Antiblack sentiment, in particular, received an ominous boost as blacks were increasingly used to fill positions vacated by strikers. In fact, the use of black workers as strikebreakers and as a threat to would-be labor organizers continued in industrial work at least until the formation of the Congress of Industrial Organizations (the CIO) in 1936, and to this day it continues in the Southern textile industry, which is perhaps the most underorganized in America. Many blacks have sometimes found it impossible to get jobs except as a result of labor-management strife.

Herbert G. Gutman, of the University of Rochester, has written extensively on the life of the ordinary workingman during the Gilded Age. He has pointed out how traditional labor historians distort the image of the American workingman by focusing on the most dramatic or the most successful episodes in his struggles. In the essay reprinted here, Gutman examines industrial workers' attempts to organize in the face of a growing alliance between industrial capitalists and state and national governments. In the process, he arrives at some surprising conclusions.

Until very recent times, the worker never seemed as glamorous or important as the entrepreneur. This is especially true of the Gilded Age, where attention focuses more readily upon Jim Fisk, Commodore Vanderbilt, or John D. Rockefeller than on the men whose labor built their fortunes. Most studies have devoted too much attention to too little. Excessive interest in the Haymarket riot, the "Molly Maguires," the great strikes of 1877, the Homestead lockout, and the Pullman strike has obscured the more important currents of which these things were only symptoms. Close attention has also focused on the small craft unions, the Knights of Labor, and the early socialists, excluding the great mass of workers who belonged to none of these groups and creating an uneven picture of labor in the Gilded Age.[1]

Labor history had little to do with those matters scholars tradition-

---

[1] See John R. Commons *et al.*, eds., *A Documentary History of American Industrial Society* (New York: Russell and Russell, 1958), IX, pp. i–viii.

"Industrial Workers Struggle for Power," by Herbert G. Gutman. From *The Gilded Age*, revised and enlarged edition, edited by H. Wayne Morgan (Syracuse, N.Y.: Syracuse University Press, 1970), pp. 31–53. Copyright 1963 and 1970 by Syracuse University Press. Reprinted by permission of the publisher.

ally and excessively emphasize. Too few workers belonged to trade unions to make the unions important. There was a fundamental distinction between wage earners as a social class and the small minority of the working population that belonged to labor organizations. The full story of the wage earner is much more than the tale of struggling craft unions and the exhortations of committed trade unionists and assorted reformers and radicals. A national perspective often misrepresented those issues important to large segments of the postbellum working population and to other economic and social groups who had contact with the wage earners.[2] Most of the available literature about labor in the Gilded Age is thin, and there are huge gaps in our knowledge of the entire period.[3] Little was written about the workers themselves, their communities, and the day-to-day occurrences that shaped their outlook. Excessive concern with craft workers has meant the serious neglect of the impact of industrial capitalism—a new way of life—upon large segments of the population.

A rather stereotyped conception of labor and of industrial relations in the Gilded Age has gained widespread credence, and final and conclusive generalizations about labor abound: "During the depression from 1873 to 1879, employers sought to eliminate trade unions by a *systematic* policy of lock-outs, blacklists, labor espionage, and legal prosecution. The *widespread* use of blacklists and Pinkerton labor spies caused labor to organize *more or less* secretly and *undoubtedly* helped bring on the violence that *characterized* labor strife during this period."[4] One historian asserts: "Employers *everywhere* seemed determined to rid themselves of 'restrictions upon free enterprise' by smashing unions."[5] The "*typical* [labor] organization during the seventies," writes another scholar, "was secret for protection against intrusion by outsiders."[6] Such seemingly final judgments are questionable: How *systematic* were lockouts, black-

[2] See Thomas C. Cochran, "The Social Sciences and the Problem of Historical Synthesis," in Fritz Stern, ed., *The Varieties of History* (New York: Meridian Books, 1956), pp. 352–56; Frank Tannenbaum, *A Philosophy of Labor* (New York: Knopf, 1951), p. 68; John Hall, "The Knights of St. Crispin in Massachusetts, 1869–1878," *Journal of Economic History,* 17 (June, 1958), 174–75.

[3] The literature is voluminous, if not always accurate or comprehensive; see Harold Williamson, ed., *The Growth of the American Economy* (New York: Prentice-Hall, 1951), p. 462; Anthony Bimba, *The Molly Maguires* (New York: International Pubs., 1932); J. Walter Coleman, *The Molly Maguire Riots* (Richmond, Va.: Garrett and Massie, 1936); George McNeil, ed., *The Labor Movement* (New York, 1892), pp. 241–67; Andrew Roy, *A History of the Coal Miners of the United States* (Columbus: J. L. Trauger, 1903); John R. Commons *et al., History of Labor in the United States* (New York: Macmillan, 1918), II, pp. 179–80; McAlister Coleman, *Men and Coal* (New York: Farrar & Rinehart, 1943), pp. 42–44; Arthur Suffern, *Conciliation and Arbitration in the Coal Industry of America* (Boston: Houghton Mifflin, 1915), pp. 7–17.

[4] Richard Lester, *Economics of Labor* (New York: Macmillan, 1947), p. 545; emphasis added.

[5] Herbert Harris, *American Labor* (New Haven: Yale University Press, 1938), p. 75.

[6] Selig Perlman, "Upheaval and Reorganization Since 1876," in Commons *et al., History of Labor,* II, p. 196.

lists, and legal prosecutions? How *widespread* was the use of labor spies and private detectives? Was the secret union the *typical* form of labor organization? Did violence *characterize* industrial relations?

It is widely believed that the industrialist exercised a great deal of power and had almost unlimited freedom of choice when dealing with his workers after the Civil War. Part of this belief reflects the weakness or absence of trade unions. Another justification for this interpretation, however, is more shaky—the assumption that industrialism generated new kinds of economic power which immediately affected the social structure and ideology. The supposition that "interests" rapidly reshaped "ideas" is misleading. "The social pyramid," Joseph Schumpeter pointed out, "is never made of a single substance, is never seamless." The economic interpretation of history "would at once become untenable and unrealistic . . . if its formulation failed to consider that the manner in which production shapes social life is essentially influenced by the fact that human protagonists have always been shaped by past situations."[7]

In postbellum America, the relationship between "interest" and "ideology" was very complex and subtle. Industrial capitalism was a new way of life and was not fully institutionalized. Much of the history of industrialism is the story of the painful process by which an old way of life was discarded for a new one so that a central issue was the rejection or modification of a set of "rules" and "commands" that no longer fitted the new industrial context. Since so much was new, traditional stereotypes about the popular sanctioning of the rules and values of industrial society either demand severe qualification or entirely fall by the wayside. Among questionable commonly held generalizations are those that insist that the worker was isolated from the rest of society; that the employer had an easy time and a relatively free hand in imposing the new disciplines; that the spirit of the times, the ethic of the Gilded Age, worked to the advantage of the owner of industrial property; that workers found little if any sympathy from nonworkers; that the quest for wealth obliterated nonpecuniary values; and that industrialists swept aside countless obstacles with great ease.

The new way of life was more popular and more quickly sanctioned in large cities than in small one- or two-industry towns. Put another way, the social environment in the large American city after the Civil War was more often hostile toward workers than that in smaller industrial towns. Employers in large cities had more freedom of choice than counterparts in small towns, where local conditions often hampered the employer's decision-making power. The ideology of many nonworkers in these small towns was not entirely hospitable toward industrial, as opposed to traditional, business enterprise. Strikes and lockouts in large cities seldom lasted as long as similar disputes outside of urban centers. In the large city, there was almost no sympathy for the city worker among the middle and upper classes. A good deal of pro-labor and anti-industrial sentiment flowed from similar occupational groups in the small towns. Small-town

---

[7] J. A. Schumpeter, "The Problem of Classes," in Reinhard Bendix and Seymour Lipset, eds., *Class, Status and Power* (Glencoe: Free Press, 1953), p. 79.

employers of factory labor often reached out of the local environment for aid in solving industrial disputes, but diverse elements in the social structure and ideology shaped such decisions.

The direct economic relationships in large cities and in small towns and outlying industrial regions were similar, but the social structures differed profoundly. Private enterprise was central to the economy of both the small industrial town and the large metropolitan city, but functioned in a different social environment. The social structure and ideology of a given time are not derived only from economic institutions.[8] In a time of rapid economic and social transformation, when industrial capitalism was relatively new, parts of an ideology alien to industrialism retained a powerful hold on many who lived outside large cities.

Men and their thoughts were different in the large cities. "The modern town," John Hobson wrote of the large nineteenth-century cities, "is a result of the desire to produce and distribute most economically the largest aggregate of material goods: economy of work, not convenience of life, is the object." In such an environment, "anti-social feelings" were exhibited "at every point by the competition of workers with one another, the antagonism between employer and employed, between sellers and buyers, factory and factory, shop and shop."[9] Persons dealt with each other less as human beings and more as objects. The *Chicago Times*, for example, argued that "political economy" was "in reality the autocrat of the age" and occupied "the position once held by the Caesars and the Popes."[10] According to the *New York Times*, the "antagonistic . . . position between employers and the employed on the subject of work and wages" was "unavoidable. . . . The object of trade is to get as much as you may and give as little as you can."[11] The *Chicago Tribune* celebrated the coming of the centennial in 1876: "Suddenly acquired wealth, decked in all the colors of the rainbow, flaunts its robe before the eyes of Labor, and laughs with contempt at honest poverty." The country, "great in all the material powers of a vast empire," was entering "upon the second century weak and poor in social morality as compared with one hundred years ago."[12]

Much more than economic considerations shaped the status of the urban working population, for the social structure in large cities unavoidably widened the distance between social and economic classes. Home and job often were far apart. A man's fellow workers were not necessarily his friends and neighbors. Face-to-face relationships became less meaningful as the city grew larger and production became more diverse and specialized. "It has always been difficult for well-to-do people of the upper and middle classes," wrote Samuel Lane Loomis, a Protestant minister, in the 1880's, "to sympathize with and to understand the needs of

[8] *Loc. cit.*

[9] Adna Weber, *The Growth of Cities in the Nineteenth Century* (New York: Macmillan, 1899), pp. 433–34.

[10] *Chicago Times*, May 22, 1876.

[11] *New York Times*, Nov. 20, 1876.

[12] *Chicago Tribune*, July 4, 1876.

their poorer neighbors." The large city, both impersonal and confining, made it even harder. Loomis was convinced that "a great and growing gulf" lay "between the working-class and those above them."[13] A Massachusetts clergyman saw a similar void between the social classes and complained: "I once knew a wealthy manufacturer who personally visited and looked after the comforts of his invalid operatives. I know of no such case now."[14] The fabric of human relationships was cloaked in a kind of shadowed anonymity that became more and more characteristic of urban life.[15]

Social contact was more direct in the smaller post–Civil War industrial towns and regions. *Cooper's New Monthly,* a reform trade union journal, insisted that while "money" was the "sole measure of gentility and respectability" in large cities, "a more democratic feeling" prevailed in small towns.[16] "The most happy and contented workingmen in the country," wrote the *Iron Molder's Journal,* "are those residing in small towns and villages. . . . We want more towns and villages and less cities."[17] Except for certain parts of New England and the mid-Atlantic states, the post–Civil War industrial towns and regions were relatively new to that kind of enterprise. Men and women who lived and worked in these areas usually had known another way of life, and they contrasted the present with the past.

The nineteenth-century notion of enterprise came quickly to these regions after the Civil War, but the social distance between the various economic classes that characterized the large city came much more slowly and hardly paralleled industrial developments. In the midst of the new industrial enterprise with its new set of commands, men often clung to older "agrarian" attitudes, and they judged the economic and social behavior of local industrialists by these values.

The social structure of the large city differed from that of the small industrial town because of the more direct human relationships among the residents of the smaller towns. Although many persons were not personally involved in the industrial process, they felt its presence. Life was more difficult and less cosmopolitan in small towns, but it was also less complicated. This life was not romantic, since it frequently meant company-owned houses and stores and conflicts between workers and employers over rights taken for granted in agricultural communities and large cities.[18] Yet the nonurban industrial environment had in it a kind

13 Samuel Lane Loomis, *Modern Cities and Their Religious Problems* (New York: Baker and Taylor, 1887), pp. 60–61, 63–66.

14 Massachusetts Bureau of Labor Statistics, *Second Annual Report 1870–1871* (Boston, 1871), p. 475.

15 See, e.g., Louis Wirth, "Urbanism as a Way of Life," in Paul Hatt and Albert Reiss, Jr., eds., *Cities and Society* (Glencoe: Free Press, 1957), pp. 36–63; Bert F. Hoselitz, "The City, the Factory, and Economic Growth," *American Economic Review,* 45 (May, 1955), 166–84.

16 "The Distribution of Wealth," *Cooper's New Monthly,* 1 (July, 1874), 7–9.

17 *Iron Molder's Journal,* Jan., 1874, 204.

18 See Ohio Bureau of Labor Statistics, *First Annual Report 1877* (Columbus, 1878), pp. 156–92.

of compelling simplicity. There the inhabitants lived and worked together, and a certain sense of community threaded their everyday lives.

The first year of the 1873 depression sharply suggested the differences between the large urban center and the small industrial town. There
was no question about the severity of the economic crisis. Its consequences were felt throughout the entire industrial sector, and production,
employment, and income fell sharply everywhere.[19] The dollar value
of business failures in 1873 was greater than in any other single year between 1857 and 1893.[20] Deflation in the iron and steel industry was especially severe: 266 of the nation's 666 iron furnaces were out of blast by
January 1, 1874, and more than 50 percent of the rail mills were silent.[21]
A New York philanthropic organization figured that 25 percent of the
city's workers—nearly 100,000 persons—were unemployed in the winter
months of 1873–74.[22]

"The simple fact is that a great many laboring men are out of work,"
wrote the *New York Graphic.* "It is not the fault of merchants and manufacturers that they refuse to employ four men when they can pay but one,
and decline to pay four dollars for work which they can buy for two and
a half."[23] Gloom and pessimism settled over the entire country, and the
most optimistic predicted only that the panic would end in the late spring
months of 1873.[24] James Swank, the secretary of the American Iron and
Steel Association, found the country suffering "from a calamity which
may be likened to a famine or a flood."[25]

A number of serious labor difficulties occurred in small industrial
towns and outlying industrial regions during the first year of the depression, revealing much about the social structure of these areas. Although
each had its own unique character, a common set of problems shaped
them all. Demand fell away and industrialists cut production and costs
to sell off accumulated inventory and retain shrinking markets. This general contraction caused harsh industrial conflict in many parts of the
country. "No sooner does a depression in trade set in," observed David
A. Harris, the conservative head of the Sons of Vulcan, a national craft

[19] A. Ross Eckler, "A Measure of the Severity of Depression, 1873–1932," *Review of
Economic Statistics,* 15 (May, 1933), 75–81; O. V. Wells, "The Depression of
1873–1879," *Agricultural History,* 11 (July, 1937), 237–49; Rendigs Fels, "American
Business Cycles, 1865–1879," *American Economic Review,* 41 (Sept., 1951), 325–49;
Alvin Hansen, *Business Cycles and National Income* (New York: Norton, 1951),
pp. 24–26, 39–41.

[20] T. E. Burton, *Financial Crises and Periods of Industrial and Commercial Depression* (New York: Appleton, 1902), p. 344.

[21] *Annual Report of the Secretary of the American Iron and Steel Association of
the Year 1874* (Philadelphia, 1875), pp. 4–5.

[22] New York Association for Improving the Condition of the Poor, *Thirty-first
Annual Report* (New York, 1874), p. 28.

[23] *New York Graphic,* Jan. 14, 1874.

[24] *American Manufacturer,* Oct. 30, 1873.

[25] *Annual Report of the Secretary of the American Iron and Steel Association for
the Year 1874,* pp. 12, 81–82.

union for puddlers and boilermen, "than all expressions of friendship to the toiler are forgotten."[26]

The *New York Times* insisted that the depression would "bring wages down for all time," and advised employers to dismiss workers who struck against wage reductions. This was not the time for the "insane imitations of the miserable class warfare and jealousy of Europe."[27] The *Chicago Times* stated that strikers were "idiots" and "criminals." Its sister newspaper, the *Chicago Evening Journal*, said the crisis was not "an unmixed evil," since labor would finally learn "the folly and danger of trade organizations, strikes, and combinations . . . against capital."[28] *Iron Age* was similarly sanguine. "We are sorry for those who suffer," it explained, "but if the power of the trade unions for mischief is weakened . . . the country will have gained far more than it loses from the partial depression of industry." Perhaps "simple workingmen" would learn they were misled by "demagogues and unprincipled agitators." Trade unions "crippled that productive power of capital" and retarded the operation of "beneficent natural laws of progress and development."[29] James Swank was somewhat more generous. Prices had fallen, and it was "neither right nor practicable for all the loss to be borne by the employers." "Some of it," he explained, "must be shared by the workingmen. . . . We must hereafter be contented with lower wages for our labor and be more thankful for the opportunity to labor at all."[30]

In cutting costs in 1873 and 1874, many employers found that certain aspects of the social structure and ideology in small industrial towns hindered their freedom of action. It was easy to announce a wage cut or refuse to negotiate with a local trade union, but it was difficult to enforce such decisions. In instance after instance, and for reasons that varied from region to region, employers reached outside of their environment to help assert their authority.

Industrialists used various methods to strengthen their local positions with workers. The state militia brought order to a town or region swept by industrial conflict. Troops were used in railroad strikes in Indiana, Ohio, and Pennsylvania; in a dispute involving iron heaters and rollers in Newport, Kentucky; in a strike of Colorado ore diggers; in two strikes of Illinois coal miners; and in a strike of Michigan ore workers.[31]

Other employers aggravated racial and nationality problems among workers by introducing new ethnic groups to end strikes, forcing men to work under new contracts, and destroying local trade unions. Negroes

---

[26] *Vulcan Record*, 1 (Sept., 1874), 12–14.

[27] *New York Times*, Oct. 27, Nov. 2, 15, 1873.

[28] *Chicago Times*, Oct. 3, Nov. 3, 1873.

[29] *Iron Molder's Journal*, 1 (Dec., 1873), 161; *Iron Age*, May 26, 1874, 14.

[30] *Annual Report of the Secretary of the American Iron and Steel Association for the Year 1874*, pp. 81–82.

[31] See Herbert G. Gutman, "Trouble on the Railroads in 1873–1874: Prelude to the 1877 Crisis," *Labor History*, 2 (Spring, 1962), 215–35; *Cincinnati Enquirer*, Feb.–March, 1874; *Chicago Times*, Nov. 12, 1873; *Chicago Tribune*, Nov. 10–20, 1874.

were used in coal disputes.[32] Danish, Norwegian, and Swedish immigrants went into mines in Illinois, and into the Shenango Valley and the northern anthracite region of Pennsylvania. Germans went to coal mines in northern Ohio along with Italian workers. Some Italians also were used in western Pennsylvania as coal miners, and in western and northern New York as railroad workers.[33] A number of employers imposed their authority in other ways. Regional, not local, blacklists were tried in the Illinois coal fields, on certain railroads, in the Ohio Valley iron towns, and in the iron mills of eastern Pennsylvania.[34] Mine operators in Pennsylvania's Shenango Valley and Tioga coal region used state laws to evict discontented workers from company-owned houses in midwinter.[35]

The social structure in these small towns and the ideology of many of their residents, who were neither workers nor employers, shaped the behavior of those employers who reached outside local environments to win industrial disputes. The story was different for every town, but had certain similarities. The strikes and lockouts had little meaning in and of themselves, but the incidents shed light on the distribution of power in these towns, on important social and economic relationships which shaped the attitudes and actions of workers and employers.

One neglected aspect of the small industrial town after the Civil War is its political structure. Because workers made up a large proportion of the electorate and often participated actively in local politics, they influenced local and regional affairs more than wage earners in the larger cities. In 1874, few workers held elected or appointed offices in large cities. In that year, however, the postmaster of Whistler, Alabama, was a member of the Iron Molder's International Union.[36] George Kinghorn, a leading trade unionist in the southern Illinois coal fields, was postmaster of West Belleville, Illinois.[37] A local labor party swept an election in Evansville, Indiana.[38] Joliet, Illinois, had three workers on its city council.[39] A prominent official of the local union of iron heaters and rollers sat on the city council in Newport, Kentucky.[40] Coal and ore miners ran for the state legislature in Carthage, Missouri, in Clay County, Indiana, and in Belleville, Illinois.[41] The residents of Virginia City, a town famous in western mythology, sent the president of the local miners' union to Con-

---

[32] *Workingman's Advocate*, March 28, June 27–July 4, 1874; John James, "The Miners' Strike in the Hocking Valley," *Cooper's New Monthly*, 1 (July, 1874), 4.

[33] *Chicago Tribune*, April 23, 1874; *Workingman's Advocate*, July 11–18, 1874; *New York World*, July 23, 1874.

[34] *Workingman's Advocate*, March 28, 1874; *Chicago Times*, Nov. 7–9, 1874; *Cincinnati Commercial*, Feb. 11, 1874; *Iron Age*, Aug. 13, 1874, 14.

[35] See Herbert G. Gutman, "Two Lockouts in Pennsylvania, 1873–1874," *The Pennsylvania Magazine of History and Biography*, 83 (July, 1959), 317–18, 322–26.

[36] *Iron Molder's Journal*, Dec., 1874, 138.

[37] *Chicago Tribune*, Nov. 19, 1874.

[38] *Workingman's Advocate*, April 14, 1874.

[39] *Ibid.*

[40] *Cincinnati Commercial*, Jan. 18, 1874.

[41] *Workingman's Advocate*, Sept. 5–12, Nov. 7, 28, 1874.

gress.[42] In other instances, town officials and other officeholders who were not wage earners sympathized with the problems and difficulties of local workers or displayed an unusual degree of objectivity during local industrial disputes.

Many local newspapers criticized the industrial entrepreneur, and editorials defended *local* workers and demanded redress for their grievances. Certain of these newspapers were entirely independent; others warmly endorsed local trade union activities.

The small businessmen and shopkeepers, lawyers and professional people, and other nonindustrial members of the middle class were a small but vital element in these industrial towns. Unlike the urban middle class they had direct and everyday contact with the new industrialism and with the problems and outlook of workers and employers. Many had risen from a lower station in life and knew the meaning of hardship and toil, and could judge the troubles of both workers and employers by personal experience. While they invariably accepted the concepts of private property and free entrepreneurship, their judgments about the *social* behavior of industrialists often drew upon noneconomic considerations and values. Some saw no necessary contradiction between private enterprise and gain and decent, humane social relations between workers and employers.

In a number of industrial conflicts, segments of the local middle class sided with workers. A Maryland weekly newspaper complained in 1876: "In the changes of the last thirty years not the least unfortunate is the separation of personal relations between employers and employees."[43] While most metropolitan newspapers sang paeans of joy for the industrial entrepreneur and the new way of life, the *Youngstown Miner and Manufacturer* thought it completely wrong that the "Vanderbilts, Stewarts, and Astors bear, in proportion to their resources, infinitely less of the burden incident to society than the poorest worker."[44] The *Ironton Register* defended dismissed iron strikers as "upright and esteemed . . . citizens" who had been sacrificed "to the cold demands on business."[45] The *Portsmouth Times* boasted: "We have very little of the codfish aristocracy, and industrious laborers are looked upon here with as much respect as any class of people."[46]

In 1873 when the depression called a temporary halt to the expansion of the Illinois mining industry, Braidwood, Illinois, was less than a dozen years old.[47] Coal mining and Braidwood had grown together, and by 1873, 6,000 persons lived in the town. Except for the supervisors and the small businessmen and shopkeepers, most residents were coal miners. Braidwood had no "agricultural neighborhood to give it support," and

---

[42] *Iron Molder's Journal*, Dec., 1874, 138.

[43] *Frostburg Mining Journal*, Nov. 25, 1876.

[44] *Cooper's New Monthly*, 1 (Jan., 1874), 16.

[45] *Iron Age*, March 5, 1874; *Cincinnati Commercial*, Jan. 29, Feb. 3, 1874.

[46] *Portsmouth Times*, Feb. 7, 1874.

[47] See Herbert G. Gutman, "The Braidwood Lockout of 1874," *Journal of the Illinois State Historical Society*, 53 (Spring, 1960), 5–28.

"without its coal-shafts" it would have had "no reasonable apology for existing." The town had three coal companies, but the Chicago, Wilmington and Vermillion Coal Company was by far the largest, and its president, James Monroe Walker, also headed the Chicago, Burlington and Quincy Railroad. This firm operated five shafts and employed 900 men—more than half the resident miners. Most of the owners did not live in the town. The miners were a mixed lot, and unlike most other small industrial towns in this era Braidwood had an ethnically diverse population. About half the miners came from Ireland. Another 25 percent were English, Welsh, and Scotch. A smaller number were Swedes, Italians, and Germans, and still others came from France and Belgium and even from Poland and Russia. There were also native-born miners. "The town of Braidwood," a contemporary noted, "is . . . nearly akin to Babel as regards the confusion of tongues." Although they came from diverse backgrounds, they were a surprisingly cohesive social community. A trade union started in 1872 was strong enough to extract a reasonable wage agreement from the three coal firms. A hostile observer complained that nearly all the voters were miners and that a majority of the aldermen and justices of the peace "are or have been miners."

The depression cut the demand for coal and created serious problems for the operators. By March, 1874, at least 25 percent of the miners were unemployed, and the town was "dull beyond all precedent." In late May the operators, led by the Chicago, Wilmington and Vermillion firm, cut the rate for digging coal from $1.25 to $1.10 a ton and cut the price for "pushing" coal from the work wall to the shaft nearly in half. They announced that the mines would close on June 1 unless the men accepted the new contract for a full year. The miners' efforts to compromise and suggestions of arbitration were summarily rejected, and the mines closed.

The Chicago, Wilmington and Vermillion company approached private labor contracting agencies in Chicago and recruited a large number of unskilled laborers, most of whom were Scandinavian immigrants and were not miners. Three days after the strike began, sixty-five Chicago workers arrived. More came two weeks later, and a few arrived daily until the end of July, when the number increased sharply. At the same time, anticipating trouble in putting the new men to work, the operators brought special armed Chicago Pinkerton police to the town.

Difficulties plagued the operators from the start. The miners realized they had to check the owners' strategy in order to gain a victory. As soon as new workers arrived, committees of miners explained the difficulty to them. "We ask the skilled miners not to work," the leader of the strikers explained. "As to green hands, we are glad to see them go to work for we know they are . . . a positive detriment to the company." All but three of the first sixty-five new workers decided to return to Chicago and, since they lacked funds, the miners and other local residents paid their rail fare and cheered them as they boarded a Chicago-bound train. By mid-July one shaft that usually employed two hundred men had no more than ten workers. At the end of July, only 102 men worked in the mines, and not one of them was a resident miner. The disaffected miners also met the challenge of the Pinkerton men. The miners appointed

a seventy-two-man committee to prevent violence and to protect company property. The mayor and the sheriff swore in twelve of these men
as special deputies, and, with one exception—when the wives of certain
miners chased and struck the son of famed detective Allan Pinkerton—
the miners behaved in a quiet and orderly manner.

Braidwood's tiny middle class "all back[ed] the miners." They denied
complaints by the owners that the miners were irresponsible and violent.
One citizen condemned the coal companies for creating "excitement so
as to crush the miners" and declared that "public sympathy" was "entirely" with the workers. The operators wanted Pinkerton and his men
appointed "special deputies" and made "merchant police" with power
to arrest persons trespassing on company properties, but the mayor and
the sheriff turned them down and deputized the strikers. Mayor Goodrich forbade parading in the streets by the Pinkerton men, and the sheriff
ordered them to surrender their rifles and muskets. He did not want "a
lot of strangers dragooning a quiet town with deadly weapons in their
hands," and feared the miners "a good deal less than . . . the Chicago
watchmen."

The operators faced other troubles. Local judges and police officials
enforced the law more rigorously against them and their men than against
the resident miners. Two new workers who got into a fight one Sunday
were arrested for violating the Sabbath law and fined fifty dollars and
court costs. Unable to pay the fine, they were put to work on the town
streets. Another, jailed for hitting an elderly woman with a club, was
fined one-hundred dollars and court costs. A company watchman was
arrested four times, twice for "insulting townspeople."

Frustrated in these and other ways by the miners and the townspeople, the operators finally turned for help to the state government, and
E. L. Higgins, the adjutant general and head of the state militia, went
to Braidwood to see if troops were needed. Higgins openly supported the
mine owners. He tried to prevent union men from talking with new
workers, and although he asked the mayor to meet him in the office of
the Chicago, Wilmington and Vermillion firm, he "never went to see
the officers of the city . . . to gain an unprejudiced account of the
strike." "If this is what the military forces and officers are kept for," one
miner observed, "it is high time . . . such men [were] struck off the
State Government payroll and placed where they belong." Mayor Goodrich reminded Higgins that neither the Braidwood nor the Will County
authorities had asked for state interference. In a bitter letter to the
Chicago Times, Goodrich wondered whether Higgins had come "in his
official capacity or as an agent of the coal company," and firmly insisted
that "the citizens of this city were not aware that martial law had been
proclaimed or an embargo placed upon their speech."

Unable fully to exercise their authority in the town and worried
about the possibility of losing the fall trade, the operators surrendered to
the strikers fourteen weeks after the struggle began. The final agreement
pleased the miners. They were especially amused when the Chicago,
Wilmington and Vermillion company agreed to send all the new workers
back to Chicago. A spokesman for the operators, however, bitterly as-

sailed the Braidwood mayor and other public officials for their failure
to understand the meaning of "peace, order, and freedom." Surely the
operators had further cause for complaint in 1877 when Daniel Mc-
Laughlin, the president of the miners' union, was elected mayor of Braidwood, other miners were chosen aldermen, and one became police magistrate.

Manufacturers in the small industrial iron towns of the Ohio Valley
such as Ironton and Portsmouth, Ohio, and Newport and Covington,
Kentucky, had similar troubles.[48] Several thousand men and fifteen iron
mills were involved in a dispute over wages that lasted for several months.
The mill owners who belonged to the Ohio Valley Iron Association cut
the wages of skilled iron heaters and roller men 20 percent on December
1, 1873. After the workers complained that the manufacturers were taking "undue advantage" of them "owing to the present financial trouble,"
their wages were cut another 10 percent. The valley mill owners worked
out a common policy; they decided to close all the mills for a month or so
in December and then reopen them under the new scale. Hard times
would bring new workers.

Although the mill owners in large cities such as St. Louis, Indianapolis, and Cincinnati found it easy to bring in new workers from the outside, it was another story in the small towns. They could hire new hands
in Pittsburgh, Philadelphia, and other eastern cities, but the social environment in Covington, Portsmouth, Newport, and Ironton made it
difficult to keep these men. Fellow townspeople sympathized with the
locked-out workers. In such an environment they were a relatively
homogeneous group and made up a large part of the total population of
the town. When workers agitated in small towns, paraded the streets, or
engaged in one or another kind of collective activity, their behavior
hardly went unnoticed.

The difficulties small-town iron manufacturers faced especially beset
Alexander Swift, owner of the Swift Iron and Steel Works in Newport,
Kentucky. Although his workers suffered from almost indescribable poverty after the factory closed, they would not surrender. When Swift
reopened the mill, he hired armed "special policemen." Some of the new
workers left town after they learned of the conflict, and the "police"
accompanied the rest to and from their work. The old workers made
Newport uncomfortable for new hands. There was no violence at first,
but many strikers and their wives, especially the English and Welsh
workers, gathered near the mill and in the streets to howl at the "black
sheep" going to and from work. The Newport workers exerted pressure
on them in "the hundred ways peculiar to workingmen's demonstrations."
Swift was embittered, for by the end of January only a few men worked
in his mill.

He was not alone. Mill owners in Covington, Ironton, and Portsmouth faced similar difficulty. Early in February, therefore, the Ohio
Valley Iron Association announced that unless the men returned to work

---

[48] See Herbert G. Gutman, "An Iron Workers' Strike in the Ohio Valley, 1873–
1874," *Ohio Historical Quarterly*, 68 (Oct., 1959), 353–70.

on or before February 20 they would lose their jobs and never again be hired in the valley iron mills. When most of the workers refused to return, they were fired. New workers were quickly brought to the towns, and Swift demanded special police protection for them from the Newport City Council, but it assigned only regular police. Crowds jeered the new men, and there were several fights. A large number of new workers again left Newport. "We never went any further with those fellows," a striker explained, "than calling them 'black sheep' and 'little lambs.'" Swift vainly appealed to the police to ban street demonstrations by the workers and their families, then armed the new men with pistols. When the strikers and their supporters gathered to jeer them, one of the imported laborers shot wildly into the crowd and killed a young butcher's helper. The enraged crowd chased Swift's men out of the city. After blaming the shooting on the failure of the Newport authorities to guard his men properly, Swift closed the mill.

These events did not go unnoticed in the Ohio Valley. The *Portsmouth Times* leveled a barrage of criticism at Swift and the other manufacturers. It asked whether or not they had a "right" to circulate the names of strikers in the same manner as "the name of a thief is sent from one police station to another." Such action was "cowardly . . . intimidation," and the *Times* asked: "Does not continued and faithful service deserve better treatment at the hands of men whose fortunes have been made by these workmen they would brand with the mark of CAIN? . . . Is this to be the reward for men who have grown gray in the service of these velvet-lined aristocrats? . . . Out on such hypocrisy!" After the shooting in Newport, the *Times* turned on Swift and called him a "bloodletter." Violence was wrong, the *Times* admitted, but "if the gathered-up assassins from the slums and alleys of the corrupt cities of the East are brought here to do deeds of lawlessness and violence, the stronger the opposition at the beginning the sooner they will be taught that the city of Portsmouth has no need of them."

Immune to such criticism, Swift continued to try to break down the strength of the Newport workers. In the end he succeeded. He realized that the only way to weaken the strikers was to suppress their power of public demonstration and therefore urged the Newport mayor to enforce local ordinances against dangerous and "riotous" crowds, asked the Kentucky governor to send state militia, and even demanded federal troops. Although the mayor banned "all unusual and unnecessary assemblages" in the streets, Swift still asked for state troops, and on March 5, the Kentucky governor ordered twenty-five members of the Lexington division of the state militia to Newport. Their arrival weakened the strikers and created a favorable environment for Swift. Street demonstrations were banned. The police were ordered to arrest "all persons using threatening or provoking language." When a number of unskilled strikers offered to return at the lower wage, Swift turned them away. He also rejected efforts by a member of the city council to effect a compromise with the old workers. A week after the troops arrived and three and a half months after the start of the lockout, Swift was in full control of the situation. New men worked in his factory, and the strikers admitted defeat.

The use of troops, however, was bitterly condemned in the Ohio Valley. A reporter for the *Cincinnati Enquirer* found that the "general opinion" in Newport was that Swift's maneuver was "little else that a clever piece of acting intended to kindle public sentiment against the strikers and . . . gain the assistance of the law in breaking up a strike." A Newport judge assailed the Kentucky governor, and a local poet sang of the abuse of public power:

> Sing a song of sixpence
>   Stomachs full of rye,
> Five-and-twenty volunteers,
>   With fingers in one pie;
>
> When the pie is opened
>   For money they will sing,
> Isn't that a pretty dish
>   For the City Council Ring?

There was less drama in the other Ohio Valley iron towns than in Newport, but the manufacturers in Portsmouth, Ironton, and Covington faced similar trouble. The old workers persuaded many new hands to leave the region. When fourteen men from Philadelphia arrived in Ironton and learned of the troubles for the first time, they left the city. Strikers paid their return rail fare. The same happened in Portsmouth, and the departing workers declared: "A nobler, truer, better class of men never lived than the Portsmouth boys . . . standing out for their rights." Nonstrikers in these towns also acted contrary to the manufacturers' interests. Each week the *Portsmouth Times* attacked the mill owners. "We are not living under a monarchy," the *Times* insisted, and the "arbitrary actions" of the employers were not as "unalterable as the edicts of the Medes and Persians."

A Covington justice of the peace illustrated something of the hostility felt toward the companies. Three strikers were arrested for molesting new hands, but he freed one and fined the others a dollar each and court costs. A new worker, however, was fined twenty dollars for disorderly conduct and for carrying a deadly weapon. He also had to post a five-hundred-dollar bond as a guarantee that he would keep the peace.

In the end, except in Newport, where Swift had successfully neutralized the power of the workers, a compromise wage settlement was finally worked out. Certain mills brought in new men, but some manufacturers withdrew the blacklist and rehired striking workers. A friend of the Ohio Valley iron manufacturers bitterly complained: "Things of this sort make one ask whether we are really as free a people as we pretend to be." This devotee of classical laissez-faire doctrine sadly concluded: "If any individual cannot dispose of his labor when and at what price he pleases, he is living under a despotism, no matter what form the government assumes."

Although hardly any Negroes worked in coal mines before 1873, soon after the depression started mine operators in the Ohio Hocking Valley recruited hundreds from border and southern cities. Some had been sparingly employed in certain Indiana and Ohio mines, but attracted little attention. It was different in the Hocking Valley in 1874. A large number of white miners struck and showed an unusual degree of unanimity and staying power. They found support from members of the local middle class, and the operators, unable to wear down the strikers, brought in Negroes. Although the miners were defeated, the problems they raised for their employers indicated much the same social environment as that in Braidwood and the Ohio Valley iron towns.

The railroad opened new markets for bituminous coal, and the years between 1869 and 1873 were a time of great prosperity. In 1870, 105,000 tons left the valley, and in 1873 just over 1,000,000 tons were shipped. Two years later, more than 20 percent of the coal mined in Ohio came from the Hocking Valley. Although entry costs were low, the ten largest firms in 1874 employed nearly two-thirds of the valley's miners.[49]

The miners fell into two social groupings. Those born in and near the valley had spent most of their lives in the mines and often held local positions of public trust and esteem. A Cincinnati reporter found that miners held "a good position in society . . . as a class" and filled "a fair number of municipal, church, and school offices." These men had seen their status depersonalized as they quickly became part of a larger labor force, dependent on a distant and uncontrollable market. They unavailingly complained when operators brought in many more miners than needed for full-time work. A perceptive observer found that many of the older miners "have worked in these mines since they were boys and feel they have an actual property right to their places." Most of the new men who flocked to the valley after 1869 came from distant areas, and a good number were from England, Wales, and Ireland. The rapid growth of the industry made it difficult to support trade unions in the valley.[50]

Economic crisis in 1873 suddenly punctured the region's prosperity. At best, miners found only part-time employment, and cash wages were less common than usual, for working miners were paid mostly in ninety-day notes and store credit. The operators complained that labor costs were too high and made the selling price of coal in a competitive but depressed market prohibitive. Talk of wage cuts, however, turned the miners toward trade unionism, and in December, 1873, they founded several branches of the newly established Miners' National Association. The operators in turn formed a region-wide trade association, and each of them posted a $5,000 bond as proof he would follow its directives. They also announced a sharp wage cut effective April 1, 1874, and entirely proscribed the new union.

49 See Herbert G. Gutman, "Reconstruction in Ohio: Negroes in the Hocking Valley Coal Mines in 1873 and 1874," *Labor History*, 3 (Fall, 1962), 243–64.
50 *Cincinnati Commercial*, May 23, June 4, 1874; Edward Wieck, *The American Miners' Association* (New York: Russell Sage Foundation, 1940), p. 141.

Prominent union leaders lost their jobs. One operator closed his supply store "for repairs," and another locked his men in a room and insisted that they sign the new wage agreement. But the union thrived. Only nine "regular" miners favored the new contract, and no more than twenty-five or thirty regulars refused to join the union. The union men agreed to the lower wage but refused to abandon their organization. The operators remained adamant and insisted that the "progress or decay" of the region hinged on the destruction of the new union—"a hydra too dangerous to be warmed at our hearth." A strike over the right of labor organization started on April 1.[51]

The strike brought trouble for the operators. Except for the *Logan Republican*, the weekly valley newspapers either supported the strikers or stood between them and the operators.[52] No more than thirty regular miners accepted the new contract on April 1, and only seventy men entered the mines that day. Local public officials declined to do the bidding of prominent operators. The New Straitsville police deputized strikers, and after Governor William Allen sent the state inspector of mines to investigate reported miner violence, country and town officials assured him there was no trouble and a committee of merchants and "other property owners" visited Allen "to give him the facts."

New Straitsville town officials joined the miners to check the effort of operator W. B. McClung to bring in from Columbus "a posse" of nine special police armed with Colt revolvers and Spencer rifles. The miners felt it "unnecessary" for armed police to come to "their quiet town," and men, women, and children paraded the streets in protest. They made it uncomfortable for McClung's police, and he promised to close his mine and return the men to Columbus. But the mayor, on the complaint of a miner, issued a warrant for their arrest for entering the town armed, "disturbing the peace and quiet." Ordered to stand trial, the nine left town after McClung's superintendent posted their bond.

Except for the Nelsonville operators, other owners closed their mines on April 1 for two months and waited out the strikers. Toward the end of May, the operators divided among themselves. A few settled with strikers, but the largest rejected arbitration and rebuked the union.[53] Compromise was out of the question, insisted the more powerful operators, and they attacked the governor for not sending militia. The triumph of the union would soon lead to the "overthrow" of "our Government and bring upon us anarchy and bloodshed that would approach, if not equal, the Communism of Paris."[54]

Unable to exert authority from within, the owners brought in between 400 and 500 Negroes in mid-June. Most came from Memphis, Louisville, and Richmond; few were experienced coal miners. They were offered high wages, told nothing of the dispute, and were generally misinformed about conditions. One employer admitted that "the motive for

[51] *Cincinnati Commercial*, May 23, 1874; *Hocking Sentinel*, Dec. 25, 1873, Jan. 8, 22, Feb. 12, 26, March 5, 1874.
[52] *Logan Republican*, April 4, 1874.
[53] *Cincinnati Commercial*, May 23, 1874; *Workingman's Advocate*, May 23, 1874.
[54] *Athens Messenger*, May 7, 1874.

introducing the Negro was to break down the white miners' strike."
Another boasted of his "great triumph over Trades-Unions" and called
the use of Negroes "the greatest revolution ever attempted by operators
to take over their own property." Gathered together in Columbus, the
Negroes then were sped by rail to one of the mines, which was turned
into a military camp. The county sheriff, twenty-five deputies, and the
governor's private secretary were also there. Apparently with the approval
of these officials, the operators armed the Negroes with "Government
muskets," bayonets, and revolvers, and placed them on "military duty"
around the property. No one could enter the area unless endorsed "by
the operators or police." In the meantime, state militia were mobilized in
nearby Athens, in Chillicothe, and in Cincinnati.[55]

Anger swept the Hocking Valley when the strikers learned of this.
The first day 1,000 miners and their families stood or paraded near the
Negro encampment. No violence occurred, but the men called across
picket lines of armed Negroes and urged them to desert the operators.
The second day even more miners paraded near the encampment and
urged the Negroes to leave. The miners succeeded in "raiding" the operators with an "artillery of words," and around 120 Negroes went back
on the operators. Two of the defectors admitted they had been "led by
misrepresentations to come North" and "wouldn't interfere with white
folks' work." They defended unions as "a good thing" and advocated
"plenty of good things" for everyone. The strikers housed the Negroes
in union lodge rooms, and with the help of local citizens raised about
five-hundred dollars to help them return South. But this was only a small
victory for the strikers. Enough Negroes remained to strengthen the
hand of the operators and to demoralize the union men. Negroes went
to other mines, even though strikers begged them not to work and
"mothers held their children in their arms pointing out the negroes to
them as those who came to rob them of their bread."[56]

Outside the Hocking Valley, the press applauded the operators. The
Cleveland Leader thought the strikers were "aliens"; the *Cincinnati Commercial* called them drunkards, thieves, and assassins. In the Hocking
Valley, however, some residents complained of the "mercenary newspaper men and their hired pimps." The valley newspapers especially
criticized the owners for using Negroes. Some merchants and other business folk also attacked the operators. Certain Nelsonville businessmen
offered aid to the strikers and unsuccessfully pleaded with the operators
to rehire all the miners. The police also were friendly, and the New
Straitsville mayor prevented the sending of militia to his town.[57]

Destruction of the union and the introduction of Negro workers did
not bring industrial harmony. There were strikes over wage cuts in 1875
and 1877, and conflict between Negro and white miners. In 1875, when
the men resisted a wage cut, the employers tacitly admitted that their

55 *Hocking Sentinel*, April 1, 1874; *Chicago Tribune*, June 30, 1874.
56 *Cincinnati Commercial*, June 13, 14, 15, 1874; *New Lexington Democratic Herald*,
    June 18, 1874.
57 *Cleveland Leader*, July 7, 1874.

power in the valley still was inadequate. Two of them, W. F. Brooks and T. Longstreth, visited Governor Allen and pleaded that he "restore order" in the valley towns. The governor was cautious, however, and sent no troops. But their pleas revealed the employers' anxieties and need for outside power.[58]

Nothing better illustrated the differences between the small town and large city than attitudes toward public works for the unemployed. Urban newspapers frowned upon the idea, and relief and welfare agents often felt that the unemployed were "looking for a handout." The jobless, one official insisted, belonged to "the degraded class . . . who have the vague idea that 'the world owes them a living.' " Unemployed workers were lazy, many said, and trifling.[59]

Native-born radicals and reformers, a few welfare officers, ambitious politicians, responsible theorists, socialists, and "relics" from the pre– Civil War era all agitated for public works during the great economic crisis of 1873–74. The earliest advocates urged construction of city streets, parks and playgrounds, rapid transit systems, and other projects to relieve unemployment. These schemes usually depended on borrowed money or fiat currency, or issuance of low-interest-rate bonds on both local and national levels. The government had aided wealthy classes in the past; it was time to "legislate for the good of all not the few." Street demonstrations and meetings by the unemployed occurred in November and December of 1873 in Boston, Cincinnati, Chicago, Detroit, Indianapolis, Louisville, Newark, New York, Paterson, Pittsburgh, and Philadelphia. The dominant theme at all these gatherings was the same: unemployment was widespread, countless persons were without means, charity and philanthropy were poor substitutes for work, and public aid and employment were necessary and just.[60]

The reaction to the demand for public works contained elements of surprise, ridicule, contempt, and genuine fear. The Board of Aldermen refused to meet with committees of jobless Philadelphia workers. Irate Paterson taxpayers put an end to a limited program of street repairs the city government had started. Chicago public officials and charity leaders told the unemployed to join them "in God's work" and rescue "the poor and suffering" through philanthropy, not public employment.[61]

The urban press rejected the plea for public works and responsibility for the unemployed. Men demanding such aid were "disgusting," "crazy," "loud-mouthed gasometers," "impudent vagabonds," and even "ineffable asses." They were ready "to chop off the heads of every man addicted to clean linen." They wanted to make "Government an institution to pillage

[58] *Cincinnati Commercial*, Oct. 3, 1874, March 22, 1875; *New Lexington Democratic Herald*, March 25, 1875; *Hocking Sentinel*, March 4, 25, 1875; *Ohio State Journal*, April 1, 1875.

[59] *New York Graphic*, Nov. 10, 1873; *Chicago Tribune*, Dec. 23, 1873; New York Association for Improving the Condition of the Poor, *Thirtieth Annual Report, 1873* (New York: 1873), pp. 41 ff.

[60] *New York Sun*, Oct. 22, Nov. 4, Nov. 20–Dec. 20, 1873; *Chicago Times*, Dec. 1– 31, 1873.

[61] *New York World*, Dec. 27, 1873; see sources in note 60.

the individual for the benefit of the mass." Hopefully, "yellow fever, cholera, or any other blessing" would sweep these persons from the earth. Depressions, after all, were normal and necessary adjustments, and workers should only "quietly bide their time till the natural laws of trade" brought renewed prosperity. Private charity and alms, as well as "free land," were adequate answers to unemployment. "The United States," said the *New York Times*, "is the only 'socialistic,' or more correctly 'agrarian,' government in the world in that it offers good land at nominal prices to every settler" and thereby takes "the sting from Communism." If the unemployed "prefer to cling to the great cities to oversupply labor," added the *Chicago Times*, "the fault is theirs."[62]

None of the proposals of the jobless workers met with favor, but the demand by New York workers that personal wealth be limited to $100,000 was criticized most severely. To restrict the "ambition of building up colossal fortunes" meant an end to all "progress," wrote the *Chicago Times*. The *New York Tribune* insisted that any limitation on personal wealth was really an effort "to have employment without employers," and that was "almost as impossible . . . as to get into the world without ancestors."[63]

Another argument against public responsibility for the unemployed identified this notion with immigrants, socialists, and "alien" doctrine. The agitation by the socialists compounded the anxieties of the more comfortable classes. Remembering that force had put down the Paris Communards, the *Chicago Times* asked: "Are we to be required to face a like alternative?" New York's police superintendent urged his men to spy on labor meetings and warned that German and French revolutionaries were "doing their utmost to inflame the workingman's mind." The *Chicago Tribune* menacingly concluded, "The coalition of foreign nationalities must be for a foreign, non-American object. The principles of these men are wild and subversive of society itself."[64]

Hemmed in by such ideological blinders, devoted to "natural laws" of economics, and committed to a conspiracy theory of social change so often attributed only to the lower classes, the literate nonindustrial residents of large cities could not identify with the urban poor and the unemployed. Most well-to-do metropolitan residents in 1873 and 1874 believed that whether men rose or fell depended on individual effort. They viewed the worker as little more than a factor of production. They were sufficiently alienated from the urban poor to join the *New York Graphic* in jubilantly celebrating a country in which republican equality, free public schools, and cheap western lands allowed "intelligent working people" to "have anything they all want."[65]

The attitude displayed toward the unemployed reflected a broader

[62] *New York Tribune*, Dec. 12, 1873.

[63] *Ibid.*

[64] *Chicago Times*, Dec. 23, 30, 1873; *Chicago Tribune*, Dec. 23–30, 1873.

[65] See *Chicago Tribune*, Dec. 29, 1873; Thurlow Weed to the Editor, *New York Tribune*, Dec. 20, 1873; *Cumberland Civilian and Times* (Maryland), Feb. 12, 1874.

and more encompassing view of labor. Unlike similar groups in small towns, the urban middle- and upper-income groups generally frowned upon labor disputes and automatically sided with employers. Contact between these persons and the worker was casual and indirect. Labor unions violated certain immutable "natural and moral laws" and deterred economic development and capital accumulation.[66] The *Chicago Times* put it another way in its discussion of workers who challenged the status quo: "The man who lays up not for the morrow, perishes on the morrow. It is the inexorable law of God, which neither legislatures nor communistic blatherskites can repeal. The fittest alone survive, and those are the fittest, as the result always proves, who provide for their own survival."[67]

Unions and all forms of labor protest, particularly strikes, were condemned. The *New York Times* described the strike as "a combination against long-established laws," especially "the law of supply and demand." The *New York Tribune* wrote of "the general viciousness of the trades-union system," and the *Cleveland Leader* called "the labor union kings . . . the most absolute tyrants of our day." Strikes, insisted the *Chicago Tribune*, "implant in many men habits of indolence that are fatal to their efficiency thereafter." Cleveland sailors who protested conditions on the Great Lakes ships were "a motley throng and a wicked one," and when Cuban cigar makers struck in New York, the *New York Herald* insisted that "madness rules the hour."

City officials joined in attacking and weakening trade unions. The mayor forbade the leader of striking Philadelphia weavers from speaking in the streets. New York police barred striking German cigar workers from gathering in front of a factory whose owners had discharged six trade unionists, including four women. Plain-clothes detectives trailed striking Brooklyn plasterers. When Peter Smith, a nonunion barrel maker, shot and wounded four union men—killing one of them—during a bitter lockout, a New York judge freed him on $1,000 bail supplied by his employers and said his employers did "perfectly right in giving Smith a revolver to defend himself from strikers."[68]

Brief review of three important labor crises in Pittsburgh, Cleveland, and New York points out different aspects of the underlying attitude toward labor in the large cities. The owners of Pittsburgh's five daily newspapers cut printers' wages in November, 1873, and formed an association to break the printers' union. After the printers rejected the wage cut and agreed to strike if nonunion men were taken on, two newspapers fired the union printers. The others quit in protest. The *Pittsburgh Dispatch* said the strikers "owe no allegiance to society," and the other publishers condemned the union as an "unreasoning tyranny." Three publishers started a court suit against more than seventy union members charg-

[66] *New York Tribune*, June 22, 1874.

[67] *Chicago Times*, Aug. 26, 1874.

[68] *New York Herald*, Nov. 2, 1873; *New York Times*, June 3, 1874; *Cleveland Leader*, June 18, 1874; *Chicago Tribune*, April 15, 1874.

ing them with "conspiracy." The printers were held in $700 bail, and the strike was lost. Pittsburgh was soon "swarming with 'rats' from all parts of the country," and the union went under. Though the cases were not pressed after the union collapsed, the indictments were not dropped. In 1876, the *Pittsburgh National Labor Tribune* charged, "All of these men are kept under bail *to this day* to intimidate them from forming a Union, or asking for just wages." A weekly organ of the anthracite miners' union attacked the indictment and complained that it reiterated "the prejudice against workingmen's unions that seems to exist universally among officeholders."[69]

In May, 1874, Cleveland coal dealers cut the wages of their coal heavers more than 25 percent, and between four- and five-hundred men struck. Some new hands were hired. A foreman drew a pistol on the strikers and was beaten. He and several strikers were arrested, and the coal docks remained quiet as the strikers, who had started a union, paraded up and down and neither spoke nor gestured to the new men. Police guarded the area, and a light artillery battery of the Ohio National Guard was mobilized. Lumber heavers joined the striking workers, and the two groups paraded quietly on May 8. Although the strikers were orderly, the police jailed several leaders. The strikers did not resist and dispersed when so ordered by the law. In their complaint to the public, they captured the flavor of urban-industrial conflict:

> The whole thing is a calumny, based upon the assumption that if a man be poor he must necessarily be a blackguard. Honest poverty can have no merit here, as the rich, together with all their other monopolies, must also monopolize all the virtues. We say now . . . we entertain a much more devout respect and reverence for our public law than the men who are thus seeking to degrade it into a tool of grinding oppression. We ask from the generosity of our fellow citizens . . . to dispute [*sic*] a commission of honest men to come and examine our claims. . . . We feel confident they will be convinced that the authorities of Cleveland, its police force, and particularly the formidable artillery are all made partisans to a very dirty and mean transaction.

The impartial inquiry proved unnecessary; a few days later several firms rescinded the wage cut, and the strikers thanked these employers.[70]

Italian laborers were used on a large scale in the New York building trades for the first time in the spring of 1874. They lived "piled together like sardines in a box" and worked mainly as ragpickers and street cleaners. They were men of "passionate dispositions" and, "as a rule, filthy beyond the power of one to imagine." Irish street laborers and unskilled workers were especially hard on Italians, and numerous scuffles between

[69] *Pittsburgh Post*, Nov. 21–30, 1873.
[70] *Cleveland Plain Dealer*, May 7–11, 1874.

the two groups occurred in the spring of 1874. In spite of the revulsion toward the Italians as a people, the *New York Tribune* advised employers that their "mode of life" allowed them to work for low wages.[71]

Two non-Italians, civil engineers and contractors, founded the New York Italian Labor Company in April, 1874. It claimed 2,700 members, and its superintendent, an Italian named Frederick Guscetti, announced: "As peaceable and industrious men, we claim the right to put such price upon our labor as may seem to us best." The firm held power of attorney over members, contracted particular jobs, provided transportation, supplied work gangs with "simple food," and retained a commission of a day's wages from each monthly paycheck. The company was started to protect the Italians from Irish "adversaries," and Guscetti said the men were willing to work "at panic prices." The non-Italian managers announced the men would work for 20 percent less in the building trades. Employers were urged to hire them "and do away with strikes."[72]

Protected by the city police and encouraged by the most powerful newspapers, the New York Italian Labor Company first attracted attention when it broke a strike of union hod carriers. Irish workers hooted and stoned the Italians, but the police provided them with ample protection. The *Cooper's New Monthly* complained that "poor strangers, unacquainted with the laws and customs and language of the country," had been made "the dupes of unprincipled money sharks" and were being "used as tools to victimize and oppress other workingmen." This was just the start. The firm advertised its services in *Iron Age*. By the end of July, 1874, it had branched out with work gangs in New York, Massachusetts, and Pennsylvania.[73]

There is much yet to learn about the attitude toward labor that existed in large cities, but over all opinion lay a popular belief that "laws" governed the economy and life itself. He who tampered with them through social experiments or reforms imperiled the whole structure. The *Chicago Times* was honest, if callous, in saying: "Whatever cheapens production, whatever will lessen the cost of growing wheat, digging gold, washing dishes, building steam engines, is of value. . . . The age is not one which enquires when looking at a piece of lace whether the woman who wove it is a saint or a courtesan." It came at last almost to a kind of inhumanity, as one manufacturer who used dogs and men in his operation discovered. The employer liked the dogs. "They never go on strike for higher wages, have no labor unions, never get intoxicated and disorderly, never absent themselves from work without good cause, obey orders without growling, and are very reliable."[74]

The contrast between urban and rural views of labor and its fullest

---

[71] *New York Toiler*, Aug. 22, 1874; *New York Sun*, July 6, 1874; Board of Health of the City of New York, *Fourth Annual Report, May 1, 1873 to April 30, 1874* (New York, 1874), pp. 96–97.

[72] *New York Times*, June 25–30, 1874; *New York Tribune*, June 2–14, 1874.

[73] *New York Sun*, June 2, 10, 1874; *New York World*, July 23–24, 1874.

[74] *Chicago Times*, May 22, 1876; *Iron Age*, April 27, 1876, 24.

role in society and life is clear.[75] In recent years, many have stressed "entrepreneurship" in nineteenth-century America[76] without distinguishing between entrepreneurs in commerce and trade and those in industrial manufacturing. Reflecting the stresses and strains in the thought and social attitudes of a generation passing from the old pre-industrial way of life to the new industrial America, many men could justify the business ethic in its own sphere without sustaining it in operation in society at large or in human relationships. It was one thing to apply brute force in the marketplace, and quite another to talk blithely of "iron laws" when men's lives and well-being were at stake.

Not all men had such second thoughts about the social fabric which industrial capitalism was weaving, but in the older areas of the country the spirits of free enterprise and free action were neither dead nor mutually exclusive. Many labor elements kept their freedom of action and bargaining even during strikes. And the worker was shrewd in appealing to public opinion. There is a certain irony in realizing that small-town America, supposedly alien and antagonistic toward city ways, remained a stronghold of freedom for the worker seeking economic and social rights.

But perhaps this is not so strange after all, for pre-industrial America, whatever its narrowness and faults, had always preached personal freedom. The city, whose very impersonality would make it a kind of frontier of anonymity, often practiced personal restriction and the law of the economic and social jungle. As industrialism triumphed, the business-man's powers increased, yet he was often hindered—and always suspect— in vast areas of the nation which cheered his efforts toward wealth even while condemning his methods.[77]

Facile generalizations are easy to make and not always sound, but surely the evidence warrants a new view of labor in the Gilded Age. The standard stereotypes and textbook clichés about its impotence and division before the iron hand of oppressive capitalism do not quite fit the facts. Its story is far different when surveyed in depth, carrying in it overtones of great complexity. And even in an age often marked by lust for power, men did not abandon old and honored concepts of human dignity and worth.

[75] See Gutman, "Two Lockouts in Pennsylvania, 1873–1874," and Gutman, "Trouble on the Railroads in 1873–1874: Prelude to the 1877 Crisis."

[76] Louis Hartz, *The Liberal Tradition in America* (New York: Harcourt, Brace, 1955), pp. 110–13, 189–227; Richard Hofstadter, *The American Political Tradition and the Men Who Made It* (New York: Knopf, 1948), pp. v–ix; John Higham, ed., *The Reconstruction of American History* (New York: Humanities Press, 1962), pp. 21–24, 119–56.

[77] Cochran, *Railroad Leaders,* p. 181.

Blacks and
Poor Whites
in the South

C. VANN WOODWARD

While there has been a great deal of controversy about the role of blacks in Reconstruction, there is no doubt that in the years after Reconstruction blacks were relegated to a distinctly degrading position. After 1865, the policies of Radical Republican Reconstruction had won for blacks in the South voting rights and a variety of political offices. However, with the coming in 1877 of what whites were to call "Redemption"—the full restoration of home-rule in the South—most black politicians were removed from office and left with no direct influence. Occasionally—before the various state governments contrived to deprive most blacks of the ballot—the black vote was mobilized against the growth of the Democratic party in the South and nationally, but after 1877 the black voice in Southern politics grew increasingly weak.

From the first days of emancipation, the masses of ex-slaves were less interested in politics than in gaining some degree of economic independence. Since their only experience was with the farm, real freedom for them depended on having their own plots of land. In early Reconstruction, there were several proposals to break up the ante-bellum plantations and to provide each freedman with the all-important "forty acres and a mule." These came to nothing, however, and the great majority of the former slaves became tenant farmers and sharecroppers and remained bound to the land through debt to the landowners. Those who tried to escape the new system of economic bondage were faced with a return to forced labor through the convict-lease system, by which the South further exploited primarily black labor.

In the postwar years, agriculture went into a slump throughout the nation, particularly in the war-ruined South. Poor whites in the South—like blacks, rural laborers for the most part—were left with little basis for self-respect aside from their feelings of superiority to blacks. Thus it became increasingly important to them to keep blacks in a subordinate position. While the black man had been a slave, the distinction in status was clear; but now that he was free, the competition for status became acute. Since both whites and blacks were in a depressed financial condition, simple economic distinctions could not be made. Insecure whites found the solution to their status problems in segregation—an institution that had hardly been necessary in ante-bellum America—and they encouraged the willing legislatures to enact laws severely restricting the activities of blacks. By the end of the nineteenth century, aided by several decisions of the Supreme Court, the segregationists had constructed a dual society in the South such that the least distinguished white was able to convince himself that he was better than the most distinguished black.

Also in the postwar years, poor whites began to drift from the fields and hills of the South into the newly developed mill towns. But industry offered them merely a new type of misery, for owners kept wages at a minimum and responded to signs of labor unrest by threatening to replace white laborers with blacks.

It is one of the tragedies of American history that poor whites and blacks were never able to join together in order to force Southern capitalism to institute some form of industrial democracy. The Populist movement in the 1890's did briefly stimulate cooperation between blacks and whites, but by early in the twentieth century even Populist leaders were emphasizing racial hatred rather than interracial cooperation. Indeed, with few exceptions, poor whites through the years have not only refused to work with blacks for common goals but have sought the blacks' subordination, with the result of depriving both labor groups of important allies in their struggle against management.

In the following selection, C. Vann Woodward, of Yale University, describes the subjugation of the freedmen and the beginnings of industrialization in the post-Reconstruction South, explaining the process by which masses of blacks and whites were trapped in poverty.

If Reconstruction ever set the bottom rail on top, it was not for long and never securely. Redemption seemed to leave little doubt that the bottom rail was again on the bottom—whatever its temporary dislocation. It remained for the New South to find what Reconstruction had failed to find:

"Blacks and Poor Whites in the South." From C. Vann Woodward, *Origins of the New South, 1877–1913* (Baton Rouge, La.: Louisiana State University Press, 1951), pp. 205–34. Reprinted by permission.

the measure of the emancipated slave's freedom and a definition of free labor, both black and white; for the white worker's place in the New Order would be vitally conditioned by the place assigned the free black worker.

Much discussion about the Negro's civil rights, his political significance, his social status, and his aspirations can be shortened and simplified by a clear understanding of the economic status assigned him in the New Order. Emancipation and Reconstruction had done little to change that picture. The lives of the overwhelming majority of Negroes were still circumscribed by the farm and plantation. The same was true of the white people, but the Negroes, with few exceptions, were farmers without land. Questionnaires from the census of 1880 revealed that in thirty-three counties of Georgia where Negro population was thick, "not more than one in one hundred" Negro farmers owned land; the same proportion was reported from seventeen black Mississippi counties; twelve others reported not one in twenty, and many not one in fifty. From Tennessee as a whole the report was that only "a very small part of the Negroes own land or even the houses in which they live"; also from Louisiana and Alabama came reports of "very few" owners.[1]

More specific information is provided for one state by the report of the Comptroller General of Georgia for the year ending October 1, 1880. Of a total of some $88,000,000 in land value, the Negroes, who made up nearly half the state's population, owned around $1,500,000. Of a total of some $23,000,000 in value put upon cattle and farm animals, the Negroes owned about $2,000,000, and of some $3,200,000 in agricultural tools, the Negroes reported a little more than $163,000.[2] It is pretty clear that as a rule the Negro farmer not only worked the white man's land but worked it with a white man's plow drawn by a white man's mule. In the next two decades the race's landholdings improved slightly, but in 1900 black Georgians had taxable titles to only one twenty-fifth of the land; only 14 per cent of the Negro farmers owned their farms, and in 1910 only 13 per cent.[3] In the South as a whole, by 1900, 75.3 per cent of the Negro farmers were croppers or tenants.[4]

The landless Negro farmers, like the landless whites, worked either for wages or for shares, under any of several arrangements. When the Alabama planter furnished tools, animals, and feed, as well as the land, his share was one half of all crops; when he furnished only the land he took one fourth of the cotton and one third of the corn. There were numerous variations, including the "two-day system" on Edisto Island, where the tenant worked two days of the week

---

[1] *Tenth Census, 1880,* V, *Cotton Production,* "Mississippi," 154–55; "Tennessee," 104–05, "Louisiana," 83–84; VI, *Cotton Production,* "Georgia," 172–73.

[2] Quoted in [Glenn W.] Rainey ["The Negro and the Independent Movement in Georgia" (manuscript in possession of its author)], Chap. I.

[3] [Robert P.] Brooks [*The Agrarian Revolution in Georgia, 1865–1912* (Madison, 1914)], 44, 122.

[4] United States Census Bureau, *Negro Population in the United States, 1790–1915* (Washington, 1918), 571–72.

for the landlord in the feudal manner.[5] The impression of uniformity in the labor system that replaced slavery would seem to have been exaggerated. As late as 1881 it was reported that in Alabama "you can hardly find any two farmers in a community who are carrying on their business alike," and frequently one planter might use several methods at once: "To one he rents, to another he gives a contract for working on shares, to another he pays wages in money, and with another he swaps work, and so *ad infinitum*." Whatever system was used "there follows the same failure, or partial failure."[6]

The share system called forth especially severe criticism from all sides as being "ruinous to the soil" and "a disgrace to farming." A large proportion of landlords preferred and used the wage system. From Tennessee in 1880 it was reported that "advocates for shares and wages are about equally divided in number." Census reports of wages paid for labor in cotton production in 1880 make no distinction between white and black workers, and there probably was little difference. Prevalent monthly wages for a man's work "from sun to sun" were $8.00 to $14.00 in Alabama; $8.00 to $15.00 in Arkansas; $6.00 to $10.00 in Florida; $5.00 to $10.00 in Georgia ($4.00 to $6.00 per month for women); $6.00 to $15.00 in Louisiana; $8.00 to $12.00 in Mississippi, South Carolina, and Tennessee; $8.00 to $15.00 in Texas. Daily wages were usually 50 cents with board, or 75 cents without. A year's wages for a man in the central cotton belt of Georgia were $60.00 to $100.00; in Tennessee they were $100.00 to $125.00. Both yearly and monthly wages included rations.[7] In 1888 it was estimated by an authority that "the regular allowance of an ordinary hand is 12 pounds of bacon and 5 pecks of meal by the month," which "would cost him twenty-three dollars in the course of twelve months."[8]

It should be noted that the year 1880, for which the wage rates are quoted, was a relatively "good" year for cotton prices. When the price fell to half that in the nineties the wages could not have been nearly so high. If a yield of only three to six bales per hand could be expected, as estimated in Arkansas in 1880, the product of a year's labor would likely bring little more than $100.00 on the market in the middle nineties. Working on shares, the cropper at that rate received about $50.00 for his year's work. Neither he nor his landlord was likely to see or handle any cash, since both were in all probability deeply enmeshed in the toils of the crop lien. They received instead meager supplies at the prices demanded of credit customers.

The tides of Negro migration that had set in during Reconstruction, as the first and most characteristic expression of freedom, continued to move in the same general directions for some years after Redemption.

---

[5] *Tenth Census, 1880*, V, *Cotton Production*, 60–66; VI, *Cotton Production*, 154–55.

[6] Montgomery *Advertiser*, August 12, 1881.

[7] *Tenth Census, 1880*, V, *Cotton Production*, "Arkansas," 104–05; "Louisiana," 83–84; "Mississippi," 154–55; "Tennessee," 104–05; "Texas," 160–61; VI, *Cotton Production*, "Alabama," 154–55; "Florida," 70–71; "Georgia," 172–73; "South Carolina," 60–66.

[8] Philip A. Bruce, *The Plantation Negro as a Freeman* (New York, 1889), 200–01.

These movements were of three kinds: from the country to the towns; from the poorer lands to the delta, bottom, and richer lands; and from the older states to the newer states of the Southwest. Intermittent complaint and a few laws against "enticing" labor persisted through the eighties. With one striking exception, however, the Negro migrations were largely from one part of the South to another. The great exodus northward did not begin until a half century after freedom.[9]

A census survey of the relation of land and labor in the cotton state of Alabama in 1880 revealed that the Negroes were most thickly concentrated upon the most fertile soil in the state, and the whites, upon the poorest soil; that the most fertile land, where the sharecropping system was most prevalent, yielded the least product, and was rapidly being exhausted; that poorer lands under cultivation by owners produced greater yield per capita and per acre; and that the white farmer was rapidly gaining on the black in the proportion of cotton produced.[10]

In spite of these facts, there was an almost universal preference among Black-Belt landlords for Negro tenants and workers. "White labor is totally unsuited to our methods, our manners, and our accommodations," declared an Alabama planter in 1888. "No other laborer [than the Negro] of whom I have any knowledge, would be as cheerful, or so contented on four pounds of meat and a peck of meal a week, in a little log cabin 14 x 16 feet, with cracks in it large enough to afford free passage to a large sized cat."[11] "Give me the nigger every time," echoed a Mississippi planter. "The nigger will never 'strike' as long as you give him plenty to eat and half clothe him: He will live on less and do more hard work, when properly managed, than any other class, or race of people. As Arp truthfully says 'we can boss him' and that is what we southern folks like."[12]

The writer who estimated the cash value of freedom for the Negro thirty years after emancipation at a little less than one dollar a year to the individual[13] overstated his point, though not so grossly as it might seem. At least such expensive luxuries as civil liberties and political franchises were beyond his reach. He knew very well that immediate, daily necessities came first—land, mules, plows, food, and clothes, all of which had to be got from a white man who oftener than not had too little himself.

In the working out of a new code of civil rights and social status for the freedman—in the definition of the Negro's "place"—Reconstruction had been only an interruption, the importance of which varied from state to state, but which was nowhere decisive. The transition from slavery to

---

[9] The exception was the "Exodus" of 1879. This has been treated by . . . [E. Merton] Coulter [*The South During Reconstruction, 1865–1877*, in *A History of the South*, VIII (Baton Rouge, 1947)], 100–01. On Negro migration, see [Vernon L.] Wharton [*The Negro in Mississippi, 1865–1890*, in the *James Sprunt Studies in History and Political Science*, XXVIII (Chapel Hill, 1947)], 106–24.

[10] *Tenth Census, 1880*, VI, *Cotton Production*, "Alabama," 64.

[11] A. W. S. Anderson, in *Proceedings of the Third Semi-Annual Session of the Alabama State Agricultural Society* (Montgomery, 1888), 93–95.

[12] Quoted in Wharton, *Negro in Mississippi*, 121.

[13] [Walter G.] Cooper [*The Piedmont Region* . . . (Atlanta, 1895)], 77.

caste as a system of controlling race relations went forward gradually and tediously. Slavery had been vastly more than a labor system, and the gap that its removal left in manners, mores, and ritual of behavior could not be filled overnight. The so-called "Black Codes" were soon overthrown, as were the laws imported by the Carpetbaggers. Redemption and Hayes's policy of *laissez faire* left the code to be worked out by Southern white men. It has already been pointed out that there was no unity of opinion among them concerning the Negro's political rights. There also existed a roughly comparable division with reference to his civil rights.

Hampton, Lamar, Nicholls, and Redeemers of that type gave their solemn pledges in the Compromise of 1877 to protect the Negro in all his rights. They were probably guilty of less hypocrisy than has been charged. The class they represented had little to fear from the Negro and at the same time considerable to gain for the conservative cause by establishing themselves in a paternalistic relationship as his protector and champion against the upland and lower-class whites. This would better enable them to control his vote (against the same white element), not to mention his labor. In 1877 J. L. M. Curry listened to a debate of the Virginia Assembly in Jefferson's neoclassic capitol. "A negro member," he recorded with evident satisfaction in his diary, "said that he and his race relied for the protection of their rights & liberties, not on the 'poor white trash' but on the 'well-raised' gentlemen."[14] Black-Belt white men were casual about their daily intimacy and easy personal relations with Negroes, an attitude that made upland Southerners uncomfortable and shocked Northerners, even Radical Carpetbaggers. So long as this old leadership retained strong influence, the racial code was considerably less severe than it later became.

In the early years of freedom saloons in Mississippi usually served both whites and blacks at the same bar; many public eating places, "using separate tables, served both races in the same room"; public parks and buildings were still open to both to a great extent; and segregation in common carriers was not at all strict.[15] The most common type of discrimination on railways was the exclusion of Negroes from the first-class, or "ladies'" car. The races were accustomed to sharing the second-class coach. In 1877, however, a South Carolinian wrote that Negroes were "permitted to, and frequently do ride in first-class railway and street railway cars" in his state. This had caused trouble at first but was "now so common as hardly to provoke remark."[16] In 1885 George W. Cable, who was sensitive regarding discrimination, reported that in South Carolina Negroes "ride in the first class cars as a right" and "their presence excites no comment," while "in Virginia they may ride exactly as white people

---

[14] Diary of J. L. M. Curry, January 13, 1877, in [The Jabez L. M. Curry Papers (Division of Manuscripts, Library of Congress)].

[15] Wharton, *Negro in Mississippi*, 232. The evolution of "caste as a method of social control" is admirably worked out by this author.

[16] Belton O'Neall Townsend, "South Carolina Society," in *Atlantic Monthly*, XXXIX (1877), 676. Commenting in 1879 on the "perfect equality" of races in Southern tramcars, a member of Parliament wrote: "I was, I confess, surprised to see how completely this is the case; even an English Radical is a little taken aback at first." Sir George Campbell, *White and Black* . . . (New York, 1879), 195.

do and in the same cars."[17] Even the ante-bellum practice of using a common cemetery continued for many years. White papers occasionally "mistered" Negro politicians, if they were "good" politicians, and a Richmond paper affirmed in 1886 that "nobody here objects to sitting in political conventions with negroes. Nobody here objects to serving on juries with negroes."[18] Even the Tillman legislation of 1891 defeated a Jim Crow bill for railway cars.

From the beginning, however, concessions to the harsher code and developing phobias of the hillbillies of the white counties had to be made. There were South Carolinians in numbers who did not share the Charleston *News and Courier*'s feeling that it was "a great deal pleasanter to travel with respectable and well-behaved colored people than with unmannerly and ruffianly white men."

It is one of the paradoxes of Southern history that political democracy for the white man and racial discrimination for the black were often products of the same dynamics. As the Negroes invaded the new mining and industrial towns of the uplands in greater numbers, and the hill-country whites were driven into more frequent and closer association with them, and as the two races were brought into rivalry for subsistence wages in the cotton fields, mines, and wharves, the lower-class white man's demand for Jim Crow laws became more insistent. It took a lot of ritual and Jim Crow to bolster the creed of white supremacy in the bosom of a white man working for a black man's wages. The Negro pretty well understood these forces, and his grasp of them was one reason for his growing alliance with the most conservative and politically reactionary class of whites against the insurgent white democracy. A North Carolina Negro wrote: "The best people of the South do not demand this separate car business . . . and, when they do, it is only to cater to those of their race who, in order to get a big man's smile, will elevate them [*sic*] to place and power." He believed that "this whole thing is but a pandering to the lower instincts of the worst class of whites in the South."[19]

The barriers of racial discrimination mounted in direct ratio with the tide of political democracy among whites. In fact, an increase of Jim Crow laws upon the statute books of a state is almost an accurate index of the decline of the reactionary regimes of the Redeemers and triumph of white democratic movements. Take, for example, the law requiring separate accommodations for the races in trains, said to be "the most typical Southern law." No state[20] enacted such a law for more than

---

[17] [George W.] Cable [*The Silent South* (New York, 1885)], 85–86. Cable was quoting the Charleston *News and Courier* with regard to South Carolina. The observation on Virginia custom is his own.

[18] Richmond *Dispatch*, October 13, 1886.

[19] Editorial, *Southland* (Salisbury, N.C.), I (1890), 166–67.

[20] The Tennessee legislature passed an act in 1875 abrogating the common law and releasing common carriers and other public servants from serving anyone they chose not to serve. A Federal circuit court declared this unconstitutional in 1880. An act of 1881 required separate first-class accommodations for Negroes, but left the two races unsegregated in second-class coaches. Stanley J. Folmsbee, "The Origin of the First 'Jim Crow' Law," in *Journal of Southern History*, XV (1949), 235–47.

twenty years after 1865. Yet in the five years beginning in 1887 one after another adopted some variation of the law: Florida in 1887, Mississippi in 1888, Texas in 1889, Louisiana in 1890, Alabama, Arkansas, Kentucky, and Georgia in 1891. These were the years when the Farmers' Alliance was first making itself felt in the legislatures of these states. Mississippi, in 1888, was the first state to adopt a law providing for the separation of the races in railway stations, and Georgia, in 1891, the first to adopt the law for streetcars.[21] These laws, though significant in themselves, were often only enactments of codes already in practice. Whether by state law or local law, or by the more pervasive coercion of sovereign white opinion, "the Negro's place" was gradually defined—in the courts, schools, and libraries, in parks, theaters, hotels, and residential districts, in hospitals, insane asylums—everywhere, including on sidewalks and in cemeteries. When complete, the new codes of White Supremacy were vastly more complex than the ante-bellum slave codes or the Black Codes of 1865–1866, and, if anything, they were stronger and more rigidly enforced.

Among the institutions of the Old Order that strained to meet the needs of the New, none proved more hopelessly inadequate than the old penitentiaries. The state was suddenly called upon to take over the plantation's penal functions at a time when crime was enormously increasing. The strain was too great. One after another of the states adopted the expedient of leasing the convicts to private corporations or individuals. In Louisiana the convict-lease system had an ante-bellum origin; in the other Southern states it was introduced by the provisional or military governments and retained by the Carpetbaggers and Redeemers.

For a number of reasons the lease system took firm roots in the New Order and grew to greater proportions. For one thing, it fitted perfectly the program of retrenchment, for under it the penitentiary not only ceased to be a heavy burden on the taxpayer but became a source of revenue to the state—sometimes a very lucrative source. The system also fitted conveniently the needs occasioned by the new criminal codes of the Redemption regimes, which piled up heavy penalties for petty offenses against property, while at the same time they weakened the protection afforded the Negro in the courts. The so-called "pig law" of Mississippi defined the theft of any property over ten dollars in value, or any cattle or swine of whatever value, as grand larceny, with a sentence up to five years. After its adoption the number of state convicts increased from 272 in 1874 to 1,072 by the end of 1877. The number in Georgia increased from 432 in 1872 to 1,441 in 1877. Additional convictions meant additional revenue instead of additional taxes. The system quickly became a large-scale and sinister business. Leases of ten, twenty, and thirty years were granted by legislatures to powerful politicians, Northern syndicates, mining corporations, and individual planters. Laws limiting hours of labor and types of work for convicts were nonexistent in some states and negligible in others, and in two states protective laws were later removed or modi-

[21] Franklin Johnson, *Development of State Legislation Concerning the Free Negro* (New York, 1919), 15, 54, 62–207; Gilbert T. Stephenson, *Race Distinctions in American Law* (New York, 1910), 216–17.

fied. Responsibility of lessees for the health and lives of convicts was extremely loose. Some states had no inspectors and in others inspection was highly perfunctory if not corrupt. Where the law permitted, the large lessees subleased convicts in small or large gangs for short periods, thus rendering responsibility to the state even more fictitious and protection of the state's prisoners all but impossible. County prisons in many cases adopted the system and in Alabama had twice as many convicts leased as the state. The South's "penitentiaries" were great rolling cages that followed construction camps and railroad building, hastily built stockades deep in forest or swamp or mining fields, or windowless log forts in turpentine flats.[22]

The degradation and brutality produced by this system would be incredible but for the amount of evidence from official sources. A report of the inspectors of the Alabama penitentiary revealed that the prisons were packed with several times the number of convicts they could reasonably hold.

> They are as filthy, as a rule, as dirt could make them, and both prisons and prisoners were infested with vermin. The bedding was totally unfit for use. . . . [It was found] that convicts were excessively and sometimes cruelly punished; that they were poorly clothed and fed; that the sick were neglected, insomuch as no hospitals had been provided, [and] that they were confined with the well convicts.[23]

A grand-jury investigation of the penitentiary hospital in Mississippi reported that inmates were

> all bearing on their persons marks of the most inhuman and brutal treatments. Most of them have their backs cut in great wales, scars and blisters, some with the skin peeling off in pieces as the result of severe beatings. . . . They were lying there dying, some of them on bare boards, so poor and emaciated that their bones almost came through their skin, many complaining for want of food. . . . We actually saw live vermin crawling over their faces, and the little bedding and clothing they have is in tatters and stiff with filth.[24]

In mining camps of Arkansas and Alabama convicts were worked through the winter without shoes, standing in water much of the time. In both

[22] *Report of the United States Commissioner of Labor, 1886, Convict Labor* (Washington, 1887), especially pp. 72–79. For a dispassionate account by a warden, see J. C. Powell, *The American Siberia; or, Fourteen Years' Experience in a Southern Convict Camp* (London, 1891), *passim*; Wharton, *Negro in Mississippi*, 237–40.

[23] *Biennial Report of the Inspectors of the Alabama Penitentiary from September 30, 1880, to September 30, 1882* (Montgomery, 1882), *passim*.

[24] Jackson *Clarion*, July 13, 1887.

states the task system was used, whereby a squad of three was compelled to mine a certain amount of coal per day on penalty of a severe flogging for the whole squad. Convicts in the turpentine camps of Florida, with "stride-chains" and "waist-chains" riveted on their bodies, were compelled to work at a trot. "They kept this gait up all day long, from tree to tree," reported the warden.[25] The average annual death rate among Negro convicts in Mississippi from 1880 to 1885 was almost 11 per cent, for white convicts about half that, and in 1887 the general average was 16 per cent. The death rate among the prisoners of Arkansas was reported in 1881 to be 25 per cent annually. An indication of what was called "moral conditions" is provided in a report of the Committee on the Penitentiary of the Georgia Legislature: "We find in some of the camps men and women chained together and occupying the same sleeping bunks. The result is that there are now in the Penitentiary twenty-five bastard children, ranging from three months to five years of age, and many of the women are now far advanced in pregnancy."[26] For the Southern convict-lease system a modern scholar can "find parallel only in the persecutions of the Middle Ages or in the prison camps of Nazi Germany."[27]

The lease system was under bitter attack, especially from the various independent parties, and repeated attempts were made to abolish or reform it. Julia Tutwiler of Alabama was a moving spirit in the reform movement. Almost everywhere, however, the reformers were opposed by vested interests within the Redemption party—sometimes by the foremost leaders of that party. Senator Brown of Georgia was guaranteed by his twenty-year lease "three hundred able-bodied, long-term men" to work in his Dade Coal Mines, for which he paid the state about eight cents per hand per day.[28] Senator Gordon was also a member of a firm leasing convicts. Colonel Colyar, leader of one wing of the Redemption party in Tennessee, leased that state's prisoners at $101,000 a year for the Tennessee Coal and Iron Company. Control over these Southern state "slaves" was the foundation of several large fortunes, and in one case, of a great political dynasty. Robert McKee, who was in a position to know all the workings of the system, wrote that the state warden of Alabama, John H. Bankhead, "grew rich in a few years on $2,000 a year," and manipulated the legislature at will. "The 'penitentiary ring' is a power in the party," he wrote privately, "and it is a corrupt power. One of the State officers is a lessee of convicts, and has a brother who is a deputy warden."[29] Former Secretary of State Rufus K. Boyd believed that the convict-lease ring was "as unscrupulous as any radical in the days of their power. . . . Are we all thieves? What

25 Little Rock *Daily Gazette*, March 24, 27, 1888; Powell, *American Siberia*, 22.

26 Georgia *House Journal*, 1879, Pt. I, 386–91.

27 Fletcher M. Green, "Some Aspects of the Southern Convict Lease System in the Southern States," in Fletcher M. Green (ed.), *Essays in Southern History Presented to Joseph Gregoire de Roulhac Hamilton* . . . (Chapel Hill, 1949), 122.

28 Georgia *House Journal*, 1879, Pt. I, 386–91.

29 Robert McKee to Boyd, February 3, 1882, in [Robert McKee Papers (Alabama Department of Archives and History, Montgomery)].

is it leading to? Who can submit to these things patiently?"[30] Yet the party continued to submit.

The convict-lease system did greater violence to the moral authority of the Redeemers than did anything else. For it was upon the tradition of paternalism that the Redeemer regimes claimed authority to settle the race problem and "deal with the Negro."

The abandonment of the Negro by his Northern champions after the Compromise of 1877 was as quixotic as their previous crusade in his behalf had been romantic and unrealistic. The *Nation* thought the government should "have nothing more to do with him," and Godkin could not see how the Negro could ever "be worked into a system of government for which you and I would have much respect."[31] The New York *Tribune*, with a logic all its own, stated that the Negroes, after having been given "ample opportunity to develop their own latent capacities," had only succeeded in proving that "as a race they are idle, ignorant, and vicious."[32]

The Supreme Court's decision in October, 1883, declaring the Civil Rights Act unconstitutional was only the juristic fulfillment of the Compromise of 1877, and was, in fact, handed down by Justice Joseph P. Bradley, Grant's appointee, who had been a member of the Electoral Commission of 1877. "The calm with which the country receives the news," observed the editor of the New York *Evening Post*, "shows how completely the extravagant expectations . . . of the war have died out."[33] A Republican who held repudiated bonds of South Carolina wrote from New York that the Civil Rights decision came "as a just retribution to the colored people for their infamous conduct" in assisting in the repudiation of the bonds; "if they expect the people of the North to fight their battles for them they can wait until doomsday," he added.[34]

It has already been pointed out that the wing of the Republican party that raised the loudest outcry against Hayes's policy of deserting the Negro promptly abandoned him itself as soon as it came to power under Garfield and Arthur and threw support to white Republicans in alliance with any white independent organization available. Repeated warnings from the South that the Negro voters were "getting demoralized," that they would "make terms with their adversaries," and that the Republican party was "losing its hold on the younger generation" were ignored.[35]

---

[30] Boyd to McKee, February 26, 1883; also Morgan to McKee, March 15, 1882; McKee to Thomas R. Roulhac, February 25, 1883, *ibid.*

[31] *Nation*, XXIV (1877), 202; Edwin L. Godkin, quoted by [Paul H.] Buck [*The Road to Reunion, 1865–1900* (Boston, 1937)], 295.

[32] New York *Tribune*, April 7, 1877.

[33] New York *Evening Post*, October 16, 1883.

[34] Letter, *ibid.*, October 20, 1883.

[35] A. J. Willard, Columbia, S.C., to J. Hendrix McLane, [?] 12, 1882; James E. Richardson to Chandler, September 14, 1884, in [William E. Chandler Papers (Division of Manuscripts, Library of Congress)]; David M. Key to Hayes, December 31, 1882, in [Rutherford B. Hayes Papers (Hayes Memorial Library, Fremont, Ohio)].

Political leaders of his own race furnished guidance of doubtful value to the Negro in his political quandary. For one thing the average cotton-field Negro voter had little more in common with the outstanding Negro politicians of the South than he had with the corporation lawyers who ran the Republican party in the North. Former Senator Blanche K. Bruce of Mississippi owned "a handsome plantation of 1,000 acres," which he operated as absentee landlord, much as had his predecessor, Senator Jefferson Davis.[36] Former Congressman James T. Rapier of Alabama was "the possessor of extensive landed interests" in that state in which he employed more than a hundred people. Former Congressmen Josiah T. Walls of Florida and John R. Lynch of Mississippi were reported to be "proprietors of vast acres under cultivation and employers of large numbers of men,"[37] and Norris Wright Cuney, Negro boss in Galveston, Texas, was the employer of some five hundred stevedores.[38] Former Senator Bruce was quoted in 1883 as saying that his party represented "the brains, the wealth, the intelligence" of the land, and that "the moneyed interests of this country would be seriously affected" by a Republican defeat.[39]

The more successful of the Negro politicians were maintained in some Federal office "of high-sounding titles and little importance" in Washington. At home they often came to an understanding with Democratic leaders of the Black Belt called "fusion," which served the interests of both by diminishing the power of the white counties in the white man's party and the authority of white leaders in the black man's party. The confusion in which this policy resulted for the average Negro voter may be imagined from the nature of the instruction Lynch gave Mississippi Republicans at a meeting in 1883. It made no difference whether the county machines decided "to fuse with the Independents instead of the Democrats, or with the Democrats instead of the Independents, or to make straight [Republican] party nomination instead of fusing with either"; it was the duty of all good party men, whatever the decision, to follow the machine, "although they may honestly believe the decision to be unwise."[40] Such instructions would not have sounded unfamiliar to followers of the white man's party.

Soon after the war Negroes began to break up into differentiated social and economic classes that eventually reproduced on a rough scale the stratified white society. Enough of a Negro middle class had emerged in the eighties to reflect faithfully the New-South romanticism of the white middle class, with its gospel of progress and wealth. A Negro paper named the *New South* made its appearance in Charleston. It warned the race against "following the *ignis fatuus* of politics," and urged the gospel of "real progress"—money-making.[41] The class of 1886 at Tuskegee

---

[36] Washington *Bee* (Negro paper), July 21, 1883.
[37] Huntsville *Gazette* (Negro paper), February 11, 1882.
[38] Maud Cuney-Hare, *Norris Wright Cuney* (New York, 1913), 42.
[39] New York *Globe* (Negro paper), February 24, 1883.
[40] Quoted in New York *Globe*, October 20, 1883.
[41] Quoted in *Nation*, XLVIII (1889), 461.

adopted the motto "There is Room at the Top,"[42] and freshman W. E. B. Du Bois found his classmates at Fisk in 1885 of the same blithe turn of mind.[43] No American success story could match the Master of Tuskegee's *Up from Slavery!*

Another considerable Negro element saw nothing better than to take refuge under the paternalism of the old masters, who offered some protection against the extreme race doctrines of the upland whites and sometimes more tangible rewards than the Republican bosses. Cleveland's administration and its Southern lieutenants encouraged this tendency among Negroes. The *Nation*, a Cleveland supporter, rejoiced that "thousands of them" had discovered "that their true interests are bound up with the interests of their old masters."[44]

Although the majority of the Negro masses remained Republican or potentially Republican voters, suspicion and criticism of the party of liberation were on the increase during the eighties. The Compromise of 1877 was described as "disillusioning"; the Civil Rights decision as "infamous," a "baptism in ice water"; Chandler's politics as "fatuous" and "degrading." There was also a growing tendency to look upon Republican tariff, railroad, and financial legislation more critically. "The colored people are consumers," said the chairman of a Colored People's Convention in Richmond. "The Republicans have deserted them and undertaken to protect the capitalist and manufacturer of the North."[45] "Neither of these parties," wrote a Negro editor, "cares a tinker snap for the poor man. They are run in the interest of capital, monopoly and repression."[46] The defeat of the Blair bill was a bitter disappointment. Professor J. C. Price, editor of a Negro journal in Salisbury, North Carolina, pointed out that "the Republican party was committed to the enactment of national legislation for the education of the masses," yet the Blair bill had been "voted down and owed its death in the Senate to Republican opposition." Under the circumstances the Negro was not impressed by the Lodge bill to re-enact Reconstruction election laws, and was more disillusioned when it was defeated. "He is beginning to distinguish between real friendship and demagoguery."[47]

In the meanwhile, the movement to make the party "respectable" was gaining ground among "Lily-white" Republicans in the South. A party leader, addressing the Lincoln Club of Arkansas on the problem of attracting "persons who have heretofore acted with the Democratic party," announced that he was seeking "a way by which they could act with the Republican party without being dominated over by the negro."[48]

[42] *Southern Letter* (Tuskegee), V (July, 1888), 3.

[43] W. E. Burghardt Du Bois, *Dusk of Dawn: An Essay Toward an Autobiography of a Race Concept* (New York, 1940), 25–27.

[44] *Nation*, XLI (1885), 369.

[45] Richmond *Dispatch*, April 16, 1890.

[46] New York *Globe*, April 5, 1884. See also, *ibid.*, October 13, 20, 27, 1883; May 3, 1884.

[47] *Southland*, I (1890), 162–63.

[48] Little Rock *Daily Gazette*, July 22, 1888.

The Republican White League of Texas believed that "the union is only safe in the hands of the Anglo-Saxon race, and that a Republican party in Texas to merit the respect of mankind must be in the hands of that race."[49] A New England traveler was grieved to report to the "kinsmen and friends of John Brown, Wendell Phillips, and William Lloyd Garrison" the words of a Southern white Republican who said, "I will not vote to make a negro my ruler. . . . I was a white man before I was a Republican."[50] Even the Northern churches in the South, stoutest proponents of the missionary phase of Northern policy, had drawn the color line by the end of the eighties.[51]

Not long after the inauguration of President Benjamin Harrison in 1889, the Negro press began to accuse him of throwing his support to the Lily-white faction of his party in the South and of not giving the Negroes their fair reward in patronage. The protest soon became bitterly critical. In January, 1890, delegates from twenty-one states met at Chicago and organized the National Afro-American League. Professor Price was elected president and T. Thomas Fortune, who was easily the foremost Negro editor of his day, was chosen secretary. In a militant speech Fortune said of the old parties that "none of them cares a fig for the Afro-American" and that "another party may rise to finish the uncompleted work" of liberation.[52] Inspired by the Chicago meeting, which established numerous branch leagues, other Negro conventions were held. In Raleigh a "Negroes' 'Declaration of Independence'" was proclaimed, declaring that "the white Republicans have been traitors to us," and the Negroes, "the backbone of the Republican party, got nothing" in the way of patronage.[53] Joseph T. Wilson, chairman of a Negro convention in Richmond, protested that his race had been "treated as orphan children, apprenticed to the rice-, cotton-, and tobacco-growers in the South." As for the Negro's political plight, "The Republican party does not know what to do with us and the Democratic party wants to get rid of us, and we are at sea without sail or anchor drifting with the tide."[54] Five such conventions were held in 1890, and all of them were said to have "declared their disaffection with existing political parties."[55] The black man was beginning to feel toward his party much the same as the Southern white man was feeling toward his—that his vote was taken for granted and his needs were ignored.

By 1890 a million Negroes were reported to have joined the Colored Farmers' Alliance. At their annual convention, held at the same time and place as the convention of the white Alliance, the black farmers took a more radical position than their white brethren, substantially affirming the

[49] Dallas *Morning News*, June 9, 1892.

[50] Charles H. Levermore, "Impressions of a Yankee Visitor in the South," in *New England Magazine*, N.S., III (1890–1891), 315.

[51] [Hunter D.] Farish [*The Circuit Rider Dismounts: A Social History of Southern Methodism, 1865–1900* (Richmond, 1938)], 214–15.

[52] New York *Age*, January 25, 1890.

[53] Richmond *Dispatch*, April 16, 1890.

[54] *Ibid.*

[55] *National Economist*, IV (1890), 234–35.

single-tax philosophy that "land is not property; can never be made property. . . . The land belongs to the sovereign people." They also leaned
even more toward political independence. Their leader reminded them:
"You are a race of farmers, seven-eighths of the colored people being
engaged in agriculture," and there was "little hope of the reformation of
either of the existing political parties."[56]

As the Populist rift in the ranks of white solidarity approached, the
Negro race was more prepared for insurgency than at any time since
enfranchisement. Leaders shrewdly calculated their opportunities. For
some of it was the chance to "teach the White Republicans a lesson"; for
others, to strike a blow against "our old, ancient and constant enemy—
the Democracy"; for still others, an experiment in joint action with white
Southerners on a platform of agrarian radicalism. The general temper
was perhaps best expressed in the slogan offered by one Negro: "Let the
vote be divided; it will be appreciated by the party who succeeds to
power."[57]

The appeal that the proslavery argument had for the poorer class of
whites had been grounded on the fear of being leveled, economically as
well as socially, with a mass of liberated Negroes. Social leveling after
emancipation was scotched by sundry expedients, but the menace of
economic leveling still remained. The rituals and laws that exempted
the white worker from the penalties of caste did not exempt him from
competition with black labor, nor did they carry assurance that the penalties of black labor might not be extended to white.

The propagandists of the New-South order, in advertising the famed
cheap labor of their region, were not meticulous in distinguishing between the color of their wares. If they stressed the "large body of strong,
hearty, active, docile and easily contented negro laborers" who con-
formed to "the apostolic maxim of being 'contented with their wages,'
and [having] no disposition to 'strike,'" they claimed the same virtues
for the "hardy native Anglo-Saxon stock." The pledge of the *Manufacturers' Record*, for example, that "long hours of labor and moderate wages
will continue to be the rule for many years to come," amounted almost
to a clause of security in the promissory note by which the New South
got capital to set up business. Additional security was not lacking. "The
white laboring classes here," wrote an Alabama booster, "are separated
from the Negroes, working all day side by side with them, by an innate
consciousness of race superiority. This sentiment dignifies the character
of white labor. It excites a sentiment of sympathy and equality on their
part with the classes above them, and in this way becomes a wholesome
social leaven."[58]

[56] *Ibid.*

[57] See opinions of several Negro leaders under the title "Will a Division Solve the
Problem?" in *Southland*, I (1890), 222–44; also Huntsville *Gazette*, March 29, 1890;
November 21, 1891.

[58] John W. Dubose, *The Mineral Wealth of Alabama and Birmingham Illustrated*
(Birmingham, 1886), 109.

It was an entirely safe assumption that for a long time to come race consciousness would divide, more than class consciousness would unite, Southern labor. Fifty strikes against the employment of Negro labor in the period from 1882 to 1900 testify to white labor's determination to draw a color line of its own. It is clear that in its effort to relegate to the Negro the less desirable, unskilled jobs, and to exclude him entirely from some industries, white labor did not always have the co-operation of white employers.[59]

In the cotton mills, at least, racial solidarity between employer and employee held fairly firm. By a combination of pressures and prejudices, a tacit understanding was reached that the cotton-mill villages were reserved for whites only. Probably no class of Southerners responded to the vision of the New South more hopefully than those who almost overnight left the old farm for the new factory. The cotton-mill millennium had been proclaimed as the salvation of "the necessitous masses of the poor whites." One enthusiastic promoter promised that "for the operative it would be Elysium itself." Historians have placed the "philanthropic incentive," undoubtedly present in some cases, high in the list of motives behind the whole mill campaign.

The transition from cotton field to cotton mill was not nearly so drastic as that which accompanied the change from primitive agriculture to modern factory in England and New England. For one thing, the mill families usually moved directly from farm to factory, and usually came from the vicinity of the mill. For another, the ex-farmer mill hand found himself in a mill community made up almost entirely of ex-farmers, where a foreigner, a Northerner, or even a city-bred Southerner was a curiosity. As late as 1907 a study revealed that 75.8 per cent of the women and children in Southern cotton mills had spent their childhood on the farm, and the 20.2 per cent who came from villages usually came from mill villages.[60]

The company-owned shanties into which they moved differed little from the planter- or merchant-owned shanties they had evacuated, except that the arrangement of the houses was a reversion to the "quarters" of the ante-bellum plantation instead of the dispersed cropper system. As pictured by an investigator in Georgia in 1890, "rows of loosely built, weather-stained frame houses, all of the same ugly pattern and buttressed by clumsy chimneys," lined a dusty road. "No porch, no doorstep even, admits to these barrack-like quarters." Outside in the bald, hard-packed earth was planted, like some forlorn standard, the inevitable martin pole with its pendant gourds. Inside were heaped the miserable belongings that had furnished the cropper's cabin: "a shackling bed, tricked out in gaudy patchwork, a few defunct 'split-bottom' chairs, a rickety table, and a

---

[59] Charles H. Wesley, *Negro Labor in the United States, 1850–1925; A Study in American Economic History* (New York, 1927), 235–38.

[60] [Elizabeth H.] Davidson, *Child Labor Legislation in the Southern Textile States* [Chapel Hill, 1939], 7–8; [Holland] Thompson [*From the Cotton Field to the Cotton Mill; A Study of the Industrial Transition in North Carolina* (New York, 1906)], 109–10; [Broadus] Mitchell [*The Rise of Cotton Mills in the South*, in Johns Hopkins University *Studies in Historical and Political Science*, XXXIX, No. 2 (Baltimore, 1921)], 173–86.

jumble of battered crockery," and on the walls the same string of red peppers, gourd dipper, and bellows. In certain mill villages of Georgia in 1890 not a watch or clock was to be found. "Life is regulated by the sun and the factory bell"—just as it had once been by the sun and farm bell. The seasons in the vocabulary of the cracker proletariat were still "hog-killin'," "cotton-choppin'," and " 'tween crops." The church was still the focus of social life, and the mill family was almost as migratory as the cropper family. The whole of this rustic industrialism moved to a rural rhythm.[61]

Mill-village paternalism was cut from the same pattern of poverty and makeshift necessity that had served for plantation and crop-lien paternalism. In place of the country supply store that advanced goods against a crop lien there was the company store that advanced them against wages, and since the weaver was as rarely able to add and multiply as was the plowman, accounts were highly informal. Mill-village workers were sometimes little further advanced toward a money economy than were cotton croppers, and payday might bring word from the company store that the family had not "paid out" that week. Pay was often scrip, good only at the company store, or redeemable in cash at intervals. Company-owned houses were usually provided at low rent and sometimes rent free. "Lint-head" fealty often carried with it certain feudal privileges like those of gathering wood from company lands and pasturing cows on company fields. The unincorporated company town, in which everything was owned by the mill corporation, was the most completely paternalistic. Here company schools and company churches were frequently subsidized by the corporation, which of course controlled employment of preacher and teacher.[62] In the smaller mills the relationship between owner and employees was highly personal and intimate, with a large degree of dependency on the part of the workers. "Not only are relations more friendly and intimate than at the North," found a Northern writer, "but there is conspicuous freedom from the spirit of drive and despotism. Even New England superintendents and overseers in their Southern mills soon glide into prevailing *laissez-faire* or else leave in despair."[63]

After all allowance has been made for the manna of paternalism, the "family wage," and the greater purchasing power of money in the South, the wages of Southern textile workers remained miserably low. The very fact that the wages of the head of a family combined with those of the other adult members were inadequate to support dependents makes the "family wage" a curious apology for the system. Wages of adult male workers of North Carolina in the nineties were 40 to 50 cents a day. Men constituted a minority of the workers, about 35 per cent in the four leading textile states in 1890; women, 40 per cent; and children between the ages of ten and fifteen years, 25 per cent. The wages of children, who entered into degrading competition with their parents, varied consider-

[61] Clare de Graffenried, "The Georgia Cracker in the Cotton Mill," in *Century Magazine*, N.S., XIX (1891), 487–88.
[62] Mitchell, *Rise of the Cotton Mills*, 225–26.
[63] De Graffenried, "Georgia Cracker in the Cotton Mill," *loc. cit.*, 487.

ably, but there is record of mills in North Carolina that paid 10 and 12 cents a day for child labor.[64] The work week averaged about seventy hours for men, women, and children. Wages were slow to improve, and did not keep pace with mounting capitalization and profits. Adult male spinners in representative mills of North Carolina who had received $2.53 a week in 1885 were getting $2.52 in 1895, and adult female spinners in Alabama got $2.76 a week in the former and $2.38 in the latter year.[65] Hourly wages for adult male spinners in the South Atlantic states were not quite 3 cents in 1890, only 2.3 cents in 1895, and a little over 3 cents in 1900; for female spinners in the same section the rate declined from about 4.5 cents an hour in 1890 to 4 cents in 1900.[66] Yet with these wages and conditions, there seems to have been no trouble in filling the company houses to overflowing. Few workers ever returned to farming permanently, and strikes were almost unheard of.

The glimpses one gets of life among this sunbonneted, wool-hatted proletariat raise doubts about the sense of *noblesse oblige* and the "philanthropic incentives" with which their employers have been credited. If paternalism sheltered them from the most ruthless winds of industrial conflict, it was a paternalism that could send its ten-year-old children off to the mills at dawn and see them come home with a lantern at night. It could watch its daughters come to marriageable age with "a dull heavy eye, yellow, blotched complexion, dead-looking hair," its "unmarried women of thirty . . . wrinkled, bent, and haggard," while the lot of them approached old age as illiterate as Negro field hands.[67] If white solidarity between employees and employer was to save the white worker from the living standard of the Negro, the results in the cotton mills were not very reassuring.

The extent to which labor in other industries shared in the prosperity of the New South is indicated by the level of wages maintained. In few industries or crafts did wages rise appreciably, and in many they were actually reduced. In the tobacco industry of the South Atlantic states, for example, cigar makers got 26 cents an hour in 1890 and 25 cents in 1900, while stemmers' wages remained at about 10 cents; in representative leather industries of the same states tanners remained on 11-cent wages, while in the South Central states their wages fell from 12.75 cents in 1890 to 11.5 cents in 1900; compositors' wages in the printing industry advanced from about 24 cents to nearly 26 cents in the South Atlantic states over the decade, from 28 cents to 29 cents in the South Central states; machinists did little better than hold their own in this period; bricklayers' wages declined from 45 cents to 43 cents in the South Central states and rose from 35 cents to about 37 cents in the South Atlantic states; carpenters in the former section got nearly 26 cents in 1890 and over 27 cents in

[64] Davidson, *Child Labor Legislation in the Southern Textile States*, 8, 16.

[65] *Eleventh Annual Report of the Commissioner of Labor, 1895–96* (Washington, 1897), 184, 235.

[66] *Nineteenth Annual Report of the Commissioner of Labor, 1904* (Washington, 1905), 385.

[67] De Graffenried, "Georgia Cracker in the Cotton Mill," *loc. cit.*, 489–93, 495; Davidson, *Child Labor Legislation in the Southern Textile States*, 12–13.

1900, while in the latter section their wages were raised from about 24 cents to about 26 cents; and wages of unskilled labor in the building trades varied from 8 cents to 12 cents an hour in the nineties.[68]

To a large extent the expanding industrialization of the New South was based upon the labor of women and children who were driven into the mills and shops to supplement the low wages earned by their men. In several states they were being drawn into industry much more rapidly than men. In representative establishments studied in Alabama the number of men increased 31 per cent between 1885 and 1895; that of women increased 75 per cent; girls under eighteen, 158 per cent; and boys under eighteen, 81 per cent. The increases over the same period in Kentucky were 3 per cent for men, 70 per cent for women, 65 per cent for girls, and 76 per cent for boys.[69] Of the 400,586 male children between the ages of ten and fourteen gainfully employed in the United States in 1890, the two census divisions of the Southern states accounted for 256,502, and of the 202,427 girls of that age at work they listed 130,546. The great majority in each case were employed in agriculture, fisheries, and mining.[70] Thousands of women who went to work in the cities lived on subsistence wages. In Charleston shops, where the average weekly earnings for women were $4.22, were "well-born, well-educated girl[s] side by side in the least attractive pursuits with the 'cracker.'" In Richmond, where women's wages averaged $3.93 a week, there was an "almost universal pallor and sallowness of countenance" among working women. In Atlanta "great illiteracy exists among the working girls. Their moral condition also leaves much to be desired. The cost of living is comparatively high."[71]

In spite of the contributions of women and children, the working family in the South seemed less able to own a house than that of any other section. Of the eighteen cities in the whole country with a percentage of home tenancy above 80, eleven were in the South. Birmingham, with 89.84 per cent of tenancy, had the highest rate in the United States; the percentage in Norfolk was 85.62, and in Macon, 84.66. In the South Atlantic states as a whole, over 75 per cent of home dwellers were tenants.[72] Interlarded with the long, shady boulevards of the "best sections" of Nashville, Norfolk, Macon, Memphis, and Montgomery were alleys lined with one- and two-room shanties of colored domestics. In the "worst sections" of every city sprawled the jungle of a darktown with its own business streets and uproarious, crime-infested "amusement" streets. Beyond, in suburban squalor and isolation, were the gaunt barracks of white industrial workers, huddled around the factories.

Conditions of public health and sanitation under which the urban

---

[68] *Nineteenth Annual Report of the Commissioner of Labor, 1904*, 374, 403, 417, 430–31, 461, 465.

[69] *United States Bureau of Labor Bulletin No. 10* (Washington, 1897), 242.

[70] *Eleventh Census, 1890, Compendium*, Pt. III, 460–62.

[71] *Fourth Annual Report of the Commissioner of Labor, 1888* (Washington, 1889), 13, 16, 24, 68.

[72] *Eleventh Census, 1890, Farms and Homes*, 29.

working classes lived cannot be grasped from general descriptions, since health improvements and safeguards were highly discriminatory within the cities. Richmond justly boasted in 1887 of her relatively high expenditures for municipal improvements, of being "the best-paved city of her population in the Union," and of the splendor of Broad, Main, and Cary streets, "yearly improved by elegant houses built for merchants and manufacturers." Yet in 1888 the United States Commissioner of Labor blamed "bad drainage of the city, bad drinking water, and unsanitary homes" for the appalling conditions of health among the working girls of Richmond.[73] New Orleans, with a long start over her sisters, easily achieved pre-eminence among unsanitary cities by the filth and squalor of her slums. The president of the State Board of Health of Louisiana reported in 1881 that "the gutters of the 472 miles of dirt streets are in foul condition, being at various points choked up with garbage, filth and mud, and consequently may be regarded simply as receptacles for putrid matters and stagnant waters. The street crossings are in like manner more or less obstructed with filth and black, stinking mud."[74]

"We have awakened, or are fast awakening, from our dream," commented a Southern editor. "We have pauperism, crime, ignorance, discontent in as large a measure as a people need. Every question that has knocked at European doors for solution will in turn knock at ours."[75] When work relief was offered at twenty cents a week by private charity in Alexandria, Virginia, "poor women were more than glad to get the work, and came from far and near, and many had to be sent away disappointed every week."[76] In New Orleans "a multitude of people, white and black alike," lived on a dole of thirteen cents a day in the nineties.[77]

Labor in the Southern textile mills, largely unorganized, has claimed a disproportionate share of the attention of scholars. The result has been a neglect of the history of labor in other industries and in the crafts, as well as an encouragement of the impression that no labor movement existed in the region at this period.

A study of the labor movement in the largest Southern city concludes that "the South, to judge by New Orleans, had craft labor movements smaller but similar to those in Northern cities," and that they were growing in power and influence in the eighties and nineties.[78] It was a period of testing unknown strength and challenging tentatively the Old-South labor philosophy of the New-South doctrinaires and their pledge to Northern investors that long hours, low wages, and docile labor were assured.

[73] *Fourth Annual Report of the Commissioner of Labor, 1888,* 24.

[74] *Annual Report of the Board of Health of the State of Louisiana . . . for the Year 1881* (New Orleans, 1881), 5–6. See also [Roger W.] Shugg [*Origins of Class Struggle in Louisiana; A Social History of White Farmers and Laborers During Slavery and After, 1840–1875* (University, La., 1939)], 282–89.

[75] New Orleans *Times,* September 13, 1881.

[76] New York *Tribune,* February 10, 1881.

[77] Shugg, *Origins of Class Struggle in Louisiana,* 297.

[78] Roger W. Shugg, "The New Orleans General Strike of 1892," in *Louisiana Historical Quarterly,* XXI (1938), 559.

However appealing white Southern labor found the doctrine of White Supremacy, it realized pretty early that "in nearly all the trades, the rates of compensation for the whites is [sic] governed more or less by the rates at which the blacks can be hired," and that the final appeal in a strike was "the Southern employer's ability to hold the great mass of negro mechanics *in terrorem* over the heads of the white."[79] Agreement upon the nature of their central problem did not bring agreement upon the proper means of dealing with it. Two possible but contradictory policies could be used: eliminate the Negro as a competitor by excluding him from the skilled trades either as an apprentice or a worker, or take him in as an organized worker committed to the defense of a common standard of wages. Southern labor wavered between these antithetical policies from the seventies into the nineties, sometimes adopting one, sometimes the other.

The rising aristocracy of labor, the railway brotherhoods, drew a strict color line. On the other hand, the Brotherhood of Carpenters and Joiners claimed fourteen Negro locals in the South in 1886. The coopers', the cigar makers', the bricklayers', the steel workers', and the carpenters' unions had by the eighties adopted the practice of "issuing . . . separate charters to Negro craftsmen wherever existing locals debarred them." The federations of deck workers in the cotton ports of New Orleans, Savannah, and Galveston overrode race barriers and admitted, equally, white and black longshoremen, draymen, yardmen, cotton classers, and screwmen. Especially successful were the efforts to organize the Negroes in New Orleans. The Central Trades and Labor Assembly of that city was said "to have done more to break the color line in New Orleans than any other thing . . . since emancipation of the slaves."[80]

Much of this temporary "era of good feeling" between black and white workingmen has been credited to the guidance of the Knights of Labor. The Knights' doctrine of interracial solidarity and democratic idealism makes the history of the order of particular significance for the central problem of Southern labor. The history of the Knights also confutes the legend of the Southern worker's indifference to unionism. As soon as the national organization of the Knights was established in 1878 it dispatched 15 organizers to the South. A quickening of Southern interest was evident in 1884, and by 1886 there were in ten states 21,208 members attached to the Southern District assembly and perhaps 10,000 more members of locals attached to national trade assemblies or directly to the General Assembly of the Knights. An incomplete list places 487 locals in the South in 1888, but there were many more. Concentrated around such cities as Birmingham, Knoxville, Louisville, New Orleans, and Richmond, locals were also scattered over rural areas and embraced cotton hands and sugar workers, black as well as white. The national convention of the Knights in 1886, the year of their greatest strength, met in Rich-

[79] [Philip A.] Bruce [*The Rise of the New South* (Philadelphia, 1905)], 164–65.
[80] Sterling D. Spero and Abram L. Harris, *The Black Worker: The Negro and the Labor Movement* (New York, 1931), 22, 43–44; Wesley, *Negro Labor in the United States*, 236–37, 255.

mond and was attended by delegates of both races from many parts of the South. The convention heard reports that "colored people of the South are flocking to us" and that "rapid strides" have been made in the South.[81]

The Knights were involved in numerous strikes in the South during the latter years of the eighties. These conflicts broke out in the coal mines of Alabama and Tennessee, in the cotton mills of Augusta, Georgia, and Cottondale, Alabama, among the sugar workers of Louisiana and the lumber workers in Alabama. The Knights' greatest strike victory, that against the Missouri Pacific system and Jay Gould in 1885, was won in considerable part in the shops of Texas and Arkansas. The Southwestern strike of 1886, which marked the climax and greatest failure of the order, broke out in Texas, and some of its most violent phases occurred there. The Knights experimented with co-operative enterprises of various kinds, though on no such scale as did the Farmers' Alliance. The order figured conspicuously in the politics of several cities. In 1886 the Workingman's Reform party, backed by the Knights, elected two blacksmiths, a cobbler, and a tanner to the city council of Richmond, and took control of nearly all departments of the government. In 1887 the Knights claimed that they had elected a congressman and eleven of the fifteen city council members in Lynchburg, a majority of the city and county officers in Macon, and several officers in Mobile. The following year they asserted that they had elected the mayors of Jacksonville, Vicksburg, and Anniston. The mayor of Anniston was a carpenter, and the council included two molders, a brickmaker, a butcher, a watchmaker, and a shoemaker. Their reforms were mild enough, but their experimental defiance of the color line was bitterly attacked in the Southern press. Under these burdens and the additional ones of lost strikes, the Knights passed into a decline in the South as in the nation. Co-operation with the Farmers' Alliance gave the order a decided agrarian color by the end of the eighties.[82]

A second peak of activity in the Southern labor movement came in 1892. It therefore coincided with the outburst of the Populist revolt and, like it, was symptomatic of popular discontent with the New Order of the Redeemers. It may be illustrated by two unrelated outbreaks of contrasting character—the general strike in New Orleans and the violent insurrection of Tennessee coal miners against the employment of convict labor.

The general strike in New Orleans, which followed the Homestead strike in Pennsylvania and preceded the Pullman strike in Chicago, has been described as "the first general strike in American history to enlist both skilled and unskilled labor, black and white, and to paralyze the life

[81] Frederic Myers, "The Knights of Labor in the South," in *Southern Economic Journal* (Chapel Hill), VI (1939–1940), 479–85. One official asserted that the order had 100,000 members in five Southern states, but this was an exaggerated claim.

[82] *Ibid.*, 485–87; Frank W. Taussig, "The South-Western Strike of 1886," in *Quarterly Journal of Economics* (Boston, Cambridge), I (1886–1887), 184–222; Dallas *Daily News*, March 2–April 23, 1886; Richmond *Dispatch*, May 18, July 2, September 30, October 3, 1886; Jackson *Clarion*, November 9, 1887; *National Economist*, II (1889), 221; *Tradesman*, XIV (May 15, 1886), 23.

of a great city." It came as "the climax of the strongest labor movement in the South."[83] New Orleans was about as well unionized as any city in the country when the American Federation of Labor began a successful drive early in 1892 that added thirty new chartered associations, thus bringing the total up to ninety-five. A new unity was achieved in the Workingmen's Amalgamated Council, a centralized but democratically elected body made up of two delegates from each of the forty-nine unions affiliated with the A. F. of L. The New Orleans Board of Trade, an organization of the merchants of the city, was as determined to maintain traditional prerogatives of hiring and firing as the labor council was to establish the right of collective bargaining.

Inspired by a victory of the city streetcar drivers that put an end to a sixteen-hour day and gained a closed-shop agreement, the so-called "Triple Alliance," consisting of the unions of the teamsters, scalesmen, and packers (which included Negro members), struck for a ten-hour day, overtime pay, and the preferential closed shop. The Workingmen's Amalgamated Council appointed a committee of five workers, including a Negro, to conduct the strike. The Board of Trade refused to recognize the unions or to deal with them in any way. The workers' committee first threatened, and finally, on November 8, called a general strike in support of the unions of unskilled workers. Forty-two union locals, with over 20,000 members, who with their families made up nearly half of the population of the city, stopped work. Each union on strike demanded recognition and a closed shop. Business came to a virtual standstill; bank clearings were cut in half. The employers openly declared that it was "a war to the knife" and that they would resort to extreme measures, including violence. Yet in spite of the hysteria kept up by the newspapers, the importation of strikebreakers, and the threat of military intervention, the strikers refrained from violence and there was no bloodshed. On the third day of the strike the governor of the state came to the aid of the capitalists with a proclamation that, in effect, set up martial law and implied that the militia would be called unless the strike was ended. The labor committee, never very aggressive, accepted a compromise which, though gaining the original demands of the Triple Alliance concerning hours and wages, forfeited the fight for collective bargaining and the closed shop. The Board of Trade, confident that labor, like the Negro, had been put in its "place," boasted that New Orleans was an open-shop city, and that the old philosophy of labor had been vindicated.[84]

The second labor struggle was fought upon a more primitive level, for the most elemental rights, and fought with savage violence. Competition with convict labor leased by corporations had been a long-standing and often-voiced grievance of labor all over the South. As a conservative paper stated the case in Alabama, "Employers of convicts pay so little for their labor that it makes it next to impossible for those who give work to free labor to compete with them in any line of busi-

[83] Shugg, "New Orleans General Strike of 1892," *loc. cit.*, 547.
[84] *Ibid.*, 547–59; New Orleans *Times-Democrat*, October 25, November 4–11, 1892.

ness. As a result, the price paid for labor is based upon the price paid convicts."[85]

In 1883 the Tennessee Coal, Iron, and Railroad Company leased the Tennessee penitentiary, containing some 1,300 convicts. Thomas Collier Platt, the New York Republican leader, was president of the company and Colonel Colyar, the Tennessee Democratic leader, was general counsel. "For some years after we began the convict labor system," said Colyar, "we found that we were right in calculating that free laborers would be loath to enter upon strikes when they saw that the company was amply provided with convict labor."[86]

Tennessee labor protested, and the legislature occasionally investigated, once reporting that the branch prisons were "hell holes of rage, cruelty, despair and vice." But nothing was done. In 1891, the miners of Briceville, Anderson County, were presented by the Tennessee Coal Mine Company with an "iron-clad" contract relinquishing employees' rights to a check weigher, agreeing to "scrip" pay, and pledging no strikes. When they turned down the contract the company ordered convicts to tear down their houses and build stockades for the convicts who were to replace free labor. The evicted miners then marched in force on the stockades and, without bloodshed, compelled guards, officers, and convicts to board a train for Knoxville. Governor John P. Buchanan, with three companies of militia, promptly returned the convicts to the stockades. A few days later more than a thousand armed miners packed the guards and convicts off to Knoxville a second time, and those of another company along with them, again without bloodshed. Only after the governor had promised to call a special session of the legislature were the miners pacified. Labor demonstrations in Chattanooga, Memphis, Nashville, and other towns demanded an end to convict labor and sent aid to the miners. Kentucky and Alabama labor, afflicted with the same evil, also became aroused. The Tennessee state convention of the Farmers' Alliance, which the governor attended, demanded the repeal of the convict-lease law. In spite of the official position of the Alliance, the fact that there were fifty-four Alliance members of the legislature, and that Governor Buchanan owed his election to the order, the special session of the legislature took no satisfactory action. After a futile appeal to the courts, the miners took the law into their own hands. On the night of October 31, 1891, they forcibly freed the convicts of the Tennessee Coal Mine Company, allowed them all to escape, and burned down the stockades. They repeated the same tactics later at two other mining companies, releasing in all some five hundred convicts. The mine operators of the area then employed free labor, gave up the "iron-clad" contract, and granted a check weigher.[87]

The insurrections of the following year made those of 1891 seem

[85] Fort Payne (Ala.) *Herald*, quoted in Birmingham *Age-Herald*, August 8, 1889.
[86] Nashville *Daily American*, August 23, 1892.
[87] A. C. Hutson, Jr., "The Coal Miners' Insurrection of 1891 in Anderson County, Tennessee," in East Tennessee Historical Society's *Publications* (Knoxville), No. 7 (1935), 105–15; Nashville *Daily American*, July 17–21, August 13, 1891.

tame by comparison. The Tennessee struggles involved more men and deeper issues than the contemporary Homestead strike, but they got little attention then or later. These insurrections broke out in Middle Tennessee at the mines of the Tennessee Coal and Iron Company, which had put its free labor on half time and employed 360 convicts full time. Miners overcame the Tracy City guards, burned the stockades, and shipped the convicts to Nashville. Inspired by this example, miners of one of the Tennessee Coal, Iron, and Railroad Company mines in Anderson County, at which convict labor had been reinstated, burned the stockades, renewed their war, and laid seige to Fort Anderson, which was occupied by militia and civil guards paid jointly by the company and the state to guard the convicts. Although the miners killed a few of the troops sent to relieve the besieged fort, the convicts were again reinstated. The final insurrection spelled the doom of the convict lease, however, for the following year the system was abolished by the legislature.[88]

By their actions the Tennessee miners, the New Orleans trade unions, and workers in the mines and foundries of Alabama, Georgia, and Virginia gave notice in 1892 that Southern labor was not going to accept the Old-South labor philosophy of the New-South leaders—not without a fight, anyway. The militancy of Southern labor also gave notice to the insurgent Southern farmer that he might seek recruits for the Populist revolt in the mines and factories as well as in the fields.

[88] A. C. Hutson, Jr., "The Overthrow of the Convict Lease System in Tennessee," in East Tennessee Historical Society's *Publications*, No. 8 (1936), 82–103; Nashville *Daily American*, August 15–23, 1892; Memphis *Appeal-Avalanche*, January 3, 7, March 1, 1892.

Anarchism and
the Assassination
of McKinley

SIDNEY FINE

Anarchy, a word that literally means "no rule," has always been seen
as a threat by established governments. In the last hundred years,
the principle of anarchy has been embodied in various political
theories, and advocates of anarchism have even attempted to form
a movement for the overthrow of coercive governments, whether
autocratic or democratic in form. Basically, anarchists hold that all
government is oppressive and should be replaced by voluntary associations of individuals and groups. On the question of how this condition should be brought about, anarchists split into two major
groups—those who believe in "propaganda of the word" and those
who believe in "propaganda of the deed." The former advocate the
use of persuasion to convince mankind that coercive government
serves no good purpose and should be abolished through peaceful
and legal methods. While this group may agree to participate in
direct-action campaigns that involve civil disobedience, their position
is nonviolent, and they rely chiefly on the rationality of their arguments to achieve their ends. Advocates of "propaganda of the deed,"
on the other hand, usually view violence as a necessary means of
overthrowing established governments. Thus they approve the practice of terrorism—random acts of violence or selective assassination
—in order to throw society into chaos, to undermine authority, and
to bring about the revolution they seek.

Throughout most of American history, there have been anarchist
practitioners of the "word" who sought to remove themselves from
governmental authority or who openly confronted government when
it seemed unduly oppressive. Indeed, perhaps the most important
anarchist in the early history of the nation was Henry David Thoreau,
who in 1845 retreated from society for two years and who, in his
Essay on Civil Disobedience, stated the anarchist case clearly: "That
government is best which governs not at all."

By the end of the nineteenth century, however, most Americans
and certainly the authorities tended to view all anarchists as violence-
prone. Although most anarchists in both Europe and America still

avoided violence, there had been an increase in terrorist activity, particularly in Europe, in the closing decades of the nineteenth century, and many anarchists who immigrated to the United States during those years supported such activity by writing and speaking, if not by acting themselves. In addition, widespread labor violence during this period was associated with immigrants, who formed the largest part of the Northern and Western labor force, and with anarchists, causing increasing hostility toward both the labor movement and anarchism. The Haymarket incident of 1886 reflected the extent to which public opinion was turning against anarchists. At an anarchist demonstration against police brutality in Chicago's Haymarket Square, a bomb exploded, killing a policeman and fatally wounding six others. Although the only evidence against them was their ideas, eight anarchists were found guilty of the crime, and four were hanged.

In 1901, a native-born, self-confessed anarchist of the "deed" assassinated President McKinley, setting off a strong reaction against anarchists in general. Indeed, after the turn of the century, anyone who admitted to anarchist beliefs was subject to arrest, and aliens suspected of anarchist sympathies were threatened with deportation. Typically, authorities seeking to harass and imprison anarchists used the legally dubious charge of "conspiracy," holding a person to belong to a conspiracy when he shared the beliefs of a person or persons who committed a violent, illegal act, whether or not the first person shared in the planning or committing of the act.

In the article that follows, Sidney Fine, of the University of Michigan, discusses the reaction against anarchists and the attempts to use the conspiracy charge in the aftermath of McKinley's assassination. Further, he notes the changes in immigration law brought about as a result of the upsurge of antiradical sentiment.

W riting in the *Outlook* of August 10, 1901, just one month prior to the assassination of President William McKinley, the newspaper correspondent Francis H. Nichols noted that since the assassination of King Humbert of Italy by the anarchist Bresci the question had been many times asked in the United States as to whether the nation's government and the President were themselves secure from anarchist attack.[1] Few though they were in number in the United States in the closing decades of the nine-

---

[1] Nichols, "The Anarchists in America," *Outlook*, LXVIII (Aug. 10, 1901), 863.

"Anarchism and the Assassination of McKinley," by Sidney Fine. From *The American Historical Review*, LX (July 1955), 777–99. Reprinted by permission of the author.

teenth century,[2] the anarchists, as Nichols suggests, were viewed with alarm by the American community. Anarchism was regarded as "the most dangerous theory which civilization has ever had to encounter," and the anarchist ranks, it was thought, were filled by common criminals and psychopaths who were prepared to resort to fire and the sword to subvert the social order and to murder public officials.[3]

In part, the American fear of anarchism was based on a lack of understanding as to the real nature of the anarchist doctrine. American writers on the subject of anarchism commonly failed to discriminate between individualist anarchists, who were, for the most part, native in origin and believed in free competition and private property (insofar as this term applied to the "total product of a given individual's labor"), and communist anarchists, who arrived late on the American scene, were generally of Russian or German origin, and favored the "collective autonomous commune." Of greater importance, there was little recognition of the fact that violence was not an integral part of the anarchist doctrine and that although some, but by no means all, communist anarchists advocated the use of force to overthrow the state, the individualist anarchists placed their faith in education and passive resistance and were unequivocally opposed to the propaganda of the deed.[4] "When we speak of the 'anarchist,' " Carl Schurz declared, "we mean to designate with that name a human being who is in a general way the enemy of all that exists, and who seeks to overthrow it by any means, however criminal and atrocious."[5] Gustavo Tosti conceded that a few anarchists were guilty of nothing more than "speculative intoxication," but these doctrinaires, he insisted, were scat-

---

[2] The historian Herbert L. Osgood thought that there were probably not more than ten thousand anarchists of all types in the United States in 1889. If anything, this estimate exaggerated anarchist strength. The grand jury impaneled to consider the Haymarket bombing reported that it had learned that the total number of anarchists in the United States who could be considered dangerous was less than one hundred and probably not more than forty or fifty. Osgood, "Scientific Anarchism," *Political Science Quarterly*, IV (March, 1889), 30; Henry David, *The History of the Haymarket Affair: A Study in the American Social-Revolutionary and Labor Movements* (New York, 1936), p. 229.

[3] See, for example, Richard T. Ely, "Anarchy," *Harper's Weekly*, XXXVII (Dec. 23, 1893), 1226; Jno. Gilmer Speed, "Anarchists in Hard Times," *Outlook*, XLVIII (Nov. 11, 1893), 840–41; Carl Schurz, "Murder as a Political Agency," *Harper's Weekly*, XLI (Aug. 28, 1897), 847; Gustavo Tosti, "Anarchistic Crimes," *Political Science Quarterly*, XIV (September, 1899), 404, 412–17; and Ernst Victor Zenker, *Anarchism: A Criticism and History of the Anarchist Theory* (New York, 1897), pp. iv–v.

[4] On the nature of anarchism, see James J. Martin, *Men Against the State: The Expositors of Individualist Anarchism in America, 1827–1908* (De Kalb, Ill., 1953), pp. 4–7, 277–78; Eunice Minette Schuster, *Native American Anarchism: A Study of Left-Wing American Individualism*, Smith College Studies in History, XVII (Northampton, Mass., 1931–32), pp. 87–92, 158–63; Zenker, p. 306; Osgood, pp. 18–30; and Victor S. Yarros, "Individualist or Philosophical Anarchism," in William D. P. Bliss, ed., *The New Encyclopedia of Social Reform* (new ed.; New York, 1908), pp. 41–45.

[5] Schurz, "Murder as a Political Agency," p. 847.

tered among "a mob of desperate criminals," and the anarchist theory itself was simply an "impulsive suggestion to crime."[6]

The popular view of anarchism and anarchists was the product to a considerable extent of a series of spectacular acts of violence perpetrated by, or attributed to, anarchists in Europe and the United States in the last quarter of the nineteenth century. In Europe, following the death in 1876 of Michael Bakunin, redoubtable advocate of pan-destruction, social-revolutionary and communist-anarchist leaders concluded that action was more important than words in making known the aims of anarchism and in arousing a "spirit of insurrection" and thus in preparing the masses for revolution. The propaganda of words came to be overshadowed by the propaganda of the deed, with the result that the bloody acts of anarchists "became the talk and, to a degree, the terror of the world." Anarchist violence in Europe reached its height in the last decade of the nineteenth century when Vaillant attempted to dynamite the French Chamber of Deputies and President Carnot of France, Prime Minister Canovas del Castillo of Spain, Empress Elizabeth of Austria, and King Humbert of Italy all lost their lives to anarchist assassins.[7]

In the United States social revolutionaries who were gravitating in the direction of communist anarchism found a leader in 1882 when Johann Most arrived in this country from England. Most was at the time an uncompromising advocate of the propaganda of the deed and was soon to author a pamphlet with the horrendous title, *Science of Revolutionary Warfare: A Manual of Instructions in the Use and Preparation of Nitroglycerine, Dynamite, Gun-Cotton, Fulminating Mercury, Bombs, Fuses, Poisons, etc., etc.* With Most taking the lead, the social revolutionaries met in congress in Pittsburgh in October, 1883, established the International Working People's Association, and issued a manifesto calling for the "destruction of the existing class rule, by all means, i.e., by energetic, relentless, revolutionary and international action."[8] It seemed to many Americans that the anarchists had indeed gone over to the attack when on May 4, 1886, a bomb exploded in Chicago's Haymarket Square killing one policeman and wounding seventy others, of whom six eventually died. Eight Chicago anarchists who were members of the I.W.P.A. were indicted for this act of murder, and, although the bomb-thrower was not identified, all eight were found guilty.[9]

More than any other event the Haymarket affair conditioned Americans to equate anarchism with violence and murder. As the historian of Haymarket has noted, this incident of terror fixed in the American mind the stereotype of the anarchist as "a ragged, unwashed, long-haired, wild-eyed fiend, armed with smoking revolver and bomb—to say nothing of the dagger he sometimes carried between his teeth."[10] The popular image

---

[6] Tosti, "Anarchistic Crimes," pp. 413–14.

[7] Paul Eltzbacher, *Anarchism*, trans. Steven T. Byington (New York, 1908), pp. 132–38, 178–79; Robert Hunter, *Violence and the Labor Movement* (New York, 1914), pp. 47–60, 77–87; David, *Haymarket Affair*, pp. 62–68.

[8] David, pp. 54–107; Charles A. Madison, *Critics and Crusaders: A Century of American Protest* (New York, 1947), pp. 166–68.

[9] David's *Haymarket Affair* is by far the best account of this subject.

[10] *Ibid.*, p. 528. See also Martin, *Men Against the State*, pp. 3–4, 6, 9; and Madison, pp. 169–70.

of the anarchist became even sharper at the time of the Homestead strike of 1892 when the Russian-born communist anarchist Alexander Berkman shot and stabbed Henry Clay Frick in a futile effort to call attention to what the assailant regarded as the wrongs of capitalism and the unfortunate plight of the workingman.[11] It mattered not that individualist anarchists deplored these acts of violence, that not all communist anarchists approved the use of force, and that even Johann Most in 1892 repudiated the propaganda of the deed in a country such as the United States.[12] To many Americans at the turn of the century it appeared that the crazed adherents of anarchism, however few their number, would stop at nothing to achieve their revolutionary ends.

The worst fears of Americans as regards anarchism seemed to be confirmed when on September 6, 1901, President William McKinley was fatally shot by a professed anarchist, Leon F. Czolgosz.[13] The assassin signed a confession in which he stated that he had killed the President because he regarded it as his duty to do so. He informed doctors who examined him that he had studied anarchism for several months, that he did not believe that there should be any "rulers," that he understood perfectly well what he was doing when he shot the President, and that he was willing to take the consequences.[14]

Although the assassin's connections with anarchism were of the most tenuous sort and although insanity rather than anarchism may have prompted his actions,[15] there was a general disposition among a public conditioned to think of anarchism in terms of Haymarket and Berkman's

---

[11] Emma Goldman, *Living My Life* (1-vol. ed.; New York, 1934), pp. 87–88.

[12] *Freiheit*, Aug. 27, 1892.

[13] McKinley was operated upon less than an hour after he was shot, staged a brief recovery, but died on September 14. For accounts of the assassination, see Louis L. Babcock, "An Account of the Assassination of President McKinley and the Trial of Czolgosz," Buffalo Historical Society *Museum Notes*, I (September–October, 1931), 2–12; Charles S. Olcott, *The Life of William McKinley* (Boston, 1916), II, 313–33; and Robert J. Donovan, "The Man Who Didn't Shake Hands," *New Yorker*, XXIX (Nov. 28, 1953), 88 ff.

[14] Babcock, pp. 10–11; Vernon L. Briggs, *The Manner of Man That Kills: Spencer-Czolgosz-Richeson* (Boston, 1921), pp. 242–46; New York *Daily Tribune*, Nov. 3, 1901.

[15] The doctors who examined Czolgosz at the time declared that he was sane, but the more extensive investigations conducted by Doctors Channing and Briggs after Czolgosz' execution suggest insanity as a more likely explanation for the crime. The subject is discussed in the following: Carlos F. MacDonald, "The Trial, Execution, Autopsy and Mental Status of Leon F. Czolgosz, Alias Fred Nieman, the Assassin of President McKinley. With a Report of the Post-Mortem Examination by Edward Anthony Spitzka," *Journal of Mental Pathology*, I (December, 1901–January, 1902), 185–94; Briggs, pp. 332–39; Walter Channing, "The Mental Status of Czolgosz, the Assassin of President McKinley," *American Journal of Insanity*, LIX (October, 1902), 268–78; Charles Hamilton Hughes, "Medical Aspects of the Czolgosz Case," *Alienist and Neurologist*, XXIII (January, 1902), 49; G. Frank Lydston, *The Diseases of Society* (5th ed.; Philadelphia, London, 1908), pp. 253–54; Allen McLane Hamilton, *Recollections of an Alienist, Personal and Professional* (New York, 1916), pp. 363, 365–66. For Czolgosz' ties with anarchism, see Briggs, pp. 284–85, 299, 316–22; Channing, pp. 245–52; Goldman, *Living My Life*, pp. 289–91; and Cleveland *Press*, Sept. 7, 1901.

attack on Frick to hold anarchism itself responsible for the death of the President and to view Czolgosz as but the instrument of an alien and noxious doctrine that regarded assassination as a legitimate weapon to employ against government and constituted authority.[16] It was therefore deemed necessary not merely to try and to execute the assassin,[17] as was promptly done, and to apprehend those who might have conspired with him, but to take action against resident anarchists in general, since they were all, in effect, accessories to the crime.

Buffalo police authorities let it be known soon after Czolgosz was apprehended that they were quite certain that fellow anarchists had aided him in the planning and execution of the crime.[18] Suspicion immediately centered upon Emma Goldman, the high priestess of the communist anarchists, and the group of Chicago anarchists associated with the publication of *Free Society*, the leading English-language communist-anarchist periodical in the United States. Czolgosz had heard Emma speak in Cleveland on May 5, 1901, and had been so impressed with her that he had sought her out in Chicago and had spoken to her briefly on July 12, 1901, as she was leaving the city. Miss Goldman introduced him to some of her Chicago anarchist friends, including Abe Isaak, Sr., editor of *Free Society*. Isaak invited Czolgosz to his home and promised to find him lodgings and a job but was unable to comply with his request for funds.[19] Although this was the last either Miss Goldman or Isaak saw of Czolgosz and although Isaak apparently came to suspect Czolgosz as a possible spy and so informed the readers of his journal on September 1, 1901, five days before the attack on McKinley, Buffalo authorities nevertheless suspected them of complicity in the assassination and requested their arrest.[20]

On the night of the assassination Chicago police arrested Abe Isaak, Sr., his wife, his son, and his daughter, and five other Chicago anarchists. All were charged with conspiracy to kill the President, although only Isaak, Sr.'s arrest had been requested by Buffalo. The following day the number of prisoners was raised to twelve with the arrest of three more

[16] See, for example, New York *Daily Tribune*, Sept. 8, 1901; Philadelphia *Press*, Sept. 16, 19, 1901; *Literary Digest*, XXIII (Oct. 5, 1901), 391; *Public*, IV (Sept. 28, 1901), 388; George Gunton, "Can We Stamp Out Anarchy?" *Gunton's Magazine*, XXI (October, 1901), 349–50; Murat Halstead, *The Illustrious Life of William McKinley Our Martyred President* (n.p., 1901), pp. 98–99, 257; *Review of Reviews*, XXIV (October, 1901), 389; Theodore L. Jouffroy, "Warnings and Teachings of the Church on Anarchism," *Catholic World*, LXXIV (November, 1901), 203; and Charles P. Neill, "Anarchism," *American Catholic Quarterly Review*, XXVII (January, 1902), 173, 178–79.

[17] For accounts of Czolgosz' trial, see New York *Daily Tribune*, Sept. 24, 25, 1901; MacDonald, "Trial of Czolgosz," pp. 181–84; and Halstead, pp. 450–61.

[18] New York *Daily Tribune*, Sept. 8, 1901; Detroit *News-Tribune*, Sept. 8, 1901; Detroit *Evening News*, Sept. 11, 1901.

[19] Goldman, *Living My Life*, pp. 290–91; *Free Society*, Oct. 6, 1901; Channing, "Mental Status of Czolgosz," pp. 247–51; Briggs, *Manner of Man That Kills*, pp. 316–19. In her Cleveland speech, Emma denied that anarchists favored violence but declared that she did not wish to condemn too severely the crimes which some anarchists had committed because of the high motives that had inspired these crimes. Cleveland *Plain Dealer*, May 6, 1901.

[20] *Free Society*, Sept. 1, Oct. 6, 1901. Czolgosz was not mentioned by name in the September 1 warning.

anarchists then residing in Chicago. The prisoners were arraigned on September 9, 1901; the men were remanded for ten days without bail, and the women, of whom there were three, were first allowed to [post] bail and then later in the day released.[21]

The bag of anarchist prisoners in Chicago was increased by one on September 10 with the arrest of Emma Goldman. Miss Goldman had been in St. Louis when news arrived that McKinley had been slain, that her Chicago friends were under arrest, and that she herself was wanted by the Chicago police for alleged participation in a conspiracy to assassinate the President. Apparently deciding to give herself up, Emma entrained for Chicago, arrived there on September 9, and was apprehended the following morning.[22]

Miss Goldman was arraigned on September 11, but bail was refused her pending a decision on a plea for writs of habeas corpus already initiated by attorneys for the Chicago anarchists. Hearings on the latter matter and on the conspiracy charge were several times postponed, chiefly because of the failure of Buffalo authorities to supply any supporting evidence. Bail was eventually fixed on September 18 at $15,000 for the Isaak group and at $20,000 for Emma. The hearings on the conspiracy charge were finally held on September 23, but since the Buffalo police had been unable to produce any evidence of conspiracy or to find any grounds for requesting extradition, the prisoners had to be released.[23]

In addition to the arrest of the Chicago anarchists and Emma Goldman, the theory that McKinley had been assassinated as a result of an anarchist conspiracy led to the apprehension of Antonio Maggio, Carl Nold, and Harry Gordon. Maggio was rumored to have predicted some time prior to Czolgosz' act that McKinley would be assassinated by October 1, 1901. After the assassination, Maggio was arrested in the territory of New Mexico by a United States marshal and bound over to a federal court on a charge of conspiracy to murder, but he was subsequently released.[24] Gordon and Nold were arrested in Pittsburgh on September 9 on request from Buffalo. Gordon had been Emma Goldman's host when she had visited Pittsburgh late in August, 1901, and Carl Nold was not only an associate of Emma's but had previously been imprisoned for complicity in Alexander Berkman's attack on Frick. Both men were released on September 11 for lack of evidence.[25]

Because Czolgosz' deed served to make an always unpopular doctrine still more unpopular, even anarchists who were not suspected by police authorities of actual participation in a conspiracy to assassinate McKinley were placed in a difficult position. Most prominent among the anarchists who although not charged with any direct complicity in the President's

[21] Chicago *Tribune*, Sept. 7, 8, 9, 10, 1901; *Free Society*, Oct. 6, 1901.

[22] Goldman, pp. 295–304; Chicago *Tribune*, Sept. 11, 1901. Emma claimed in her autobiography that she had planned to give the Chicago *Tribune* an exclusive interview for $5,000 before giving herself up and expected to use the money to fight the case. Goldman, p. 298.

[23] Goldman, pp. 305–11; Chicago *Tribune*, Sept. 12, 13, 14, 19, 24, 25, 1901; *Free Society*, Oct. 6, 1901.

[24] Chicago *Tribune*, Sept. 10, 13, 15, 1901; New York *Daily Tribune*, Sept. 9, 13, 14, 1901, Apr. 13, 1902.

[25] Philadelphia *Press*, Sept. 12, 1901; Chicago *Tribune*, Sept. 10, 12, 1901.

assassination nevertheless felt the sting of the law as its consequence was the fiery communist anarchist, Johann Most. Most, who had several times been jailed both in Europe and America for his revolutionary utterances, was this time the victim of an embarrassing coincidence. In the September 7 issue of his journal, *Freiheit*, an issue which had been printed on September 5 and distributed on September 6 several hours before the assassination, he had included as filler material a piece entitled "Mord contra Mord" (Murder against Murder), which consisted of extracts from articles published in 1849 by the German revolutionary Karl Heinzen in which the latter accepted tyrannicide as the " 'chief means of historical progress.' " "The greatest of all follies in the world," the *Freiheit* extract declared, "is the belief that there can be a crime of any sort against despots. . . . Despots are outlaws . . . to spare them is a crime. . . . We say murder the murderers. Save humanity through blood, poison and iron." Most, who had used Heinzen's articles as filler material before, noted parenthetically that the views therein expressed were "still true today."[26]

When Most learned of the assassination of McKinley, he ordered the withdrawal from circulation of the issue of *Freiheit* in question; but a few copies had already been sold, and Most's troubles had begun. He was arrested on September 12 and jailed and four days later was ordered by a New York City police court magistrate to stand trial in the Court of Special Sessions.[27] Within a few days Most was back in jail, this time having been arrested at a picnic on a charge of inciting to riot. The complaint was dismissed, however, when it turned out that the only evidence in the possession of the prosecution was a large red flag seized at the place of the arrest.[28]

Exonerated of one charge, Most now had to stand trial for his publication of the Heinzen article. He was charged with the violation of Section 675 of New York's penal code, a catch-all section which made it a misdemeanor to commit an act which "seriously" disturbed "the public peace" or "openly" outraged "public decency" and for which no other punishment was provided in the code. Most's attorney, the socialist Morris Hillquit, argued that the Heinzen piece was directed against kings rather than against the elected officials of a democracy, that it was over fifty years old, and that it had been reprinted many times. His client's freedom of the press, he insisted, was being abridged by the application of the vague terms of Section 675.[29]

Unimpressed by Hillquit's argument, Justice Hinsdale on October 14 sentenced Most to one-year imprisonment on Blackwell's Island. The justice pointed out that Section 675 was applicable to the teachings of

---

[26] *Freiheit*, Sept. 7, 1901; Morris Hillquit, *Loose Leaves from a Busy Life* (New York, 1934), pp. 123–25; Rudolf Rocker, *Johann Most: Das Leben Eines Rebellen* (Berlin, 1924), pp. 401–03; Carl Wittke, *Against the Current: The Life of Karl Heinzen (1809–1880)* (Chicago, 1945), pp. 73–75.

[27] *Freiheit*, Sept. 21, 1901; Hillquit, p. 125; New York *Daily Tribune*, Sept. 13, 14, 15, 17, 1901.

[28] *Freiheit*, Sept. 28, Oct. 5, 1901; New York *Daily Tribune*, Sept. 24, 30, Oct. 1, 3, 1901.

[29] Hillquit, pp. 125–27.

anarchy, which he defined as "the doctrine that the pistol, the dagger and dynamite may be used to destroy rulers." It was unnecessary, Hinsdale asserted, to prove any connection between the publication of the article and the assassination of McKinley: the offense was the same as if the latter had never occurred since the advocacy of crime was in itself a crime irrespective of whether there was any connection between the advocacy and an overt act.[30]

The decision of the lower court was upheld on appeal by both the appellate division of the Supreme Court[31] and the Court of Appeals. Speaking for the Court of Appeals, Justice Vann argued that the article in question "held forth murder as a duty and exhorted . . . readers to practice it upon their rulers." "The courts," Vann added significantly, "cannot shut their eyes to the fact that there are elements in our population, small in number but reckless and aggressive, who are ready to act on such advice and to become the assassins of those whom the people have placed in authority." The justice also pointed out that although the New York constitution guaranteed the freedom of the press, it specifically exempted abuses of this right and certainly did not authorize the publication of articles like the Heinzen piece.[32] Sentence was pronounced on June 20, 1902, and thus a chain of events whose most important link was the assassination of McKinley by an avowed anarchist ended in the imprisonment for one year of Johann Most.[33]

Anti-anarchist sentiment also made itself felt in the Pacific Northwest, where the object of disapprobation was the small anarchist colony of Home, in Pierce County, Washington. Following the President's assassination, Tacoma newspapers directed a storm of abuse at the little colony, and it appeared for a time as if steps would be taken to destroy it. The Tacoma *Ledger* equated anarchy with crime and assassination and refused to print a letter from James F. Morton, one of the leading figures of the colony and the editor of its journal, *Discontent,* which set forth the peaceful character of the individualist anarchists. In a front-page headline of September 11, the Tacoma *Evening News* asked the question, "Shall Anarchy and Free Love Live in Pierce County?" and, as if to answer this query, a Loyal League was formed in the county whose announced object was "the annihilation of anarchists and Anarchism."[34]

[30] People *v.* John Most, 16 N.Y. Crim. Reports (1903), 105–11; New York *Daily Tribune,* Oct. 15, 1901.

[31] People *v.* Most, 71 App. Div. N.Y. 160 (1902); *Freiheit,* Apr. 19, 1902.

[32] People *v.* Most, 171 N.Y. 423 (1902), 428–32. "Most was convicted," Hillquit wrote, "not so much because of the fortuitous and ill-timed reprint of the hoary Heinzen article as for his general anarchist propaganda." Hillquit, p. 127.

[33] Before the Court of Appeals handed down its decision, Most once again found himself in the toils of the law. At a farewell meeting called in his honor, he applauded the anarchist William McQueen's attack on government in general and the United States government in particular. He was arrested when the meeting was over but was released three days later. *Freiheit,* May 10, 1902; Rocker, *Most,* p. 413; *Free Society,* May 18, 1902.

[34] E. E. Slosson, "An Experiment in Anarchy," *Independent,* LV (Apr. 2, 1903), 779–85; *Discontent,* Sept. 25, Oct. 2, 1901; Tacoma *Evening News,* Sept. 11, 1901. Morton was a *summa cum laude* graduate of Harvard and the grandson of the Rev. S. F. Smith, author of "America."

Although violence was avoided, Home Colony was nevertheless sub-jected at this time to a series of petty persecutions by public authorities which must be viewed in the light of the prevailing sentiment as regards anarchism. Shortly after the assassination the federal government, in two separate actions, brought several members of the colony to trial for viola-tion of the Comstock Act;[35] and, in addition, postal authorities took steps to impede the dissemination of the colony's journal. Efforts in the latter direction culminated in the abolition of the Home post office on April 30, 1902, and in the forced suspension of further publication of *Discontent*.[36]

The desire of Pierce County inhabitants to purge the anarchists from their midst was shared by the residents of the little coal-mining town of Spring Valley, Illinois, which numbered some three hundred to five hun-dred anarchists among its population of seven thousand and according to at least one Chicago newspaper was "the banner anarchist city of the United States."[37] Like most of the town's inhabitants, the anarchists were Italian in origin and, like many of the foreign-language anarchist groups in the United States, accepted violence as a legitimate method of further-ing the anarchist cause. Their organ, *L'Aurora*, extolled Czolgosz' deed, and *L'Aurora*'s editor, Ciancabilla, hailed Czolgosz as a martyr. This was more than Spring Valley's nonanarchist inhabitants could bear, and it was therefore decided at a mass meeting of September 21 to suppress *L'Aurora* and to drive its editor from town. After the meeting a delegation went to wreck the offices of the journal only to find that the equipment had been removed to one of the nearby coal mines. A few days later Cianca-billa was ordered to leave the community, but he refused to do so. How-ever, he was arrested on September 27 by a United States deputy marshal on a charge of publishing lottery advertisements in his journal and thereby violating postal regulations. He was jailed when unable to provide $5,000 bail and was eventually fined $100. Pressed for funds, *L'Aurora* was forced to suspend publication, and its editor went to work for *Free Society*.[38]

Throughout the United States in the days and months after Mc-Kinley's assassination anarchists were made the objects of vilification and abuse and sometimes of outright violence. On the night of September 15 a band of thirty armed men raided the anarchist settlement of Guffey Hollow, Pennsylvania, and forced twenty-five anarchist families to leave the area.[39] The same night a mob attacked the office of the New York Yiddish-language anarchist organ, *Freie Arbeiter Stimme*, did considerable damage to property, and caused those present in the office to flee for their lives.[40] Cleveland police suppressed the meetings of the Liberty Associa-

---

[35] As amended in 1876 the Comstock Act provided penalties for sending through the mails printed materials or pictures of an indecent character.

[36] For the details with respect to these matters, see *Discontent*, Nov. 13, 20, Dec. 18, 1901, Jan. 1, Mar. 19, 26, Apr. 23, 30, 1902; and *Lucifer*, Aug. 7, 1902. Home was without an official journal until March 11, 1903, when the *Demonstrator* made its first appearance.

[37] (Chicago) *Sunday Inter-Ocean*, Sept. 29, 1901.

[38] *Ibid.*; *Free Society*, Oct. 6, Dec. 22, 1901; *Discontent*, Jan. 1, 15, 1902; Halstead, *McKinley*, p. 77; Chicago *Tribune*, Sept. 16, 22, 28, 1901.

[39] Halstead, p. 83; New York *Daily Tribune*, Sept. 18, 1901.

[40] *Freie Arbeiter Stimme*, Sept. 20, 1901, Feb. 16, 1951.

tion, the anarchist group before which Emma Goldman had delivered the speech that Czolgosz claimed had influenced him.[41] The Ithaca *Journal* advised inhabitants of Ithaca to boycott Henry Bool, a well-to-do local furniture dealer and individualist anarchist, and both the *Journal* and the Ithaca *Daily News* refused to print communications from Bool which set forth the nonviolent character of individualist anarchists. "We all hold you in the highest esteem and believe you to be absolutely honorable and honest in your convictions," the business manager of the *Daily News* informed Bool, "but the public pulse, at the present time, will not stand anything in the line of the doctrine of anarchy."[42]

In Rochester, where Emma Goldman's family resided and where Emma was an occasional visitor, Justice Davy of the New York Supreme Court ordered a grand-jury investigation of the city's one hundred anarchists and directed that "every person found to be a member of the local society was to be indicted for conspiracy to overthrow the government." After considering the matter, however, the grand jury reported that it had not obtained sufficient evidence to justify bringing in any bills of indictment, but it recommended continuation of the investigation.[43] The Newark Excise Board, after an incident involving two anarchists in a local saloon, decided not to award any licenses to anarchist establishments and to revoke licenses granted to establishments that permitted anarchists to congregate on their premises and to demonstrate against government.[44] The anarchists Charles Martino and Mrs. Quintevalli were driven from their homes in Union Hill, New Jersey.[45] The mayor of Paterson, New Jersey, residence of a numerous colony of Italian-born anarchists, and the chiefs of police of such cities as Boston, New York, and Philadelphia announced that they were prepared to "go to the extreme lengths of law" in dealing with the "reds."[46]

Accepting the doctrine of guilt by family association, the landlord of Czolgosz' family in Cleveland ordered his tenants to move, and the Cleveland *Leader* demanded that the assassin's father, who had a city job digging water trenches, be fired.[47] Even as late as May, 1903, when Theodore Roosevelt was visiting Los Angeles, the police, on the advice of the

[41] *Free Society*, Dec. 29, 1901; *Freiheit*, Dec. 14, 1901.

[42] Henry Bool, *Henry Bool's Apology for His Jeffersonian Anarchism*, pp. 4–12, 25; M. M. Dayton to Bool, Oct. 8, 1901, Bool Papers, Joseph A. Labadie Collection, University of Michigan. See also Bool to George E. Priest, Nov. 2, 1901, *ibid.*; and Steven T. Byington to Bool, Nov. 9, 1901, Byington Papers, Labadie Collection.

[43] *Literary Digest*, XXIII (Oct. 5, 1901), 391; New York *Evening Post* (semi-weekly edition), Oct. 31, 1901.

[44] New York *Daily Tribune*, Sept. 16, 17, 19, 1901; Halstead, *McKinley*, pp. 83–84, 92.

[45] New York *Daily Tribune*, Sept. 18, 1901. The mayor of Cliffside Park, New Jersey, ordered Mrs. Bresci, the wife of Humbert's assassin, to move from the area but after consulting legal authorities reconsidered his decision. *Ibid.*; Philadelphia *Press*, Sept. 20, 1901.

[46] New York *Daily Tribune*, Sept. 7, 8, 10, 11, 24, 1901; Halstead, *McKinley*, pp. 77–79; Philadelphia *Press*, Sept. 10, 15, 1901; New York *Evening Post* (semi-weekly edition), Sept. 9, 1901.

[47] New York *Daily Tribune*, Sept. 14, 1901; *Public*, IV (Sept. 28, 1901), 386.

Secret Service, arrested John Czolgosz, Leon's brother, and kept him in custody until the President left the city.[48]

Although anarchists bore the brunt of the resentment engendered by Czolgosz' assassination of McKinley, they were not the only ones to suffer the wrath of the public. The socialists in particular were subjected to considerable annoyance,[49] a fact which is probably accounted for by the tendency of the unthinking to identify socialism with its ideological opposite, anarchism. As a Baptist clergyman wrote to the anarchist Henry Bool: "Anarchists, Socialists, and Communists are all one to the general public,—and all enemies of the present social order as they regard it."[50] Quite apart from ideological factors, all persons who made derogatory remarks about the martyred President in the weeks after the assassination were likely to find themselves in trouble.[51]

The attacks on individual anarchists did not, of course, dispose of "the monster of anarchy," popularly viewed as the real cause of the President's death, any more than did the trial and execution of the President's assassin. There was, however, no lack of suggestions as to how this problem might be met. The solution most frequently proposed in the months after the assassination was the exclusion from the United States of anarchist immigrants, a proposal based on the erroneous but widely held assumption that anarchism was not indigenous to the United States and one which over-

---

[48] New York *Daily Tribune*, May 8, 9, 1903.

[49] For evidence on this point, see *Worker*, Oct. 6, 1901; Philadelphia *Press*, Sept. 10, 22, 1901; Detroit *Evening News*, Sept. 16, 1901; *Discontent*, Oct. 2, Nov. 27, 1901; New York *Daily Tribune*, Sept. 14, 18, 21, 1901; New York *Weekly Tribune*, Sept. 26, 1901; and Chicago *Tribune*, Sept. 10, 1901.

[50] R. T. Jones to Bool, Nov. 5, 1901, Bool Papers.

[51] The newspapers of the time are replete with evidences of this fact. Two of the more important persons who were affected were Detroit's single-tax advocate, Tom Bawden, and Maryland's Senator Wellington. Bawden was arrested on September 10 and fined for a speech in which he declared: "He [Czolgosz] is one of the many throughout the country who know that they are oppressed. I wish to God that there were a lot more just such men in the country." Detroit *Evening News*, Sept. 11, 17, 1901. Senator Wellington's remark that he was "totally indifferent in the matter" of the assassination brought his expulsion from the Union League Club of Maryland and inspired a demand that he be expelled from the Senate. *Literary Digest*, XXIII (Sept. 21, 1901), 337–38. A particular object of criticism after the assault upon McKinley was the Hearst press. Hearst's New York *Journal* had been exceedingly reckless in its criticisms of McKinley ever since 1896, and at times it appeared even to sanction assassination as a means of ridding the country of the President. A boycott of the Hearst papers was declared by many groups after the assassination. Frank Luther Mott, *American Journalism: A History of Newspapers in the United States Through 260 Years: 1690 to 1950* (rev. ed.; New York, 1950), pp. 540–41; *McKinley the Martyr: Extracts from Mr. Hearst's Papers* . . . (n.p., n.d.). The apogee of folly amidst the general hysteria following the attack on the President was attained by the Virginia Constitutional Convention, which on September 17, 1901, decided to omit the guarantee of free speech contained in the Virginia Bill of Rights in good part because of its belief that it was the right of free speech that had led to the death of the President. Cooler heads eventually prevailed, however, and the section in question was restored. *Nation*, LXXIII (Sept. 26, 1901), 235–36.

looked the obvious fact that the President's assassin was native born.[52] The corollary of the thesis that immigrant anarchists be excluded was the strongly held view that anarchists already in the United States (many advocates of this idea would have included citizens as well as aliens) be banished, preferably to some Pacific island.[53] It was also proposed that assaults on the president and other high-placed federal officials should constitute a federal offense regardless of where perpetrated, should be punished more severely than assaults on private persons, or should be regarded as treason, that a detail of Secret Service men be assigned to guard the president, that the law deal severely with those who by the spoken or written word advocated violence and the assassination of public officials or urged the overthrow of the government by force, that anarchist publications be banned and anarchist meetings suppressed, that anarchist assassins be made to suffer cruel and unusual punishments or even be subjected to lynch law, that anarchism be treated by international agreement as piracy, and that anarchists be subjected to "police control."[54] Few indeed were the

[52] *Public Opinion*, XXXI (Sept. 19, 26, 1901), 360, 390; *Literary Digest*, XXIII (Sept. 21, 1901), 335; Chicago *Tribune*, Sept. 7, 1901; Philadelphia *Press*, Sept. 9, 12, 1901; New York *Daily Tribune*, Sept. 8, 9, 10, 1901; Chicago *Post*, Oct. 28, 1901; Boston *Globe*, Dec. 12, 1901; Halstead, *McKinley*, p. 107; Lew Wallace, "Prevention of Presidential Assassinations," *North American Review*, CLXXIII (December, 1901), 723-24; *Gunton's Magazine*, XXI (October, 1901), 302-04, 353.

[53] *Congressional Record*, 57 Cong., 1 sess., p. 216; "An Anarchist Experiment Station," *Independent*, LIII (Nov. 7, 1901), 2661-63; Andrew D. White, "Assassins and Their Apologists," *ibid.*, LIV (Aug. 21, 1902), 1990; Halstead, *McKinley*, pp. 100-01; *Public Opinion*, XXXI (Sept. 19, 26, Dec. 19, 1901), 360, 390, 781-82; *Literary Digest*, XXIII (Sept. 21, Oct. 5, 1901), 335, 391; Chicago *Tribune*, Sept. 7, 11, 1901; Philadelphia *Press*, Sept. 10, 1901; New York *Daily Tribune*, Sept. 8, 9, 10, 12, 18, 23, 1901; Boston *Globe*, Dec. 12, 1901.

[54] Eugene Wambaugh, "The Nation and the Anarchists," *Green Bag*, XIII (October, 1901), 461-62; S. C. T. Dodd, "Congress and Anarchy: A Suggestion," *North American Review*, CLXXIII (October, 1901), 433-36; Edgar Aldrich, "The Power and Duty of the Federal Government to Protect Its Agents," *ibid.*, CLXIII (December, 1901), 746-57; George C. Holt, "The Defects of the United States Criminal Law," *Independent*, LIII (Sept. 26, 1901), 2282-85; Wallace, "Prevention of Presidential Assassinations," pp. 723-26; J. M. Buckley, "The Assassination of Kings and Presidents," *Century*, XLI (November, 1901), 142; Arthur T. Pierson, "The Spirit of Anarchy and the Weapon of Assassination," *Missionary Review of the World*, XXIV (November, 1901), 803; "Anarchism and the Law," *Independent*, LIII (Sept. 12, 1901), 2187-89; "Anarchy and Its Suppression," *Harper's Weekly*, XLV (Oct. 5, 1901), 997; *Educational Review*, XXII (October, 1901), 321-22; "Anarchism—Its Cause and Cure," *Outlook*, LXIX (Oct. 5, 1901), 253-54; *Gunton's Magazine*, XXI (October, 1901), 304-05; New York *Daily Tribune*, Sept. 8, 9, 11, 12, Oct. 16, 18, 1901; Chicago *Tribune*, Sept. 7, 8, 9, 10, 11, 15, 16, 23, 24, 26, 29, Oct. 5, 16, 1901; Philadelphia *Press*, Sept. 8, 9, 10, 11, 12, 16, 19, 1901; Chicago *Post*, Oct. 28, 1901; Detroit *Evening News*, Sept. 16, 1901; Boston *Globe*, Dec. 12, 1901; *Public Opinion*, XXXI (Sept. 12, 19, 26, 1901), 324, 359-60, 390; *Literary Digest*, XXIII (Sept. 21, Oct. 5, 1901), 335-36, 391-93; *Nation*, LXXIII (Sept. 26, 1901), 235; Robert A. Pinkerton, "Detective Surveillance of Anarchists," *North American Review*, CLXXIII (November, 1901), 609-17; Secretary of the Treasury, *Annual Report on the State of the Finances for the Fiscal Year Ended June 30, 1902* (Washington, 1902), p. 52.

persons who distinguished between philosophical anarchists and anarchists who advocated the use of force and between anarchist thought and anarchist crime, who protested proposed curbs on anarchists which trenched on constitutional guarantees, and who castigated Americans who seemed ready to barter away the essentials of freedom in the interests of security against a minor and temporary danger.[55]

It remained for Congress, and such state legislatures as saw fit to act, to transform suggestions into legislation and to devise appropriate measures for dealing with anarchism and particularly with its more violent manifestations.[56] The opening shot in the campaign of the federal government to cope with the problem presented by the assassination of McKinley was fired by the nation's new president, Theodore Roosevelt, in his first message to Congress. Roosevelt, who believed "that we should war with relentless efficiency not only against anarchists, but against all active and passive sympathizers with anarchists,"[57] declared that McKinley had been killed "by an utterly depraved criminal belonging to that body of criminals who object to all governments, good and bad alike." Both the advocates of anarchy and the apologists for anarchism were, he insisted, "morally accessory to murder before the fact." Roosevelt suggested to Congress that it exclude from the United States anarchists who extolled assassination and that it deport alien anarchists who espoused this view. The federal courts, he recommended, should be given jurisdiction over attempts on the life of the president or officials in the line of presidential succession, and he thought that even unsuccessful attempts should be severely punished. Roosevelt also proposed that treaties be drawn up making anarchy an offense against the law of nations similar to piracy and the slave trade.[58]

The Fifty-seventh Congress was confronted not only by the recommendations of the President but by a multitude of anti-anarchy bills presented by its own membership. Debate was, however, confined to the Ray Bill in the House and the Hoar Bill in the Senate. The former provided the death penalty for persons who killed the president, vice-president, those in the line of presidential succession, and ambassadors of foreign countries accredited to the United States while these officials were per-

---

55 Particularly noteworthy as a deplorer of the popular hysteria was Louis F. Post, editor of the single-tax journal the *Public*. See, for example, *Public*, IV (Sept. 14, 21, 28, Oct. 12, 1901), 353–55, 371, 388–94, 422–24. Moderate views were also expressed by the social gospelers R. Heber Newton, Washington Gladden, and Lyman Abbott; by Illinois' former governor, John Peter Altgeld; by the editor of the *Arena*, B. O. Flower; and by such journals as the New York *Evening Post*, the Detroit *Evening News*, the *Nation*, and the *Chautauquan*.

56 For earlier attempts by Congress to deal with the problem of anarchism, see J. C. Burrows, "The Need of National Legislation Against Anarchism," *North American Review*, CLXXIII (December, 1901), 727–45.

57 Roosevelt to Henry Cabot Lodge, Sept. 9, 1901, Elting E. Morison, *et al.*, eds., *The Letters of Theodore Roosevelt*, 8 vols. (Cambridge, 1951–54), III, 142.

58 Hermann Hagedorn, ed., *The Works of Theodore Roosevelt*, 24 vols. (memorial edition; New York, 1923–26), XVII, 93, 96–99.

forming their official duties, or because of their official character, or because of their "official acts or omissions." Attempts to accomplish the
above were to be punished by not less than ten years' imprisonment. Persons who aided, incited, or conspired with anyone to perpetrate such
deeds were to be deemed principal offenders, and accomplices after the
fact were to receive sentences of from one to twenty-five years. Fines
and imprisonment were stipulated for persons who advocated or justified
the killing or assaulting of public officials. Persons who disbelieved in or
who were opposed to "all organized government," or who were members
of organizations entertaining such beliefs, or who advocated the killing
of public officials because of their official character were not to be permitted to enter the United States, nor were they to be naturalized.[59]

The Hoar Bill was of somewhat narrower scope than its House
counterpart. It provided the death penalty for persons who willfully killed
or attempted to kill the president, the vice-president, any officer upon
whom the duties of the president might devolve, or the sovereign of a
foreign nation. Persons instigating or counseling such crimes or conspiring
to accomplish same were to be imprisoned for twenty years, whereas persons who by the spoken or written word threatened to kill or advised the
killing of any of the aforesaid were to receive ten-year terms. Accomplices after the fact were to be punished as principals. Further to insure
the safety of the president, the measure provided that the secretary of
war was to detach officers and men from the regular army to guard the
chief executive. The Hoar Bill passed the Senate on March 21, 1902, by a
vote of 52 to 15, despite protests from southern senators that to make an
assault upon high-placed federal officials a federal offense constituted an
invasion of the domain of the states and that to provide greater punishment for such attacks than for attacks upon ordinary persons was to
enact class legislation.[60]

The House Committee on the Judiciary, to which the Hoar Bill was
referred, found the measure unacceptable. In reporting the bill back to the
House on April 4, it preserved only the Senate number of the measure
and substituted for the original text the Ray Bill with one new section
added. The latter stipulated that in prosecutions under the act for attacks
on the president, vice-president, or persons in the line of presidential succession, it was to be presumed, unless the contrary was proved, that these
officials were, at the time of the commission of the alleged offenses, engaged in the performance of their official duties. Congressman Ray of
New York explained that the Hoar Bill was unconstitutional insofar as it
defined and punished as crimes offenses against high officials simply because of their office irrespective of whether they were engaged in the
performance of official duties, and that it threatened the nation's liberty
by theoretically permitting the secretary of war to assign the entire
regular army to the task of guarding the president.[61] Objections in the

---

[59] *House Reports, No. 433,* 57 Cong., 1 sess., pp. 16–18.
[60] *Congressional Record,* 57 Cong., 1 sess., pp. 1495, 2269, 2275–76, 2288, 2299, 2356,
    2428–35, 2483–92, 2907, 2953–63, 2995–3006, 3045–66, 3113, 3115–23, 3126–29.
[61] *House Reports, No. 1422,* 57 Cong., 1 sess., pp. 1–12.

House to the new version of the Ray Bill were similar to those voiced in
the Senate with respect to the Hoar Bill, but the measure passed on June
9, 1902, by a vote of 179 to 38.[62]

Prompted by its Committee on the Judiciary, the Senate refused to
concur in the House amendments to its bill, and the measure had to be
referred to a conference committee. The latter's report, which recommended a bill somewhat closer to the House version than to the original
Senate measure, was not submitted to the House until February 19, 1903,
and to the Senate until four days later. It provided the death penalty for
persons who caused the death of the president, vice-president, and anyone
upon whom the duties of the presidency had devolved, and a similar penalty for causing the death of foreign ambassadors and ministers accredited
to the United States and officials in the line of presidential succession provided they were engaged in the performance of their official duties or
were killed because of their official character or duties or because of their
official acts or omissions. The measure further provided that any person
who aided or advised the killing of the officials named or conspired with
any person to this end, as well as accomplices after the fact, should be
deemed principal offenders. The remaining sections of the measure were
derived from the Ray Bill.[63]

The conference report was accepted by the House on February 20,
1903, but it ran into difficulties in the Senate. Senator Hoar of Massachusetts asked his colleagues to accept the report without debate, but when
the measure was taken up on March 3, 1903, the last day of the session,
Senator Bacon of Georgia insisted that it was an altogether different proposal from the one previously considered by the Senate and must therefore be debated at length. Hoar pressed for a vote, but when Senator
Teller of Colorado assured him that the measure would not pass, Hoar
withdrew his motion, and the measure died. Thus, although the House
and Senate had separately approved bills designed to deal with one or
another aspect of the problem of anarchy, the two houses, in the press
of business during the closing hours of the session, were unable to agree
on a compromise measure.[64]

The country was not, however, to be without some congressional
legislation on the subject of anarchy. Since there was relatively little
difference of opinion in the Congress or in the nation as a whole with
regard to the necessity of shutting off the alleged flow of anarchist immigrants, it is not surprising that this legislation took the form of anarchist-
exclusion amendments to the immigration legislation. Section 2 of a measure designed to regulate the immigration of aliens into the United States,
which was passed by the House on May 27, 1902, added to the list of
excluded immigrants "anarchists, or persons who believe in or advocate
the overthrow by force or violence of all governments, or of all forms of
law, or the assassination of public officials." At the instigation of Senator

---

[62] *Congressional Record*, 57 Cong., 1 sess., pp. 3701, 6235–45, 6246–52, 6283–6305, 6332–
60, 6361, 6392–6420, 6421–26, 6450–59, 6460–67, 6468–76, 6506–08.

[63] *Ibid.*, pp. 6564–65, 6838; *ibid.*, 57 Cong., 2 sess., p. 2407.

[64] *Ibid.*, 57 Cong., 2 sess., pp. 2419–20, 2703–04, 2953, 2956–64.

Bacon, the Senate, while retaining Section 2, added to the measure as Section 38 the much more sweeping provisions of the Ray Bill, which excluded not only advocates of the forcible overthrow of government but also persons who disbelieved in or were opposed to all government, or who were members of or affiliated with organizations teaching such views, or who advocated the assassination of public officials because of their official character, forbade such persons to become naturalized, and fined those who aided such individuals either to enter the United States or to become naturalized. It was in this form that the measure ultimately passed the Congress on March 3, 1903, receiving the approval of the President the next day.[65]

The inability of Congress to agree on legislation for the control of domestic anarchists was not matched by three of the states: New York, New Jersey, and Wisconsin. New York became the first state to take action when its governor signed into law on April 3, 1902, a measure which struck at criminal anarchy, defined as "the doctrine that organized government should be overthrown by force or violence, or by assassination of the executive head or of any of the executive officials of government, or by any unlawful means." It was made a felony punishable by not more than ten years' imprisonment, or by a fine of $5,000, or both to advocate criminal anarchy by the written or spoken word, to justify assassination so as to advocate criminal anarchy, to organize, or help to organize, or become a member of, or voluntarily assemble with any group formed to advocate such doctrines, and for two or more persons to assemble to advocate or teach such doctrines. It was made a misdemeanor punishable by two years' imprisonment, or $2,000 fine, or both for the owner or caretaker of a hall or building to permit its use for an assemblage advocating criminal anarchy.[66]

Enacted as a result of pressures stemming from the assassination of McKinley and designed to curb anarchists who were addicted to violence, the New York criminal anarchy law turned out to be of singularly little significance as an anti-anarchist measure. Although there were some abortive attempts to apply it to anarchists in the years after McKinley's death[67] and although the measure figured in a minor slander suit,[68] it lay dormant for all practical purposes until it was applied in 1919 not to an anarchist but to a prominent leader of the Left Wing Section of the Socialist party (later Communist party), Benjamin Gitlow, who had published a manifesto advocating the destruction of the existing state and its

---

[65] *House Reports, No. 982,* 57 Cong., 1 sess., pp. 2–3; *Congressional Record,* 57 Cong., 1 sess., pp. 2984, 6014, 6044; *Senate Reports, No. 2119,* 57 Cong., 1 sess.; *Congressional Record,* 57 Cong., 2 sess., pp. 2805–06, 2809, 2867–68, 2894–95, 2918–19, 2949–50, 3010–11, 3077; *United States Statutes at Large,* XXXII, 1214, 1221–22.

[66] Clevenger-Gilbert, *Criminal Law and Practice of New York . . . as Amended to End of Legislative Session of 1948* (official edition; Albany, N.Y., 1948), Penal Law, Article 14, Sections 160–64.

[67] *Freiheit,* Apr. 12, 26, May 10, 17, 24, 1902; *Free Society,* May 18, 1902; Goldman, *Living My Life,* pp. 390–92, 396.

[68] Von Gerichten *v.* Seitz, 94 App. Div. N.Y. 130 (1904).

replacement with a dictatorship of the proletariat. Although Justices Pound and Cardozo of the New York Court of Appeals protested that to advocate the dictatorship of the proletariat was not to advocate criminal anarchy and that the statute in question aimed historically only at the latter, the court ruled that Gitlow was guilty under the terms of the act of 1902.[69] The case was appealed to the United States Supreme Court, which in a celebrated opinion, Holmes and Brandeis dissenting, upheld the constitutionality of the New York law and maintained that the defendant had not been deprived of the liberty guaranteed to him by the Fourteenth Amendment.[70]

Twenty-seven days after the New York criminal anarchy law was approved, New Jersey responded by legislation to the existing anti-anarchist sentiment by enacting a statute which went further than the New York law in that it struck not only at the advocacy of the overthrow of government by force but also at the encouragement of "hostility or opposition to any and all government." The measure punished by a fine of not more than $2,000, or imprisonment at hard labor for not more than fifteen years, or both any person who advocated anarchy, as defined, or who belonged to an organization, or attended a meeting, or circulated literature which had this purpose in view. The death penalty or, at the discretion of the jury, life imprisonment was to be imposed on persons who assaulted "with intent to kill and with intent thereby to show his or her hostility or opposition to any and all government," or who incited or aided others to assault, or who conspired to kill the president, vice-president, any official in the line of succession to the presidency, the governor of New Jersey or the chief executive of any state, or the heir apparent or presumptive to the throne of any foreign state.[71]

The third and last state to fall in line was Wisconsin, which on May 22, 1903, put into effect a measure modeled almost word for word upon the New York law.[72] Thus did the attack on McKinley inspire legislation which was to serve as a precedent for the criminal anarchy and criminal syndicalist laws of a later day.

The anarchists themselves were far from agreed in their reaction to the President's assassination. Individualist anarchists, as might have been expected, unequivocally condemned Czolgosz' action, disavowed any connection between anarchism and assassination, and insisted that they sought to achieve their objectives by "peaceful persuasion." "It cannot be too emphatically insisted on," declared James F. Morton, "that there is absolutely nothing in the Anarchist philosophy which constitutes, directly or

[69] People v. Gitlow, 234 N.Y. 132 (1922).

[70] Gitlow v. N.Y., 268 U.S. 652 (1925).

[71] Revised Statutes of New Jersey Effective December 20, 1937, 4 vols. (n.p., 1938), Title 2, pp. 483–84.

[72] Journal of Proceedings of the Forty-sixth Session of the Wisconsin Legislature. In Senate. 1903 (Madison, 1903), p. 1285; Wisconsin Statutes, 1949 (20th ed.; Racine, n.d.), Ch. 347.14–347.18, pp. 3119–20.

indirectly, an incitement to assassination. This is true in the fullest sense, without reservation or equivocation."[73]

Communist anarchists, on the other hand, were divided in their attitude toward the assassination as toward the question of the use of force in general. Generally speaking, however, they were more inclined to accept Czolgosz' act than were the individualist anarchists and, at the very least, tended to picture the deed as "a part of that great human tide constantly rising against oppression in direct response to natural law." Emma Goldman thus found it possible to "bow in reverenced silence before the powers" of the assassin's soul, and Kate Austin accepted the assassination "as the supreme protest of a brave and generous heart against 'the curse of government.'" Free Society apologized to the assassin for having suspected that he was a spy and, after some equivocation on the subject, concluded that "the logic of revolutionary thought" required anarchists to accept deeds such as that of Czolgosz.[74] The individualist anarchist Edwin C. Walker justly complained that Free Society was "through and through . . . a scarcely-veiled apology for the killing of McKinley."[75]

If anarchists were of different minds in their estimate of Czolgosz' deed, they were united in their opposition to the various proposals put forward after the assassination for dealing with the anarchist problem in the United States. Anarchism, they insisted, could not be stamped out by legislative or administrative fiat, as was being suggested. Since laws and persecution were powerless to kill a real truth, just as they were unnecessary to demolish error, anarchism would survive despite all the measures that might be taken to combat it.[76] Concentrating increasingly on the

---

[73] Discontent, Sept. 18, 1901. See also ibid., Sept. 25, Oct. 9, 1901; Bool, Henry Bool's Apology for His Jeffersonian Anarchism; Henry Bool's Creed, reprint from the Weekly Ithacan of Oct. 24, 1901; Who's Who? A Discussion Between an Autocratic Democrat and a Government-by-Consent Anarchist . . . ; Free Comrade, November, 1901; Lucifer, Sept. 14, 21, 28, Oct. 31, 1901.

[74] Free Society, Oct. 6, 13, Dec. 8, 15, 1901, Mar. 9, Oct. 12, 26, 1902; Chicago Tribune, Dec. 6, 7, 1901; New York Daily Tribune, Nov. 28, 1901. Czolgosz' action is also defended in Jay Fox, Roosevelt, Czolgosz and Anarchy (New York, 1902). Most's Freiheit reiterated its view that propaganda of the deed should not be employed in countries such as the United States where other kinds of propaganda were still possible to anarchists. Freiheit, Sept. 14, 21, Oct. 5, 1901. See also Down with Anarchists (New York, 1901), a pamphlet prepared by Most. For criticism of Czolgosz' act by other communist anarchists, see Goldman, Living My Life, pp. 323–24 (views of Alexander Berkman), Philadelphia Press, Sept. 12, 1901 (views of Carl Nold), Chicago Tribune, Sept. 7, 1901 (views of Oscar Neebe and Lucy Parsons), and Freie Arbeiter Stimme, Sept. 13, 20, 27, 1901. Emma Goldman was particularly disturbed at the attitude toward the assassination assumed by English-speaking and Jewish anarchists but was satisfied with the reaction of French, Italian, and Spanish groups. Goldman, pp. 316, 318.

[75] Walker to Bool, Dec. 15, 1901, Bool Papers.

[76] Philadelphia Evening Bulletin, Oct. 14, 1901; Free Society, Dec. 29, 1901, Apr. 20, June 8, 1902, Mar. 29, Nov. 15, 1903; Discontent, Oct. 2, 9, Dec. 18, 1901; Freiheit, Nov. 30, 1901, Mar. 15, 22, 1902; Constitutional Freedom or New Jersey Tyranny—Which? (n.p., [1902]).

free-speech aspects of the problem, anarchists charged that the attack on them was but a prelude to efforts to suppress all unpopular views, all expressions of dissent. Americans were urged to resist this tendency and to check any encroachment on the right of free speech.[77]

The anarchists were provided with an opportunity to exploit their free-speech views when the federal government enforced for the first time the anarchist-exclusion sections of its new immigration legislation by arresting the English anarchist and trade-unionist John Turner, who had arrived in New York in October, 1903. A series of lectures was arranged for Turner by American anarchists, the first of which was delivered in New York on October 23, 1903, on the subject of trade unionism and the general strike. At the conclusion of his address Turner was arrested for having entered the United States in violation of the immigration legislation. Turner was searched, and on his person were found a copy of *Free Society*, a pamphlet prepared by Johann Most, and a schedule of lectures indicating that he was to have spoken on such subjects as "The Legal Murder of 1887" and was to have addressed a mass meeting with Most in commemoration of the hanging of the Haymarket anarchists.

The day following his arrest Turner received an administrative hearing before a board of special inquiry of the Department of Commerce and Labor and was ordered deported. This decision was upheld by the Secretary of Commerce and Labor and, on appeal, by the Circuit Court of the United States for the Southern District of New York.[78]

Pending deportation Turner was held at Ellis Island. He was locked in a 9 by 6 foot cage designed for insane immigrants and for a time could be visited only by his counsel and not even by him on a private basis.[79] Wishing to push the case to the United States Supreme Court, the anarchists, with Emma Goldman taking the lead, asked Turner if he would be willing to remain at Ellis Island while his case was appealed. Turner agreed to remain, not, he said, because he thought the case would be decided in his favor but because he believed that public opinion might be sufficiently aroused to bring about the repeal of the legislation in question or to forestall his being deported.[80]

On November 14, 1903, a group of Turner's supporters, several but not all of whom were anarchists, formed themselves into a Free Speech League and assumed direction of his case. The League engaged Clarence Darrow and his partner, Edgar Lee Masters, as counsel for Turner and decided to concentrate its attention on the free-speech aspects of the affair. "The sole question at issue," the League informed the public, "is: Shall the Federal Government be a Judge of beliefs and disbeliefs?"

[77] James F. Morton, Jr., *Do You Want Free Speech?* (Home, Washington, [1903]); George Pyburn, *The Conspiracy Against Free Speech and Press* (New York, 1902); *The Free Speech League, Its Declaration* (n.p., [1902]). These three pamphlets are available in the Labadie Collection.

[78] United States *ex rel* John Turner *v.* William Williams, *Brief and Argument of Appellant* (Chicago, 1904), pp. 4–7; *Free Society,* Oct. 25, 1903.

[79] *Free Society,* Nov. 29, Dec. 6, 1903; *Demonstrator,* Dec. 1, 1903; *Public,* VI (Feb. 20, 1904), 722.

[80] *Free Society,* Nov. 22, 1903; Goldman, *Living My Life,* pp. 347–48.

"Tyranny," it declared, "always begins with the most unpopular man or class and extends by degrees: it should be resisted at the beginning."[81]

That the anarchists were beginning to win a measure of outside support by playing up the free-speech angle of the Turner case was clearly evidenced when they arranged a mass meeting in New York City's Cooper Union on December 3, 1903, to protest the threatened deportation of John Turner. Although the anarchists had provided the impetus for the meeting, the list of vice-presidents for the affair included such prominent nonanarchists as Felix Adler, Ernest H. Crosby, Henry George, Jr., Franklin Giddings, Henry D. Sedgwick, Jr., Horace White, Carl Schurz, and the Reverend Leighton Williams. Resolutions were adopted at the meeting which protested "so much of the Immigration Law as authorizes the exclusion and deportation of an alien solely because of his opinions" and also the administrative process by which Turner had been seized and detained.[82] Similar meetings were held in Philadelphia and in Buffalo, and the government's actions were also protested by several labor organizations.[83]

Criticism of the immigration legislation insofar as it provided for the exclusion of peaceful anarchists was also voiced by some of the leading newspapers and magazines in the country. The New York *Evening Post*, the New York *Daily News*, the New York *World*, the Springfield *Republican*, the *Independent*, and the *Outlook* all argued that in barring aliens from the country because of their opinions alone, the federal government was striking at the vital principle of freedom of speech and freedom of thought.[84]

Criticisms of this sort failed, however, to sway the nation's highest court, which took up the Turner case on April 6, 1904. In his majority opinion upholding anarchist exclusion, Chief Justice Fuller rejected the argument of Darrow and Masters[85] and declared that Congress has the power to exclude aliens and to prescribe terms for their entry, that it can deport those who have entered in violation of the law, that it can have

[81] *Free Society*, Nov. 22, 1903; Goldman, pp. 348–49; Free Speech League, *The Imprisonment of John Turner. Free Speech and the New Alien Law* (n.p., 1903). The anarchist Edwin C. Walker had organized a Free Speech League on May 1, 1902, which was closely related to the new League in terms of personnel. See undated pamphlet in the Labadie Collection giving demands and constitution of the 1902 organization.

[82] *Free Speech and the New Alien Law* ([New York], 1903); *Free Society*, Dec. 13, 1903.

[83] *Free Society*, Dec. 13, 20, 1903, Jan. 3, 10, 24, 31, Feb. 7, 1904; *Public*, VI (Dec. 26, 1903, Feb. 13, 20, 1904), 594–95, 717, 723. For the Buffalo meeting, see newspaper clippings in envelope labeled "John Turner Case," Labadie Collection.

[84] Views of New York *Post* and New York *Daily News* cited in *Free Speech and the New Alien Law;* views of Springfield *Republican* cited in *Demonstrator*, Dec. 30, 1903; New York *World*, Jan. 31, 1904; "Liberty of Opinion Denied," *Independent*, LV (Dec. 10, 1903), 2940–41; *Outlook*, LXXV (Nov. 21, 1903), 678–79; *ibid.*, LXXVII (May 28, 1904), 205–06. But see also *Literary Digest*, XXVII (Dec. 19, 1903), 855–57.

[85] United States *ex rel* John Turner *v.* William Williams, *Brief and Argument of Appellant*, pp. 24–187.

executive officers enforce these provisions, and that such action does not deprive aliens of due process of law or of freedom of speech or of the press. Fuller thought that it was not an unjustifiable inference from the evidence in the case that Turner contemplated the use of force to attain his ideals, but he insisted that the act would have been constitutional even if Turner had been merely a philosophical anarchist, because it was to be presumed that "Congress was of [the] opinion that the tendency of the general exploitation of such views is so dangerous to the public weal that aliens who hold and advocate them would be undesirable additions to our population."

In a separate concurring opinion Justice Brewer declared that since it appeared that Turner was an anarchist of the type who sought the overthrow of the government by force, it was unnecessary to consider what his rights would have been were he simply a philosophical anarchist. It is difficult to see how Brewer could have maintained this position in view of the language of Section 38.[86]

With the trial of John Turner and the upholding by the Supreme Court of the constitutionality of the anti-anarchist provisions of the immigration legislation of 1903, the anti-anarchist phase of the assassination of William McKinley was brought to a close. The passions engendered by the assassination had long since been quieted, and now the issue as a whole ceased to be of public interest. Traces of the affair remained only in the legislation enacted by Congress and the states of New York, New Jersey, and Wisconsin and in the writings of the communist anarchists who chose to add Leon Czolgosz to their list of anarchist martyrs.[87]

The lot of the anarchist in this country remained a troubled one, however, and when the United States entered World War I the federal government intensified the attack upon anarchism which it had initiated following the assassination of McKinley. Alarmed at the implications of the Russian Revolution of 1917 and overly concerned with the threat to the nation's stability represented by alien radicals, Congress in 1917 and 1918 provided for the deportation of "aliens who are members of the anarchistic and similar classes" and in so doing adopted a solution for the anarchist problem much discussed after Czolgosz' attack on McKinley. Acting under the authority of this legislation, federal officials in late 1919 and early 1920 arrested approximately three thousand aliens for possible deportation. The great majority of this number were apparently communists or suspected communists, but anarchists were also included in the total; and when the *Buford* on December 21, 1919, sailed for Finland and Russia, fifty-one anarchists were among its cargo of 249 deportees. The most prominent of the "Red Ark's" anarchist passengers were Emma Goldman and Alex-

---

[86] U.S. *ex rel* John Turner *v.* Williams, 194 U.S. 279 (1904), 289–90, 293–94, 296.

[87] For the martyrization of Czolgosz by communist anarchists, see particularly [Voltairine de Cleyre], *McKinley's Assassination from the Anarchist Standpoint* (n.p., [1907]); and the October issues of *Mother Earth* for 1906, 1908, 1910, 1911, 1912, 1913, and 1916. For an expression of individualist anarchist disgust with communist-anarchist martyrization of Czolgosz, see Edwin C. Walker, *Liberty vs. Assassination* (New York, [1906]).

ander Berkman, both of whom had but recently completed jail terms of twenty-one months for violation of the Espionage Act.[88]

Insofar as anarchists had associated themselves with the syndicalist-minded Industrial Workers of the World, they also ran afoul of the criminal syndicalist laws[89] enacted by various state governments during the war years and immediately thereafter. As a result of this combined assault of state and federal governments between 1917 and 1920, the anarchist movement in the United States was almost completely disrupted; and although the subject of anarchism was to be a factor in the celebrated Sacco-Vanzetti case, anarchism no longer attracted significant public attention after 1920.[90] The fears which it had at one time inspired had by the end of the second decade of the twentieth century been transferred to the far more serious problem of communism, and it was the communist dictatorship of the proletariat rather than the anarchist propaganda of word or the deed that now seemed to constitute the more important threat to the nation's security.

[88] Jane Perry Clark, *Deportation of Aliens from the United States to Europe* (New York, 1931), pp. 216–21; Louis F. Post, *The Deportations Delirium of Nineteen-Twenty: A Personal Narrative of an Historic Official Experience* (Chicago, 1923), p. 27.

[89] Twenty states enacted such laws between 1917 and 1920. Eldridge Foster Dowell, *A History of Criminal Syndicalism Legislation in the United States* (Baltimore, 1939), p. 21. In addition, Massachusetts and Vermont adopted criminal anarchy laws in 1919. Zechariah Chafee, Jr., *Free Speech in the United States* (Cambridge, 1941), pp. 585, 595.

[90] Madison, *Critics and Crusaders,* pp. 170–71.

Suggestions for Further Reading

For a general introduction to the Gilded Age, see Ray Ginger, *Age of Excess** (Macmillan, 1965), and Fred A. Shannon, *The Centennial Years: A Political and Economic History of America from the Late 1870s to the Early 1890s** (Doubleday, 1967). Perhaps the best introduction to the period, but a study that continues into the twentieth century, is Robert Wiebe, *The Search for Order, 1887–1920** (Hill and Wang, 1967). T. C. Cochran and William Miller deal with the economic development of the United States during the postwar years in *The Age of Enterprise** (Macmillan, 1942).

The impact of certain social and political theories that appeared late in the nineteenth century and the conflicts they engendered are discussed in Richard Hofstadter, *Social Darwinism in American Thought** (University of Pennsylvania Press, 1944); Sidney Fine, *Laissez Faire and the General Welfare State: A Study of Conflict in American Thought, 1865–1901** (University of Michigan Press, 1956); and Henry F. May, *Protestant Churches and Industrial America** (Harper and Row, 1949).

The standard treatment of immigration in the United States is M. A. Jones, *American Immigration** (University of Chicago Press, 1960). Special problems of the new immigration in the period after the Civil War are dealt with in Barbara Miller Solomon, *Ancestors and Immigrants** (Harvard University Press, 1956); John Higham, *Strangers in the Land: Patterns of American Nativism, 1860–1925** (Rutgers University Press, 1955); and Moses Rischin, *The Promised City: New York's Jews, 1870–1914** (Harvard University Press, 1962).

The industrialists of the postwar years are viewed harshly in Matthew Josephson, *The Robber Barons: The Great American Capitalists, 1861–1901** (Harcourt Brace Jovanovich, 1934). Useful biographies of leading industrial figures are Allan Nevins, *John D. Rockefeller* (2 vols.; Scribner's, 1940), and Joseph Frazier Wall, *Andrew Carnegie* (Oxford University Press, 1970). For a penetrating fictional treatment of a businessman by a contemporary author, see William Dean Howells, *The Rise of Silas Lapham** (Houghton-Mifflin, 1885).

Two contemporary works that provide valuable insight into life in the late nineteenth century are Edward Bellamy's utopian novel, *Looking Backward, 2000–1887** (Ticknor, 1888), and Jacob Riis's *How the Other Half Lives: Studies Among the Tenements of New York** (Scribner's, 1890).

The standard history of the American workingman is John R. Commons et al., *History of Labour in the United States* (4 vols.; Macmillan, 1918–35). A specialized survey of labor during the

* Available in paperback edition.

Gilded Age is Norman J. Ware, *The Labor Movement in the United States, 1860–1895** (Appleton-Century-Crofts, 1929). For the philosophy behind the labor movement, see Gerald N. Grob, *Workers and Utopia: A Study of Ideological Conflict in the American Labor Movement, 1865–1900** (Northwestern University Press, 1961), and Herbert G. Gutman, "Protestantism and the American Labor Movement: The Christian Spirit in the Gilded Age," *American Historical Review*, Vol. 62 (October, 1966), 74–101.

Important labor conflicts are treated in Leon Wolff, *Lockout: The Story of the Homestead Strike of 1892** (Harper and Row, 1965); Almont Lindsey, *The Pullman Strike: The Story of a Unique Experiment and of a Great Labor Upheaval** (University of Chicago Press, 1942); D. L. McMurray, *Coxey's Army: A Study of the Industrial Army Movement of 1894** (Little, Brown, 1929); and R. V. Bruce, *1877: Year of Violence** (Bobbs-Merrill, 1959).

Several of C. Vann Woodward's essays on the post-bellum South have been collected under the title *The Burden of Southern History** (Louisiana State University Press, 1960). Woodward describes the development of segregation in the South in *The Strange Career of Jim Crow** (2d rev. ed.; Oxford University Press, 1966). The special problems faced by Southern blacks after the war are considered in Vernon L. Wharton, *The Negro in Mississippi, 1865–1890** (University of North Carolina Press, 1947); G. B. Tindall, *South Carolina Negroes, 1877–1900** (University of South Carolina Press, 1952); and Charles E. Wynes (ed.), *The Negro in the South since 1865** (University of Alabama Press, 1965). Rayford W. Logan provides a survey of attitudes toward Afro-Americans during the Gilded Age in *The Negro in American Life and Thought: The Nadir, 1877–1901* (Dial, 1954), published in paperback under the title *The Betrayal of the Negro.** Postwar attitudes and political activities of Southern whites are considered in Lawrence J. Friedman, *The White Savage: Racial Fantasies in the Postbellum South** (Prentice-Hall, 1970); A. D. Kirwan, *Revolt of the Rednecks: Mississippi Politics, 1876–1925** (University of Kentucky Press, 1951); and Paul Lewinson, *Race, Class and Party: A History of Negro Suffrage and White Politics in the South** (Oxford University Press, 1932). The plight of the American farmer is explored in Fred A. Shannon, *The Farmer's Last Frontier: Agriculture, 1860–1897** (Holt, Rinehart and Winston, 1945), and in Theodore Saloutos, *Farmer Movements in the South, 1865–1933** (Universtiy of California Press, 1960).

General treatments of anarchism are found in George Woodcock, *Anarchism: A History of Libertarian Ideas and Movements** (World, 1962); James Joll, *The Anarchists** (Little, Brown, 1964); and the collection of documents edited by Irving Louis Horowitz, *The Anarchists** (Dell, 1964). The American anarchist tradition is examined in James J. Martin, *Men Against the State: The Expositors of Individual Anarchism in America, 1827–1908** (Adrian Allen Associates, 1953), and in Henry J. Silverman (ed.), *American Radical Thought: The Libertarian Tradition** (Heath, 1970). Conflicts between anarchists and the establishment are treated in Henry David, *The History of the Haymarket Affair: A Study in the American Social-Revolutionary and Labor Movements* (Holt, Rinehart and Winston, 1936), and in Louis Adamic, *Dynamite: The Story of Class Violence in America** (Viking, 1935).

The Early
Twentieth Century

The IWW Fight
for Free Speech
on the West Coast

MELVYN DUBOFSKY

For the most part, organized labor in America has been content to seek economic advantage for itself. On a few rare occasions, however, labor unions have participated in movements to restructure American society as a whole in order to bring about a more equitable distribution of wealth and more humane conditions of life. The Knights of Labor, organized in 1869, was such an organization. A radical utopian union, it opened its membership to all workers, regardless of race, sex, age, nationality, or type of work. Its program included not only the typical labor demands, such as the eight-hour day and the abolition of child labor, but also demands for equal pay for both sexes, an income tax, and prohibition of the sale of alcoholic beverages. At the peak of its strength, the Knights had over 700,000 members. But a reputation for violence and radicalism caused it to decline rapidly after about 1885, and by the middle of the 1890's it had virtually disappeared.

The next significant radical labor organization was the Industrial Workers of the World (the IWW), better known as the Wobblies. The IWW was founded in 1905 as an outgrowth of the Western Federation of Miners. The purpose of the new organization, according to its chairman and guiding spirit, William D. ("Big Bill") Haywood, was to reorganize American government and economic life. The Wobblies advocated what has been called anarcho-syndicalism—that is, the organization of society into cooperative labor groups that would control the means of production, distribution, and exchange. In other words, they believed in socialism without the state. The IWW avoided political action, however, and concentrated on trying to organize the bottom strata of the American labor force, particularly the unskilled migrant workers of the Western mining, lumber, and agricultural industries. Like the Knights, the IWW was open to workers of all races, sexes, ages, nationalities, and types of work.

The Wobblies were perhaps the most colorful labor organization in American history, partly because of their leadership. One of the most renowned of the Wobbly leaders was Joe Hillstrom, also known as Joe Hill, who composed many of the marching songs used by future industrial workers in organization drives. Hill is perhaps best known for a statement he made just before his execution on a contrived murder charge in Utah: "Don't mourn for me. Organize." It was this spirit that captured the imagination of thousands of wandering workingmen in the West and that later spread to the East, where the IWW organized several successful strikes in northern mill cities.

Almost from the inception of the IWW, the United States government as well as local governments and industries made every effort to destroy it. Although the Wobblies did not advocate violence, they stressed direct action in their organizing campaigns, and the violent reactions they sometimes evoked on the part of the authorities earned them the charge of fomenting violence. In 1917, with the approval of President Wilson, the Justice Department attacked the IWW headquarters, confiscated all records, and arrested the leaders on charges of sedition, espionage, and interference with the war effort. Though the case against them was nonexistent, the Wobbly leaders were found guilty and imprisoned. The movement was thus effectively suppressed. Subsequently, many of the Wobbly leaders joined the Communist party to continue their work for social change.

Melvyn Dubofsky, of the University of Wisconsin, has written a richly textured and exhaustive study of the IWW entitled **We Shall Be All: A History of the Industrial Workers of the World,** a chapter of which is reprinted here. This selection, dealing with the Wobblies' doctrine that the streets belong to the people and that all people have the right to free speech, gives an indication of the spirit that activated the movement as well as of the vicious response it drew from the dominant forces in American society.

Quit your job. Go to Missoula. Fight with the Lumber Jacks for Free Speech," the *Industrial Worker* encouraged its readers on September 30, 1909. "Are you game? Are you afraid? Do you love the police? Have you been robbed, skinned, grafted on? If so, then go to Missoula, and defy the police, the courts and the people who live off the wages of prostitution." Thus did the IWW proclaim the first of its many fights for free speech.

"The IWW Fight for Free Speech on the West Coast." Reprinted by permission of Quadrangle Books from *We Shall Be All: A History of the Industrial Workers of the World* by Melvyn Dubofsky, pp. 173–97. Copyright © 1969 by Melvyn Dubofsky.

Many years after the IWW's free-speech fights had faded from public memory, Roger Baldwin, founding father of the American Civil Liberties Union, recalled that the Wobblies

> wrote a chapter in the history of American liberties like that of the struggle of the Quakers for freedom to meet and worship, of the militant suffragists to carry their propaganda to the seats of government, and of the Abolitionists to be heard. . . . The little minority of the working class represented in the I.W.W. blazed the trail in those ten years of fighting for free speech [1908–1918] which the entire American working class must in some fashion follow.[1]

For Wobblies free-speech fights involved nothing so abstract as defending the Constitution, preserving the Bill of Rights, or protecting the civil liberties of American citizens. They were instigated primarily to overcome resistance to IWW organizing tactics and also to demonstrate that America's dispossessed could, through direct action, challenge established authority. To workers dubious about the results achieved by legal action and the reforms won through political action, the IWW taught the effectiveness of victories gained through a strategy of open, yet nonviolent confrontations with public officials. Roger Baldwin perceived as much when, writing long before the post-1954 civil rights movement had made the strategy of confrontation a commonplace of American protest movements, he commented about the IWW's approach: "Far more effective is this direct action of open conflict than all the legal maneuvers in the courts to get rights that no government willingly grants. Power wins rights—the power of determination, backed by willingness to suffer jail or violence, to get them."[2]

The IWW and its members did challenge the law and endure violence and imprisonment to win free speech—that is, the right for their soapboxers to stand on street corners, or in front of employment offices, and harangue working-class crowds about the iniquities of capitalism and the decay of American society. But behind the right to speak freely lay more important IWW goals. Many Wobblies considered street speaking the most effective means of carrying their gospel to Western workers. They had solid evidence for this belief. Experience had demonstrated that it was almost impossible for organizers to reach timber workers, construction hands, and harvesters out on the job where watchful employers harassed "labor agitators" and where workers were scattered over a vast geographical area. Only in the city did Western workers concentrate in sufficiently large numbers to be reached effectively by the handful of organizers proselytizing for the IWW, and only in the city did the "agitator" have a measure of freedom to recruit without interference by employers. Many an IWW recruit—among them, Richard Brazier, who

[1] IWW, *Twenty Five Years of Industrial Unionism* (Chicago, 1930), p. 20.
[2] *Ibid.*

later became a leader in the Northwest and also a member of the general executive board—testified to how urban soapboxers such as Joe Ettor aroused his initial interest in the IWW. The IWW and the Western workers also had a common enemy in the city: the employment agent or "shark." These "sharks," against whom the IWW directed most of its street-corner harangues, controlled employment in agriculture and lumber. With anti-union employers they maintained the heavy labor turnover among the unskilled workers—one on the way, one on the job, one leaving—that kept labor organization out of the fields and forests, wages low, and working conditions primitive. The heavy labor turnover guaranteed substantial commissions to the employment agencies that located jobs for the unemployed, as well as large payoffs to cooperating managers and foremen. If the IWW could break the links connecting the "shark," the employer, and the transient laborer, it could loosen the heavy chain of economic circumstances that kept the Western worker in semi-bondage.

Breaking the hold of the employment agencies on the job market would be the initial step in improving working conditions and raising wages, results which would themselves insure a sharp rise in IWW membership. With this in mind, IWW organizers, conceding that industrial conflict belonged in the *shop*, not on the street, stressed: ". . . To carry the war into the shop we must first get into the shop—in this case the camp. To control the source of supply in the industrial cities by forcing the employers to hire men through the I.W.W. is a great step in the direction of industrial control."[3] Put differently, this meant that Western migratories had to be organized before going out on the job, which might last only a few days; and this, in turn, could be accomplished only by controlling the employment agencies, or abolishing them and replacing them with IWW hiring halls. Here is the primary reason the IWW demanded free speech in Spokane, Fresno, Missoula, Aberdeen, Minot, Kansas City, and scores of other Western cities where migratories laid over between jobs, or patronized employment agencies to find new jobs. Three of these many free-speech struggles reveal the pattern of IWW confrontations and their role in the history and development of the organization: Spokane, 1909–1910; Fresno, 1910–1911; and San Diego, 1912.

The first significant IWW struggle for free speech erupted in Spokane, Washington, the hub of the Inland Empire's agricultural, mining, and lumber industries and the central metropolis for all of western Washington, western Oregon, and northern Idaho. Here employers came to locate labor for the mines of the Coeur d'Alenes, the woods of the interior, and the farms of the Palouse and other inland valleys. Migratory workers came to rest up in Spokane during the winter after a long hard harvest summer or an equally arduous season of railroad construction work. In Spokane workers discovered cheap skid-row hotels and cheaper whisky and women to spend their skimpy savings on. When spring approached and savings dwindled, the migratories could turn to the "sharks,"

[3] *Industrial Worker,* June 3, 1909, p. 2; August 5, 1909, p. 3.

who for a price offered another season of employment out in the countryside or forest.

What the IWW accomplished in Spokane was in some respects truly
remarkable. Recruiting largely among workers whose lives were often brutal and violent and who had a view of masculinity somewhat akin to the
Latin idea of *machismo,* the IWW channeled working-class hostility toward employment agencies into constructive courses. Soapboxers warned
angry workers that broken heads and shattered windows would not put
the "sharks out of business." No! they thundered. "There is only one way
you can get out of their hold. That is by joining the I.W.W. and refusing
to go to them for jobs."[4]

The IWW's message was heard. Overalls Brigade "General" J. H.
Walsh had come to Spokane after the 1908 convention, and within six
months rejuvenated a previously moribund IWW local. The revitalized
union leased expensive new headquarters which included a large library
and reading room, ample office space, and an assembly hall seating several
hundred. It held inside propaganda meetings four nights a week, operated
its own cigar and newsstand, and even featured regular movies: from
conventional one-reelers to illustrated rebel songs and dry economic lectures. When local authorities restricted street speaking, the Spokane local
published its own newspaper, the *Industrial Worker,* which reached a
wide local working-class audience. Walsh's local even retained a Spokane
law firm on a yearly retainer, as well as maintaining a voluntary hospital
plan for members. All this was supported from March to April 1909 by
the dues of twelve hundred to fifteen hundred members in good standing
and double that number on the local's books.[5] For the first time, or so it
now seemed, a labor organization had succeeded in reaching the Inland
Empire's migratory workers.

IWW growth brought an immediate and inevitable reaction from
Spokane's employers, "sharks," and officials. In March 1909 the city council, acting on complaints from the chamber of commerce, prohibited
street-corner orations by closing Spokane's streets to Wobblies and all
other "revolutionists." It did so partly because the soapboxers castigated
organized religion and partly because IWW oratory had a greater effect
than "respectable" citizens realized upon "the army of the unemployed
and poorly paid workers." Spokane's city council's action was in accord
with the observation made by a later federal investigator that the IWW's
right to speak should be restricted when the organization denounced
"everything we have been taught to respect from our earliest days . . .
all kinds of religions and religious sects. . . ."[6] Christianity and patriotism
thus became the employment agents' first line of defense against the IWW

---

[4] *Industrial Union Bulletin,* February 27, 1909, p. 1; J. H. Walsh in *ibid.,* February
21, 1909, p. 1.

[5] *Industrial Worker,* April 29, 1909, p. 5.

[6] Daniel O'Regan to Dr. Charles McCarthy, November 10, 1914, United States Commission on Industrial Relations Papers, Department of Labor, Record Group 174,
National Archives (hereafter cited as CIR Papers); Charles Grant, "Law and Order
in Spokane," *Industrial Worker,* March 18, 1909, p. 3.

onslaught. Thus, Spokane's initial street-speaking ordinance allowed religious groups, most notably the Salvation Army, the IWW's major competitor, the right to speak on the city's streets.

The IWW maintained that its organizers would continue speaking
until the ordinance was repealed or made binding upon all organizations.
On March 4 the city council placed religious groups under the ban, but
the IWW remained unsatisfied. That very day J. H. Walsh himself
mounted a soapbox and addressed his "fellow workers and friends," only
to be hauled off to jail by local police. Later he was tried, convicted, and
fined for violating the local street-speaking ordinance. For the next
several days, as Walsh's legal appeals moved through the various courts,
Wobblies spoke on Spokane's streets—and were promptly arrested and
jailed. As the number of those arrested rose, so did the fines and the
length of imprisonment. In March 1909 Spokane's jail filled with Wobblies, ten to twelve men crammed in cells built to accommodate only
four. The free-speech prisoners, fed a diet of bread and water twice daily,
could neither lie nor sit down. One Wobbly later recalled: "The misery
in those cells was something never to be forgotten. . . ."[7]

But the Wobblies refused to give up the struggle. Instead, they sang
revolutionary songs, refused to work on the jail rock pile, held daily
business meetings, made speeches, and preserved their militancy even
within the prison walls. Those who passed by Spokane's jail during those
March days must have thought it an odd prison, when they heard the
words of the "Red Flag" or the "Marseillaise" filtering out from behind
the bars.

As spring approached, the migratories began to leave Spokane for the
countryside. Under these circumstances, city authorities released the imprisoned Wobblies, while state courts considered the constitutionality of
Spokane's street-speaking ordinance. Spring and summer were not the
time for the IWW to contend for free speech: it had to wait for its members to return for another winter in the city.

With the bulk of the migratories temporarily away, Spokane's
officials acted to avert another winter of discontent and tumult. On
August 10 the city council enacted a revised law that allowed religious
groups to hold street meetings but required all other organizations to
obtain permits before doing so. The *Industrial Worker* promptly warned
the city fathers that the IWW would not ask permission to speak on
streets its members had built. "The toad-eaters who make up the Spokane city council are afraid of the I.W.W.," a Wobbly rhetorician noted
in an editorial. "Even the devil is not afraid of the Starvation Army."[8]
Thus a renewed clash between Wobblies and public authorities awaited
summer's end.

Summer ended, the migratories returned to Spokane, and IWW soapboxers again took to the streets. The inevitable followed. On Monday,
October 25, the police arrested Jim Thompson for street speaking without
a permit. The IWW promptly demanded the inalienable right of free

---

[7] Grant, "Law and Order," p. 3.
[8] *Industrial Worker*, August 12, 1909, p. 1.

speech and also declared that it would send as many men to Spokane as were needed to win its struggle. Despite the IWW's threat and a legal ruling declaring the revised street-speaking ordinance discriminatory and unconstitutional, the battle continued to rage. On November 1, the day of the legal decision ruling the ban on speaking unconstitutional, the IWW initiated round-the-clock street meetings. Spokane's police promptly arrested each speaker who mounted a soapbox. Before long the city jail held every local IWW leader: Walter Nef, Jim Thompson, James Wilson, C. L. Filigno, and A. C. Cousins. Those not hauled off a soapbox were picked up in a police raid on IWW headquarters, which also netted three female sympathizers. The arrested Wobblies went to jail peaceably, for, as the *Industrial Worker* advised its readers, "it must be understood that any person, at any time, who would try to incite disorder or 'rioting' is an enemy of the I.W.W. Nothing of the kind will be tolerated at this time."[9] Passive resistance and confrontation tactics as a form of direct action were being put to the test in Spokane.

The city fathers used every instrument of power they controlled to thwart the IWW. Before the battle ended almost four hundred Wobblies had been jailed. For a time, public officials reasoned that if they could incapacitate the IWW's leaders, the fight would dissipate. Such reasoning lay behind the city's decision to raid IWW headquarters on November 3, and to arrest local Wobblies on criminal conspiracy charges; it was also behind the move to arrest the editors of the *Industrial Worker*. None of this decisively stifled the Wobblies, however, for as one policeman remarked: "Hell! we got the leaders, but damned if it don't look like they are all leaders."[10]

After their arrest Wobblies received a further taste of Spokane justice. When Frank Little appeared in court, the presiding magistrate asked him what he had been doing at the time of his arrest. "Reading the Declaration of Independence," Little answered. "Thirty days," said the magistrate. The prosecuting attorney demanded that the IWW "feel the mailed fist of the law," which for those leaders charged with criminal conspiracy meant four to six months in jail. For most Wobblies arrested for disorderly conduct the sentence was thirty days, then release, followed by further street speaking and another thirty-day sentence. This legal treatment, most Wobblies thought, justified their definition of government "as the slugging committee of the capitalist class."[11]

In Spokane, indeed, slugging soon became more than merely rhetorical. Arresting police officers used their clubs liberally. Jail life proved even worse: twenty-eight to thirty Wobblies would be tossed into an

[9] *Ibid.*, October 27, 1909, p. 1; November 3, 1909, pp. 1–2.
[10] *Ibid.*, November 10, 1909, p. 1.
[11] These descriptions of Spokane justice come from Elizabeth Gurley Flynn, "The Fight for Free Speech at Spokane," *International Socialist Review*, X (December 1909), 483–89; Flynn, "The Shame of Spokane," *ibid.* (January 1910), pp. 610–19; S. Sorenson to V. St. John, n.d., CIR Papers.

eight-by-six-foot sweatbox, where they would steam for a full day while staring at bloodstained walls.[12] After that they would be moved into an ice-cold cell without cots or blankets. Those who did not weaken from the heat of the first cell often collapsed from the chill of the second. Because Spokane's regular jails could not accommodate the hordes of IWW prisoners, the city converted an unheated, abandoned schoolhouse into a temporary prison. There in mid-winter jailers offered scantily clad prisoners two ounces of bread daily, soft pine for a pillow, and hardwood for a bed. Inside the schoolhouse guards woke the inmates at all hours of the night and then chased them from room to room. Under these conditions some Wobblies fell ill; others, no longer able to stand the strain, collapsed in the middle of the floor; still others maintained their spirits by walking around in a circle singing the "Red Flag." Once a week the school's jailers marched the prisoners out in order to have them bathe for allegedly sanitary reasons. Taken to the city jail, the Wobblies were stripped, thrust under an ice-cold shower, and then, frequently in frigid weather, marched back to their unheated prison.

The IWW estimated that, as a result of this treatment, 334 of the 400 men in prison for 110 days (from November through March) were treated in the emergency hospital a total of 1,600 times. Many left prison with permanent scars and missing teeth; the more fortunate walked away with weakened constitutions.

When police repression and prison brutality failed to weaken the Wobblies' resistance, the authorities resorted to different tactics. After raiding and closing IWW headquarters, they denied every hall in Spokane, except Turner Hall, to the Wobblies. Police seized copies of the *Industrial Worker* and arrested the men—even the boys—who peddled the paper. Unable to function in Spokane, the IWW moved its headquarters and all its defense activities to Coeur d'Alene City under the direction of Fred Heslewood, and published the *Industrial Worker* in Seattle. In the face of relentless repression, the IWW resisted.

The IWW ultimately triumphed because of the spirit and determination of its members. When IWW headquarters pleaded for volunteers to fight for free speech, scores of Wobblies descended upon Spokane. One Wobbly left Minneapolis on November 10, traveling across North Dakota and Montana atop a Pullman car despite sub-zero temperatures. Arriving in Spokane on November 21, somewhat chilled but ready to fight, he was arrested by police two days later. He was not alone: hundreds like him came to Spokane, and hundreds more were ready to come. All intended

---

[12] This account is drawn from Sorenson to St. John, CIR Papers; Robert Ross to CIR, September 19, 1914, CIR Papers; Spokane Free Speech Committee to United Brotherhood of Carpenters and Joiners of America, January 9, 1910, Department of Justice Files, Record Group 60, National Archives (hereafter cited as D/J 60); Flynn, "Shame of Spokane," pp. 610–19; Fred Heslewood, "Barbarous Spokane," *International Socialist Review*, X (February 1910), 705–13; *Industrial Worker*, November 1909–March 1910.

to make the free-speech fight an expensive and difficult proposition for Spokane's taxpayers. "Let them cry quits to their Mayor and police force if they do not relish it," threatened the Wobblies. "We can keep up the fight all winter."[13]

No one better exemplified this IWW spirit than the "Rebel Girl," Elizabeth Gurley Flynn.[14] Only nineteen years old and recently released from a Missoula jail (where another free-speech battle had ended), she was several months pregnant when she arrived in Spokane in November 1909. Local papers described her at that time as a "frail, slender girl, pretty and graceful, with a resonant voice and a fiery eloquence that attracted huge crowds." Another observer pictured her as a little woman, Irish all over, with "the Celt in her grey-blue eyes and almost black hair and in the way she clenches her small hands into fists when she's speaking." To Woodrow Wilson, she described herself in 1918 as

> an humble and obscure citizen who has struggled for democracy as her vision glimpsed it and who has suffered for espousing an unpopular and much misrepresented point of view. . . . For seven years I have supported my child, and helped to educate two sisters . . . and a brother. . . . This . . . has been a labor of love, but it is rather incompatible with the popular conception of a "labor agitator."[15]

Elizabeth Gurley Flynn, however, was all agitator. Daughter of immigrant Irish parents, at fifteen or sixteen she made her first speech as a "materialistic socialist" before her father's radical club in Harlem; at seventeen she had been arrested for street speaking in New York; and at nineteen she was jailed, first in Missoula, then in Spokane. So adept an agitator was she that the Spokane authorities considered her the most dangerous and effective of Wobbly soapboxers. When a young attorney suggested to the city fathers that she not be tried along with the men on charges of criminal conspiracy, the local officials responded: "Hell, no! You just don't understand. She's the one we are after. She makes all the trouble. She puts fight into the men, gets them the publicity they enjoy. As it is, they're having the time of their lives."[16]

Spokane brought Elizabeth Gurley Flynn to trial on charges of criminal conspiracy with a young Italian Wobbly named Charley Filigno. Not unexpectedly, the jury declared on February 24, 1910: "Filigno, guilty. Elizabeth Gurley Flynn, not guilty." An enraged prosecutor demanded of the jury foreman, "What in hell do you fellows mean by

[13] Sorenson to St. John, CIR Papers; Flynn, "Free Speech Fight," p. 488.

[14] The following sketch is based on Elizabeth Gurley Flynn, *I Speak My Own Piece* (New York, 1955); B. H. Kizer, "Elizabeth Gurley Flynn," *Pacific Northwest Quarterly*, LVII (July 1966), 110–12; "E. G. Flynn: Labor Leader," *Outlook*, CXI (December 15, 1915), 905.

[15] Quotations are from Kizer, "Flynn," p. 111; *Outlook*, p. 905; E. G. Flynn to Woodrow Wilson, January 10, 1918, File 188032–146, D/J 60.

[16] Kizer, "Flynn," pp. 111–12.

acquitting the most guilty, and convicting the man, far less guilty." To which the foreman calmly replied: "She ain't a criminal, Fred, an' you know it! If you think this jury, or any jury, is goin' to send that pretty Irish girl to jail merely for bein' bighearted and idealistic, to mix with all those whores and crooks down at the pen, you've got another guess comin'."[17]

But looks can be deceiving, and in Elizabeth Gurley Flynn's case they certainly were. After the fight in Spokane she proceeded to bigger and better battles. She was with the IWW at Lawrence, Paterson, and Everett. Still later, with Roger Baldwin, she helped found the American Civil Liberties Union, and fought to defend the rights of the poor and the exploited. Her vision of democracy as she glimpsed it took her from the Socialist party to the IWW to the ACLU and ultimately in the 1930's to the Communist party. During the forties and fifties she became American communism's leading female advocate as well as the only woman ever sentenced to a prison term under the Smith Act. While in Moscow attending a Soviet party congress in her capacity as chairman of the American Communist party, she died on September 5, 1964, at the age of seventy-four. From her first speech before the Harlem Socialist Club as a teen-ager to her last talk as a Communist, Elizabeth Gurley Flynn remained true to what she allegedly told theatrical producer David Belasco, upon turning down a part in a Broadway play: "I don't want to be an actress! I'm in the labor movement and I speak my own piece."[18]

The piece she spoke in Spokane in the winter of 1909–1910 aided the IWW immeasurably. She won national attention and sympathy that no male agitator could. Her clash with local authorities, her arrest, and the despicable treatment she received in jail made nationwide headlines. She exemplified the IWW's determination to win free speech in Spokane. If repression could not break the spirit of a pregnant, slightly built, teenage girl, how could it crush the Wobblies' free-speech fighters flooding into Spokane in an unending stream?

Yet the Spokane struggle continued through the winter of 1910, as public officials resorted to further repressive measures. On February 22 Spokane officials crossed the state line into Idaho, raided IWW defense headquarters in Coeur d'Alene City, and arrested Fred Heslewood on a fugitive warrant. In response the IWW advised its members: "Let us go to Spokane, fill their jails and overthrow the whole tottering edifice of corruption misnamed the Spokane City Government." Five thousand volunteers were asked to demonstrate their contempt for the "slugging committee of the capitalist class."[19]

Faced with this unrelenting nonviolent resistance, city officials finally weakened. From the IWW's point of view, Spokane's authorities chose

---

[17] Quoted in *ibid.*, p. 112.
[18] Flynn, *I Speak My Own Piece*, p. 53.
[19] *Industrial Worker*, March 5, 1910, p. 1; February 26, 1910, p. 2.

a propitious moment for compromise, for by the end of February the Wobblies also were weakening in their resolve. St. John and other IWW officials found it harder and harder to recruit volunteers for the Spokane fight. When spring came it would be even more difficult. Acting the part of realists, not visionary revolutionaries, a three-man IWW committee, including William Z. Foster, a new member, approached Spokane's mayor to discuss peace terms. The mayor at first proved unresponsive. He approved the IWW's defense of free speech, yet stressed that street speaking would not be tolerated when it interfered with the normal flow of traffic or the business of citizens—a decision that would be made by responsible public officials. The mayor further reminded the IWW committee that only the city council and the courts could determine the constitutionality of city restrictions on street speaking. Somewhat ominously, he warned that continued IWW free-speech activities would be more stringently repressed. The Wobblies, in turn, threatened that the "IWW is going to use the streets of Spokane or go down fighting." In truth, neither side had much stomach for continued warfare. For one thing, the city could not stand the expense of several hundred individual legal trials, including the ensuing appeals; for another, the IWW had exhausted campaigners and it lacked new recruits to take up the slack. Thus, on March 3, 1910, after a series of conferences between IWW representatives and various city officials, peace came to Spokane.[20]

The IWW won its major demands. Indoor meeting places would no longer be denied to the organization, and it could also hold peaceful outdoor meetings without police interference. Spokane agreed to respect the IWW's right to publish the *Industrial Worker* and to sell it on the city's streets. Complicated terms were also devised to secure the release of those Wobblies still in prison. Significantly, the authorities assured the IWW that free speech would be allowed on city streets in the near future. Until the council enacted new speaking ordinances, it barred street corners to religious groups: the Salvation Army as well as the IWW would have to await the passage of a free-speech statute later that year.

Wobblies also won the secondary demands which had undergirded their fight for free speech. In the midst of the battle, Spokane officials had initiated reforms in the employment agency system, rescinding the licenses of the worst of the "sharks." After the battle, public officials throughout the Northwest attempted to regulate private employment agencies more closely.[21]

As viewed by the Wobblies, the Spokane free-speech fight had been an impressive triumph for the twin principles of direct action and passive resistance. The discipline maintained by the free-speech fighters and the

[20] *Ibid.*, March 5, 1910, p. 1; March 12, 1910, p. 1; William Z. Foster, *Pages from a Worker's Life* (New York, 1939), pp. 143–45; Foster, *From Bryan to Stalin* (New York, 1937), pp. 41–42.

[21] E. G. Flynn, "Latest News from Spokane," *International Socialist Review*, X (March 1910), 828–34; *Industrial Worker*, March 12, 1910, p. 1; March 19, 1910, p. 1.

passivity with which they endured brutalities won the respect of many parties usually critical of or hostile to the IWW. During the struggle local socialists, Spokane's AFL members, and WFM miners in the Coeur d'Alenes, as well as "respectable" townspeople, contributed money, food, or just plain sympathy to the Wobbly cause. Passive resistance also showed what migratory workers who lacked the franchise might accomplish by more direct means. *Solidarity* grasped the lesson of Spokane when it observed: "By use of its weakest weapon—passive resistance—labor forced civic authorities to recognize a power equal to the state." If labor can gain so much through its crudest weapon, it asked, "what will the result be when an industrially organized working class stands forth prepared to seize, operate, and control the machinery of production and distribution?"[22]

But free speech on the streets of Spokane did not guarantee successful labor organization among the workers of the fields, woods, and construction camps of the Inland Empire. In 1910 the IWW had only learned how to attract migratory workers during their winter layovers in town; it had not yet hit upon the secret of maintaining an everyday, effective labor organization out on the job among workers who moved freely. It had not yet discovered how to survive when employers set armed gunmen upon "labor agitators" and summarily discharged union members. Victory in Spokane did, however, inspire the soapboxers and organizer-agitators so prominent within the IWW to carry their campaigns for free speech to other Western cities where migratories gathered to rest or to seek employment.

One such city was Fresno, California, where ranchers from the lush San Joaquin Valley came to acquire labor for their vegetable and fruit farms. In Fresno, as in Spokane, lonely men recently returned from a season of fruit picking or construction work spent their hard-earned funds on whisky and women. Here Wobbly soapboxers found an audience ready for the IWW's gospel.

Fresno had become the most active IWW center in California, and no other local in the state could compare to Fresno Local 66 in size of membership or in militancy of spirit. Late in 1909 and early the following year, Local 66 had unexpected success in organizing Mexican-American railroad laborers and migratory farm hands—a development not at all to the liking of city officials, the management of the Santa Fe Railroad, or the ranchers. As Wobblies continued to hold open street meetings and to win more recruits for their organization, minor skirmishes with the police rose in number—so much so that by May 1910 the local IWW forecast a full-scale free-speech fight. Fresno, indeed, was ready for the challenge. Its police chief had revoked the IWW's permit to hold street meetings and had threatened to jail on vagrancy charges any man without a job (serving as an IWW official was not considered employment). This led Frank Little, the leading local Wobbly, to predict that when the summer harvest ended, Wobblies would invade Fresno to battle for free speech.[23]

That fall a struggle similar in all basic respects to the one recently terminated in Spokane erupted in Fresno. In this case no money would be wasted on lawyers and defense funds; whatever funds the Fresno local obtained would be used to keep Wobblies on the streets, the local court docket crowded, and Fresno's pocketbook empty. "All aboard for Fresno," announced the *Industrial Worker* on September 10, "Free Speech Fight On."

Fresno's town fathers responded to the IWW invasion just as their civic neighbors to the north had done. First, they closed every hall in the city to the Wobblies, who were thus compelled to re-establish headquarters in a large rented tent outside the city limits. Fresno police followed up with a series of wholesale arrests which, by mid-November, temporarily broke IWW resistance. By the end of the month, though, the Wobblies were back on the streets in increasing numbers, and the more men Fresno arrested, the more Wobblies seemed to materialize. Fresno learned the hard way that arrests did not subdue militant Wobblies. Worse yet, the city discovered that it had no statute forbidding street speaking, thus invalidating the charges upon which the bulk of the arrests had been made. With the city thus deterred from legal action, mob action resulted. On the evening of December 9 a large mob gathered outside the city jail, where it severely beat a number of Wobblies who had come to visit imprisoned fellow workers. Its martial spirit duly aroused, the mob promptly marched out to the IWW's tent camp and put it to the torch. That evening, St. John wired Fresno's mayor: "Action of 'respectable mob' will not deter this organization. . . . Free speech will be established in Fresno if it takes twenty years."[24]

Met by mob violence, the IWW counseled passive resistance, advising its fighters: ". . . Remember despite police brutality, don't retaliate in kind." So disciplined did the Wobblies remain that the *Sacramento Bee*, itself a bitter and sometimes unrestrained critic of the IWW, commented: ". . . When the good citizens and the authorities of any city countenance such outrages as those committed by the Fresno mob, the I.W.W. may be said to shine by comparison."[25]

Despite legal and extra-legal repression (Fresno on December 20 had enacted an ordinance banning street speaking), Wobblies continued to arrive in town in increasing numbers. Moving in and out of Fresno, and also in and out of jail, they encountered repression and brutality. What kept them coming and going was the same spirit and determination that motivated their leader in Fresno—Frank H. Little.

[23] W. F. Little to *Industrial Worker*, May 21, 1910, p. 4; F. H. Little to Editor, May 27, 1910, *ibid.*, June 4, 1910, p. 1; F. Little to Editor, May 29, 1910, *ibid.*, June 11, 1910, p. 2; Daniel O'Regan to Charles McCarthy, November 10, 1914, CIR Papers.
[24] *Industrial Worker*, September 3, 1910, p. 1; October 1, 1910, p. 1; October 8, 1910, pp. 1, 4; October 5, 1910, p. 4; November 9, 1910, p. 3; November 17, 1910, pp. 1, 3; November 30, 1910, p. 4; December 6, 1910, p. 4; V. St. John to Mayor of Fresno, December 9, 1910, in *ibid.*, December 15, 1910, p. 1; cf. O'Regan to McCarthy, November 10, 1914, CIR Papers.
[25] Quoted in *Industrial Worker*, December 22, 1910, p. 1.

If Elizabeth Gurley Flynn was the "Rebel Girl," Frank Little was the "hobo agitator." More than any other individual he personified the IWW's rebelliousness and its strange compound of violent rhetoric, pride in physical courage (the *machismo* element), and its seemingly contradictory resort to nonviolent resistance. Part American Indian, part hardrock miner, part hobo, he was all Wobbly. A tall, spare, muscular man with a weatherbeaten yet ruggedly handsome face, Little looked the complete proletarian rebel. As James P. Cannon, an old friend who fought with Little in Peoria and Duluth, remembered him: "He was always for the revolt, for the struggle, for the fight. Wherever he went he 'stirred up trouble' and organized the workers to rebel. . . . He was a blood brother to all insurgents . . . the world over."[26]

This one-eyed rebel[27] never occupied a comfortable union office or kept books like his close associates, St. John and Haywood; instead, he always went where the action was. From 1900 to 1905 he fought in the major WFM industrial conflicts, joining with that union's militants and following them into the IWW, where he remained when the WFM withdrew. In 1909 he was in Spokane, the following year in Fresno. In later years Little would turn up in San Diego, Duluth, Butte—anywhere Wobblies fought for a better world. Whenever miners, harvesters, or construction workers needed a leader, Little was available. When fear immobilized workers, he set an example for others to follow. His utter fearlessness brought him to Butte in 1917 to aid rebellious copper miners. By this time he was an ailing rheumatic, bearing the vestiges of too many beatings and too many jailings, and hobbling about on crutches as the result of a recently broken leg. Yet Little remained the active agitator—an agitator apparently so terrifying to the "respectable" that on August 1, 1917, Montana vigilantes lynched him and left his body dangling from a railroad trestle on Butte's outskirts.

In 1910–1911 he was still a reasonably healthy man. He demonstrated in Fresno how a man unafraid, a man whose life had already taken him, and would later take him again, from one violent incident to another, could also lead a struggle based entirely on the moral suasion of passive resistance. Little proved in Fresno, as the IWW proved in so many other places, that even the potentially violent, given a good cause and a compelling ideology, could set an example of peaceful direct action.

Frank Little instilled his own rebelliousness in those who fought for free speech with him in Fresno. Only dedication and courage approximating Little's can account for teen-age Herbert Minderman's ability to

[26] James P. Cannon, *Notebook of an Agitator* (New York, 1958), pp. 32–36.
[27] W. D. Haywood and Charles Lambert, who served with Little on the IWW's last pre-war general executive board, were also prominent one-eyed Wobblies.

withstand the tortures endured by Wobbly prisoners in Fresno's jail. Minderman kept a daily diary which described in some detail the course of the Fresno struggle and the punishments inflicted upon IWW prisoners.[28] As Minderman described it, imprisonment had no appreciable effect on the Wobbly spirit. In jail Wobblies sang rebel songs, held propaganda meetings, and transacted the somewhat irregular business of Local 66. They talked so cantankerously and sang so loudly that their jailers took unusual steps to silence the noisy ones. A guard gagged one Wobbly with his own sock, causing a government investigator to comment: "The severity of this punishment can be understood only by one who is familiar with the rank and file of I.W.W.'s and knows how rarely they bathe."[29] Wobblies responded to repression within the jail by mounting what they labeled a "battleship," which meant continuous yelling, jeering, and pounding on cell bars and floors until the guards felt compelled to use more forceful measures.

The sheriff thus denied his prisoners adequate sleeping gear, tobacco, reading materials, and decent food. When this failed to still the tumult, he resorted to physical force. Firemen appeared at the city jail with a 150-pound pressure hose, which was turned upon the cell holding the Wobblies. Prisoners tried to protect themselves by erecting a barricade of mattresses. But the pressure of the water swept the mattresses away and drove the Wobblies against the cell wall. Some Wobblies sought refuge by lying flat on the floor, but the hose was aimed down upon them, the stream of water then thrusting them up into the air like toothpicks. Even the most rebellious soon had enough of this treatment. Yet the firemen maintained the water pressure for fully a half-hour, and before they left almost every prisoner found his clothes in shreds and his body black and blue. The Wobblies spent the remainder of that chill December night up to their knees in water.

Some Wobblies broke under these tactics, promising to leave town if released. But most refused to compromise. They served out their time and then returned to Fresno's streets to soapbox.

The IWW's refusal to terminate its struggle had the same effect in Fresno as it had had earlier in Spokane. Each prisoner demanded a jury trial, managed his own defense, and challenged as many prospective jurors as possible. Wobblies used every delaying tactic their limited legal knowledge made available. On a good day Fresno's courts might try two or three men; however many Wobblies they sentenced, it seemed more were always on the docket. To make matters worse, still more Wobblies were always on the road to Fresno. Although the IWW found it harder to attract volunteers than it had been in Spokane, nevertheless many Wobblies shared the militancy of Little and young Herbert Minderman and set off to join their fellow workers

---

[28] The following account comes largely from Minderman's diary of the Fresno fight and O'Regan's verification of it in O'Regan to McCarthy, November 10, 1914, CIR Papers.

[29] O'Regan to McCarthy, CIR Papers.

in Fresno.[30] This eventually became too great a burden for the city's taxpayers, its judges, and its businessmen.

Fresno's officials finally weakened in their resolve to repress their antagonists. Again, IWW leaders proved realistic and able negotiators. Well aware that local authorities hated to compromise while under pressure, the Wobblies allowed secret and informal talks to proceed. These conferences began on February 25 when a local citizens' committee visited the Fresno jail in order to ascertain the IWW's truce terms. In less than two weeks the citizens' committee and city officials consented to the release of all IWW prisoners and to a guarantee of the organization's right to speak on Fresno's streets. Finally, on March 6 Local 66 wired IWW headquarters: "The Free Speech Fight is over, and won. . . . Complete victory."[31]

What the IWW won in Fresno was not precisely clear. No public settlement terms were announced, either by the local IWW or by Fresno's citizens' committee. Moreover, for the next several years Local 66 and Fresno disappeared from mention in the IWW press; Frank Little left the area to fight IWW wars elsewhere, and the San Joaquin Valley's fruit pickers remained unorganized, overworked, and underpaid. In brief, an inglorious and inconclusive climax. In Fresno as in Spokane, the IWW had learned how to contact the migratories in town but not how to organize them on the job. Local 66 had succeeded in making its headquarters a community center for the West's dispossessed, yet it failed to carry the organization into the surrounding countryside where it was most needed.

As propaganda, however, the IWW may have gained something from the Fresno struggle. In a conflict which lasted over six months but cost less than $1,000, the IWW received enormous national publicity. Although the Fresno conflict did not attract quite the nationwide attention that Elizabeth Gurley Flynn had focused on Spokane, it did reinforce the image of the IWW as an organization that used passive resistance to defend clear constitutional rights. It demonstrated once again that the most exploited and dependent groups in American society could act for themselves—and act peaceably at that—as well as that they also had the power—nonpolitical power, of course—to alter the prevailing arrangements of the local community. Yet the Fresno fight left behind no effective labor organization to capitalize upon the IWW's apparent "victory," and no immediate membership growth followed this new triumph for free speech.[32]

---

[30] Albert Tucker to Vincent St. John, September 21, 1914, CIR Papers; cf. Thomas Whitehead to Editor, *Solidarity*, March 4, 1911, p. 1; and E. M. Clyde to Editor, *ibid.*, April 8, 1911, p. 4; *Industrial Worker*, February 23, 1911, p. 1; March 2, 1911, p. 1.

[31] *Industrial Worker*, March 9, 1911, p. 1; *International Socialist Review*, XI (April 1911), 634–36.

[32] Hyman Weintraub, "The IWW in California," unpublished master's thesis, University of California, Los Angeles (1947), pp. 23–32.

The Spokane and Fresno victories led Wobblies to contend for free speech elsewhere, though with uneven success. Almost always these fights were associated with efforts to organize lumber workers and migratory harvesters. In one tragic case the IWW's campaign for free speech was entirely unrelated to the objectives of labor organization. In San Diego in 1912 the IWW learned the limits of passive resistance, as well as the folly of concentrating its limited power on tangential causes.

In 1912 San Diego was a comfortable city of fifty thousand, mostly well-to-do devotees of the area's ideal climate. It had a small and contented working class and no important or large industries threatened by labor difficulties. No migratories drifted into town *en masse* to spend the winter, and no ground seemed less fertile for IWW efforts. As IWW martyr-bard Joe Hill noted: "A town like San Diego for instance where the main 'industry' consists of 'catching suckers' [tourists] is not worth a whoop in Hell from a rebel's point of view."[33] Indeed, never did the number of Wobblies in San Diego exceed a few hundred. Yet those few, as a contemporary journalist commented, "goaded the authorities and the populace into a hysterical frenzy, into an epidemic of unreasoning fear and brutal rage, into a condition of lawlessness so pronounced that travelers fear to visit the city."[34]

For years E Street between Fifth and Sixth Avenues in the heart of downtown San Diego had served as a sort of Hyde Park Speakers' Corner. Every evening socialists and anarchists, savers and atheists, suffragists and Wobblies, harangued the faithful from their accustomed spots on the corner. But in December 1911 San Diego's city council, acting upon a grand-jury recommendation, closed the downtown area, the so-called "congested district," to street meetings. In response, Wobblies, socialists, single-taxers, and even the local AFL men created a broad coalition called the Free Speech League. From the day the anti-street-speaking ordinance took effect, February 8, 1912, police and League members clashed over the right of free speech. By February 12, ninety men and women had been arrested, and by February 15, 150 prisoners languished in city and county jails. Day and night for the next several weeks, the League held free-speech meetings and the police arrested speakers, until the county as well as the city jails were crowded beyond normal capacity.[35]

Before long, what began as a common struggle by a broad coalition of anti-establishment organizations became a largely IWW-led struggle. Although the non-Wobbly groups continued to participate in the San Diego struggle, the public, locally and nationally, associated the conflict with the IWW. The battle did, in fact, feature the tactics the IWW had

[33] Joe Hill to E. W. Vanderleith, n.d., Frank Walsh Papers, Box 7, New York Public Library, Manuscript Division.
[34] Walter V. Woehlke, "I.W.W.," *Outlook*, CI (July 6, 1912), 512.
[35] Mary A. Hill, "The Free Speech Fight at San Diego," *Survey*, XXVIII (May 4, 1912), 192–94.

tested successfully in Spokane and Fresno. Again Wobblies threatened to fill the jails and crowd the court dockets until a financially drained city surrendered. Again the Wobblies looked to passive resistance to accomplish their aims. One IWW bard, an early, perhaps premature version of Dr. Seuss, advised: "Come on the cushions; Ride up on top; Stick to the brakebeams; Let nothing stop. Come in great numbers; This we beseech; Help San Diego to win *Free Speech!*"[36]

Although San Diego had less to fear from the Wobblies than either Spokane or Fresno, it nevertheless acted more savagely to repress free speech. No brutality proved beyond the imagination of San Diego's "good" citizens. What the police could not accomplish by stretching the local law's elastic fabric, private citizens, acting as vigilantes, did. Even discounting the predictable exaggeration of the reports in the *Industrial Worker* and *Solidarity*, repression proved the rule in San Diego. The city's citizens learned from the mistakes previously revealed in Spokane and Fresno. San Diego would not be invaded by armies of Wobblies, nor bankrupted by scores of prisoners who resided in jail as beneficiaries of the public purse and who demanded costly individual trials. San Diego devised just the remedy for these IWW tactics. Several nights a week vigilantes visited the jails, seized a group of free-speech prisoners, and escorted them beyond the county line. To any Wobbly who dared to return, and to those who attempted to join the fight, the vigilantes promised worse treatment.[37]

San Diego's brand of viligante justice has been described best by some of the Wobblies who experienced it. On the night of either April 4 or 5,[38] 1912, Albert Tucker and 140 other men, half of whom were under twenty-one years of age, hopped a freight train out of Los Angeles bound for San Diego. About one o'clock that morning the train slowed down and Tucker noticed on either side of the freight cars about four hundred men armed with rifles, pistols, and clubs of every variety. Tucker has vividly portrayed what ensued.[39]

> The moon was shining dimly through the clouds and I could see pick handles, ax handles, wagon spokes and every kind of club imaginable swinging from the wrists of all of them while they also had their rifles leveled at us . . . the only sign of civilization was a cattle corral. . . . We were ordered to unload and we refused. Then they closed in around the flat car which we were on and began clubbing and knocking and pulling men off by their heels, so

---

36 *Industrial Worker*, February 22, 1912, p. 4; February 29, 1912, p. 4; March 7, 1912, p. 4.

37 Hill, "Free Speech Fight," pp. 193–94; Woelke, "I.W.W.," p. 531; among other non-IWW sources.

38 Tucker was not certain of the precise date when he wrote his account of these events two years later.

39 A. Tucker to Vincent St. John, September 21, 1914, CIR Papers.

inside of a half hour they had us all off the train and then bruised
and bleeding we were lined up and marched into the cattle corral,
where they made us hold our hands up and march around in the
crowd for more than an hour. . . . They marched us several times,
now and then picking out a man they thought was a leader and
giving him an extra beating. Several men were carried out unconscious . . . afterwards there was a lot of our men unaccounted for
and never have been heard from since. The vigilantes all wore
constable badges and a white handkerchief around their left arms.
They were drunk and hollering and cursing the rest of the night.
In the morning they took us out four or five at a time and marched
us up the track to the county line . . . where we were forced to
kiss the flag and then run a gauntlet of 106 men, every one of which
was striking at us as hard as they could with their pick ax handles.
They broke one man's leg, and everyone was beaten black and blue,
and was bleeding from a dozen wounds.

The man with the broken leg, Chris Hansen, himself a veteran of other
IWW free-speech fights, also described what happened that night: "As I
was lying there I saw other fellows running the gauntlet. Some were
bleeding freely from cracked heads, others were knocked down to be
made to get up and run again. Some tried to break the line only to be
beaten back. It was the most cowardly and inhuman cracking of heads I
ever witnessed. . . ."[40] "Thus did San Diego," in the words of anti-IWW
journalist Walter Woehlke, "having given its money to mark the historic
highway [El Camino Real] with the symbols of love and charity, teach
patriotism and reverence for the law to the travelers thereon."[41]

That all of this vigilante violence had occurred with the connivance
of local public officials soon became known to the entire nation. Governor Hiram Johnson, Progressive politician extraordinary, under pressure
from the AFL, the Socialist party, the IWW, and many influential Californians, some of whom had played a prominent role in his election, dispatched special investigator Harris Weinstock to San Diego. Weinstock's
investigation corroborated all the Free Speech League's charges of police
and vigilante brutality. A thoroughly outraged Weinstock compared San
Diego's behavior to the worst excesses of the tsarist Russian regime.[42]

This public condemnation notwithstanding, San Diego vigilantes
continued their previous activities. Early in May 1912 police fatally
wounded an IWW member. On May 15 anarchist Emma Goldman and
her manager-lover, Ben Reitman, arrived in town to lend their voices to
the struggle. When they debarked at the railroad station they found a
howling mob, including many women, screaming: "Give us that anarchist;
we will strip her naked; we will tear out her guts." That evening vigilantes
abducted Reitman from his hotel room. Placing him in the back seat of a

[40] Chris Hansen to Vincent St. John, n.d., CIR Papers.
[41] Woehlke, "I.W.W.," p. 531.
[42] Harris Weinstock, *Report to the Governor of California on the Disturbance in the City and County of San Diego in 1912* (Sacramento, 1912).

speeding auto, they tortured him as they sped out of town. About twenty miles beyond San Diego's limits the vigilantes stopped the car, got out, and proceeded to a second round of torture. As later described by Reitman, this is what happened: "With tar taken from a can [they] traced I.W.W. on my back and a doctor burned the letters in with a lighted cigar. . . ." Afterward, Reitman ran the gauntlet, and then he kissed the American flag and sang the "Star Spangled Banner." Beaten, bruised, and degraded, he dragged himself away clad only in his underwear, "because the Christian gentlemen thought that I might meet some ladies and shock them."[43]

Despite their militancy and the sympathy they received as a result of the kind of treatment described above, Wobblies lacked the power to alter conditions in San Diego. The state had the power, but it used it to condemn, not to reform. The federal government also had the power, but in 1912, unlike a half-century later, its power was not at the disposal of peaceful protesters being abused by local or state authorities.

In 1912 it was San Diego's public officials, not the beaten and intimidated Wobblies, who turned to the federal Justice Department for support. Early in May city police superintendent John Sehon asked Attorney General George Wickersham for federal assistance in local efforts to repress the subversive, un-American IWW. Well before that date Sehon had been cooperating with the federal attorney for southern California (John McCormick) and with private detectives appointed by a citizens' committee controlled by sugar king John Spreckels and anti-union Los Angeles newspaper magnate Harrison Grey Otis. Sehon, the federal attorney, and the private detectives searched for evidence linking the IWW to an alleged plot to overthrow the constituted authorities in San Diego and Washington, D.C., and also to join the Mexican Revolution, the aim here being to capture Lower California for the IWW. Where these diligent investigators could not find evidence, they manufactured it. On May 4 Sehon informed the Justice Department that Wobblies were congregating across the nation—275 in Los Angeles, 140 outside San Diego, 1,060 at various points in the state, and other bands in Chicago, Kansas City, and Oklahoma City—preparing "to overthrow the Government and take possession of all things. . . ." Armed with guns and dynamite and led personally by St. John and Haywood, the Wobblies, according to Sehon and United States Attorney McCormick, had organized "a criminally treasonous" conspiracy which had to be nipped in the bud by federal authorities.[44]

---

[43] Emma Goldman, *Living My Life* (New York, 1934), pp. 495–501; Richard Drinnon, *Rebel in Paradise: A Biography of Emma Goldman* (Chicago, 1961), pp. 135–36.

[44] John L. Sehon to George Wickersham, May 2, 1912, File 150139–7; F. C. Spaulding to Wickersham, May 3, 1912, File 150139–8; code message, John McCormick to Wickersham, May 4, 1912, File 150139–6, and May 6, 1912, File 150139–13, all in D/J 60.

Fortunately, Attorney General Wickersham remained calm and collected. Despite strong pressure from one of California's senators and from San Diego's congressman, Wickersham realized that the IWW posed no threat to American stability or security. What little disorder had occurred in San Diego, local authorities could manage, and the Attorney General certainly knew that San Diego had not been hesitant in its use of repression. But as a Republican politician with a presidential election upcoming, Wickersham mollified southern California Republicans by allowing McCormick to continue his federal investigation for evidence of IWW subversion.[45]

Throughout the summer of 1912, San Diego officials tried unsuccessfully to involve the Justice Department in the local conflict. McCormick even impaneled a Los Angeles grand jury to take evidence in an attempt to indict Wobblies for criminal conspiracy. In the opinion of a Justice Department official in Washington, McCormick's grand jury proved no more than that Wobblies "are apparently self-confessed liars and lawbreakers, but there is nothing indicating a specific attack upon the Government of the United States." After having allowed McCormick and his Republican supporters to have their fun, Wickersham ordered federal proceedings against the IWW dropped.[46]

At this juncture southern California's "reactionary" Republicans went over the Attorney General's head, carrying their case for federal repression of the IWW directly to President William Howard Taft. F. W. Estabrook, a prominent member of the Republican National Committee and an industrialist whose own factory had earlier been struck by the IWW, compared the California labor situation to that in Chicago in 1894 when Cleveland dispatched troops to crush the Pullman strike. He suggested to the President "that this matter [the San Diego conflict] is of the greatest importance, not only in a political way . . . but . . . it is time that vigorous action, whenever opportunity occurs, should be taken to stamp out the revolutionary methods of this anarchistic organization." More to the point, Estabrook assured Charles Hilles, Taft's secretary, that vigorous anti-IWW action would guarantee California's votes for Taft in the November election; furthermore, he added, such action would weaken the cause of the Hiram Johnson Progressive Republicans, who supported Theodore Roosevelt and the Progressive party in the 1912 election.[47]

---

[45] Senator John D. Works to Wickersham, May 4, 1912, and Wickersham's reply of May 6, 1912, File 150139–10; Congressman J. C. Needham to Wickersham, May 4, 1912, and Wickersham's reply, May 6, 1912, File 150139–12; Mayor James W. Wedham to Wickersham, May 5, 1912, and Wickersham's reply, May 6, 1912, File 150139–11; Wickersham to McCormick, May 6, 1912, File 150139–13; Wickersham to Senator Works, May 9, 1912, File 150139–14, all in D/J 60.

[46] McCormick to Wickersham, June 28, 1912; William R. Haar to Wickersham, July 5, 1912, and Wickersham's reply, July 6, 1912, File 150139–20; Wickersham to Senator Works, August 27, 1912, File 150139–26, all in D/J 60.

[47] F. W. Estabrook to Charles D. Hilles, September 5, 1912 (with enclosure: Charles H. DeLacour to Estabrook, September 5, 1912), File 150139–28, D/J 60.

Taft was receptive to Estabrook's suggestions. Political intrigue and his desire to be re-elected apparently clouded his usually clear mind, for Taft wrote as follows to Wickersham on September 7:

> There is not any doubt that that corner of the country is a basis for most of the anarchists and the industrial world workers [*sic*], and for all the lawless flotsam and jetsam that proximity to the Mexican border thrusts into those two cities. . . . We ought to take decided action. The State of California is under an utterly unscrupulous boss [Hiram Johnson], who does not hesitate . . . to [have to] do with these people and cultivate their good will, and it is our business to go in and show the strong hand of the United States in a marked way so that they shall understand that we are on the job.[48]

In other words, Taft expected repression of the IWW to win California's electoral votes.

Lacking presidential ambitions himself, Wickersham remained calm. Acceding to Taft's desire to investigate IWW subversion, the Attorney General nevertheless discounted the overblown reports and rumors emanating from southern California. Indeed, he maintained at the very end of the San Diego affair just as he had at the beginning: "I know of no reason why the [Justice] Department should take any further action."[49]

Although the federal government refused to intervene in San Diego, and Taft won neither California's votes nor re-election, the IWW continued to suffer at the hands of police and also private citizens. No agency of government was prepared in 1912 to defend the civil liberties of citizens who flaunted the traditions and rules of America's dominant classes.

Still, the IWW and its free-speech allies fought on. Pleading for funds and volunteers, they obtained money but precious few men. Even with a diminishing supply of manpower and close to defeat, the Wobblies remained defiant. Upon being sentenced to prison, one Wobbly, Jack White, proclaimed: "To hell with your courts; I know what justice is."[50]

Courtroom defiance was no substitute for victory. By October 1912, nine months after the inauguration of the free-speech fight, downtown San Diego remained vacant and lonely at night. "The sacred spot where so many I.W.W.'s were clubbed and arrested last winter," wrote Laura Payne Emerson, "lies safe and secure from the unhallowed tread of the hated anarchist, and in fact, from all other human beings." And she la-

---

[48] Taft to Wickersham, September 7, 1912, File 150139–29, D/J 60.
[49] Wickersham to Taft, September 16, 1912, and to C. D. Hilles, September 16, 1912, File 150139–31; Charles DeLacour to Wickersham, November 22, 1912, with marginal note by W.R.H. (William R. Haar?), File 150139–35, all in D/J 60.
[50] *Solidarity*, August 24, 1912, p. 3.

mented: "They have the courts, the jails and funds. What are we going to do about it?"[51]

Some Wobblies still counseled passive resistance, "the trump card that we hold and the vigilantes cannot use." Other Wobblies had their doubts. A crippled Chris Hansen vowed from his hospital bed: "My lesson is passive resistance no more." Albert Tucker, another survivor of the vigilantes' gauntlet, declaimed: "If I ever take part in another [free-speech fight] it will be with machine guns and aerial bombs." There must be, Tucker reasoned, "a better way of fighting and better results. . . ."[52] Similar frustration with nonviolent tactics appeared in a warning the *Industrial Worker* delivered to San Diego's public officials on April 4, 1912. "Take warning! Sehon, Wilson, Utley, Keno—take heed members of the 'vigilance committee'—Your names will be spread, broadcast! Reparation will be exacted! He laughs best who laughs last!"

Yet IWW threats and violence always remained rhetorical; the beatings suffered by nonviolent Wobblies, on the other hand, were very real. They hardly seemed worth it when the object to be gained, free speech, of and by itself brought no improvement in working conditions and added few members to the IWW. It seemed worth even less when, as Joe Hill remarked, San Diego was "not worth a whoop in Hell from a rebel's point of view."

If the battles in Spokane and Fresno demonstrated the effectiveness of nonviolence, San Diego starkly revealed the weakness of passive resistance as a tactic when the opposition refused to respect common decency and when no higher authority would intervene on behalf of the oppressed. Well before their defeat in San Diego, however, many Wobblies had had second thoughts about their organization's involvement in free-speech fights. At the time of the Spokane conflict, W. I. Fisher wrote to the *Industrial Worker:* "If we are to have a strong union we have to go to the job where the workers are and begin our agitation. . . . It is only where we control or are seeking control of the job that we can build up a lasting economic power." In 1911, during the Fresno struggle, Pacific Coast IWW representatives meeting in Portland voiced their opposition to unnecessary free-speech campaigns when more effective work remained to be accomplished in organizing and educating "wage slaves" on the job.[53]

But the IWW could not avert further free-speech fights. In the Far West and in other regions where migratory workers congregated, street speaking continued to be the most effective means for spreading the IWW gospel and for winning new recruits to the organization. After all, the migratories attracted to the IWW as a result of the 1909–1912 free-speech fights would become the dedicated Wobblies who later spearheaded the IWW's successful penetration of the woods and the wheat fields during the World War I years. Other motives also kept Wobblies on their soap-

---

[51] Quoted in *Industrial Worker*, October 17, 1912, p. 4.

[52] *Ibid.*, August 18, 1912, p. 2; Tucker to St. John, September 21, 1914, and Hansen to St. John, n.d., CIR Papers.

[53] *Industrial Worker*, January 15, 1910; A. Tucker to Vincent St. John, September 21, 1914, CIR Papers.

boxes. They were, to be sure, as much agitators as organizers, as much propagandists as labor leaders, and they needed their street corners and soapboxes in order to denounce capitalist society and "bushwa" morality. Wobblies also felt compelled to compete with the Salvation Army's street-corner preachers, who counseled the oppressed to be humble and content while awaiting their reward in heaven. In response to this advice, the IWW gospelers preached "a little less hell on earth" for exploited workers.

The Washington
Race Riot, 1919

ARTHUR I. WASKOW

The racial division of American society has produced untold misery in this country and has given rise to a pattern of urban racial violence that seems virtually endemic to the United States. Episodes of racially motivated violence have marked American history almost from its beginnings, ranging from lynchings by whites in the South to more recent black ghetto uprisings in the North. There is evidence that genuine "race riots"—a distinct form of racial violence in which members of both races enter into active conflict—took place in New York City as early as 1712.

During the period between the beginning of the First World War and the end of the Second World War, race riots were the characteristic form of racial violence, reaching a peak in the year 1919. Indeed, James Weldon Johnson, the executive director of the NAACP, called the summer of 1919 the "Red Summer" because of the blood that flowed in the streets. At least twenty-two race riots broke out that summer in American cities, both North and South.

Several factors helped to build up the racial hostilities that exploded in 1919. First, the war had spurred a large migration of blacks from rural areas of the South to Northern cities, where many new jobs in commerce and industry were open to blacks for the first time. In addition to opening up new industries, the war mobilization cut off the normal flow of immigrant labor to the North, requiring the active recruitment of black workers. Furthermore, many native whites who might have filled the new positions were drawn into military service, thus permitting blacks to get a foothold in the war industries. When the war ended, demobilization produced a wave of unemployment, and blacks were often the first to be fired. Competition for jobs became acute and led to bitter feeling. Racial tension was increased as returning whites sought to restore the racial patterns that had been altered by the war.

In the vanguard of increasingly militant Northern blacks were those who had served in the armed forces during the war. Although the American military discriminated against black troops in a number of ways, and although there had been many racial incidents both at home and abroad during the war, black soldiers felt they had earned a share of the benefits of American society, and they were not inclined to be pushed around without fighting back. Upon their return to this country, several black soldiers, some in army uniform, were lynched by angry mobs. Such atrocities added to the blacks' determination to struggle against their attackers and to hold on to the meager gains they had made during the war.

On May 10, 1919, a riot in Charleston, South Carolina, marked the beginning of the Red Summer, which lasted until the end of September. The major riots of the summer took place in Washington, D.C.; Chicago, Illinois; Longview, Texas; Knoxville, Tennessee; and Omaha, Nebraska. The Chicago riot was the most costly in terms of life, leaving fifteen whites and twenty-three blacks dead and many others wounded. But the Washington riot was particularly startling, because it took place in the nation's capital and because it began, not in some remote sector of the city, but on Pennsylvania Avenue midway between the Capitol and the White House.

Arthur I. Waskow, of the Institute for Policy Studies in Washington, includes a description of the Washington riot in his comparative study of the race riots of 1919 and the sit-ins of the 1960's, entitled **From Race Riot to Sit-In.** Among other things, he points out the crucial role of federal troops in provoking the spread of violence and then entering the struggle on the side of the whites. As Waskow notes elsewhere, provocative police activity was common to almost all the riots that took place during that summer.

The first of the 1919 riots to attract great national attention occurred in Washington, D.C., where a summer of increasing tension between Negroes and whites culminated in an explosion in mid-July.

Relations between the races in the capital had been affected by the accession of the southern-oriented Wilson administration and by the World War. Beginning in 1913, Negroes in the federal service had been segregated at work by their new southern supervisors, where they had never been segregated before; and there had been stirrings of anger among

Washington's Negroes over the suddenly more "southern" outlook of their lives.[1]

Then, with the coming of the war, job prospects changed again. As Emmett Scott, secretary-treasurer of Howard University, described the situation, the war boom in federal employment in Washington gave additional jobs to whites, some of whom left private jobs which Negroes then took over. Negroes were both angered by civil-service discrimination against them and rewarded with a sudden surge in income and self-respect in private employment, where some skilled laborers among them made more money than the white civil servants. Some whites in their turn resented this sudden twist of events.[2] Scott's analysis was confirmed by Louis Brownlow, a commissioner of the District of Columbia, who felt that jealousy among whites at the relatively greater prosperity of Negroes since the war had stirred bitterness between the races.[3]

The fact that Washington's population had been swelled during the war by a major influx of southern whites and a moderate influx of southern Negroes, the one group still intending to "teach any fresh 'nigger' his place" and the other determined to be free or to win revenge, exacerbated the racial tensions within the city.[4] The Negroes' sense of independence was strengthened by their service in France during the war, frequently under officers who had been trained in the Reserve Officers Training Corps (ROTC) at Washington's Howard University.[5]

The existing conflicts were brought to a boil by opportunistic journalism. The *Washington Post,* then published by Ned McLean, was bitterly antagonistic to the District of Columbia government and especially to the top command of the police force. McLean especially objected to tough police enforcement of Prohibition. He began hounding the police through his newspaper, and in the summer of 1919 began to criticize them for not controlling a "crime wave" of assaults and robberies. The *Post* kept the idea of a "crime wave" alive by sensationalizing the usual summer crime statistics and playing up ordinary cases of assault. Prominent among these were alleged instances of attempts by Negroes to rape white women.[6]

On July 9, the Washington branch of the NAACP sent a letter to all four daily newspapers in the city, "calling their attention to the fact that

[1] John Hope Franklin, *From Slavery to Freedom* [New York, 1947], pp. 445–46; Constance McLaughlin Green, *Washington: Capital City* [Princeton, 1963], pp. 218–26.

[2] *New York World,* Aug. 10, 1919, NAACP MSS. [From the preface to *From Race Riot to Sit-In:* "I am grateful to Roy Wilkins of the NAACP for permission to use these files."]

[3] *New York Call,* July 26, 1919, NAACP MSS.

[4] *Amsterdam News,* Aug. 6, 1919, NAACP MSS.

[5] Author's interview with Rayford W. Logan, 1959.

[6] Louis Brownlow, *A Passion for Anonymity* [Chicago, 1958], p. 84; author's interview with Brownlow, 1959; Herbert J. Seligmann, *The Negro Faces America* [New York, 1920], pp. 120–22; *New York Call,* July 26, 1919, *Baltimore Herald,* July 8, 1919, NAACP MSS.

they were sowing the seeds of a race riot by their inflammatory head-lines." According to the branch, only one newspaper answered—the *Star* —and that acknowledged the justice of the complaint.[7] The next day, however, the *Times* printed a news story emphasizing the NAACP's interest in bringing to justice all Negroes accused of crime, and leaving out its criticism of the tendency of the press to identify particular Negro criminals with the entire Negro population.[8]

The tension continued to increase. Suspects were arrested in some of the attempted rape cases and then released to the accompaniment of more attacks on police "laxity" by the *Post*.[9] On Saturday, July 19, the *Post* featured another case of alleged assault with the headline, "NEGROES AT-TACK GIRL . . . WHITE MEN VAINLY PURSUE." The body of the story de-scribed an "attack" in which two Negroes jostled a secretary on her way home, tried to seize her umbrella, and "frightened at her resistance to their insulting actions," fled. The paper also reported that the chief of police, Major Raymond W. Pullman, had ordered all young men "found in iso-lated or suspicious parts of the city after nightfall" held for questioning.[10]

The incident reported by the *Post* on Saturday morning bore deadly fruit on Saturday night. The girl "attacked" was the wife of a man in the naval aviation department. Two hundred sailors and Marines decided to avenge the slight to his and their honor by lynching two Negroes who had been suspected of the attack but released by the police. The sailors began a march into southwest Washington, stopping every Negro they met and beating several, both men and women. Civilians began to join the march, and when one Negro and his wife fled to their home the mob followed and attempted to break in through hastily set up barricades.[11]

At that point, both District and military police responded to a riot call and dispersed the mob. Ten arrests were made: two of white Navy men, and eight of Negroes who were "held for investigation." When three more Negroes were later stopped on the street by District police pa-trolling the area, one of them fired at the policemen and wounded one of them. This last event was the first use of violence by Negroes on Saturday night, although the eight-to-two arrest rate might be imagined to have indicated a higher rate of lawbreaking by Negroes.[12] It is hard to avoid concluding that the unneutral behavior of the police had much to do with the Negro attack on them and with the later increase in violence from both Negroes and whites.

On Sunday morning, the Washington branch of the NAACP asked Josephus Daniels, the Secretary of the Navy, to restrain the sailors and Marines who had led the attack. They warned of a more serious clash if no action were taken.[13] But none was taken. Indeed, Daniels' later diary

[7] *Philadelphia Public Ledger*, July 28, 1919, NAACP MSS.

[8] *Washington Times*, July 10, 1919, NAACP MSS.

[9] *Washington Post*, July 19, 1919, NAACP MSS.

[10] *Ibid.*

[11] *Washington Times*, July 20, 1919, NAACP MSS.

[12] *Ibid.*

[13] *Philadelphia Public Ledger*, July 28, 1919, NAACP MSS.

notes on the riot suggested that he blamed most of it on the Negroes and was not greatly interested in protecting them.[14]

On Sunday night the situation exploded. Shortly before 10 P.M., a policeman arrested a young Negro on a minor charge at a heavily trafficked corner on Pennsylvania Avenue, halfway between the Capitol and the White House. While the policeman waited for the patrol wagon, "hundreds of men in khaki and blue and many negroes" crowded around. The Negro under arrest was snatched away from the police by several white men and beaten over the head. The police recovered him and dispersed the crowd, but arrested no whites. Down the street, a few minutes later, another fight broke out between white servicemen and Negro civilians. This time three Negroes were badly injured.[15]

From then on, the violence multiplied. Soldiers and sailors marched up Pennsylvania Avenue, chasing and beating Negroes, yanking them off streetcars, and growing ever more belligerent. The police, few in number and aided only by a handful of soldiers detailed as a provost guard, scarcely interfered, except to arrest about fifteen men, white and Negro, on charges of disorderly conduct. Most Negroes fled, but some fought back. At midnight, the soldiers and sailors had to return to their barracks. But after 1 A.M., even more violent struggles broke out at several corners in the downtown area, with white as well as Negro civilians involved in these clashes.[16]

In reporting the riot on Monday morning, the *Washington Post* gave it the leading place and large black headlines. The paper added a crucial paragraph:[17]

> It was learned that a mobilization of every available service man stationed in or near Washington or on leave here has been ordered for tomorrow evening near the Knights of Columbus hut on Pennsylvania Avenue between Seventh and Eighth Streets. The hour of assembly is 9 o'clock and the purpose is a "clean up" that will cause the events of the last two evenings to pale into insignificance.

No explanation was made of where the "orders" came from, and the publication of this notice brought the strongest condemnation of the *Post* from the Negro community and the District officials.[18]

---

[14] On Sunday night he wrote there had been a "riot—race—following negro assaults on white women," and on Monday, out of all the many cases of racial violence going in both directions, selected to note in his diary only that "carriage full of negroes drove by Naval Hospital and wantonly fired into party of convalescent sailors and marines." E. David Cronon [ed.], *The Cabinet Diaries of Josephus Daniels, 1913–1921* [Lincoln, 1963], p. 427.

[15] *Washington Post*, July 21, 1919, *Washington Times*, July 21, 1919, NAACP MSS.

[16] *Ibid.*, *Washington Post*, July 21, 1919, NAACP MSS.; *Washington Star*, July 21, 1919, *Washington Bee*, July 26, 1919.

[17] *Ibid.*

[18] Author's interviews with Brownlow, Campbell Johnson, and West A. Hamilton, 1959; Edward H. Lawson, "Teaching How to Riot," in *The American Teacher*, Oct. 1919, NAACP MSS.

During the day on Monday, a flurry of meetings were held and statements issued on the violence of Sunday night. The George Washington Post of the American Legion condemned the participation of servicemen or ex-servicemen in the nightly race riots.[19] The NAACP asked the Secretary of War to investigate and punish the guilty soldiers. It also sent a committee to the District commissioners and the chief of police to ask for more effective action by the police to protect Negroes. Herbert J. Seligmann of the NAACP's national office in New York arrived in Washington to get firsthand information on the riot.[20] Pastors of Negro churches, meeting under the sponsorship of the National Race Congress, condemned the police force for taking "no precaution that a competent and efficient police department would have employed," and demanded that the War and Navy departments cancel the leaves of all servicemen in the Washington area.[21]

In Congress, members of the Senate and House committees on the District of Columbia expressed their hope that the riots would cease or be suppressed, but did not recommend any specific action. Congressmen not on these committees were more specific. A Florida congressman demanded a congressional investigation of the failure of the police to apprehend Negro assailants of white women, arguing that this failure had caused the riot. A New York congressman demanded that the Army, Navy, and Marine Corps prevent their men from joining the riots, and received assurances from three high-ranking officers that servicemen would be prevented from participating in any renewal of the riots Monday night. Two other members of the House demanded that the President declare martial law.[22]

District Commissioner Brownlow met with Secretary of War Newton D. Baker and Army Chief of Staff Peyton March in order to plan for the use of troops to quell the rioting. Brownlow told the press that co-operation between the District police and the Army was certain to end the trouble. He said preparations had been made to bring troops in from Army camps in the District and even from Camp Meade, Maryland, if necessary, to police the District. Brownlow also urged Washingtonians to stay out of the downtown area Monday night. No general cancellation of servicemen's leaves was announced, but base commanders were told to detain in barracks all men "without a good excuse for leave."[23]

While this flurry of conferences and statements continued, the first riot cases were being disposed of in police court. Four Negroes who had been arrested Sunday night on charges of disorderly conduct and unlawful assembly were set free. A white sailor was found guilty of disorderly conduct in organizing the original mob march on Saturday night, and was turned over to the Navy for punishment.

19 *Washington Post*, July 22, 1919, NAACP MSS.
20 *Philadelphia Public Ledger*, July 28, 1919, NAACP MSS.
21 *Washington Post*, July 22, 1919, NAACP MSS.; *Washington Star*, July 22, 1919.
22 *Washington Times*, July 21, 1919, NAACP MSS.; *Washington Star*, July 22, 1919.
23 *Washington Times*, July 21, 1919, NAACP MSS.

During Monday afternoon, Negroes who were alarmed by the *Post*'s "mobilization notice" began to arm themselves. Guns were bought in Washington and Baltimore. "Alley Negroes," some of them soldiers from the Negro regiment recruited in Washington, took out the rifles they had used in France.[24] One story that persisted for decades had it that officers at the Howard University ROTC prepared to give arms and ammunition to the Negro population if it should become necessary.[25] During the day came the first evidence of the new determination of Negroes to "fight back" and even to attack. One mob of twenty-five or thirty boarded a streetcar and beat the motorman and conductors. Others fired from a speeding automobile on sailors in the Naval Hospital grounds. Still others set out in a gang for the Navy Yard, presumably to be on hand when employees finished work; but these were dispersed by the police before they could reach the Yard.[26]

But Monday afternoon was only a faint prelude. That night, despite the precautions and the public statements, the riot was renewed, in a form far worse than before. Four men were killed outright, eleven others mortally or seriously wounded. Of these fifteen, six were white policemen, one a white Marine, three white civilians, and five Negro civilians. Dozens of others sustained injuries that were less serious but required hospitalization. Three hundred men were arrested for riotous behavior or for carrying concealed weapons.[27]

The force that had been set up to cope with the riots was made up of 700 Washington police and 400 soldiers, sailors, and Marines organized as an emergency provost guard. Few servicemen took part in the Monday night disturbances. But a surging mob of 1,000 white civilians made repeated attempts to break through a cavalry cordon in order to attack the Negro residential areas, once almost doing so after massing at the Treasury and marching past the White House. But several cavalry charges broke up these attempts. Whenever the mob found Negroes in the downtown area, the Negroes were savagely beaten. Police were able only to keep the mob moving, not to disperse it. Some Negroes caught in this melee responded to attack by firing pistols at the mob.[28]

Meanwhile, in the Negro areas Negroes were beating white men, and were firing upon passing streetcars and automobiles from houses along the way. Eight or ten automobiles were manned by armed Negroes and were used as armored cavalry in lightning attacks on white residential districts, randomly firing at houses and people. Other automobiles were used by whites in the same fashion, and at least one running dogfight was reported between Negroes and whites in two such cars. Several policemen were wounded or killed while trying to arrest armed Negroes or to raid houses that had been used as sniper centers.[29]

On Tuesday, a startled press was calling for "uncompromising meas-

[24] Lawson, *loc. cit.*; memo from Seligmann to NAACP staff, NAACP MSS.
[25] Author's interview with Campbell Johnson, 1959.
[26] *Washington Times*, July 21, 1919, NAACP MSS.
[27] *Washington Post*, July 22, 1919, NAACP MSS.; *Washington Star*, July 22, 1919.
[28] *Ibid.*
[29] *Ibid.*

ures," for more military patrols, even for martial law.[30] The District commissioners rejected suggestions that President Wilson be asked to declare martial law, and instead worked out plans for much more forceful military support of the civil government.[31] President Wilson called in Secretary of War Baker, who then arranged with General March, Secretary of the Navy Daniels, and the Washington police chief to order into the District additional troops from Camp Meade, Marines from Quantico, and sailors from two ships lying in the Potomac. In command of these augmented military forces was placed Major General William G. Haan, who ordered troops into every section of the city.[32]

Early in the evening, Baker and Brownlow conferred on the troop dispositions. Haan, accompanied by Police Chief Pullman, drove through the city to inspect the troops. Haan announced publicly that he was satisfied that the situation was well in hand, with one third of his force on actual patrol and two thirds in reserve with speedy transport available to be hurried to any danger point.[33] But privately he talked with military men in New York about the possibility that troops might have to be sent from there.[34] In effect, these arrangements all but supplanted local police, who had become suspect to the Negro community, by the more nearly neutral federal troops.

General Haan also exerted himself to control the city's newspapers, on the theory that much of the riot was "merely a newspaper war." He later wrote a brother officer, "When I got them [the newspapers] to agree to say approximately what I wanted them to say, which was the truth, then soon everything was over."[35]

While these military preparations were being made, the Negro community took steps both to protect its members and to reduce the chance of violence. The NAACP's local legal committee arranged to defend many Negroes who had been arrested for carrying weapons, protesting against the arrests of many such men "while the white men from whom they were attempting to protect themselves were not molested." Another NAACP committee visited Brownlow to report that Negro prisoners after being arrested "were often beaten up and abused by the police officers." They asked to be deputized to visit various precinct stations to see that Negro prisoners were treated well, but Brownlow spoke with the police authorities and later said full provision had been made through regular channels for correct treatment of prisoners.[36] Other Negro leaders visited

---

[30] *Washington Post*, July 22, 1919, *Washington Star*, July 22, 1919, *Washington Times*, July 22, 1919, NAACP MSS.

[31] *Ibid.*

[32] *Washington Post*, July 23, 1919, NAACP MSS.; Cronon, *Cabinet Diaries of Josephus Daniels*, pp. 427–28; *Washington Times*, July 23, 1919, *Washington Star*, July 23, 1919.

[33] *Ibid.*

[34] William G. Haan to Major Gen. Thomas H. Barry, July 30, 1919, Haan MSS., Wisconsin State Historical Society.

[35] *Ibid.*

[36] *Philadelphia Public Ledger*, July 28, 1919, NAACP MSS.

Capitol Hill to ask for a congressional investigation of what they thought was police antagonism to Negroes, exemplified by the failure of the police to hire a single Negro patrolman in four years.[37] Police captains in the heavily Negro precincts met with local Negro leaders and arranged for the early closing of moving-picture theaters, near-beer saloons, and poolrooms in the Negro areas. Leading Negro ministers urged their congregations to keep off the streets.

Minor efforts to prevent another outbreak were made within the federal bureaucracy. The Commerce Department urged all its employees to keep off the street at night and to discuss the subject of race relations "temperately."[38] In the Division of Negro Economics in the Labor Department, the assistant director was asked to get in touch with leading Negro ministers in Washington and try to arrange a meeting with white clergymen that might produce a joint statement to calm the public. The Assistant Secretary of Labor advised against letting even the slightest "tinge" of official sanction be lent to any activity involving the race riot; but he suggested that names of ministers who might be interested could be given as "a personal matter" to an outsider who could then make the contacts himself.[39]

All these efforts at peace-making and order-keeping finally bore fruit on Tuesday night, July 22. Two thousand federal troops, the admonitions for self-control, and an intermittent driving rain together succeeded in preventing crowds from gathering. Only two important incidents marred the night. One Negro tried to escape arrest and was shot, but not seriously hurt, by a Marine on patrol. Two white men on guard duty as officers of the Home Defense League (a police reserve created during the war) were shot, and one of them was killed, when they attempted to halt a Negro for questioning. But aside from these events, a night of rumors and alarms held little violence. "Several times," according to one newspaper, "the cavalry galloped through the streets to answer calls for assistance and found on their arrival that they were not needed." Toward morning, as it became clear that there would be little trouble, and as the wet streets made more and more difficulty for the cavalry detachment, it was withdrawn and put on reserve. At dawn the infantry and naval patrols were withdrawn.[40]

The relaxation allowed Secretary Baker to write the President on Wednesday that the situation was finally in hand. Baker explained that the one death had grown "out of no controversy or excitement but . . . an unprovoked and impulsive act, perhaps the act of a man of unstable mind, deranged by excitement growing out of the general situation." He

[37] *Washington Post*, July 23, 1919, NAACP MSS. See also *Washington Bee*, July 26, 1919, and Aug. 2, 1919, on Negroes' suspicion of the police.

[38] E. W. Libby to C. E. Stewart, July 22, 1919, Justice Dept. MSS., National Archives.

[39] Karl G. Phillips to George E. Haynes, July 22, 1919, Labor Dept. MSS., National Archives.

[40] *Washington Post*, July 23, 1919, NAACP MSS. See also *Washington Star*, July 23, 1919, Wilson MSS., Library of Congress.

reported that the attitude of the Negroes, particularly their leaders, had been helpful. As for Wednesday evening, Baker said he had instructed Haan to keep his troops on duty at points from which they could quickly meet any emergency.[41]

The rest was anticlimax. Several members of the NAACP staff visited Senator Arthur Capper, a Kansas Republican, Wednesday and won his support for a congressional investigation of race riots and lynching.[42] On Thursday, a coroner's jury held one Negro for murder of a white Marine, although the Negro claimed he had drawn his pistol in self-defense against a mob and had hit the Marine accidentally.[43] But by Thursday it was clear that the riot was over, and attention turned to the prevention of future riots.

In considering the future, both General Haan and Police Chief Pullman emphasized the need for troops to police the capital in order to prevent or cope with a recurrence of any sort of mob violence. As the authorities pointed out, "disturbances in national capitals abroad and the general feeling of unrest throughout the world, coupled with the fact that the United States has assumed the position of the leading democratic nation, all demand that no small causes be allowed to throw the city into a state of lawlessness."[44] In line with this strong-police approach to the prevention of violence, Police Chief Pullman and Commissioner Brownlow asked Congress to increase the number and the pay of policemen.[45]

Negroes reacted somewhat differently. One pamphlet issued soon after the riots crowed about the "heroic resistance" of the young Negroes who "defied the point of bayonets, the sting of blackjacks and the hail of bullets in defending themselves." This pamphlet insisted that only the abolition of the "Mobocratic Lyncherized system . . . of Jim Crow" would ultimately satisfy Washington's Negroes.[46] Even the far more cautious and conservative statement issued by Emmett Scott of Howard University and Judge Robert Terrell of the Municipal Court placed the blame for the riots on the white mob and called Negro retaliation deplorable but natural. Scott and Terrell specified that interracial co-operation to prevent riots must be based on mutual sharing of the rewards of American life, rather than on Negro subordination.[47]

A middle position of Negro indignation, somewhere between the Scott-Terrell caution and the pamphleteer's anger, was taken by the NAACP. The national office wrote Attorney General A. Mitchell Palmer to ask whether he intended to proceed against the *Washington Post* for

[41] Newton D. Baker to Woodrow Wilson, July 23, 1919, Wilson MSS., Library of Congress.

[42] Memo from Seligmann to NAACP staff, NAACP MSS.

[43] *Washington Post*, July 25, 1919, NAACP MSS.; *Washington Star*, July 24, 1919.

[44] *Washington Post*, July 25, 1919, NAACP MSS.

[45] *Ibid.*; *Washington Star*, July 30, 1919.

[46] Edgar M. Grey, *The Washington Riot* [New York, 1919], in Schomburg Collection, New York Public Library.

[47] *Washington Star*, July 27, 1919, NAACP MSS.

inciting to riot by printing its "mobilization notice." (The answer was no.)[48]

Similarly moderate criticism came from a Washington Negro minister, who asked Palmer to intervene in behalf of Negroes accused of carrying concealed weapons who were being charged "unreasonable" bonds and jailed for "extreme" periods. Palmer did write the district attorney for Washington, who said he would make sure that no such discrimination took place.[49] Requests of the same type that discrimination against Negroes be avoided in the post-riot trials came from Congressman Isaac Siegel, a New York Republican, who reported that a number of letters from both whites and Negroes had called the matter to his attention. Siegel received assurances of fair treatment.[50]

But the courts continued to hand down sentences that seemed severe to the Negro community, and in September a group of Negro ministers gathered what were reported to be 30,000 signatures on a petition for presidential clemency. The leader of the drive said he would present the petition to the President, on Wilson's return from his nationwide tour for the League of Nations.[51] But that tour ended in Wilson's physical breakdown, and nothing more was heard of the bid for executive clemency.

As was to be expected, the four days of rioting in the national capital stirred thought and feeling all across the United States. Much of it focused on the problems of official and private violence, but some dealt with the issues of racial equality and subordination that were basically in conflict.

One of the widespread reactions outside Washington, as it had been a strong reaction inside Washington, was to demand tougher policing of the city. Criticism of Congress for not providing enough money to attract enough able men to the police force was the response of several newspapers as far away as Rochester and Minneapolis,[52] and of United States senators from California and Kansas.[53] "A larger, better drilled and more ably commanded police organization" in Washington was called for by

[48] John R. Shillady to A. Mitchell Palmer, July 25, 1919, Robert P. Stewart to Shillady, July 29, 1919, Justice Dept. MSS.

[49] J. Milton Waldron to Palmer, Aug. 1, 1919, Palmer to Waldron, Aug. 8, 1919, Palmer to John E. Laskey, Aug. 8, 1919, Laskey to Palmer, Aug. 12, 1919, Justice Dept. MSS.

[50] Isaac Siegel to Palmer, July 30, 1919, Stewart to Siegel, Aug. 1, 1919, Stewart to Laskey, Aug. 1, 1919, Laskey to Palmer, Aug. 4, 1919, Justice Dept. MSS.

[51] *Washington Herald*, Sept. 2 and 9, 1919, NAACP MSS.; NAACP *Branch Bulletin*, October, 1919, in files of Senate Judiciary Committee, Legislative MSS., National Archives.

[52] Rochester newspaper, no name, July 26, 1919, *Minneapolis National Advocate*, Aug. 2, 1919, NAACP MSS.

[53] Senators James Phelan and Arthur Capper, quoted in *Washington Post*, July 22, 1919, NAACP MSS.

the *New York Herald.*[54] The *Utica Press* translated Washington's troubles into a demand that Utica enact a law preventing the promiscuous sale of firearms.[55] And the *New York Globe* summed up the entire approach embodied in demands for a larger police force when it said: "There is nothing to be done but to quiet the rioters by force. We make no pretense nowadays of settling the race question; we simply keep it in abeyance."[56]

This emphasis upon the need for a *strong* police was countered by many Negroes and some whites with demands for a *neutral* police. W. E. B. Du Bois, editor of *The Crisis*, insisted that Washington policemen were notoriously anti-Negro, and had intervened to stop the riots only when whites began to get the worst of the battles.[57] The *Amsterdam News* cited the rejection of Negro candidates for the Washington police force and the failure to use existing Negro patrolmen in the riot when "their moral influence would have been valuable" as evidence of the "antipathy of Washington police toward negroes."[58] What the partiality of the Washington police had meant to Negroes and would continue to mean in the future was spelled out by the *New York Commoner:* "As the police have failed to protect the Negroes of the capital there is but one course open. Let every Negro arm himself and swear to die fighting in defense of his home, his rights and his person. In every place where the law will not protect their lives, Negroes should buy and hoard arms."[59] This analysis of the Washington riot as an index of the Negroes' readiness to fight back on their own when the police would not protect them was echoed by James Weldon Johnson of the NAACP staff. He said that if Washington had had officers with "the courage to enforce the law against the white man as well as against the colored," the Washington riot would have ended the Saturday it began, and Negroes would not have gone on the offensive Monday.[60] White newspapers like the *New York Call* and *New York Globe* agreed that where Negroes felt unprotected by the law, they were now prepared to protect themselves.[61]

Judgments differed when the press tried to evaluate this new readiness to fight back. Some papers, like the *Commoner*, applauded the new atmosphere. The *Pittsburgh Courier* said proudly that Negroes had learned "a bullet in Washington has no more terrors than . . . in the Argonne."[62] Others, especially white newspapers, saw it as an inevitable but not especially laudable response of self-defense.[63] But some white editors warned

54 *New York Herald*, July 26, 1919, NAACP MSS.

55 *Utica Press*, July 25, 1919, NAACP MSS.

56 *New York Globe*, July 23, 1919, NAACP MSS.

57 *New York Tribune*, July 23, 1919, NAACP MSS.

58 *Amsterdam News*, Aug. 6, 1919, NAACP MSS.

59 *New York Commoner*, July 23, 1919, NAACP MSS.

60 *Washington Post*, July 25, 1919, NAACP MSS.

61 *New York Call*, July 25, 1919, *New York Globe*, July 29, 1919, NAACP MSS.

62 *Pittsburgh Courier*, July 26, 1919, NAACP MSS. See also United Civic League Press Service release, July 30, 1919, NAACP MSS.

63 *New York World*, July 23, 1919, *Des Moines Evening Tribune*, July 22, 1919, *New York Tribune*, July 23, 1919, *New York Call*, July 25, 1919, NAACP MSS.

that "any Negro in his senses ought to know that violence is the last thing in the world that can help his cause." The *New York Globe* and the *New York World* argued that every appeal that Negroes made should be to the law, to its impartiality if possible, but always to the law. "Oppressed as they are, they cannot free themselves by force," the *Globe* insisted.[64]

The alternative to self-defense was transformation of the police power into a neutral force. To some people, the Washington riot seemed a demonstration of the need for the federal government to provide that neutral police force. Specifically, it was argued that federal anti-lynching legislation would force local and state police to defend Negroes against white lynch mobs. The distinction between the partiality of the Washington police and the relative impartiality of the federal troops once they intervened as an official unit was not lost on observers. Thus, showing his respect for federal impartiality, a Negro who had in 1916 led a delegation from the African Methodist Episcopal Church to see the President now wrote him a long, impassioned letter begging for a law to make lynching a federal crime.[65] The *New York Post* and the *Survey* similarly argued for a neutral federal intervention to end lynching, in order to prevent "a terrible race war."[66]

There were, of course, some commentators who saw the problem as much deeper than the provision of a more powerful or more neutral police force, and who believed more basic change was necessary. But there were disagreements on the direction that basic change should take.

To some, a letup in racial violence was hard to imagine short of the attainment of racial equality. Thus a writer in *The American Teacher* called for an end to the segregation that had kept not only Washington's schoolchildren but her whole society cut into two warring parts.[67] Several French newspapers and a New York magazine espoused racial equality as the goal but warned that its achievement would probably require successive race riots to urge the process on, for the "antipathy of whites towards blacks grows stronger in direct ratio to the amount of progress made by the Negro race."[68]

To a number of other editors, North and South, it seemed clear that Negro insubordination was the cause of the riots and that a return of order could only be accomplished if the Negro would go back to and stay in his place. The *New York Times*, for example, mourned the passing of that Washington in which "the negroes, before the great war, were well behaved, . . . even submissive."[69] The *Brooklyn Eagle* similarly headlined its report, "RACE WAR IN WASHINGTON SHOWS BLACK AND WHITE

[64] *New York Globe,* July 29, 1919, *New York World,* July 29, 1919, NAACP MSS.

[65] J. G. Robinson to Woodrow Wilson, July 26, 1919, Justice Dept. MSS.

[66] *New York Post,* July 23, 1919, *Survey,* Aug. 2, 1919, NAACP MSS.

[67] Edward H. Lawson, "Teaching How to Riot," *The American Teacher,* Oct. 1919, NAACP MSS.

[68] *Young Democracy,* Aug. 1, 1919, *L'Homme Libre* and *L'Avenir,* quoted in *Chicago Tribune,* July 25, 1919, NAACP MSS.

[69] *New York Times,* July 23, 1919, NAACP MSS. [© 1919 by The New York Times Company. Reprinted by permission.]

EQUALITY NOT PRACTICAL," and went on to blame the riot on the full employment, high wages, and increasing independence that Washington Negroes had won from the war.[70] Newspapers in Syracuse and Albany[71] were no more cautious in assuming Negro inferiority and the need to control Negroes who acted as if they were equal than were newspapers in Memphis and Nashville.[72] A more official southern view of the relative places of whites and Negroes in society was set forth by the Alabama legislature. By joint resolution, the legislature chided the white leadership of the North for trying to act by "purely idealistic and theoretical considerations," rather than in a "practical way." This theoretical spirit, the legislators said, had led to the kind of hatred between the races in the "disordered" North that did not exist in the South.[73]

Having aroused these thoughts across the nation, the Washington riot faded away. The talk of an investigation came to nothing, the *Washington Post*'s attack on the District of Columbia administration and police chief had no lasting effect, and race relations in the capital underwent no overt change, either in the direction of equality or of subordination for Negroes. According to some who lived through the riots, there was a new self-respect among Negroes, a readiness to face white society as equals because Negroes had fought back when they were attacked.[74] The Washington riot demonstrated that neither the silent mass of "alley Negroes" nor the articulate leaders of the Negro community could be counted on to knuckle under, even in a largely southern city with a hostile police force and a press that had been harping on the unforgivable "Negro" crime.

[70] *Brooklyn Eagle*, July 27, 1919, NAACP MSS.

[71] *Syracuse Herald*, July 24, 1919, *Albany Argus*, July 24, 1919, NAACP MSS.

[72] *Nashville Banner*, July 22, 1919, Memphis Press, July 24, 1919, NAACP MSS.

[73] Montgomery, Alabama, newspaper, no name, no date, NAACP MSS.

[74] Author's interviews with Campbell Johnson, West A. Hamilton, and Rayford W. Logan, 1959.

Feminism

as a

Radical Ideology

WILLIAM L. O'NEILL

Some standard narrative histories of America give the impression that the only issues capable of stirring women to organize politically were prohibition and women's suffrage. This is certainly not the case, although it is true that overconcentration on these issues and the heavy publicity that centered around them tended to divert attention from other aspects of feminism that may have been of more profound importance both for the women of America and for society at large.

At the time of the 1848 convention on women's rights in Seneca Falls, New York—the event from which the women's rights movement usually dates itself—feminists saw disfranchisement as only one of a whole array of serious legal and social disabilities faced by women. Women were not allowed to own property—in most cases, not even the clothes they wore. A working wife was not allowed to keep her wages but was required to turn them over to her husband. In the case of separation or divorce, a woman had no legal claims on her husband and was not allowed to keep the children. She had no legal status, which meant that she was not permitted to bring suit or to give testimony in the courts. Often, she was not permitted to inherit property or to make a will. She was barred from public office and excluded from public life generally. For the most part, women lacked opportunities for education, vocational training, and professional employment. The national consensus was that women belonged in the home, and determined efforts were made to see that they stayed there.

In the beginning, there was a good deal of confusion and disagreement among the feminists as to the best method of improving their situation. Some women instituted petition campaigns and direct lobbying in their respective states. Others sought the help of friendly legislators, hoping to bring informal influence to bear. Eventually, most of the efforts of the women's movement were focused on securing the right to vote, for it seemed that only the use of the franchise could generate the pressure necessary to eliminate legal discrimination against women.

In retrospect, it may be difficult to understand why the idea of female suffrage was so furiously opposed by the American public, both male and female, in the closing years of the nineteenth century. The opponents of female suffrage often used the argument that women were too frail, too pure, too noble, to participate in the political arena. Indeed, the Gilded Age was one of the most corrupt periods in American political life, and men may actually have seen the extension of the franchise as a step toward the corruption of a new segment of society. Or, believing their own rhetoric, they may have feared that women voters would force overly rigorous reforms on the existing political and social structures. In the South, the vote of black women was viewed as an even more unthinkable threat to the status quo than the vote of white women. Any explanation that could be given here would be simplistic. But, generally, the opposition to the women's movement can be understood as part of a wide-ranging defensive reaction against the breakdown of the traditional family system that was proceeding, hand in hand with urbanization, in the entire Western world.

When women's suffrage was finally achieved in 1920, after over half a century of struggle, the women's movement was too divided within itself to mobilize the new vote for any better purpose than prohibition. Because class interests tended to take precedence over sex interests, women voters failed to function as a specific political interest group. On the contrary, they tended to join the men in conventional party politics and hence had virtually no effect on national policy. Having won a major victory, many of the feminist leaders retired from the public eye, and the agitation for women's rights largely died out, to be revived only in the 1960's.

In the following article, William L. O'Neill, of the University of Wisconsin, argues that the lack of a significant ideology was a chief factor in the failure of the women's rights movement of the late nineteenth and early twentieth centuries to have any major impact on American life.

Several years ago, in his cogent and provocative essay on the changing place of women in American life, Carl Degler argued that feminism

"Feminism as a Radical Ideology" by William L. O'Neill was originally published in *Dissent: Explorations in the History of American Radicalism*, edited by Alfred F. Young, © 1968 by Northern Illinois University Press. Reprinted by permission of the publisher.

failed because it was unable to construct a viable ideology.[1] Feminism, however, produced an immense literature, and much of it was ideological in that it attempted to frame the "woman question" in such a way as to force solutions.[2] Instead of writing off this material as inadequate—although it was—I think something is to be gained from tracing the principal lines of thought that feminism developed in order to pinpoint the weaknesses that permitted it to collapse once equal suffrage had been secured.

Because feminism was such a widespread, indistinct, poorly defined phenomenon, feminists never developed a precise vocabulary. Indeed, the vagueness of their language reflected larger confusions of thought and perception that kept them from building a successful ideology. No historian, to my knowledge, has found it necessary to remedy this defect, but, because I intend to show that there were several kinds of feminism, a word about terms is necessary.

The phrase most commonly used by women in the nineteenth and early twentieth centuries to describe their expanding activities was "the woman movement." This movement included not only those things pertaining to women's rights but almost any act or event that enlarged woman's sphere, increased her opportunities, or broadened her outlook. It covered everything from woman suffrage and social reform down to the individual accomplishments of gifted, ambitious women. "Feminism," a more limited word, related specifically to the advancement of women's legal and political rights. The feminist movement, in turn, was broadly divided into two wings, but, because feminists themselves did not recognize this until the very end of the period, i.e., in the 1920's, I have coined the phrases "social feminism" to describe that part of the movement that put social reform ahead of women's rights and "hard-core" or "extreme feminists" to describe those who put women's rights before all else. A "suffragist" was simply one who worked for equal suffrage, irrespective of her views on other questions.[3]

During much of its history feminism was considered extremely radical; indeed, suffragists did not triumph until after they had persuaded the public that they constituted a "bourgeois, middle-class, . . . middle-of-the-road movement."[4] Although equal suffrage was an absurdly controversial issue, and there was little basis for the repeated charge that it

---

[1] See Carl N. Degler, "Revolution Without Ideology: The Changing Place of Women in America," in *The Woman in America* (Boston, 1965), pp. 193–210. The best guide to the history of women's rights is Eleanor Flexner, *Century of Struggle* (Cambridge, Mass., 1959). A good analysis of the movement's thought in its salad days is Aileen S. Kraditor's *The Ideas of the Woman Suffrage Movement* (New York, 1965).

[2] See, for example, Professor Degler's evaluation of the movement's best ideologue, "Charlotte Perkins Gilman on the Theory and Practice of Feminism," *American Quarterly*, 8 (Spring, 1956): 21–39.

[3] "Suffragette" was the English equivalent of "suffragist." The former term was used in America mainly as a derisive term by critics of woman suffrage.

[4] "A Bourgeois Movement," *The Woman Citizen*, July 7, 1917, p. 99.

was revolutionary, for a long time there was good reason to think that the feminist program—of which suffrage was only a part—had revolutionary implications. This was so because, by the Victorian era, women were locked into such a tight domestic system—their role so narrowly defined—that granting them real equality was impossible without overhauling the entire social structure. Full equality required drastic readjustments on two levels. If women were to have an equal chance with men to develop themselves, not only would they need equal educational and vocational opportunities but they would somehow have to be relieved of the domestic obligations that bound most of them to the home. And, because every system encourages the attitudes that are appropriate to it, the whole complex of ideas and assumptions that "justified" women's inferior status would have to be changed.

At the beginning of the nineteenth century the only acceptable roles for women were domestic; there was virtually nothing for them to do except stay at home or hire out as maids, governesses, and, before long, teachers. A handful made other places for themselves, but until the middle of the century they were too few to affect the system. The cultural rationale that kept women in the home, however, was more complex and demands further attention. The Victorian woman was part of a network of ideas, prejudices, and religious emotionalism that simultaneously degraded and elevated her. "The cult of true womanhood" (as one historian calls it) emphasized women's piety, purity, submissiveness, and domesticity. Religious work was almost the only form of outside activity permitted women because it did not take them away from their "true sphere." "From her home woman performed her great task of bringing men back to God."[5] Woman, it was believed, was morally and spiritually superior to man because of her highly developed intuition, refined sensibilities, and especially because of those life-giving maternal powers that defied man's comprehension. But woman was physically weaker than man, inferior to him in cognitive ability, and wholly unsuited to the rough world outside the home. This was just as well, however, because women were largely responsible for "The Family," the chief adornment of Christian society and the foundation of civilized life.[6]

Although the concept of women as wan, ethereal, spiritualized creatures bore little relation to reality by mid-century, when women operated machines, worked in the fields, hand-washed clothing, and toiled over kitchen ranges, it was endorsed by science and by religion. A vast and constantly growing body of polemical literature was churned out by physicians, clergymen, and journalists in support of this thesis. Even fashion conspired to the same end; the bustles and hoops and the corsets and trailing skirts in which women were encased throughout much of the century seemed designed to hobble them and prevent all but the most desperate from leaving their homes for long. (The weight of metal,

[5] Barbara Welter, "The Cult of True Womanhood: 1820–1860," *American Quarterly*, 18 (Summer, 1966): 162.
[6] For a more complete description of this idea, see my *Divorce in the Progressive Era* (New Haven, 1967), pp. 58–61.

cloth, and bone that women were expected to bear should itself have disproved the notion that they were peculiarly delicate creatures, but of course it did not.) Feminine "delicacy" was considered the visible evidence of their superior sensibilities, the "finer clay" of which they were made. Women who were not delicate by nature became so by design. In the end, the fashion was self-defeating for it aroused fears that women would become so ornamental as to be incapable of discharging their essential functions. The Civil War helped wake middle-class women from "their dream of a lady-like uselessness," and in 1861, when Vassar College was founded, its trustees put physical education at the head of their list of objectives.[7]

The Victorian idealization of women was self-defeating in another and more important way. The Victorians attempted to compensate women for their domestic and pedagogic responsibilities by enveloping them in a mystique that asserted their higher status while at the same time guaranteeing their inferiority; hence the endless polemics on the moral purity and spiritual genius of woman that found its highest expression in the home and that had to be safeguarded at all costs from the hopelessly corrupting effects of the man-made society without. But, as William R. Taylor and Christopher Lasch have suggested,

> the cult of women and the home contained contradictions that tended to undermine the very things they were supposed to safeguard. Implicit in the myth was a repudiation not only of heterosexuality but of domesticity itself. It was her purity, contrasted with the coarseness of men, that made woman the head of the home (though not of the family) and the guardian of public morality. But the same purity made intercourse between men and women at last almost literally impossible and drove women to retreat almost exclusively into the society of their own sex, to abandon the very home which it was their appointed mission to preserve.[8]

Thus the "woman movement" had its origins in the sexual segregation that Victorians considered essential for an ideal domestic system. Beginning with church societies and a few women's clubs, associationism grew and grew, until by the end of the century millions of women were caught up in it, and their old isolation was broken.

As we noted earlier, the woman movement was not the same thing as feminism. Women who worked for their church or met in literary societies were, however, indirectly helping themselves by developing aspirations that promoted the larger growth to come. They began to press for more education and to manifest intellectual and literary interests. The acute Englishwoman, Harriet Martineau, noted that "in my progress through the country [America] I met with a greater variety and extent

[7] Amy Louise Reed, "Female Delicacy in the Sixties," *Century*, 68 (October, 1915): 258–70.

[8] "Two 'Kindred Spirits': Sorority and Family in New England, 1839–1846," *New England Quarterly*, 36 (March, 1963): 35.

of female pedantry than the experience of a lifetime in Europe would afford." This pedantry, she hastened to add, "was not to be despised in an oppressed class, as it indicates the first struggle of intellect with its restraints; and it is therefore a hopeful symptom."[9]

Even more hopeful, of course, was the next step that these developments made possible: the formulation of a distinct women's rights movement. In the 1830's women were stirred by the currents of reform that were sweeping the country, and those who were moved to action discovered that their status as women told against their ambitions as abolitionists, temperance workers, or whatever. Sarah M. Grimké was inspired to write the first American feminist tract of consequence[10] because some clergymen objected to her anti-slavery work. Elizabeth Cady Stanton was started on her career as a women's rights leader after she was denied a seat, by reason of her sex, at a World Anti-Slavery Convention in London. Susan B. Anthony became a feminist after she was discriminated against by her male colleagues in the temperance movement.

In 1848 these separate streams of dissent came together at the first Women's Rights Convention in Seneca Falls, New York. The "Declaration of Sentiments" that was adopted by the meeting indicated another element that infused the early feminist movement: the libertarianism of the age of reform. Modeled in part on the Declaration of Independence, this manifesto declared that "the history of mankind is a history of repeated injuries and usurpations on the part of man toward woman, having in direct object the establishment of an absolute tyranny over her."[11] It was, in fact, a decidedly radical document—not that it called for an end to private property, or anticipated a good society along socialist lines, but in storming against every iniquity from votelessness to the double standard of morals it made demands that could not be satisfied without profound changes in the social order. The most sophisticated feminists appreciated, in some measure at least, that they were not merely asking for their rights as citizens, that what they wanted called for new institutions as well as new ways of thinking. They seem to have been feeling their way toward a new domestic order. Mrs. Stanton, who denounced marriage as "opposed to all God's laws," wanted to begin its reformation by liberalizing divorce.[12] The magazine she and Susan B. Anthony ran after the Civil War, *Revolution*, was full of references to the "marriage question" at a time when no orthodox person was willing to admit that there was a marriage question.

Logic alone had forced extreme feminists to sail these dangerous

[9] In *Society in America*, 3 vols. (London, 1837), 3: 107.

[10] *The Equality of the Sexes and the Condition of Women* (Boston, 1838).

[11] *History of Woman Suffrage*, 1: 70. This immense documentary history of the suffrage movement from 1848 to 1920 ran to six fat volumes and was published between 1881 and 1922. The first three volumes (1881, 1882, 1887) were edited by Elizabeth Cady Stanton, Susan B. Anthony, and Matilda Joslyn Gage. Volume 4 (1902) was edited by Susan B. Anthony and Ida Husted Harper, and volumes 5 and 6 (1922, 1922) by Miss Harper.

[12] A letter to Lucy Stone, November 24, 1856, in *History of Woman Suffrage*, 1: 860.

waters because even then it was clear that if women were fully emancipated by law, their domestic obligations would nevertheless prevent them from competing with men on an equal basis. There were only two (by no means mutually exclusive) ways of dealing with this problem: either women must be supported by the kind of welfare measures (guaranteed maternity leaves with pay, family allowances, and the like) that the advanced social democracies have devised, or marriage and the family must be more flexibly defined.

Because the first alternative did not exist in the mid-nineteenth century, far-sighted women had to consider how the essential domestic institutions could be revised to free women from the tyranny of home and family; they had some precedents to guide them. For their own reasons the Mormons practiced polygamy, while the Shaker communities went to the opposite extreme by abolishing not only marriage but sexual relations as well. A number of perfectionist groups explored the varieties of free love, such as John Humphrey Noyes, who (at Oneida, New York) combined the equality of the sexes, perfectionism, socialism, and "complex marriage" (the sharing of spouses) in a bizarre but strikingly successful way. In such an atmosphere it was natural for the boldest feminists to flirt with radical approaches to the domestic problem. It is impossible to tell where these speculations would have led Mrs. Stanton and her followers, but the Victoria Woodhull affair suggests a likely possibility.

Victoria Woodhull and her equally vivid sister, Tennessee Celeste Claflin, burst upon the New York scene in 1868. Although nominally lady stockbrokers, they were agitators and evangelists by persuasion, and enthusiasts for everything radical, or just plain wild—socialism, spiritualism, or women's rights. Their magazine, *Woodhull and Claflin's Weekly*, promoted such causes, as well as the peculiar interests of their mentor, Stephen Pearl Andrews, a self-proclaimed universal philosopher and linguist. The surprising thing about the raffish sisters is that they rapidly became celebrated champions of the cause of women, admired by such shrewd and experienced figures as Elizabeth Cady Stanton and Susan B. Anthony. In 1871, for example, Victoria Woodhull persuaded a congressional subcommittee to hold hearings on woman suffrage, and she testified before it with great effect.

Their *Weekly* was interested in marriage from the beginning. Stephen Pearl Andrews believed in free love in the usual Victorian sense (that is, in extramarital sexual relationships contracted as a matter of principle), and the Claflin sisters had practiced free love long before they understood its theoretical possibilities. Having thrown out a good many hints, Mrs. Woodhull finally called a mass meeting and on the stage of Steinway Hall declared herself a free lover. She seems to have been genuinely astonished at the ferocious reaction to this public confession; newspapers hounded her, cautious feminists snubbed her, and the sisters fell on hard times, financially and emotionally. Victoria struck back by disclosing that Henry Ward Beecher, the most famous preacher of the day and a good friend of woman suffrage, had been having an affair with the wife of Theodore Tilton, Mrs. Woodhull's friend, her biographer, and perhaps her lover. The ensuing scandal destroyed the Claflins and the

Tiltons; but Beecher survived it, thanks to his great reputation, considerable courage, and influential friends.[13]

The effect of this debacle on the suffrage movement's fortunes is
hard to determine because the cause was already in bad shape when the
Claflins took it in hand. Suffragists had been disappointed at the end of
the Civil War when they were asked to sacrifice votes for women to
secure votes for Negro men. Some of them refused to admit that the
freedman's need was greater than theirs and, because of this and other
frictions, the suffrage movement had divided into two organizations: the
staid, Boston-based American Woman's Suffrage Association and the more
aggressive National Woman's Suffrage Association, led by Miss Anthony
and Mrs. Stanton. Both groups were tarnished by the Beecher-Tilton
affair, but the AWSA suffered less because it had always been anti-Claflin.
The NWSA came in for a larger measure of abuse because of its closer
association with the sisters, but the unquestionable virtue and integrity of
its leaders saved it from total eclipse. It used to be thought that the affair
had set back equal suffrage for decades; today, however, the movement's
temporary decline seems to have been only one feature of the conservative
backlash of the Gilded Age. Suffragists had expected too big a reward for
their services during the Civil War as nurses, propagandists, and sanitary
commission volunteers. The country was grateful to them, but not all
that grateful—as the defeat of woman suffrage in the hotly contested
Kansas referendum of 1866 demonstrated. In freeing and enfranchising
the Negro, America, it seemed, had exhausted its supply of liberalism.

The Woodhull affair had one lasting effect, however: it reaffirmed
the general conviction that suffrage politics and radical speculations, particularly those affecting marriage and the family, did not mix. In consequence the movement, although it never disowned the social goals that
women's votes were presumably to implement, emphasized the most
conservative aspects of the suffrage question. The vote was shown to be
compatible with the existing domestic economy, and—at best—with those
reforms that would elevate and refine domesticity to the level of perfec-
tion for which society yearned. Suffragists thereafter, vigorously resisting
the temptation to think seriously about the domestic institutions that
ruled their lives, made sexual orthodoxy their ruling principle.

In the long run these shocks had two important consequences:
feminism rapidly became more conservative and more altruistic. Its conservatism—not the doing of Victoria Woodhull—stemmed from the tight-
ening up of morals and manners that occurred in the high Victorian era.
Bills like the Comstock Act (1873) made it impossible for John Hum-

---

[13] For a compact description of these events, see Robert E. Riegel, *American
Feminists* (Lawrence, Kan., 1963), pp. 144–50. A recent biography of Victoria
Woodhull is Johanna Johnston's *Mrs. Satan: The Incredible Saga of Victoria C.
Woodhull* (New York, 1967). The best single source on these events is the
Weekly itself, a fascinating publication that deserves more attention than most
historians have given it.

phrey Noyes and other sexual radicals to use the mails, choking off the lively debate that had flourished earlier. The porous or open quality that had characterized American life in the age of reform gave way to the censorious prudery we associate with Victorianism. It is very likely that the extreme feminists would have had to abandon their tentative explorations, if only because of social purity. Earlier there had been sporadic attempts by organized women to eliminate the double standard of morals by holding men to a higher level of conduct. The radical feminists who toyed with free love approached the same goal from an opposite direction, by proposing a sort of convergence in which men and women would occupy a middle ground between the old extremes of absolute license and complete chastity. After the war, however, all doubts as to which line feminists would follow were relieved by the social purity movement, which enlisted the energies of public-spirited women all over the country in a crusade to abolish prostitution and infidelity.[14] Mrs. Stanton continued to advocate free divorce, to the great embarrassment of her younger followers, but she was very much the exception.

At the same time that feminists abandoned their more advanced positions they took on a great range of activities that often had little to do with women's rights. Extreme feminists, for example, displayed a keen sense of self-interest in the struggle over Negro suffrage after the Civil War. The Stantonites as a rule were more radical and more sensitive to the needs of others than the Boston faction, but when they were forced to choose between the Negroes' interests and their own they unflinchingly went down the line for feminist objectives.

The feminism of later years, however, was much more generous and diffuse. A hardy band of suffragists fought the good fight for the vote while most feminists devoted themselves to charities, philanthropies, and reforms. As social workers, settlement house residents, members of women's clubs, advocates of the reform of child labor and women's working conditions, of municipal government, public health, education, and housing, and as temperance workers and conservationists they submerged their interests as women in a sea of worthy enterprises. These social justice activities became the principal justification for feminism and are what historians most admire about the movement, but feminists paid a high price for their good deeds in two important ways. First, these activities drained off personnel from the women's rights movement and protracted the suffrage struggle. Second, they led to ideological confusions that played a large role in the collapse of feminism once the vote was won.

Social feminism also perpetuated the confusion between class and sex, that false sense of solidarity that characterized the entire woman movement. In a way this was natural, because all women suffered from disabilities that were imposed upon men only discriminatingly. It was not possible to have a "man movement" because most men enjoyed all the rights and opportunities that God and nature presumably intended them

---

[14] For this important but little-studied reform, see David Jay Pivar's "The New Abolitionism: The Quest for Social Purity, 1876–1900" (Ph.D. diss., University of Pennsylvania, 1965).

to have. Equal rights for women, however, did not mean the same thing to a factory girl that it meant to a college graduate, and feminists invariably refused to admit that differences in station among women were of any importance. In the beginning this hardly mattered, because the early feminists were mainly bourgeois intellectuals who were struggling to improve their own immediate circumstances. As the woman movement matured, however, its sociological evasions and self-deceptions attained critical proportions.

This analytic failure, which was characteristic of a movement that (with the notable exceptions of Elizabeth Cady Stanton and Charlotte Perkins Gilman) produced few intellects of the first rank, was compounded by an insistence that women were united in a selfless sisterhood by their maternal capacities, real or potential. "Women," it was declared over and over again, "stand relatively for the same thing everywhere and their first care is naturally and inevitably for the child."[15] Maternity was not only a unifying force but the enabling principle that made the entrance of women into public life imperative. As another suffragist put it in 1878, "the new truth, electrifying, glorifying American womanhood today, is the discovery that the State is but the larger family, the nation the old homestead, and that in this national home there is a room and a corner and a duty for mother."[16] Not only was the nation a larger home in need of mothering, but, by impinging upon the domestic circle, it made motherhood a public role.

As Jane Addams saw it, "many women today are failing properly to discharge their duties to their own families and household simply because they fail to see that as society grows more complicated it is necessary that woman shall extend her sense of responsibility to many things outside of her own home, if only in order to preserve the home in entirety."[17] Thus the effort to escape domesticity was accompanied by an invocation of the domestic ideal: women's freedom road led in a circle, back to the home from which feminism was supposed to liberate them. Feminism was made respectable by accommodating it to the Victorian ethos that had forced it into being.

Given the plausibility and flexibility of this contention, women were (perhaps inevitably) lured into using it to secure their immediate aims; but in retrospect it does not seem to have been an unqualifiedly successful ploy. The Women's Christian Temperance Union is a case in point. Although one historian recently hailed Frances Willard's "supreme cleverness" in using "this conservative organization to advocate woman suffrage and child labor laws and other progressive legislation always in the name of purity and the home,"[18] the history of the WCTU illustrates the weakness of an argument that begins by

---

[15] Mrs. Ellis Meredith at the 1904 NWSA convention, in *History of Woman Suffrage*, 5: 101.

[16] Elizabeth Boynton Harbert, *ibid.*, 3: 78–79.

[17] "Woman's Conscience and Social Amelioration," in Charles Stelzle, ed., *Social Applications of Religion* (Cincinnati, 1908), p. 41.

[18] Andrew Sinclair, *The Better Half* (New York, 1965), p. 223.

accepting the opposition's premise. In conceding that better homes were of equal importance to feminists and anti-feminists alike, these women reduced their case from one of principle to a mere quarrel over tactics. All the opposition had to do to redeem itself was prove that its tactics were superior. This apparently is what happened to the WCTU after the death of Frances Willard (which coincided with a significant change in its social composition), when new leaders came to believe that temperance was more crucial to the home than suffrage, child welfare, and other progressive causes. Perhaps this new orientation would have come about in any event, but surely such WCTU suffragists as Frances Willard made it much easier by their willingness to utilize the cult of domesticity in pursuit of quite separate and distinctively feminist objectives.

The truth was that while these feminists resented the demands made upon them in their roles as wives and mothers, they were insufficiently alert to the danger presented by even a partial accommodation to the maternal mystique. Gravely underestimating the tremendous force generated by the sentimental veneration of motherhood, they assumed they could manipulate the emotions responsible for the condition of women without challenging the principles on which these feelings rested. Moreover, while denying that under the present circumstances mothers could be held accountable for the failings of their children, they implied that, once emancipated, women could legitimately be indicted for their progenies' shortcomings. In 1901 Susan B. Anthony declared that "before mothers can rightfully be held responsible for the vices and crimes, for the general demoralization of society, they must possess all possible rights and powers to control the conditions and circumstances of their own and their children's lives."[19] Her remark would seem to mean that, once granted political equality, mothers would have to answer for all the ills of society. This was a great weight to lay on female posterity, and such statements contributed to the unhealthy and unrealizable expectations that feminism encouraged.

A further hazard of the feminist emphasis on motherhood was the support it lent the notion that women were not only different from men, but superior to men. Julia Ward Howe, a moderate and greatly admired feminist, persistently implied that emancipation was intended to make women better mothers as well as freer persons.

> Woman is the mother of the race, the guardian of its helpless infancy, its earliest teacher, its most zealous champion. Woman is also the home-maker, upon her devolve the details which bless and beautify family life. In all true civilization she wins man out of his natural savagery to share with her the love of offspring, the enjoyment of true and loyal companionship.[20]

---

[19] In *History of Woman Suffrage*, 5: 5–6.
[20] Florence Howe Hall, ed., *Julia Ward Howe and the Woman Suffrage Movement* (Boston, 1913), p. 158.

Definitions like this left men with few virtues anyone was bound to admire, and inspired women to think of themselves as a kind of super-race that had been condemned by historical accident and otiose convention to serve its natural inferiors.

Such indeed was the case with women who, encouraged by the new social sciences (especially anthropology, which demonstrated that matriarchies had existed and may once have been common, if not universal), took themselves with a new seriousness that few men could share. Elizabeth Cady Stanton argued that prehistoric women had been superior to men, or at least equal to them, but that Christianity, and especially Protestantism, had driven the feminine element out of religion and had subordinated women to the rule of men. Society thereby had lost the beneficent moral and conservative forces of the female intellect and the mother instinct.[21]

With this line of argument Walter Rauschenbush, no enemy of women's rights, was compelled to take issue. Alarmed by what he regarded as the feminists' moral pretensions, he wrote: "Many men feel that women are morally better than men. Perhaps it is right that men should instinctively feel so. But it is a different matter when women think so too. They are not better. They are only good in different ways than men."[22] Rauschenbush believed in the emancipation of women, but he reminded his readers that the feminine virtues could easily be exaggerated, and that in recent times both Christian Science and theosophy had demonstrated a particular appeal to women even though both stressed authority and unexamined belief.

As Rauschenbush's observation suggests, the attempt to demonstrate women's superior nature led nowhere. In essence it was just one more variation of the Victorian mystique, another way of exploiting the belief that woman's unique power was rooted in the mystery of her life-giving capacities. Taken one way, it led back to a preoccupation with motherhood. Read differently, it supported so complete a rejection of men that women could retain their integrity and spirituality only in spinsterhood. Or—by subscribing to the principles of Ellen Key, who elevated motherhood even above marriage and made the right to have illegitimate children the central aspect of feminism —women could have their cake and eat it too.[23] They could realize their generative and instinctual potential without an unseemly dependence on the contaminating male. Deliberately having an illegitimate child necessitated an act of masculine cooperation, and in a delicious reversal of ancient custom man became an instrument of woman's purpose and his ungoverned passion the means to her full emancipation. This was radicalism

---

[21] See her paper, "The Matriarchate, or Mother-Age," in Rachel Foster Avery, ed., *Transactions of the National Council of Women of the United States* (Philadelphia, 1891), pp. 218–27.

[22] "Moral Aspects of the Woman Movement," *Biblical World*, 42 (October, 1913): 197.

[23] See esp. Key's *Love and Marriage* (New York, 1911).

with a vengeance, but a radicalism that had curiously little to do with the normal objects of revolutionary ardor.

Most organized women, however, were neither radical nor especially feministic. The woman movement as a whole, and most social feminists in particular, were satisfied with the comparatively modest programs of the WCTU and the General Federation of Women's Clubs. These programs, despite the fears of conservatives, were no threat to what Mrs. Gilman scornfully called the domestic mythology; in fact, they rested largely on the domestic and maternal mystique that was characteristic of the Victorian era. Not only did organized women continuously invoke "home and mother," for the most part their serious enterprises dealt with such related social matters as pure foods and drugs, child welfare, and working mothers. Whenever suffragists were able to tie in the ballot with a specific problem of special interest to women, they gained adherents. Through most of the nineteenth century suffragists maintained that women were entitled to vote as a matter of right and that they needed the vote to protect themselves and to advance the causes that were important to them. Neither argument was very persuasive in the age of Victoria, and always the suffragists' greatest obstacle was the indifference of their own sex.

As late as 1908 Theodore Roosevelt could comfortably, and quite rightly, say that "when women as a whole take any special interest in the matter they will have suffrage if they desire it."[24] But only a few years later the picture had changed entirely. In 1914 the General Federation of Women's Clubs endorsed women suffrage in the name of its two million members; in 1917 membership in the NWSA soared to something like two million; and in that same year 500,000 women in New York City alone put their signatures to a suffrage petition. By 1917 it was obvious that women wanted the vote, and by 1920 they had it.

Few feminists seemed to realize that although winning the vote had been a feminist victory, it had not been won for feminist reasons. Suffragists had merely persuaded the organized middle-class women, who had become a potent force for reform in the Progressive era, that they needed the vote in order to secure the healthier and broader domestic life that was their main objective; feminists had not, however, convinced bourgeois women that they were greatly deprived and oppressed and that they had vast unrealized capabilities. From a strictly feminist point of view, the vote had been wrongly obtained. It neither reflected nor inspired a new vision of themselves on the part of most American women. Moreover, the suffrage could not but demoralize feminists who had worked so hard for so long, only to find that success had little effect upon the feminine condition.

The immediate consequence of feminine emancipation, then, was the fading away of the woman movement as it became apparent that the

[24] In a letter to Lyman Abbott, dated November 10, 1908, published in "An Anti-Suffrage Meeting in New York," *Remonstrance* (January, 1909), p. 3.

great organizations had less in common than they supposed. Moreover, the organizations themselves were changing in character. The WCTU was obsessed with prohibition (although it did not entirely lose interest in other social problems during the 1920's). The NWSA was transformed into the League of Women Voters; and although the league struggled valiantly to advance the old causes beloved of women reformers, it lacked the drive, funds, and numerical membership of its predecessor. The General Federation suffered least, because it had always been less committed to major reforms than its sister groups, and if its member clubs slackened their efforts, the national leadership continued to support the federation's traditional interests. The best evidence of the movement's decline was the fate of the Women's Joint Congressional Committee, which had been formed in 1920 to lobby for bills in which organized women took a special interest. Although it enjoyed some success (it helped keep Muscle Shoals [a federal hydroelectric project in Alabama] out of private hands and it preserved a measure of federal support for mothers' pensions and other welfare programs), it lost more battles than it won, especially in the crucial struggle to ratify the Child Labor Amendment.

In the 1920's the split between social feminism and hard-core feminism emerged as a fundamental distinction. During the voteless years a common interest in women's suffrage and a general if vague commitment to women's and children's welfare had saved feminists from having to choose between equal rights and social reform. Then, in the twenties, a sharp cleavage opened between feminists in the League of Women Voters and the Joint Committee—which labored mainly for civic-virtue and welfare measures—and the militant Woman's Party, which singlemindedly pursued a narrow program that was signified by the title of its periodical *Equal Rights*. The most divisive feature of the Woman's Party program was its espousal of an equal rights amendment to the Constitution. Social feminists were alarmed by the Lucretia Mott Amendment (as the Woman's Party called it) because of the possibility that the courts would define equal rights as equal treatment. If this happened, the entire array of protective legislation that had been enacted for the benefit of working women during the Progressive era would be swept away. Inasmuch as the courts had already interpreted the Clayton Act to the disadvantage of working men, had twice declared congressional child labor bills unconstitutional, and had struck down minimum wage laws for women, this was not an unreasonable fear. The Woman's Party insisted that equal rights and equal treatment would not be confused, or, if they were confused, so much the better: protective laws discriminated against working women by denying them the competitive advantages of men, who could work whatever jobs and hours they pleased. In reality the competition issue was relevant mainly to business and professional women who had to function in the job market as individuals. It hardly applied to wage-earning women, who could not bargain individually over wages, hours, or working conditions. Thus, feminists of every kind discovered that women did not constitute a real social class but were subject to the same distinctions that obtained among men.

Throughout the decade, and indeed long afterward, an unseemly struggle was waged over equal rights and protective legislation, but this quarrel was only symptomatic of the deeper confusions into which the entire movement had fallen as a result of the Nineteenth Amendment. It was not merely a question of whether complete equality was more risky than advantageous, nor even where, having won the vote, feminism ought to go, but what being a woman in America really meant. In short, feminists had traveled a long, circuitous, ascending path—to find themselves in 1920 about where they had been in 1830. They had not failed to better their condition along the way, but in avoiding fundamental questions for the sake of immediate advantages they had merely postponed the inevitable confrontation with themselves. Now the day of reckoning was at hand.

In the 1920's, then, it became clear that the anti-suffragists had been right all along in saying that the vote would neither change the lives of women as individuals nor greatly aid the causes in which organized women were most interested. Most women soon lost interest in overthrowing such remaining barriers to full emancipation as the WP urgently, and the LWV rather perfunctorily, called to their attention. The surviving hard-core feminists abandoned the fight for social justice (except for themselves), while the social feminists devoted themselves to such causes as peace, poverty, and prohibition, which had little to do with the status of women.

Under these circumstances it was no longer possible to speak with accuracy of a "woman movement," and the term fell into disuse, although such organizations as the International Woman's Suffrage Alliance and the International Council of Women perpetuated the cosmopolitan and cooperative spirit that had been such a striking and useful feature of the old movement. Hard-core feminism, on the other hand, contracted in size and spirit, so that it came to resemble its own mid-Victorian predecessor.

In the 1920's the movement's focus of interest shifted from organized to unorganized women, from the sober clubwoman and earnest social worker to the flapper. This in turn signaled a rebirth of the old popular sociology that considered women only as individual members of an undifferentiated mass. Although the greatest achievement of the woman movement had been to expand the definition of woman, the movement had only modified, not rejected, the biological imperatives of the Victorian ethos; and when the movement began to subside it left the contradiction between woman's sexual identity and her unique persona to be resolved, if possible, in a wholly new context. This new environment was created partly by feminism's successes, partly by its failures, and to a large extent by things over which it had no control. The movement admired daring and independence, to a degree, but it associated these qualities with large and generous purposes. The "new woman" of the twenties was indeed bold and venturesome—but in pursuit of what the older generation considered trivial if not ignoble objectives. The woman movement wanted to eliminate the double standard in morals by making men practice the sexual ethics they preached. The flapper also endorsed a single standard of morality, but she wanted sexual ethics to conform to reality rather than the reverse. Most of all, of course, young women in the postwar era were molded by the characteristic novelties of the period: the ebbing of reform, the demoralizing aftermath of the "war to end war," the emergence of mass society and mass culture, the new technology, and the higher standard of living that permitted the merchandising of pleasure on an immense scale.

The change in feminine sexual behavior was not only the most sensational aspect of these changes but a striking evidence of the shift in women's lives from organization to individuality. Woman suffrage had been a public question that enlisted collective energies; sexuality was a private concern that women had, perforce, to cope with as individuals. Our own atmosphere is so sexually charged and we hear so much about the "sexual revolution" that it is easy to forget the significant changes that took place more than a generation ago. Not only was sex discussed publicly and with a previously forbidden candor in the twenties, there is good reason to think that people, especially women, experienced sex in a different manner. At the end of the decade a gynecologist remarked that in 1885 his typical patient was "the woman 'who would rather die than be examined.' In the early nineties the patient instantly covered the least bare spot, with the sheet, but in 1920 full exposure is taken for granted by the young."[25] In another of those remarkable studies that preceded the Kinsey reports a psychiatrist discovered that the sexual experiences of one hundred women correlated with their year of birth. In his admittedly small and arbitrary example, of fifty women who had been born before 1890 only seventeen had engaged in either pre- or extramarital intercourse, compared with thirty of the fifty women who were born after 1890. It seemed to him that the sexual behavior of men and women was converging.[26]

These few bits of evidence lend substance to the feeling of most contemporary observers that important changes in the sexual patterns of the young were taking place during the 1920's. But the new sexuality was accompanied by new attitudes of even greater importance. A juvenile court referee wrote that the younger generation did not admire its parents. The old maxim that age and experience command respect no longer carried weight. Girls and young women were much more aggressive in finding husbands than their mothers were. They expected to work after they were married, mostly for the added income, but they were vague about what they would work at and reluctant to train for particular occupations. A girl "intends to marry at a more specific date if she can bring it about, have a definite number of children at desirable intervals, and earn a definite sum toward the upkeep when she needs to." Most

[25] Robert Latou Dickinson and Lura Beam, *A Thousand Marriages* (Baltimore, 1931), pp. 12–13.

[26] See Gilbert V. Hamilton, *A Research in Marriage* (New York, 1929). Although Hamilton's sample was a small one, his findings "parallel those of Kinsey for the same grouping of subjects 20 years later" (in Aron Krich, ed., *The Sexual Revolution* [New York, 1965], p. xii).

disturbing of all, the younger generation had rejected the idealism of the previous generation. "So for lack of other vision they believe in themselves."[27]

Over and over again the same refrain was heard. Even when girls expressed more or less traditional sentiments, they did so for sensible reasons, which were very different from the principled stands of their mothers. Thus a study of 252 middle-class girls disclosed that although they thought chastity good and promiscuity undesirable, they generally advanced practical rather than moral arguments for this position. Only one girl in three said that in every case she would disapprove of a friend's affair.[28]

A thoughtful ex-suffragist writer of the League of Women Voters (which was distressed by its difficulties in recruiting young members) pointed out that "the feministic movement isn't at all smart among the juniors. But it is interesting to observe that such rights as the old feministic movement has already won for the females of the species, the young accept as a matter of course. Especially when these rights mean personal and individual privileges."[29] Her informants used the First World War, much as a later generation would use The Bomb, to deflate what they regarded as the moral pretensions of their elders and expose the uselessness of their advice.

At least one young woman struck closer to home when she bluntly observed that the previous generation always put off its own ambitions until after some job of reform had been done. "They were all going to return to their personal knitting after they had tidied up the world. Well look at the world! See how they tidied it up! Do you wonder that our generation says it will do its personal knitting first?" Indeed, this girl expressed a high degree of moral fervor in proclaiming her amoral credo:

> But we're not out to benefit society, to remold existence, to make industry safe for anyone except ourselves, to give any small peoples except ourselves their rights. We're not out for submerged tenths, we're not going to suffer over how the other half lives. We're out for Mary's job and Luella's art, and Barbara's independence and the rest of our individual careers and desires.[30]

In one sense this outburst suggests that there was a feminist equivalent of Dada: an insistence that the private vision takes precedence over the social will, that art exists for its own sake and woman for her own sake, a repudiation of the grand causes and glorious rhetoric that had moved the older generation. It was also a logical conclusion to the feminist hardline.

[27] Eleanor R. Wembridge, "The Girl Tribe—An Anthropological Study," *Survey* (May 1, 1928), p. 198.

[28] See Phyllis Blanchard and Carlyn Manasses, *New Girls for Old* (New York, 1937), chap. 5. (This book was completed in 1930 but was not published until 1937.)

[29] Anne O'Hagan, "The Serious-minded Young—If Any," *Woman's Journal*, 13 (April, 1928): 7.

[30] *Ibid.*, p. 39.

We have seen how dismaying this attitude was to the social feminists who had viewed women's rights as only one aspect of the good society that women could bring into being if given the chance, but it was almost as disconcerting to those who saw feminism as an end in itself. A collective impulse is not the same thing as a social movement, and to the privatized young women of the twenties, luxuriating in their emancipation, the demand of the Woman's Party that they rise up and strike another blow for freedom seemed ludicrous and anachronistic. They had all the freedom they could use; the problem was what to do with it. Having rejected both the woman movement's thesis that the purpose of emancipation was service and the feminists' call to compete fiercely with men at every occupational level, what else remained?

What remained, as events would soon demonstrate, was the "feminine mystique." The feminine mystique, as Betty Friedan recently defined it in her lively polemic, is not much different from the nineteenth century's cult of domesticity. It too glorifies the role of woman as wife and mother, finds domestic impulses at the heart of woman's nature, and warns against the dangers of feminine competitiveness. It updates the old familial ideology, however, in several ways. Feminine emancipation brought with it a better-educated womanhood, with higher cultural and aesthetic expectations. Because the home could no longer be defended with religious sentimentalities, moral authorities joined with the mass media to depict the home (in the words of an advertising man) as "the expression of her creativeness. We help her think of the modern home as the artist's studio, the scientist's laboratory."[31] Women were encouraged to regard child-rearing and home economics as complicated, lofty enterprises that demanded a skillful mixture of exact science and aesthetic inspiration. This development, already well under way in the Progressive era, required almost no effort to convince bewildered young women in the post-suffrage era that the home—cleansed of its imperfections by modern science, capitalism, and enlightened thought—was a fit object for their attention and a worthy challenge to their sharpened talents.

The task of pouring old wine into new bottles was made easier by psychoanalysis, which offered a popular solution to the problem of reconciling sexual freedom with the necessary limitations of domestic life. The woman movement had drawn a line between eroticism and sex. It accepted, with qualifications, the role of women as fundamentally determined by sex, but it vigorously rejected any suggestion that sexuality was a human right. As it turned out, however, motherhood and sensuality were largely compatible with one another. Premarital intercourse could be and was justified as preparation for that perfect physical union that modern science insisted was a necessary ingredient of married bliss. Freud seemed not only to rationalize a sexuality that society would in any case have to live with, he did this in the context of a remarkably conventional view of feminine nature. Freud, after all, was a Victorian, and his Ameri-

31 In Betty Friedan, *The Feminine Mystique* (New York, 1963), p. 217.

can popularizers translated his concept of women as inherently passive, dependent, and childlike creatures as meaning that women were most in harmony with their true natures when they functioned as sexually fulfilled housewives.[32]

Thus the popular science of the twentieth century recapitulated the popular science of the nineteenth century in discovering that the laws of nature decreed woman's sphere to be the home. The revolution in morals was, then, no revolution at all. Without for a moment denying the importance of that measure of erotic libertarianism that was gained in the 1920's, and admitting that the emancipation of women really broadened their opportunities (although most of the broadening took place before 1920), woman in the twentieth century looks surprisingly like woman in the nineteenth century.[33]

With the emergence of the feminine mystique we can see more clearly the ideological failure that kept feminists from preventing the collapse of their movement. This failure consisted largely of an inability to determine where their interests lay. Because they could not clearly define their problem, they could not devise a successful strategy for solving it. The most perceptive of the first-generation feminists understood that overcoming the prohibitions that confined them to the home made it necessary for them to challenge the polarized definitions of male and female nature upon which the prohibitions rested. This meant, in practice, denying that there were any important differences between the sexes, apart from the inescapable fact that only women bear children. So direct a challenge, of course, provoked extreme responses, which frightened all but the bravest women, but led the more far-sighted among them to consider what would happen if the formal barriers were removed. Obviously, women would still be at a disadvantage because of their maternal obligations, and in the first half of the nineteenth century there was only one way this handicap could be minimized: marriage and the family would have to be reorganized. Because the Woodhull affair had vividly demonstrated the risks inherent in this line of thought, feminists withdrew to a more defensible position, which enabled them (so they believed) to exploit the successes of the woman movement. The movement, and especially its social feminist divisions, employed a sort of moral judo against the masculine establishment by relating its goals to the Victorian stereotype. Woman, the argument ran, needed to be free in order to fulfill her larger destiny as mother of the nation.

---

[32] For an exceptionally astute critique of Freud's views on women, see Ronald V. Sampson, *The Psychology of Power* (New York, 1966).

[33] Physically (or outwardly), of course, modern women look very different from their Victorian predecessors, thanks especially to the revolution in women's dress that was completed in the twenties. The early feminists placed great emphasis on dress reform, but they gave this up after the "Bloomer fiasco," even though such men as Gerrit Smith thought it was the most desperately needed reform of all. Certainly few other changes that were desired by women have benefited so many people for so long a time. Ironically—as was so often the case—women were liberated from the crippling burdens of their dress by accident rather than by intent; fashion, not reason, called the turn.

This strategy, however, was fatal to the feminists' long-range objectives. Although social feminism promoted many desirable reforms, few of them did much for women's rights, and when social feminism secured a notable feminist objective (such as equal suffrage), it did so in ways that undermined the movement's larger program. Moreover, this alliance with the woman movement led to such confusions and evasions among feminists that it prevented them from formulating an ideology that was adequate to the complex circumstances in which they found themselves. From the outset, feminists had defined their position negatively; they were against a host of specific disabilities—unequal laws, closed professions, votelessness—and their concentration on these barriers made them vulnerable to the opportunism that characterizes political movements, which puts action ahead of theory. Their need for allies, as well as their intellectual failures, made it even harder for them to resist the blandishments of the woman movement. It is a historiographical cliché that in America such opportunism is normal, even desirable, but pragmatism (as political expediency is always called) has the defects of its virtues. If ideological formlessness promotes flexibility, moderation, and useful alliances, it also blurs the vision and encourages what can be a fatal confusion between ends and means.

After women's suffrage was won, feminists discovered that it cost more than anyone a generation earlier could have foreseen. Social feminism was discredited when the vote failed materially to assist organized women in getting what they wanted. Hard-core feminism suffered for lack of an issue that could rouse women as equal suffrage had—and also because, in calling upon women to consider their own interests first, it went against the whole tradition of selfless altruism that had become firmly associated with organized womanhood. Valuable and ennobling as this tradition was, it prevented women from addressing their problems as women, from coming to terms with their disadvantaged status, and from organizing effectively to deal with it. The decline of the woman movement after 1920 further discredited organization along sex lines as an approach to public questions. Thus the post-suffrage era was characterized by the view that women were so different from men that real integration was out of the question, by the failure of organization as a distinctively feminine tactic, and by a general refusal to recognize that women constituted a disadvantaged group that was entitled to pursue its interests in the way that minority groups have historically done in America.

Since 1930 American women have lost ground in relation to their peers in other industrial societies and in relation to their position in the twenties. Not only Russia and Scandinavia but most of western Europe have a higher percentage of women who are physicians than does the United States. There are more women in Parliament than in Congress. The number of women pharmacists and dentists is negligible here but noteworthy in Sweden and France. The percentage of A.B. and Ph.D. degrees awarded to women in America has declined since 1920. Today the percentage of women who work is larger than ever before, but their occupational segregation is as great as it was in 1900, and the dollar gap between the incomes of working men and women has been rising steadily since World War II. Measured by almost any index, the position of American women, almost half a century after their formal emancipation, is neither enviable nor admirable. Countless articles and books, most notably Betty Friedan's, have in recent years documented these points and made us aware that feminism has failed and that the conditions it struggled against remain.[34]

If my analysis is correct, modern women will have to do two things to secure equality of opportunity and treatment. They must organize in a serious, deliberate, and self-interested fashion, which would seem obvious were it not for the fact that women's right to function as a pressure group is generally denied. Most Americans will admit that individual Negroes and workers may improve their circumstances without affecting the overall position of Negroes and workers in the slightest, but this principle is rarely applied to women, who are expected to deal with their problems by going to college, taking a job, undergoing psychotherapy, or by finding another personal solution.

The reason for this analytical myopia seems to be related to the same anxieties that kept Victorian society from penetrating to the heart of the woman question. The woman movement allayed the nineteenth century's worst fears by showing that formal emancipation and a high degree of organization were largely compatible with the existing social order. Unfortunately this development, tactically sound though it was, disregarded what was most fundamental and important about feminism as a response to modern conditions. It now appears that the unrest of women is directly related to those fundamental institutions, monogamy and the conjugal family, that the Victorian world was so determined to preserve. In theory women today are free to do as they please; in practice, their heavy obligations as wives and mothers prevent them from exercising the rights they nominally enjoy.

This brings me to the second task that confronts a new feminist movement, should one emerge from the present unrest. Before women can organize effectively they must clearly understand what it is they mean to effect. They must construct an ideology that will be superior to anything that has been seen in America; but those who now are engaged in the field of women's rights seem to me insufficiently aware of this need. Such organizations as the President's Commission on the Status of Women and its counterparts on the state level, the National Woman's Party (which still is working to secure equality of women by constitu-

---

[34] For the declining position of women, see also Degler's essay cited in n. 1. Mabel Newcomer, *A Century of Higher Education for American Women* (New York, 1959), also is illuminating. For the position of women workers, Mary Keyserling's "Facing the Facts About Women's Lives Today" (*New Approaches to Counseling Girls in the 1960's* [Washington, D.C., 1966], pp. 2–10) is compelling. Sex discrimination is accurately demonstrated in Edward Gross, "*Plus ça change* . . . The Sexual Structure of Occupations over Time," a paper Gross delivered to the 1967 meeting of the American Sociological Association in San Francisco, Calif.

tional amendment), and Mrs. Friedan's National Organization for Women operate too much as their predecessors did. They see the problem in negative terms and they appear to take it for granted that the basic questions have been answered—that we know who women are, what they can do, and what they need.

More than anything else, women must understand the Victorian roots of their situation. The social feminist route (marvelous as it was from a humanitarian point of view) led to a dead end. The radical feminist solution was aborted before it had a real chance to work, but it may well be the key to a genuine feminist renaissance. Radical feminism was suppressed because it threatened to revolutionize the domestic structure, as it still does. I think, however, that the whole of the American experience shows that nothing less profound will give women the freedom in fact that we concede them only in theory.

It may be that little can be done along these lines, that woman's dilemma is one of those facts of life that simply have to be endured. But if a social revolution is wanted, and a drastic change in the position of American women would amount to just that (however unrelated it may seem to the economic problems that are the usual objects of radical concern), it must be preceded by deep and serious thought which up to this point has been conspicuously absent. To put it another way, feminism must have its Marx before it can expect a Lenin.

Suggestions for Further Reading

Works that survey various portions of the early twentieth century are Robert Wiebe, *The Search for Order, 1877–1920** (Hill and Wang, 1967); Henry F. May, *The End of American Innocence** (Knopf, 1959); William E. Leuchtenberg, *The Perils of Prosperity, 1914–32** (University of Chicago Press, 1958); and Frederick Lewis Allen, *Only Yesterday** (Harper and Row, 1931). Perhaps the best description of the conflicts engendered in American life during this period is given in novelist John Dos Passos' monumental trilogy, *U.S.A.** (Houghton-Mifflin, 1937).

Studies of the Progressive period include Richard Hofstadter, *The Age of Reform: From Bryan to F.D.R.** (Knopf, 1965); John Chamberlain, *Farewell to Reform: The Rise, Life and Decay of the Progressive Mind in America** (Day, 1932); Gabriel Kolko, *The Triumph of Conservatism** (Free Press, 1963); and James Weinstein, *The Corporate Ideal in the Liberal State, 1900–1918** (Beacon, 1968). Contemporaneous works of interest are Lincoln Steffens, *The Shame of the Cities** (McClure, Phillips, 1904); John Spargo, *The Bitter Cry of Children** (Macmillan, 1904); Robert Hunter, *Poverty** (Macmillan, 1904); and Herbert Croly, *The Promise of American Life** (Macmillan, 1909).

Patrick Renshaw has written a short history of the IWW entitled *The Wobblies** (Doubleday, 1967). Apart from Melvyn Dubofsky's work, *We Shall Be All: A History of the Industrial Workers of the World* (Quadrangle, 1969), the best available source of information on the Wobblies is the collection of documents from the movement edited by Joyce L. Kornbluh, *Rebel Voices: An I.W.W. Anthology** (University of Michigan Press, 1964). On the history of labor in the early twentieth century, see John Laslett, *Labor and the Left: A Study of Socialist and Radical Influences in the American Labor Movement, 1881–1924* (Basic Books, 1970); Irving Bernstein, *The Lean Years: A History of the American Worker, 1920–1933** (Houghton-Mifflin, 1960); and David Brody, *Labor in Crisis: The Steel Strike of 1919** (Lippincott, 1965).

Federal attempts to suppress radicals at the conclusion of the First World War are described in R. K. Murray, *The Red Scare: A Study in National Hysteria, 1919–1920** (University of Minnesota Press, 1955), and in two works by Stanley Coben, *A. Mitchell Palmer: Politician* (Columbia University Press, 1963) and "A Study in Nativism: The American Red Scare of 1919–20," *Political Science Quarterly*, Vol. 79 (March, 1964), 52–75. For a more general study, see William Preston, Jr., *Aliens and Dissenters: Federal Suppression of Radicals, 1903–1933** (Harvard University Press, 1963). The most significant anarchist trial of the twentieth century

* Available in paperback edition.

is closely examined in G. L. Joughin and E. S. Morgan (eds.), *The Legacy of Sacco and Vanzetti** (Harcourt Brace Jovanovich, 1948).

Arna Bontemps and Jack Conroy consider the migration of blacks to urban areas early in the new century in *They Seek a City* (Doubleday, 1945), expanded and published in paperback under the title *Anyplace But Here.** Also of interest is the contemporaneous work by Emmett J. Scott, *Negro Migration During the War** (Oxford University Press, 1920). Studies of the black migration that focus on specific cities include Gilbert Osofsky, *Harlem: The Making of a Ghetto** (Harper and Row, 1966); Allan H. Spear, *Black Chicago: The Making of a Negro Ghetto, 1890–1920** (University of Chicago Press, 1967); and Constance M. Green, *The Secret City: A History of Race Relations in the Nation's Capital** (Princeton University Press, 1967).

Racial strife is the subject of Allen Grimshaw (ed.), *Racial Violence in the United States* (Aldine, 1969). For studies of specific race riots, see the report of the Chicago Commission on Race Relations, *The Negro in Chicago: A Study of Race Relations and a Race Riot* (University of Chicago Press, 1922); William M. Tuttle, Jr., *Race Riot: Chicago in the Red Summer of 1919* (Atheneum, 1970); and Elliott M. Rudwick, *Race Riot at East St. Louis, July 2, 1917** (Southern Illinois University Press, 1964). Organized antiblack agitation is described in David Chalmers, *Hooded Americanism** (Doubleday, 1965), and in Kenneth Jackson, *The Ku Klux Klan in the City, 1915–1930** (Oxford University Press, 1968).

An expanded version of the essay by William L. O'Neill that is reprinted in this volume was published under the title *Everyone Was Brave: The Rise and Fall of Feminism in America* (Quadrangle, 1969). Other histories of American feminism include Andrew Sinclair, *The Emancipation of the American Woman** (Harper and Row, 1965), originally published under the title *The Better Half;* Eleanor Flexner, *Century of Struggle: The Woman's Rights Movement in the United States** (Harvard University Press, 1959); Robert E. Riegel, *American Feminists** (University of Kansas Press, 1963); and Aileen Kraditor, *The Ideas of the Woman Suffrage Movement* (Columbia University Press, 1965). A history of the movement written by the leaders themselves is Elizabeth Cady Stanton et al., *The History of Woman Suffrage* (6 vols.; Fowler and Wells, 1881–1922). Aileen Kraditor has edited a valuable collection of documents from the movement entitled *Up from the Pedestal: Selected Writings in the History of American Feminism** (Quadrangle, 1968). Two important publications by leading feminists are Charlotte Perkins Gilman, *Women and Economics** (Small-Maynard, 1898), and Carrie Chapman Catt and Nettie Rogers Shuler, *Woman Suffrage and Politics** (Scribner's, 1923). Good biographies of feminist leaders are Mary Gray Peck's *Carrie Chapman Catt* (Wilson, 1944) and Alma Lutz's *Created Equal: A Biography of Elizabeth Cady Stanton* (Day, 1940) and *Susan B. Anthony: Rebel, Crusader, Humanitarian* (Beacon, 1959).

Depression

The Organization of
Black and White Farm Workers
in the South

VERA RONY

While the nation as a whole returned to prosperity and "normalcy" in the 1920's, an ominous development was taking place on American farms. Long before the Depression came to the attention of the public through the dramatic crash of the stock market, the agricultural sector of the American economy was caught in a serious financial squeeze. The South, perennially the most depressed sector of American agriculture, was the first area afflicted by the great Depression that was eventually to affect the whole of American society.

Within the South, the groups that found themselves in the worst straits as a result of the agricultural decline were the rural share-croppers, tenant farmers, and wage laborers, both white and black. Of these, the whites probably fared a little better than the blacks, if only because they had more to fall back on when their condition grew desperate. The position of farm labor had been declining since the Civil War, as bad crop management and careless agricultural practices destroyed more and more arable land. The repeated planting of cotton and tobacco had drawn so much nourishment out of the soil that it would have been difficult to reclaim the land for cotton with the help of the most advanced agricultural techniques of the day, and these were not available to the masses of farmers. Furthermore, the land had been stripped of timber and exposed to erosion to the point that countless acres had been removed from cultivation, ruined even for replanting with trees.

As the amount of productive land dwindled, even the landowning whites were driven into tenancy and sharecropping on large estates; blacks, few of whom had ever owned land, had rarely escaped the plantations in the first place. By 1920, 60 percent of Southern farms were operated by tenant farmers, and white and black alike were caught in the thrall of rural poverty. When the full force of the Depression struck the rural South, thousands stood in danger of actually starving to death.

The first glimmers of hope for the landless poor of the rural South came from an unlikely quarter—the Northeastern-immigrant political tradition of radicalism. Members of both the Socialist and the Communist parties, many of them first- and second-generation Americans, went into the South and attempted to organize poor whites and blacks so that they could effectively confront the plantation owners with demands for reasonable compensation for their labor. Native Southern liberals, carrying on the domestic tradition of dissent and radical thought, sometimes joined with the political radicals from the North in attempts to bring about labor unity and reform.

This organizing activity resulted in the 1930's in the formation of sharecropper and tenant-farmer unions that used agricultural strikes to lend weight to their demands. At about the same time, the New Deal programs of relief, recovery, and reform were developed, ostensibly to aid the nation's farmers as well as other depressed groups. However, the bulk of the government's agricultural program consisted in paying landowners to take land out of cultivation. The owners were under no obligation to pass a share of the government money along to their tenants, and they rarely did so.

The story of the organizing work among the rural poor in the South is sensitively told by Vera Rony, formerly of the League for Industrial Democracy and currently on the faculty of the State University of New York at Stony Brook, in an article prepared for **New South,** an excerpt of which appears here. Miss Rony tells of the organization of the Southern Tenant Farmers Union and of its struggle for survival during the Depression years. In addition, she describes attempts to ensure that at least some of the economic benefits of the New Deal were passed along to those who needed them most.

Federal agricultural policy has changed little since the Depression years, with the result that in the South today, many plantation owners receive hundreds of thousands of dollars for holding land out of cultivation. Little of this money is seen by the tenants, whose work is rendered superfluous by the subsidy program.

*To realize the earth's generosity to those who have joy in sowing
and reaping gives a deep sense of security and a faith in the rightness of things.*

> JULIA PETERKIN, quoted in Howard Odum's
> *Southern Regions of the United States,*
> University of North Carolina Press, 1936

Mr. H. L. Mitchell

*Dear Secretary, I find some awful sad news about one of our
brothers on Mr. Boss Dulaney's place, a pig was killed on the highway I don't know just how long it had been killed but it had
spoiled and had been taken to the woods on a wagon and brother
george wells wandered his way to the woods and carried it home
and cleaned it for to have something to exist on for food and later
on the same brother Wells was walking down the highway and
found a great water snake with a dead turtle and he run the snake
off the turtle and carried it home and had his wife to clean it and
eat it. . . .*

> ISAAC SHAW, sharecropper, 1936;
> from *The Disinherited Speak, Letters from Sharecroppers,*
> Workers Defense League pamphlet, circa 1937

> *A Negro is a very hard working man*
> *They work like slaves on the white man land*
> *The Negro works all the week long and*
>   *the white man drinks his liquor*
> *And when its time to pay the Negro*
>   *is called a Nigger*

> DOROTHY ANN WATTS, high school student,
> Issaquena, Mississippi, in the *Issaquena
> Freedom Fighter,* August, 1965

In prime television time, the day after Thanksgiving in 1960, the image of
a famous newscaster appeared on the CBS channel. Slightly saturnine,
humane, his natural elegance in chiaroscuro contrast to the dusty road,

"The Organization of Black and White Farm Workers in the South." Reprinted
by permission of Quadrangle Books from a forthcoming book by Vera Rony. Copyright © 1967 by Vera Rony. The article from which this excerpt is taken appeared
originally in *New South,* Summer 1967.

battered trucks, and milling people behind him, Edward R. Murrow intoned:

> This scene is not taking place in the Congo. It has nothing to do with Johannesburg or Capetown. This is a shape-up for migrant workers. The hawkers you hear are chanting the going piece rate at the various fields. This is Belle Glade, Florida. This is the way the humans who harvest the food for the best-fed people in the world get hired. One farmer looked at this and said, "We used to own our slaves, now we just rent them."

Harvest of Shame, television's first major probe of the soft underbelly of American affluence, was under way.

Thousands of viewers blissfully unaware of the years of horror pictures to come—the terrified and terrifying demonstrators, the blasted ghettos—responded with outrage and pity to these itinerant poor. But among a handful of knowledgeable viewers, the response was different. "Waal, it's a fine thing, of course," rumbled veteran farm labor spokesman H. L. Mitchell, in that slow, deep, flat-out delivery more evocative of Oklahoma than of his native Tennessee. "You know, the March of Time made a movie about southern farm workers in 1936. Millions of people saw it. It was gonna make a whale of a difference. . . ."

The history of agricultural labor in the South is the record of millions of people, of no single color or culture, to whom none of the miracle-making capabilities of America have made much difference. More graphically than Negroes alone, they illustrate the limits of traditional American meliorism. For they were stigmatized by no particular mythology or history; their sole handicap lay in the usefulness of their poverty to those who have wielded power in the South from 1877 until today. Leslie Dunbar says, ". . . The civil rights movement and the reforms coming from it are the culmination of a liberal era which began with the Great Depression. Civil rights was the final item on the agenda of modern liberalism." The record below should illustrate how irrelevant the liberalism of the '30's was for the southern poor of *both* races. In so doing, it suggests that, for the South, the final item on the liberal agenda may be more complex, far-reaching—and color blind—than civil rights alone.

"A SOCIALIST DRY CLEANER FROM TYRONZA"

After the new Business Bourbons broke the back of Populism near the turn of the century, there were only sporadic economic rebellions among the small farmers, tenants, and laborers of the most densely populated rural area in America, the Cotton Belt. Yet this vast, 125-million-acre span, stretching south from the Carolinas through the Atlantic states and west through Tennessee, Arkansas, Oklahoma, and Texas, sustained the poorest people in the United States. At the height of national prosperity, just before the Crash, farm families as a whole were earning one-third as much as urban families, or an average of $1,240 per year; farm families in the cotton states averaged $620. Since this figure includes planters and yeoman farmers as well as tenants, the last group must have survived at the subsistence level, if that.

Yet, being Southerners, many of them undoubtedly cherished, like the tenant-farming Mitchells, a modestly legendary explanation of their situation. H. L. Mitchell tells it this way:

> The founder of our family came from Northern Ireland to Charleston about 1750. Like my grandfather, he was a Baptist preacher. On his way to this country he was shipwrecked off the coast of South Carolina. The story is told that he had a bag of gold and a Bible but lost the gold. None of the Mitchells ever had any money afterward.

But nothing else in Mitch's childhood was legendary—by regional standards. At the age of eight in Halls, Tennessee, he was chopping cotton and picking strawberries at 50¢ for a ten-hour day. About the same time, he learned that a Negro who had hit his father in a work dispute was promptly shot to death and his body dropped in the Obion River. By the time he was ten, he had seen his first lynching, and five years later, his second. But there, the adult was foreshadowed:

> They piled wooden boxes and pieces of wood around him and saturated the pile with oil. I was up near the front and I heard the man pleading for his life. As he stood there he gave what was alleged to be the distress call of the Masonic Order: "O God, is there no help for the widow's son?" Some leaders of the mob were Masons and they hesitated. But someone in the crowd yelled, "O hell, he's just a nigger Mason, let's burn him," and he set a match to the pile. Along with many others, I was sick and I never had any more use for the Masons.

In 1927, having completed his apprenticeship in the fields and four years of high school, Mitchell took a wife and moved to Tyronza, Arkansas, near Memphis, to begin his adult life as a sharecropper. However, he discovered that the housing provided by the large plantations dominating the area was such that "when it rained outside, it poured inside." Between the indoor weather and the outhouses, Mitchell abandoned sharecropping. Resurrecting an old pressing machine from his father's junkpile, he opened a dry-cleaning establishment.

In the beginning, the thriving little enterprise left him little time for reading—a prime avocation—or crackerbarrel discussion with gas station owner Henry Clay East, his Vergil on the local scene. But by 1931, Tyronza, like the rest of the South, had succumbed to the Great Depression. Mitchell and his friend found themselves with abundant time for thought and plenty to think about. Farm prices were plunging like an avalanche and burying American agriculture in the economic debris. Between 1929 and 1932, produce prices had declined by more than 50% and net farm income by two-thirds. For rural America as a whole, it was a grave crisis—for the dominantly agrarian South, it was a catastrophe. And like most southern problems, it had not arrived overnight.

DOWN IN THE DITCH TOGETHER

When the southern "agrarians" sought surcease from the Depression by resurrecting the plantation ideal, Howard Odum reminded them that it was not the 200,000 planter-aristocrats who revived the South after the Civil War, but millions of yeoman farmers, industriously cultivating their 100-acre plots. By 1880, these sturdy citizens comprised more than two-thirds of all southern agriculture, yet their prospects had grown exceedingly dim. The small farmer's difficulty was sadly circular: He needed capital, but southern banks, tied to a one-crop economy, were too undercapitalized to offer him the high-risk loans he required. Thus he was thrown back on credit merchants who demanded mortgages on his crops, thereby "converting the southern economy into a vast pawn shop." This burden of debt was further compounded by the low price of cotton, and the high price of tariff-inflated manufactures from the North. The resultant hardship and loss erupted in the Populist revolt. Said its thundering prophet, Tom Watson:

> You were born in plenty and spent your childhood in plenty. I had it too. Then you lost your houses. The sheriff's red flag was planted at your front gate. You and yours took down the family pictures from the wall, picked some favorite flowers from the grave and took your weary march out into a strange, cold world.

After 1896, when the insurgent, interracial phase of the Populist rebellion had been stoned, shot, and niggered to death, the farmer's weary march led most often to dependency. In 1880, about one-third of southern farms were tenant operated; by 1920, the figure had risen to 60%. As the South slid into the trough of the Depression, one-third of its cotton fields were claimed by the banks and insurance companies, while 5½ million dispossessed whites competed with 3½ million Negroes "for the new kind of slavery involved in tenancy."

For tenancy was, of course, a "boss and black" institution—the prosperous white South's adaptation to Negro "freedom." The black family, lacking land, mule, or hoe, went to work for the planter, who wanted steady labor without paying wages. As rent, the planter deducted one-third to one-half of the tenant's[1] crop, and for "furnish"—credit for seed, fertilizer, equipment, food, etc. (usually bought at the plantation store)— he took another 25% to 50%. A 1932 study of Negro tenants in Alabama showed that almost 90% "broke even" or "went into the hole." Only some 10% received any cash for their year's labor.

---

[1] Share tenants and sharecroppers are used interchangeably here because of their similarly subservient status. Technically, tenants furnished their own equipment and animals and usually paid 25% of their crop as rent, whereas croppers, who owned neither, paid as much as 50%.

A Delta folk tale relates the experience of a wily sharecropper who was determined to beat the system. Shoving his four bales onto the scale, he watched the planter compute the supervision, "furnish," and interest charges, at the end of which that worthy informed him that, as usual, he had broken even. He wouldn't get a penny. Gleefully, the tenant tossed a hidden fifth bale onto the scale. "Dawggone," said the planter, "now I'll have to figger the whole thing over agin."

Nor did the planter's control stop at the purse strings. He also decreed what was to be planted, in what manner, where marketed, and what schooling, if any, the tenants' children would receive. In [*The Emergence of the New South*], Professor George Tindall says of this period, "The long shadow of slavery still fell across the vassals of King Cotton, white and black." But why did the once independent, self-respecting white tenants acquiesce? How were they restrained from rebellion? A famous social document, *The Collapse of Cotton Tenancy*, explains:

> Because of his economic condition, and because of his race, color, and previous condition of servitude, the rural Negro is helpless before the white master. . . . This fixed custom of exploitation of the Negro has carried over to the white tenant. . . . Yet it has been impossible to bring about any change, even to get the poor white workers to take a stand, since any movement for reform is immediately confused with the race issue.

Booker T. Washington said it more succinctly: "The only way to keep a man in a ditch is to get down there with him." So there they were, nine million of them—one of every four Southerners—living in the leaking, rotting shacks, eating the salt pork and hominy, bearing the ague which was malaria and the runs which were pellagra and the torpor which was hopelessness. When a minister investigating the high incidence of disease questioned a planter about the open-surface privies scattered over the tenant landscape, the planter assured him, "All that a sharecropper needs is a cotton patch and a corn cob." He said nothing about color.

In 1931, the statistics were not yet collected nor the causal relationship explored. But in Tyronza, Arkansas, it was enough to have eyes—and heart. Mitchell and East pored over the social nostrums of the day: Huey Long's "Every Man a King," and Gerald L. K. Smith's "Share the Wealth," reposing their confidence at last in the tiny blue books published for a nickel by Haldemann-Julius: "Clay ate up those little blue books," recalls Mitchell, "and if a customer came in, he'd slip them under his newspaper, so they would think he was reading the *Memphis Commercial Appeal*. The next thing I knew, he was out in the street telling everybody that the solution to all the problems of the world was a socialist society."

When Norman Thomas brought his presidential campaign to Memphis in 1932, the 5,000 people who turned out to hear him included the two theoreticians from Tyronza. Shortly thereafter, the Socialist Party boasted a branch in northeast Arkansas. "We probably had as many members in the Tyronza local as the Socialist Party has in the whole country today," says Mitchell. "There must have been a thousand of us, mostly sharecroppers—black and white. I think it was the educational work we did there that later made it possible to organize the union on an inter-racial basis." However, his neighbors were not yet ready for a union. That required a final, precipitating grievance which was supplied, ironically, by none other than the immortal champion of the Common Man and newly elected President of the United States, Franklin D. Roosevelt.

FDR, THE PLANTERS, AND THE PEASANTS

In *FDR and the South,* Professor Frank Freidel comments, "Few figures have more significantly shaped southern destinies than a New Yorker who liked to think of himself as also a Georgian by adoption." There follows a vivid evocation of Roosevelt's affection for Warm Springs and the rural South as a whole:

> Roosevelt enjoyed relaxing in the magnificent country house of Cason Callaway, one of the largest of the textile manufacturers and a benefactor of Warm Springs, listening to the singing of Negro musicians dressed like old-time plantation hands. Also, Roosevelt dreamed of turning the miserably debt-ridden small farmers, sharecroppers, and field hands . . . into self-sustaining, self-supporting small farmers, each on his own homestead. It was one of Roosevelt's fondest dreams.

We hear a wild snicker from the young militants, and it *does* sound preposterous 35 years later, but FDR cannot be dismissed as a caricature "white liberal." His Secretary of Agriculture, Henry A. Wallace, had, as Arthur Schlesinger, Jr., puts it, "one lobe of his brain attuned to idealism," while the undivided reformist zeal of brilliant Undersecretary Rexford G. Tugwell accounted for such departmental doers and shakers (in their divers and sometimes dubious ways) as Jerome Frank, Frederick C. Howe, Gardner (Pat) Jackson, C. B. Baldwin, Lee Pressman, and Alger Hiss.

But Roosevelt also had his priorities: The country had to be hoisted from the economic abyss without delay, and the Congress upon which the task depended was dominated by such southern hierarchs as Senators Joe Robinson (D., Ark.), the majority leader, and Pat Harrison (D., Miss.), Carter Glass (D., Va.), and Cotton Ed Smith (D., S.C.), chairmen of the Commerce, Appropriations, and Agriculture Committees, respectively. Nothing better illustrates what James MacGregor Burns has termed "the insuperable difficulties of Roosevelt's middle way" than the impact of the Agricultural Adjustment Act upon the South.

The sixth measure enacted by Congress during the historic Hundred Days, the AAA became law on May 12, 1933. "If the NRA was the main-spring of the New Deal in shop and factory, the AAA was its counterpart on the farm." When Agriculture Secretary Wallace rhapsodized that it was "a contrivance as new in the field of social relations as the first gasoline engine in the field of mechanics," and his aide, Mordecai Ezekiel, called it "the greatest single experiment in economic planning under capitalist conditions ever attempted by a democracy in time of peace," a paralyzed nation took them at their word. It was no time to inquire who would benefit from the experimental planning executed by the new contrivance.

In retrospect, the answer is clear enough; the historical verdict is unanimous. The object of the AAA was to restore farm prices to the same ratio they bore to non-farm prices in the period 1909–1914. To this end, processing taxes were levied which financed the restriction of farm production, chiefly by paying benefits to farmers who agreed to produce less. In the vernacular, "Kill every third pig or plow every third row under." In drafting the law, the desperate need for speed and his own agricultural background led Wallace to rely on the advice of the major farm organizations, the American Farm Bureau and the National Grange. The Farmers Union, representing the smaller farmers, was scarcely consulted, while the unorganized tenants, croppers, and field hands were totally ignored.

Since AAA contracts were drawn with those who controlled the land, the sharecropper could benefit only from the gradual rise in produce prices and the "parity" payments on his share of the crop. In practice, the planter received 90% of the government payments since he did "the reckonin" (excerpt from a letter to Mitchell):

> we poor people . . . of Shiloh . . . had a pretty tight time last Saturday. we got that cent and a half subsidy what was Due us, our boss man Mr. McCracken paid it off. he call us in a Dark Room, and his window Shades pull near down. we coulden see how to read. had his two boys Standing By his side. we just could see how to sine the papers. we dident get justers.

Many planters invested their government checks in machinery, which confronted the tenants with wholly new hazards: They could be "tractored" off the land or thrown from it by reduced cultivation. The law failed to provide firm safeguards against either fate. No apathy could withstand so many provocations; the decades of silence gave way to food riots, relief demonstrations, and Socialist campaigns.

LAUNCHING THE MOVEMENT, 1934 VINTAGE

Although the worried planters had not yet learned how to equate Socialism with Satan, they knew how to keep Socialist candidates off the ballot and Socialist voters away from the ballot boxes. As evictions got under way, frustration mounted. A Socialist organizer dispatched to the scene wrote Norman Thomas: "Here you will find the true proletariat; here you will find inarticulate men moving inresistibly towards revolution."

In February, 1934, Thomas came to Tyronza to see for himself. He toured the woebegone cabins and talked to croppers who had received their eviction notices due to AAA crop reductions. In a passionate speech at the Tyronza High School, he blasted the government program. Mitchell recalls a detail of the scene:

> One sharecropper came in and stopped at the door. I was acting as kind of an usher, and I pointed out a vacant seat. He said he didn't have long to stay, he just thought he'd look in. He had his week's rations of groceries in his arms, a sack of flour, some meal, and so on, and there was a fellow standing next to him. When Norman started to talk, this man had never realized the conditions under which he himself lived. His eyes were fixed on this stranger up there on the platform who was talking about him. Finally he just handed all of his groceries to the fellow next to him and went over and took a seat and sat through the meeting.

To the local Socialists, Thomas suggested that political efforts be soft-pedalled in favor of an economic organization to defend the interests of sharecroppers.

On July 26, 1934, seven black men and eleven whites, including Mitchell and East, met on a plantation just outside Tyronza and formed "the union"—they didn't know what else to call it. Some of the whites had belonged to the Ku Klux Klan. Some of the Negroes were veterans of a black sharecroppers union in nearby Elaine—and of the violence which met their cautious attempts to negotiate with the planters. With that in the foreground, and a half-century of alienation in the background, these eighteen men decided matter-of-factly that the only viable union of sharecroppers was an interracial one. Being Southerners, they next considered the utility of hanging a planter or two by way of example. But a white man who favored less thorough methods was elected chairman, a Negro minister became second in command, and an Englishman from Bristol was chosen treasurer. The by-laws, modeled on an old Wobbly union, proclaimed, "The land should belong to the people who work on it." The South hadn't seen its like since Populism!

Unsurprisingly—in this remarkable region where time does not equal change—this new plantocracy v. tenant struggle was in many ways a small-scale replica of the earlier conflict. Connoisseurs of Populism who recall the "Western" style rescue (TV should consider doing some "Southerns") of Populist minister H. S. Doyle, a Negro militant threatened with lynching in Thomson, Georgia, by "fully two thousand" armed white comrades will recognize the first major ordeal of the new Southern Tenant Farmers Union.

Two organizers, both ministers but one white and one black, were arrested near Marion, Arkansas. Ward Rodgers, the white man, was escorted to the county line; C. H. Smith was thrown into jail. Mitchell realized that in Smith's case there was not a moment to lose, but the union had not yet acquired a lawyer. A frantic wire to the American Civil Liberties Union netted three possibilities, all in Memphis. Mitchell and East rushed over there, only to be promptly refused by two attorneys. "I greatly admire you fellows," said one, "but I was in the Lost Battalion in the Argonne Forest, and I'm one Jew[2] who isn't going over to Crittenden County to get a Nigra out of jail when he's charged with organizing a union." Finally the highly respected C. T. Carpenter undertook the case and hurried over to Crittenden County.

As he confronted the notorious Sheriff Curlin, an unusual number of ancient cars, trucks, and wagons discharged their burden of white union members in front of the courthouse. Inside, the sheriff allowed as how he was not about to release Reverend Smith. Time passed; the sheriff remained adamant. Then slowly, imperceptibly, the little clumps of quiet, lounging, tobacco-chewing men began to coalesce. No southern sheriff, Faulkner tells us, needs to look out of his window to see it happen; he is born knowing. But this time it was different. That night a great rally was held to celebrate Reverend Smith's release, and to hear how he had endured the fists and rubber hose of the law without betraying the union.

"That's how it began," says Mitchell, "and that's pretty much how it stayed." Negro unionists bore the brunt of the violence, but whites were not exempt. "Planters . . . padlocked church doors and packed school houses with bales of hay to deter union rallies. Their riding bosses flogged sympathetic croppers and drove them from their plantations. The Harahan Bridge, spanning the Mississippi at Memphis, became the gateway to safety for union organizers." The union begged the Justice Department for protection, but none came. Early in 1935, Reverend Rodgers was warned to "stop teachin' niggers to read, write an' figger" or prepare to meet his Maker. Incensed, Rodgers told a union rally that unless the government put a stop to such intimidation, he "would lead a group to lynch every planter in Poinsett County." When the crowd roared assent, Mitchell hurriedly stepped in and restored order. But Rodgers was arrested before he left the platform. A planters' jury, hastily assembled in a local store, convicted him of blasphemy, anarchy, and attempted overthrow of the government.

The Rodgers case produced national headlines, hundreds of new union members, and money and moral support from near and far. On this swell of popular indignation, Norman Thomas returned to Arkansas. But he got no further than his first speech in Birdsong, where he was surrounded by planters and police yelling that "no Gawd-damn Yankee bastard" was going to lecture Arkansas. Brandishing the state constitution and protesting, Thomas retreated from the platform and the state. But as the French say, he drew back only to jump farther—and in a different direction.

ALLIES LIKELY AND UNLIKELY

It was by now clear that the sharecroppers' problems would not be solved by orderly local reform. For the aggrieved Southerner the sole recourse, then as now, was Washington. There, in the feisty, argumenta-

---

[2] Another time when a plantation mob cornered three union officials, it was an attorney named Goldberger who was singled out for a beating.

tive stronghold of the New Deal, the sharecroppers attracted a pride of champions outstanding even in an era of political wizardry: Norman Thomas, Will Alexander, Rexford Tugwell, Jerome Frank, and *Bruder-schaft*—a formidable, and very mixed, bag of allies. Of these, Thomas was the first and, in the nature of his part, the most outspoken. In one of those paradoxes which are the delight of a large and variegated society, this leader of the urban, second-generation American Socialist Party would play perhaps his most organic and creative role as the spokesman of the rural, bedrock native Southern Tenant Farmers Union.

After his first trip to Arkansas in 1934, Thomas wrote to Secretary of Agriculture Wallace, "What about the sharecroppers driven from the land. . . . Has the Administration any plans for them other than the pious hopes written into the contracts with the landlords?" When Wallace, relying on his "other lobe which responded avidly to the Farm Bureau, the Extension Service, and Senator Joe Robinson of Arkansas," replied in the negative, Thomas looked for heavier artillery. He found it in a League for Industrial Democracy study which reported that, as a result of the AAA, 15% to 20% of all sharecroppers were already thrown off the land.

Wallace responded with aplomb—he ordered more research. Although studies conducted independently by Mrs. Mary C. Myers of the AAA and Dr. Calvin B. Hoover of Duke University reinforced the earlier finding, the Agriculture Department made no move. Within the department, however, there was considerable commotion. From the outset, Tugwell's Young Turks had sworn allegiance to the sharecroppers. The AAA's ineffectual Section 7a—urging that wherever possible participating landlords retain the same number of tenants they had when the program began—was inserted only at the insistence of Jerome Frank's deputy, Alger Hiss. Others in the group included liberals Frederick Howe and Pat Jackson, and Communists Lee Pressman, Nathan Witt, and John Abt.

Had the folks back in Birdsong met this last clutch of allies, they might have felt the same misgivings as the old department hands: "Too Ivy League, too intellectual, too Jewish." And one can imagine their response to the brilliant Lee Pressman's deathless challenge: "But what does this code do for the macaroni growers?" Nonetheless, in this engagement the Communists' usefulness cannot be argued. Later the party appears in another role and perhaps another light.

By February, 1935, intensifying pressure from Thomas and the Rodgers case convinced the militants it was time to act. As soon as AAA Administrator Chester Davis left town, Hiss issued a reinterpretation of Section 7a: Landlords were obligated to retain the *same* tenants for the duration of their AAA contract. Davis returned, envisioned a planter uprising, became apoplectic, and cancelled the reinterpretation. He also fired all the insurgents except Hiss, whom he considered industrious and misled. Wallace and Roosevelt expressed the highest regard for the dismissed men, but raised no finger to reinstate any of them. During the resultant hue and cry, Norman Thomas obtained an interview with the President, who confessed he hadn't read the controversial Section 7a, twitted Thomas, "Now, Norman, you're not as good a politician as I am," and concluded, "There is a new generation growing up in the South. We've got to be patient."

In Marked Tree, Arkansas, on the night of March 25, forty masked night riders fired into the home of union attorney Carpenter. Five days later, a gang of armed men pistol-whipped a group of Negro men and women as they left church. A rival union movement was initiated by one J. Green who, obviously impressed by the news from Europe, proposed that his followers wear green shirts with swastikas. As Mitchell addressed a union meeting to expose the planter financing of the prospective Green Shirts, a man in the audience rose and pulled out a gun. At once, the unionist next to him grabbed his arm, thereby deflecting the bullet to the platform floor, two inches in front of the astounded Mitchell. The union had no choice but to move to Memphis and "go underground."

Now Norman Thomas no longer spoke only about economic reform. He wired Wallace that "only a miracle can prevent bloodshed" and requested intervention. When that proved fruitless, he went to Washington to plead his case in person, and when that too failed, he wrote FDR a personal letter describing the situation in Arkansas and expressing concern that the Agriculture Department was "frankly in fear of the power of southern senators." Thomas also pressed Sen. Robert F. Wagner, then drafting his Magna Carta for labor, to include "these virtual slaves" in its protection, but Wagner replied regretfully that to do so would doom the legislation. Thomas did, however, elicit one action from Washington: Wallace gave the New York *Times* an interview condemning the bitterness aroused by "Communist and Socialist agitators in the South."

In this crisis, the beleaguered sharecroppers received unexpected reinforcements—a fresh, well-equipped squad of supporters, led by one of the most knowledgeable and effective of southern activists, "Dr. Will" Alexander. Coming from the powerful religious tradition which has spawned so many southern reformers, Alexander allied himself with Dr. Charles S. Johnson of Fisk, for scholarship, and Edwin R. Embree of the Rosenwald Fund, for cash, to create "the triumvirate which ruled the liberal South during the Thirties and Forties." By 1934, Dr. Will had added the sharecroppers to a personal jurisdiction ranging from the directorship of the South's first Commission on Interracial Cooperation to the formation of Dillard University.

Aided by the University of North Carolina's great regional sociologists (and Rockefeller money), Alexander and Johnson launched a systematic study of farm tenancy in the South. By the beginning of 1935, they had the facts; they also knew about the ordeal of the STFU, the frustrations of Thomas, and the *Realpolitik* paralysis of FDR. They were ready to go to work. Staked this time by the Rosenwalds, Alexander and Embree migrated to Washington, took a posh suite at the Hay-Adams, and embarked on the inside approach—a systematic wining and dining of the decision-makers in the Agriculture Department. This traditional lobbying was abetted in March by the publication of a masterly popularization of their research findings, *The Collapse of Cotton Tenancy*. It was no accident that its dire conclusions were front-paged across the country—the Hay-Adams team had hired a professional publicist. The New York *Times* now took up the cry with a series of rousing on-the-spot reports from Arkansas. As Dr. Will had planned, the sharecropper issue, which had always had heat, was now acquiring depth and dimension.

No King Canute, Roosevelt—who read not only the *Times* but also Dr. Will's book, of which he approved—was casting about for a solution. With typical Rooseveltian deftness, he found one which at once embodied his concern for the small farmer, placated Thomas and the Left, and pleased favorite Brain Truster Tugwell, still disgruntled over the ouster of his disciples. On April 30, 1935, FDR established the Resettlement Administration, to be directed by Tugwell. With that done, the President moved to protect his other flank: A "spontaneous" demonstration was to take place in Washington to "counteract unfavorable impressions of the AAA."

This, too, could be understood. "In his first two years, FDR achieved the exalted position of being president of all the people. Could it last?" By 1935, the answer was emerging. In the near future, an old associate would say, "The brain trusters caught the Socialists in swimming and ran away with their clothes," and Thomas would retort, "Roosevelt has not carried out any Socialist platform except on a stretcher." But FDR had one trump card left, the reviving economy—and agriculture led all the rest. Between the drought and the AAA, farm prices had increased by two-thirds, farm income by one-half, and cash receipts had doubled. Small wonder that neither Dr. Will's statistics, nor publicity, nor sentiment deterred Roosevelt from defending his most successful program.

Hearing about the AAA demonstration, Pat Jackson proposed that the STFU counter with a demonstration of its own. Only nine union members came, but they picketed the Department of Agriculture and made history; it was the first time a government bureau was so honored. When the cops tried to disperse the singing black and white demonstrators, Jackson—then in his volcanic, bullhorn-voiced prime—dispersed the cops. In an "unscheduled" address to *his* demonstrators, the President denounced those "with special axes to grind" who "were lying about the farm program." But the sharecroppers and their supporters had already made their impact: The Washington *Post* chose to salute "The Nine vs. the Three Thousand."

By July, 1935, the Resettlement Administration was ready to "coordinate and initiate all government programs in land utilization, rural rehabilitation and resettlement, and suburban resettlement." Tugwell, having taken Dr. Will's measure over many a beefsteak and Baked Alaska at the Hay-Adams, invited the Southerner to serve as his assistant. In the same month, the Senate opened hearings on a bill to provide tenants with government loans for farm purchase. The champion of the Common Man was at last remembering his debt-ridden Georgia neighbors. From the long-range view, it was a promising first anniversary for the Southern Tenant Farmers Union—and its motley, untiring supporters.

MEANWHILE, BACK AT THE PLANTATION . . .

It has often been remarked that the long view is not very edible. For the cotton-picking season opening in the fall of 1935, planters were offering 40¢ and 50¢ for 100 pounds of cotton. Thus the average worker who picked about 150 pounds in a day stretching from "can to can't" would earn less than $1 per day. There was no question of negotiating with the planters; by now they were accusing the union of planning the overthrow of "white supremacy, Christianity, the American flag, and the sanctity of home and family ties." In late September, when cotton was at its peak, delegates from the STFU's approximately thirty locals voted to strike. As Mitchell recalls:

> On the night before, the strike handbills were distributed all over the plantations at the same time—on fence posts, telephone poles, barn doors, everywhere—saying that strike was on and stay out of the fields. Five thousand of our people stayed home. In three Arkansas counties where we had just a few members, the state labor department man said he saw only five people working—in all three counties.

The planters held out for ten days; then they raised wages to 75¢ per 100 pounds. Although there was neither negotiation nor other recognition of the union, word of the triumph spread and the preventive wage raise, given in hopes of forestalling further unionization, extended rapidly over Arkansas. Sometimes this tactic works for the employer; this was one of the other times. The union enjoyed a membership explosion: Locals were organized so fast that the Memphis office couldn't keep track of them. In Muskogee, Oklahoma, a not quite full-blooded Cherokee named Odis Sweeden was squatting in his outhouse when he glanced at the newspaper underfoot and learned about the STFU's successful strike. He tore out the union's address, volunteered his services, and began to build an organization in dust-bowl Oklahoma that eventually comprised seventy-five locals. By the end of 1935, the STFU reported a membership of 25,000 in 200 locals scattered over six states.

Elated by this unexpected success, the union presented its next demand early in 1936: Wages for chopping and weeding cotton must be raised to $2 per day. The planters responded by evicting one hundred sharecroppers. As they camped in the snowdrifts, Pat Jackson called for a congressional investigation. His outrage, striking a spark in Sen. Robert LaFollette, inspired the most thorough investigation of civil liberties violations ever undertaken in the U.S. But the sharecroppers' civil liberties were not placed under the microscope of the LaFollette Committee. As its exceptionally courageous chairman said to Mitchell: "If we go in there, those southern congressmen will simply stop our appropriations."

As the ides of May came and went and the planters remained obdurate, the STFU called its second strike. Like the contemporaneous sit-downs of the auto workers, this effort had verve and originality. The picketing was done in "Marches": Unionists were lined up one behind the other, about eight feet apart, forming a very long, thin line, which marched down the road from one plantation to the other, singing and calling to those in the fields to join them. Marchers would cover 20 to 25 miles each day, with their lines lengthening and snaking out as the sun set.

The planters also displayed ingenuity, although of a somewhat antiquarian nature. In Earle, Arkansas, city marshal Paul Peacher not only arrested thirteen pickets, mainly Negro, but forced them to work out their sentences on his farm. A federal grand jury found him guilty of eight counts of violating the anti-slavery laws. When two white union sympathizers, the Rev. Claude Williams . . . and Miss Willie Sue Blagdon, undertook to search for Negro unionist Frank Weems, who disappeared after being beaten on the picket line, they were caught and whipped by "unknown assailants." Naturally, the disappearance of Weems, a black man, made no ripple, but the attack upon the whites was headlined across the nation. Clay East, leaving the Forrest City (Arkansas) courthouse after providing bail for some pickets, was recognized and set upon by a gang of riding bosses. He was flat on his back and fighting with his feet when the state patrol finally rescued him. "Clay was a very athletic type of person," sighs Mitch admiringly.

If the National Guard, called out four days after the strike began, did little to prevent such violence, it did serve the traditional function of keeping the nervous Nellies on the job and off the picket line. When Thomas again pleaded with Roosevelt to intervene, the President replied that he had requested the governor to investigate. "Like asking Capone to investigate the underworld," growled Thomas. He next urged FDR to make good use of his invitation to the Arkansas Centennial Celebration in June, but Roosevelt's conventional address skirted both labor standards and civil liberties.

In July the strike collapsed, having "made no dent at all." Still, the union had continued to galvanize its constituency and the liberal community as a whole. At year's end, the STFU boasted 6,000 new members (initiation fee, 25¢; annual dues, $1), for a total of 31,000 men and women, black and white, in Arkansas, Tennessee, Oklahoma, Missouri, North Carolina, Mississippi, and Texas. And it had aroused sufficient interest to warrant a March of Time documentary, which made no bones about the price exacted in pain and terror for the privilege of trying to better oneself on the southern plantation.

THE LEGISLATIVE FRONT: A NOBLE FAILURE, A 'SAVIOR WITHOUT A FLOCK,' A DUBIOUS VICTORY

At the time the movie, together with the other publicity, *did* seem to "make a whale of a difference." With the 1936 elections approaching and the issue vivid in the public mind, FDR moved to fulfill his legislative commitment to the sharecroppers. A Presidential Committee on Farm Tenancy was appointed, headed by Wallace and including (thanks to the machinations of Pat Jackson) a representative of the STFU. For Norman Thomas and Mitchell, the major issue confronting this committee was whether its legislative recommendations would be limited to the acquisition of land by tenants—"the subsidization of an American peasantry on subsistence farms," said Thomas—or would provide also for rural co-operatives. Both men were convinced that only the latter could compete successfully with the increasingly mechanized plantations. Although the STFU had many friends on the committee, including Tugwell and the southern triumvirate, the cooperative proposals were foredoomed. As far as Congress was concerned, co-ops had been given a more than fair trial by Tugwell's Resettlement Administration and had proved a sad, funny—and costly—flop. Thus even before the committee met, the STFU's primary objective was engulfed by one of the angriest controversies of the New Deal.

The ninety-nine "community" programs begun at the nadir of the Depression to relocate the jobless and landless represented a "back to the land" movement dear to the heart of the President, who once said, ". . . The salvation of America lies with the country men and boys. . . . They have more time to think and study for themselves." For Tugwell, who became their chief mentor and symbol, the community projects had a larger, almost apocalyptic significance. To them he brought a social philosophy as distinct from the Marxist orientation of Thomas and Mitchell as from the socio-economic regionalism of Alexander and the southern contingent. A former economics professor, Tugwell was a prophet of the planned economy and an enemy of laissez faire. But unlike the Marxists, he sought no new parties or movements to achieve these ends. Essentially elitist, he believed that an astute and determined president, surrounded by equally astute and determined planners, could revolutionize society.

The community projects—whether subsistence farms, rural-industrial, all-rural, or suburban—represented for Tugwell, says historian Paul Conkin, "the idea of cooperation, which was to replace competition and extreme individualism . . . as the new institution best suited for the modern environment. No more concerted public effort was ever made in the U.S. to develop cooperatives of all kinds." A glance at some of these projects will illustrate what happened when soaring idealism encountered unleavened reality.

At Arthurdale, a community for stranded miners in West Virginia which became Mrs. Roosevelt's pet Resettlement project, a White House aide ordered fifty prefabricated houses, which turned out to be totally useless. Thereupon the dauntless First Lady called in an architect and an interior decorator, all without consulting the local sponsors or the project director, who promptly resigned in protest. In Penderlea, a rural project in North Carolina, settlers discovered that it would take them over forty years to buy their farms, during which they had to submit to detailed home budgets and farm plans, and bank accounts held jointly with the project manager. At Penderlea and Arthurdale, the new schools were developed along the latest progressive lines proposed by consultant John Dewey; in both places the settlers demanded a return to tradition.

At Jersey Homesteads, the government spent $200,000 for a factory to produce concrete blocks; when production started, the factory collapsed. A Special Skills section brought handicrafts, fine arts, and entertainment to the projects; at Penderlea the settlers returned special records made for them, requesting hillbilly music instead. At Westmoreland, the director suggested that Special Skills people be sent only at local request, so "that we do not burden the community with more advantages than they can absorb at one time." Between the solicitous social workers, the questionnaire-asking sociologists, and the beagle-nosed reporters, one mountaineer said, "It got so a man couldn't set down to his sow belly and turnip greens without some stranger peeking in at the window or walking in to ask fool questions."

Of such stuff are headlines made, but there were more fundamental problems: The government loaned four million dollars to the communities for cooperative factories of the latest design, all of which proved financial failures. Five hosiery mills lost $64,000, a woodworking plant almost $191,000, a pants factory about $214,000, and the Arthurdale tractor plant closed after one year with a loss of more than $106,000. Even Jersey Homesteads, the only settlement with a homogeneous, New York Jewish population, whose elan is echoed in the little inaugural march for the garment factory which replaced the concrete block fiasco:

> Production, cooperation
> Freedom for every nation,
> Here, there, and everywhere,
> This is our claim:
> Workers' Aim, Workers' Aim.

The all-glass, air-conditioned factory failed in its first year of operation. An equally dire fate befell the all-rural co-ops, which were mainly in the South.

"Bad management," said Mitchell, pointing to successful consumer co-ops undertaken by the STFU and Sherwood Eddy's Delta Co-op in Mississippi. True, in some cases, but mainly *outside* management, and so much of it! Seeking only refuge from the economic storm, the unsuspecting settlers were deluged by a Niagara of planters, supervisors, managers, educators, and recreators—all with the best intentions. Who could tolerate it? (It is a comment on the selective writing of our history and the explosive social potential of "participation" that, despite this experience, the concept was virtually ignored until the civil rights revolution, thirty years later.) The damaging impact of Washington's paternalism was reinforced by the repeated reshuffling of the sponsoring agencies, with attendant confusion; the unfamiliarity of all agencies with the techniques of social planning (another lesson unlearned); and most important, the contradictory aims of the Resettlement Administration and the settlers.

Whereas the STFU and the Delta Co-op farmers chose freely to cooperate, the overwhelming majority of the government's 10,000 settlers wished only to participate in the American Dream—to own their own home or farm. When their low earnings and the government's long-term purchase policy thwarted this purpose, no planning or helping could palliate their frustration.

These developments had not run their full course when the Presidential Committee on Farm Tenancy began its investigations in November, 1936, but they were sufficiently advanced to provide ammunition for the gathering legions of Roosevelt haters. Articles entitled "Hull House in the Hills," "The Fuller Life at Arthurdale," "Four Million Dollar Village," and "Back to Capitalism" chronicled the government's pratfalls, with only an occasional bow to its intentions and problems. Nor did they advertise that Resettlement's anti-segregationist, pro-poor people, and anti-privilege philosophy motivated much of their fury.

For all of this Tugwell was, unfortunately, an ideal lightning conductor. A dashing symbol of the New Deal who "suffered neither fools nor Congressmen gladly and often publicly confused the two," he was denounced in the press as both a "wild man from Moscow" and an ineffectual academician. By the end of 1936 an anti-Tugwell Club was formed in Chicago, cracks were circulating about the "Unsettlement Administration," and a devastating series of articles entitled "Utopia Unlimited" had appeared in the Washington *Post*. An isolated, "tragic figure, a savior without a flock," Tugwell proved the final undoing of the cooperative ideal as a viable political program. By the time the committee convened, he had decided to resign, leaving the Resettlement Administration in the hands of the less controversial Will Alexander.

Predictably, the Farm Tenancy Committee's report stressed the importance of private farm ownership and Congress showed little patience with other alternatives. In July, 1937, the Bankhead-Jones Act established a Farm Security Administration within the Department of Agriculture to provide government loans to selected tenants for farm rehabilitation and purchase. The Resettlement Administration was to be absorbed by the new agency and its community projects completed; no further social experiments would be undertaken.

In its minority report to the Farm Tenancy Committee, the STFU had said: "We strongly dissent from the 'small homestead' philosophy as the solution for the majority of southern agricultural workers. It is the more readily accepted by the present landlords because they know it to be relatively ineffective and . . . harmless from their point of view." For the union, which claimed "that we workers in the fields, through our unions, through our strikes, and through our willingness to stand up against beatings, espionage, and all manner of terror . . . have brought the attention of the country to our problems," the Farm Security Administration was a dubious victory.

In addition, the FSA, like most poverty programs, was hamstrung by inadequate funds. The proposed annual budget of $50 million was reduced to $10 million in 1938, $25 million in 1939, and $50 million thereafter. Roosevelt, confronting an increasingly hostile Congress, offered little resistance, despite Secretary Wallace's admission that even at the

$50 million rate, it would take 230 years to find farms for all the existing tenants, at $4,000 per farm! Also, the program was to be administered by county committees, notoriously dominated by the Farm Bureau. Said the STFU: "The county agent is, generally speaking, the servant of the land-owning business interest from whom he gets a large portion of his pay, rather than the servant of the mass of the people in the farming areas."

The union found only one bright spot in the FSA picture, and his name was Alexander. The new director, a former farm boy who believed that "if a man didn't know the feel of an ax-handle, he couldn't understand America," yarn-spinning, genial, pragmatic Dr. Will made the most of his mandate. As a key member of the Farm Tenancy Committee, he had made sure that FSA would combine, for the first time, credit toward farm purchase with technical aid, thus motivating the ambitious tenant to learn better farming methods. In the South, this meant preaching the Odum-Vance gospel of crop diversification as a means of renewing the exhausted land and finally releasing the region from the tyranny of cotton.

In their engaging biography of Alexander, Miss Dykeman and Mr. Stokely describe the salvation of the Pettways of Gee's Bend, Alabama, begun early in the New Deal and brought to fruition by the FSA. Living in isolation in the giant ox-bow bend of the Alabama River below Selma, these 100 families descended from the slaves of the now deserted Pettway Plantation were living on wild plums in the winter of 1933. After that, they were kept alive by the relief agencies and Resettlement, but FSA investigated and decided to invest in the Pettways. Loans were made for seed, fertilizers, chickens, pigs, cows, and mules—and for re-purchase of their 12,000 acres, long foreclosed.

By 1941, 97 families had repaid their loans and owned their 100-acre farms, in a county where only 20% of farms were operator owned. They had diversified their crops and built a new school, general store, community center, and health center. When Dr. Will and their particular FSA mentor, Chapel Hill's much-loved Pete Hudgens, came to visit they were greeted by a spiritual composed in their honor, "Go Down to the Ferry and I'll Pray," each verse of which celebrated an FSA benefit.

Unlike his predecessor, Dr. Will realized that his offensive in the field would be brought up short unless he secured his political flanks. To inform the public he enlisted writers like John Fischer, now editor of *Harper's*, and James Agee, who, with FSA photographer Walker Evans, created from this experience the classical *Let Us Now Praise Famous Men*. With his bourbon-and-branch-water charm, Dr. Will also won the support of the majority leader, Arkansas' Senator Joe Robinson. Altogether, Dr. Will's FSA was a shrewd, practical, and imaginative operation.

Yet, by 1940, the country's war-bred prosperity had begun its customary work: The public was fast losing interest in the poor and dispossessed. Congress, sensing this, turned a more receptive ear to the Farm Bureau, now openly antagonistic to FSA. This was quite a switch from its 1934 position, when a collapsing agriculture caused its president to question even that most sacred of cows, rugged individualism.

It is a pity that historian Conkin's summation of the indictment levelled at FSA was not published until 1959, when Dr. Will was no longer here to enjoy it:

> The FSA aided the lowest and most helpless class of farmers, from the migrant laborers in California to southern sharecroppers. But the cotton plantations, the truck farms, and the large orchards were dependent upon these very same cheap laborers and croppers that the FSA was aiding through rehabilitation loans or resettlement opportunities. At the same time . . . the support to local cooperatives often threatened the profit of private processors and retailers. Thus those who feared competition or who were about to lose their cheap labor were naturally opposed to FSA.

Dr. Will's account was pithier. His colleagues in the Farm Bureau had, he said, "the attitude that the medicine man in Africa would have towards someone who tried to give penicillin for boils." Realizing that the times were no longer propitious for penicillin, Dr. Will resigned in 1940. The agency struggled along until 1946, when it finally succumbed to the protracted attacks of southern congressmen.

During the eight years of its life, the FSA made more than half a million rehabilitation loans to southern tenants, or more than half of all such loans granted. Of the farm purchase loans, 30,809—more than two-thirds of all loans granted—were funneled into the South. For the 1,831,000 southern tenant families reported by the census in 1935, this represents farm assistance for 27.6% and aid in purchasing farms for 1.6%. After all the publicity and protest and dedication, it turned out that the New Deal's assault on one of the most severe aspects of "the nation's Number One economic problem" (as FDR termed the South) was a chimera.

For the next twenty years, Congress turned its back on the southern rural poor, with a single exception: In 1956, social security coverage was extended to all non-migratory farm workers.

ACKNOWLEDGMENTS

The writer has profited immeasurably from long-standing association with several principals of this story, including Norman Thomas, H. L. Mitchell, Daniel Pollitt, and the late Pat Jackson. For their grace under the pressure of repeated, lengthy interviewing, thanks are due Messrs. Victor Bussie, Claude Ramsey, Nicholas Zonarich, James Pierce, and Ralph Helstein. May I also express my warm appreciation to Mrs. Robin Ulmer of the National Sharecroppers' Fund's Atlanta office, Mrs. Glenda Bartley and Mrs. Jane De Lung of the Southern Regional Council, and Miss Katherine Cheape of the University of North Carolina (Chapel Hill) Library for their creative and unstinting assistance.

BIBLIOGRAPHY

CBS Reports, *Harvest of Shame*, November 25, 1960.

Leslie W. Dunbar, *A Republic of Equals* (Ann Arbor: University of Michigan Press, 1966).

Howard W. Odum, *Southern Regions of the United States* (Chapel Hill: University of North Carolina Press, 1936).

George W. Tindall, [*The Emergence of the New South*, Volume X in *A History of the South* (Baton Rouge: Louisiana State University Press, 1967)].

H. L. Mitchell, Columbia University Oral History Collection.

C. Vann Woodward, *Tom Watson, Agrarian Rebel* (New York: Oxford University Press, 1963).

Charles S. Johnson, Edwin R. Embree, and W. W. Alexander, *The Collapse of Cotton Tenancy* (Chapel Hill: University of North Carolina Press, 1935).

Frank Freidel, *FDR and the South* (Baton Rouge: Louisiana State University Press, 1965).

Arthur M. Schlesinger, Jr., *The Coming of the New Deal* (Boston: Houghton Mifflin, 1958).

James MacGregor Burns, *Roosevelt: The Lion and the Fox* (New York: Harcourt, Brace and Company, 1956).

Jerold S. Auerbach, "The Organizing Drive of the Southern Tenant Farmers Union in Arkansas," Paper delivered at the November 13, 1964, meeting of the Southern Historical Association.

M. S. Venkataramani, "Norman Thomas, Arkansas Sharecroppers, and the Roosevelt Agricultural Policies, 1933–1937," *Arkansas Historical Quarterly*, XXIV (Spring, 1965).

David A. Shannon, *The Socialist Party in America* (New York: The Macmillan Co., 1955).

The Disinherited Speak, Letters from Sharecroppers, Workers Defense League Pamphlet (New York: Workers Defense League, undated, circa 1937).

Paul K. Conkin, *Tomorrow a New World: The New Deal Community Program* (Ithaca, New York: Cornell University Press, 1959).

Wilma Dykeman and James Stokely, *Seeds of Southern Change: The Life of Will Alexander* (Chicago: the University of Chicago Press, 1962).

Farm Tenancy: Report of the President's Committee (Washington, 1937).

Southern Tenant Farmers Union Papers, Southern Historical Collection, University of North Carolina, Chapel Hill. (In the interest of brevity, no separate and detailed citations are made for this major source. Such information will gladly be supplied to interested readers.)

The Growers Attack
Migrant Labor Organizations
in California

CAREY McWILLIAMS

Migrant farm workers have been and remain perhaps the most consistently depressed segment of the American labor force. Wandering from harvest to harvest, up and down both coasts, these low-paid agricultural laborers never have enough steady work to maintain even a passable standard of living. Their children rarely stay in one place long enough to have successful school experiences; instead, they tend to pass the school years in the fields, while local truant officers look the other way. Because they have no home base, the migrant workers seldom have a chance to exercise their political rights; and because they are relatively few in number, they have little economic or social influence in the areas they traverse. Their labor serves primarily to put money in the pockets of those engaged in large-scale agriculture—the current "agribusiness."

An important factor in the success of large-scale agriculture in this country has been the cooperation of local, state, and national political and law-enforcement authorities with landowners. In industrial labor disputes, government forces have generally supported the factory owners and managers against the workers. They have demonstrated an even more negative attitude toward agricultural workers, as witnessed by the persistence of chattel slavery as a form of agricultural labor until the second half of the nineteenth century. In this volume, we have already considered the condition of free farm laborers in the South after Reconstruction. The convict-lease system, vagrancy laws, and other laws drastically limited the freedom of the individual workingman, turning the postwar South into a near-feudal state. In the South the emphasis was on making the labor force stay put, but in the West the important thing was to keep the labor force in motion—up through California, into Oregon and Washington, and back again, following the harvests of the fruits and vegetables for which the West Coast is famous.

Through the years, much of the migrant labor population in California has been of non-European ancestry. Mexican-Americans, in particular, have often found that the only work available to them was

at harvest time. Frequently, the structures of society have been mar-
shaled against these minority populations in a manner suggestive of
Jim Crow in the South. Segregated schools, segregated housing, and
clearly discriminatory social and political practices have severely restricted their freedom of movement all along the West Coast. In
addition, they have borne the brunt of vigilante justice and lynch
law in the West—practices in which California has taken second place
only to the South. Indeed, the lawlessness of the mining camps and
of San Francisco's Barbary Coast in the nineteenth century is legendary. Currently, although large-scale agriculture has replaced mining
as the state's leading industry, the patterns of coalition against
minority workers' groups on the part of public officials, law-enforcement authorities, and leaders of business and industry remain much
as they were in the nineteenth century.

Only in recent years has there been a successful drive to organize
migrant farm workers into a viable economic force in California.
Cesar Chavez and his Mexican-American grape-pickers have formed
the United Farm Workers Organizing Committee (the UFWOC), which,
after several years of striking against great odds, has been able to
negotiate a contract with growers that promises to bring some improvement in the standard of living of both union members and other
migrant agricultural laborers. The UFWOC is now turning its attention to crops other than grapes in an attempt to provide migrant
workers with some measure of economic security throughout the
year.

Carey McWilliams, editor of **The Nation,** wrote extensively about
the situation of farm labor in California during the Depression. In the
following selection from his book **Factories in the Field,** first published in 1939, he provides a vivid contemporaneous description of
the difficulties faced by the migrant workers of the 1930's as they
struggled for a better way of life.

Following the great wave of strikes which swept California in 1933, the
farmers of the State began to form new organizations with which to combat the instinctive struggle of the State's 250,000 agricultural workers to
achieve unionization. Farmers have never lacked organization in California;

"The Growers Attack Migrant Labor Organizations in California." From Carey
McWilliams, *Factories in the Field: The Story of Migratory Farm Labor in California* (Boston: Little, Brown, 1939), pp. 230–63. Reprinted by permission of the
author.

in fact, they have long set the pace for organizational activities among American farmers. They were pioneers in the field of co-operative marketing. Today every crop is organized through a series of co-operative organizations, many of which are institutions of great power and wealth. For a great many years these organized farm groups have held the balance of political power in the State through their control of the State Senate. Holding a veto power on all State legislation, they have dictated to governors and defied the will of the people of the entire State. In addition to co-operative marketing organizations, the canning and packing houses have long been organized into powerful trade associations and, in 1926, the Western Growers Protective Association was formed, for the purpose of consolidating various smaller organizations of shippers and growers in the State. Shortly after the 1933 trouble, in February, 1934, American Institutions, Inc., was organized in California by Mr. Guernsey Frazer, a prominent American Legion official, for the purpose of selling the large shipper-growers a high-pressure pro-Fascism legislative program. This attempt to impose Fascism from the outside, so to speak, was not successful, but, by 1934, the large growers themselves recognized the necessity of organizing for the primary purpose of fighting labor organization. The organization which they effected, Associated Farmers of California, Inc., which today has membership in California of 40,000, has played an important role in the social history of the West. Inasmuch as it is the first organization of its type to appear in the United States, and as it has many points of similarity with organizations of a like character in Nazi Germany,[1] it warrants careful scrutiny.

"FROM APATHY TO ACTION"

In 1933 the California Farm Bureau Federation and the State Chamber of Commerce appointed a joint committee to study farm-labor conditions in the State. At the conclusion of this survey the farmers of Imperial Valley—"the Cradle of Vigilantism"—formed a voluntary association known as Associated Farmers, "pledged to help one another in case of emergency. They agreed to co-operate to harvest crops in case of strikes and to offer their services to the local sheriff immediately as special deputies in the event of disorders arising out of picketing and sabotage." As soon as this group was organized, the State Farm Bureau and the State Chamber of Commerce each designated a representative to go from county to county "explaining the Associated Farmers idea to local Farm Bureaus, businessmen, and peace officers." Within one year, twenty-six counties had formed associated farmer groups, and, on May 7, 1934, a convention was held in Fresno for the purpose of creating a Statewide organization. I have a stenographic report of this organization meeting. It was presided over by S. Parker Frisselle [Mr. Frisselle was the first

[1] See "The Fascist Threat to Democracy," by Robert A. Brady, *Science and Society*, Vol. II, No. 2.

president and served for two years; his successor was Colonel Walter E. Garrison], who stated that the finances for the organization would unquestionably have to come from the banks and utility companies. The initial funds were, in fact, raised by Mr. Earl Fisher, of the Pacific Gas & Electric Company, and Mr. Leonard Wood, of the California Packing Company. At this meeting, it was decided that farmers should "front" the organization, although the utility companies and banks would exercise ultimate control.

Today the Associated Farmers have their headquarters in San Francisco and branch offices in practically every county of the State.[2] Each farmer is supposed to pay one dollar a year, as membership dues, and an additional dollar for each thousand dollars a year spent in wages. In some counties, dues are levied on the basis of so many cents per ton of fruit and vegetables harvested. Every member pledges himself, "in case of trouble," to report at the local sheriff's office.

> Under agreement with the local sheriffs, no volunteer farmer will be asked to carry a gun or throw a gas bomb, even if he is deputized. He is armed with a pick handle about twenty inches long. A good many of the Associated Farmers would prefer fire-arms. But they have been overruled by cooler heads who say that in the heat of defending their homes by invading strike pickets, the embittered farmers might use their guns too effectively and turn public opinion against the organization.

The "idea" back of these mobilizations, according to Mr. Taylor, "is to muster a show of force when required." How effectively some of the mobilizations have been organized may be indicated by the fact that in the Salinas strike, 1,500 men were mobilized for deputy duty in less than a day; in the Stockton strike, 2,200 deputies were mobilized in a few hours and in Imperial Valley 1,200 deputies were recently mobilized on a few minutes' notice. When one realizes that in 1933 a large percentage of the farm lands in Central and Northern California were controlled by one institution—the Bank of America—the irony of these "embittered" farmers defending their "homes" against strikers becomes apparent.

An efficient espionage system is maintained by the Associated Farmers. In 1935, I inspected the "confidential" files of the organization in San Francisco. At that time, they had a card-index file on "dangerous radicals" containing approximately one thousand names, alphabetically arranged, with front- and side-view photographs of each individual, including notations of arrests, strike activities, affiliations, and so forth. Each reference contained a number which referred to a corresponding identification record in the archives of the State Bureau of Criminal Identification. Sets of this file have been distributed to over a hundred peace officers in the State and lists have been sent to members of the association. Local offices or branches of the Associated Farmers maintain elaborate records

[2] See "The Right to Harvest," by Frank J. Taylor, *The Country Gentleman*, October, 1937.

of a similar nature, including a "check-up" system whereby workers with a reputation for independence may be readily identified and rousted out of the locality. The State Bureau of Criminal Identification, the State Highway Patrol, and local law-enforcement agencies work in the closest co-operation with agents of the association; in a sense, the association may be said to direct the activities of these public agencies. The State Bureau of Criminal Identification had its private investigators sleuthing for the Tagus Ranch in the San Joaquin Valley and it employed, at one time or another, the various stool pigeons upon whose testimony the Sacramento criminal-syndicalism prosecution was based.

In addition to its espionage activities, the Associated Farmers maintain a carefully organized propaganda department. Regular bulletins, heavily larded with "anti-Communist" information, are sent to the members; special articles are reprinted and distributed throughout the State; and a steady flow of statements and releases are supplied to the press. In recent years, the association has begun to dabble in a more ambitious type of propaganda. One of its spokesmen, Mr. John Phillips, a State Senator, recently visited Europe. Upon his return, Mr. Phillips published a series of articles in the *California Cultivator* (February 1 and 15, 1936), on his travels. One article was devoted to Mr. Phillips' impressions of the Nazis (he was in Nuremberg when the party was in session). Mr. Phillips particularly noticed the new type of German citizenship—the *Reichsburger*—under which "you simply say that anybody who agrees with you is a citizen of the first class, and anybody who does not agree with you is a non-voting citizen." His admiration for Hitler is boundless: "I would like to tell you how the personality of Hitler impressed me and how I feel that he has a greater personal appeal, a greater personal influence on his people than many of the nations realize." "Hitler," he said in a speech on January 18, 1938, "has done more for democracy than any man before him." Some years ago, Frances Perkins, Secretary of Labor, issued a statement repudiating a circular which the Associated Farmers had distributed in which they had attempted to make out, by reference to a faked marriage license, that she was a Jewess. Throughout California in 1936 and 1937, the Associated Farmers sponsored and organized meetings for the Reverend Martin Luther Thomas, of Los Angeles, who heads a "Christian American Crusade," and who is a notorious anti-Semite and Red-baiter. As a result of Mr. Thomas' harangues, the authorities in Riverside County employed a special detective, at a salary of $1,800 a year, to spy on the "subversive activities" of school children in the Riverside public schools. Mr. Phillips, who is frequently teamed with the Rev. Mr. Thomas at anti-Communist meetings sponsored by the Associated Farmers, was, for a time, holding a county office in Riverside County, designated as "labor co-ordinator." More recently the Associated Farmers have sponsored Samuel J. Hume, of the California Crusaders, who has spoken throughout the State inveighing against labor organization.

Shortly after its formation, the Associated Farmers launched a campaign, in the rural counties, for the enactment of the anti-picketing and so-called "emergency-disaster" ordinances. Anti-picketing ordinances have, as a consequence, been enacted in practically every rural county.

The alleged justification for the "emergency-disaster" ordinances, which provide for a mobilization of all the forces of the community in case of a "major disaster," was the earthquake which occurred in Southern California in March, 1933. Today practically every county in the State, and most of the cities and towns, have such ordinances in effect. There is nothing in the wording of most of these ordinances to prevent their use in case of a "strike," which, in the eyes of the farmers during harvest, is certainly a "major disaster." The ordinances provide, in elaborate detail, for the formation of a kind of "crisis," or extra-legal governmental machinery, which is to come into existence, with broad powers, upon the declaration by the appropriate executive officer in the community that a state of emergency exists. The purpose back of the campaign for the enactment of these ordinances has been clearly indicated. For example, on December 18, 1936, the county counsel in Los Angeles was instructed to draft legislation which "would permit counties to spend funds for erecting concentration camps for use during major disasters." Thus the governmental apparatus for a kind of constitutional Fascism actually exists in California today.

It would be suggested, of course, that I am exaggerating the importance of these ordinances and misstating the purpose for which they were enacted. But other evidence exists which points to the real intention back of these measures. Concentration camps are to be found in California today. I described, in some detail, such a camp in an article which appeared in *The Nation* (July 24, 1935). It is located a few miles outside of Salinas, California. Here a stockade has been constructed which is admittedly intended for use as a concentration camp. When local workers inquired of the shipper-growers why such a curious construction had been established, they were told that it was built "to hold strikers, but of course we won't put white men in it, just Filipinos." A similar stockade at one time existed at the farm factory of the Balfour-Guthrie Company (a large British-owned concern) at Brentwood, California. During a strike at this farm in 1935, "a substantial fence surmounted by plenty of barbed wire" was built about the workers' camp, with "the entrance guarded night and day." When questioned about this camp, the growers protested that "agitators continually refer to it as a stockade, a cattle corral, or a prison, and its inhabitants as slaves or prisoners." Mr. P. S. Bancroft, President of the Contra Costa unit of the Associated Farmers, in defending the camp, said that "obviously the fence and guard were there to keep the lawless element out, not to keep the contented workmen in." When the striking workers in the Imperial Valley set up a camp and strike headquarters in 1934, however, the camp was raided by local police, because, to quote from the *Shipper-Grower Magazine* (March, 1934), "it was a concentration camp in which the workers were being kept against their wishes." The burning question, therefore, would seem to be: When is a concentration camp not a concentration camp? At the Tagus Ranch, in 1934,[3] a huge moat was constructed around an orchard in order "to protect the properties," with armed guards stationed at the entrance and

[3] See United Press stories for July 9 and July 21, 1934.

with a machine gun mounted on a truck. "All roads leading to the ranch with the exception of the main entrance, where guards are stationed, are blocked by barbed wire and flooded with water by dikes. Fifty old employees report nightly to the ranch manager regarding the conduct of employees under suspicion." There is much similar evidence, all tending to show that the great farm factories of California take on the appearance of fortified camps under military surveillance whenever a strike is threatened.

Throughout the year 1934 the Associated Farmers stimulated many "trial mobilizations." On July 23, 1934, Sheriff O. W. Toland at Gridley announced that a "trial mobilization" of American Legion men and special deputies had come off perfectly: "All Legionnaires were at the hall in ten minutes and in forty-five minutes the entire assembly was present." Many Legion Posts throughout the State practiced similar mobilizations which were timed to coincide with organizational activity among agricultural workers. From Merced, on July 14, 1934, came word that the California Lands, Inc. (Bank of America), and the California Packing Company had demanded forty extra deputy sheriffs, "equipped sufficiently to cope with violence." From Hanford, July 16, 1934, came the report that county officials had organized an Anti-Communist League "to co-operate with county officers in case of emergencies." Most of this viligante recruiting has been done by elected officials, sheriffs and district attorneys, and peace officers. For example, in 1934 Sheriff Howard Durley, according to the *Fillmore Herald*, "prepared to organize a county-wide vigilante group for the purpose of handling emergencies. Approximately 200 special deputies were sworn in, chosen from prepared lists, and these will be organized into smaller units of ten men each in all sections of the county." I could quote an abundance of similiar evidence.

In the following year, 1935, the strategy was carried a point further, when the growers began to order "preventive" arrests. On December 30, 1935, the Sheriff of Imperial Valley (where 4,000 gun permits had been issued in the summer), at the opening of the winter harvest season, "launched a valley-wide roundup of professional agitators, Communists and suspects *to avert a possible strike* among lettuce workers." Commenting upon this move, the *Los Angeles Times* stated editorially: "Professional agitators who are busily engaged in fomenting new labor trouble in the Imperial Valley winter lettuce [harvest] will find the authorities ready for them. Sheriff Ware and his deputies have *the jump on them this time*," i.e., arrests were made before a strike could be called and in advance of the season.

Needless to say, the Associated Farmers have a powerful legislative lobby in Sacramento and an elaborate legislative program. In general, they have sponsored the enactment of laws restricting labor's right to organize on the avowed theory that such legislation "would help cut down the cost of labor"; the incorporation of all labor unions; laws prohibiting sympathetic strikes; measures designed to prevent the unionization of governmental and utility-company employees; provisions limiting the right of strikers to relief; and a number of other measures, such as laws making it illegal to interfere with the delivery of food or medical supplies, outlawing the Communist Party, and prohibiting all picketing. At present, the farm groups are fighting strenuously against a proposal for a unicameral legislative body in California, for, under the present system, they actually hold a legislative veto through their control of the State Senate. Until this hold is broken, democratic processes cannot function.

SANTA ROSA

Encouraged by their success in 1934 in crushing unionization activities among agricultural workers, the Associated Farmers determined in 1935 to stamp out the last vestiges of revolt and to prevent an organizational campaign from getting under way. As part of this strategy, they organized a systematic terrorization of workers in the rural areas on the eve, so to speak, of the various crop harvests. Without waiting for organizational activity to start, and in advance of the season, fiery crosses burned on the hilltops and wholesale arrests were made, usually accompanied by an elaborate Red-baiting campaign in the local press to build up the idea, in the mind of the community, that grave danger threatened. In February, 1935, the leaders of the Associated Farmers sponsored the formation in Sacramento of the California Cavaliers, a semi-military organization, which announced that its purpose was to "stamp out all un-American activity among farm labor." Mr. Herman Cottrell, an official of the Associated Farmers and an organizer of the California Cavaliers, publicly stated: "We aren't going to stand for any more of these organizers from now on; anyone who peeps about higher wages will wish he hadn't." As the harvest season approached, statements such as the foregoing were accompanied by overt acts of terrorization. At San Jose, on June 10, 1935, on the eve of the apricot-crop harvest, three fiery crosses blazed on the hills near a workers' camp where, two years previously, a mob of vigilantes had raided the camp, kidnaped a score of "radical" leaders, held them for two hours, beaten them, and then driven them across the county line. Confident that they had the situation well in hand, the Associated Farmers, in a radio broadcast on June 14, 1935, told their members "to go ahead and don't worry about agitators this season."

In general this confidence was justified, for 1935 was marked by only one major "incident," that of Santa Rosa. In August, the workers, assembled in the Santa Rosa and Sebastopol sections for the apple harvest, voted to strike. As the season was somewhat delayed, the growers ignored the strike vote until some two hundred packing-house employees decided to join the pickers in a general walkout. On August 1, 1935, two Communist Party officials were speaking at a mass meeting of pickers and packing-house workers in Santa Rosa, when the hall was raided by a group of 250 vigilantes, who jerked the speakers from the platform, broke up the meeting, and engaged in a general free-for-all fight with the workers. As the crop matured and workers were not immediately forthcoming in the superabundance demanded by the growers, a delegation of orchard owners went to the relief agencies and demanded that a large number of relief clients be dropped from the rolls and ordered into the orchards. A few days later, on August fifth, a committee of six men, "saying they represented 300 vigilantes," called on the local WPA administrator and demanded that "all Communists, Reds, and radicals" be dropped from the payroll of the WPA, stating that if this ultimatum were not complied with in forty-eight hours, they would take matters into their own hands. The WPA administrator stalled for time, and the committee reluctantly agreed to extend the deadline.

On August 23, 1935, "with sunset this evening set as the new deadline," a mob of vigilantes seized Solomon Nitzburg and Jack Green, together with three other men, dragged them through the streets of Santa Rosa, and, after the three men had kissed the American flag on the courthouse steps and promised to leave the community, released them. Nitzburg and Green, refusing to comply with the demand, were kicked, beaten, tarred and feathered, and paraded around the courthouse in Santa Rosa, and driven out of the county. In seizing Nitzburg, the mob fired volley after volley of rifle fire through his home, and followed up this attack with the use of tear-gas bombs. The entire evening of August twenty-third was a Saturnalia of rioting, intimidation, and violence, described as "the wildest scene in the history of Sonoma County." The whole affair was carried out brazenly, with no attempt at concealment, and the *San Francisco Examiner*, which played up the incident as provocatively as possible, openly stated that "the tar and feather party was hailed in Sonoma County as a direct American answer to the red strike fomentors." The leaders of the mob consisted of the following men: a local banker, the Mayor, the head of the local Federal Re-employment Bureau, several motor cops, a member of the State Legislature, numerous American Legionnaires, and the President of the local Chamber of Commerce. Later twenty-three business and professional men in the community were indicted in connection with the riot, but were quickly acquitted; and, later, when Nitzburg and Green sued for damages, the court found in favor of the defendants.

Santa Rosa, the first major "incident" after the Cannery and Agricultural Workers Industrial Union had been smashed in 1934, was significant of the rising tide of potential Fascism in California. The division of social forces was clear-cut. On the one hand were the migratory workers in the field and the packing-house employees who were, for the most part, local residents, together with a few miscellaneous local sympathizers. Arrayed against this group were a few large growers and the packing-house companies utilizing the local townspeople as a vigilante mob to crush a pending strike. The form of constitutional government was swiftly brushed aside and mob rule openly sanctioned. This exhibition of Fascist insurrection not only went unpunished, but received open public support throughout the State and the tacit approval of State officials. The strike, of course, was crushed. In fact, the strike was crushed so thoroughly that it backfired on the growers. "The mob action," according to the United Press, "of the vigilantes has frightened away from the county so many workers that the county is 20 per cent under the number of pickers needed. Pay was increased one-fourth cent a pound, with payment of transportation, to induce pickers to come here, but the increase has had little effect in this regard." Soon the local growers were wailing about a "labor shortage" and announcing that four thousand pickers were needed immediately "to save the crop." This demonstration of the short-sightedness of employer violence, however, made no impression upon the Associated Farmers, who continued to use the Santa Rosa technique throughout 1935, 1936, and 1937.

THE BACKYARD STRIKE

Residents of Los Angeles, reading accounts of farm-labor dis-turbances in the rural counties, were formerly in the habit of regarding these riotous affairs as a peculiar manifestation of rural backwardness, a phenomenon restricted to the "heat" counties where, in the summer, people may be expected to act irrationally. This illusion was brutally dispelled, however, in the spring of 1936. In April and May of that year, tear-gas bombs began to explode and riot guns to bark in the vacant-lot areas adjacent to golf courses; and motorists along the highways leading into Los Angeles were privileged to witness as ugly an exhibition of strikebreaking as one could imagine. The occasion was a strike of celery workers.

The strike started on April twentieth, when approximately 300 Mexican workers left the fields after the growers' association (chiefly made up of Japanese growers) refused to meet their demands: 30 cents an hour, instead of the prevailing wage of 22½ cents, and a 60 per cent closed shop. Although the strikers were few in number (a total of about 2,000 workers was involved), the strike was suppressed with typical ruth-lessness. To suppress the strike, the authorities marshalled a force of ap-proximately 1,500 armed men—policemen, deputy sheriffs, and guards. When the strikers attempted to move from their strike headquarters in Venice to the near-by celery fields, the Los Angeles Red Squad, under the leadership of Captain William ("Red") Hynes, on three successive days broke the caravan procession before it could get started. When the strikers returned to their headquarters, they were pursued by the police, who tossed tear-gas bombs into the shack with children playing on the lot outside. As workers attempted to flee from the shack, they were seized and beaten. On April twentieth, police fired on a group of strikers as they were leaving for the fields. One worker was shot and another was badly burned when an officer fired a tear-gas gun at his chest from a distance of five or six feet. Throughout the following week, squads of police cars toured the fields, firing volleys of shot over the heads of any strikers they could locate. In the Dominguez hills near San Pedro, in the backyard, so to speak, of the beautiful Palos Verdes estates, a miniature battle was staged when a mob of police officers and armed farmers con-verged on a group of strikers huddled in an abandoned barn. So many arrests were made of strikers that the newspapers could not keep track of them. I estimated that at least one third of the total number of workers on strike were arrested, at one time or another (not all of them, of course, were actually prosecuted). The practice of making wholesale arrests amounted, in this case, virtually to arresting all strikers. Strikers who were injured had great difficulty in receiving medical attention and, when they finally succeeded in getting some attention at the Los Angeles County Hospital, they were turned over, after treatment, to Red-squad officers for "interrogation." One day, during the strike, a "strike-guard" fired at persons whom he suspected of being pickets and wounded a golfer on a near-by course. The guard later said it was all a mistake: He had fired at a "rabbit."

The strike was significant in that, in this instance, many of the growers wanted to sign the union agreement but were prevented from doing so by pressure from the large farm groups in the State who ordered them "to fight it out." John Anson Ford, of the Los Angeles County Board of Supervisors, charged that funds which the county turns over each year to the Los Angeles Chamber of Commerce to advertise the general charm of Southern California were used to employ agents to visit the growers and urge them not to sign the union agreement. This interesting and lively tableau was enacted not in the Imperial or San Joaquin Valley, but on the vacant lots of suburban Los Angeles. The workers, however, received no more protection in metropolitan Los Angeles than they received in the lawless farm counties of the State.

Unlike previous agricultural strikes in California, where factual data have been difficult to obtain, the celery workers' strike is well documented. Before the strike was called, the Los Angeles County Relief Administration and the WPA, under the direction of Dr. Towne Nylander, made a survey of wages and working conditions among the agricultural workers in Los Angeles County. This report clearly reveals the basic social pattern.

A survey was made of 745 families, 93.2 per cent Mexican, 6.8 per cent white. Of this group, 88.3 per cent were employed exclusively in agriculture and received compensation from no other source. The average yearly employment for those engaged exclusively in agricultural work was found to be 30.7 weeks per year. By reference to parallel studies made in 1928, it was discovered that the average duration of agricultural employment in that year, for migratory workers of the type under investigation, was 33.1 weeks per year—indicating that the working period for migratory labor is declining. The group engaged in part-time non-agricultural employment succeeded in obtaining only 14.7 weeks per year of outside work, so that the average duration of employment from all sources was 31.7 weeks per year. The report indicated, moreover, that of the sample investigated, 75.7 per cent of the families had only one worker, contrary to reports of the employment of huge families with a large total annual family income. The nine-hour day seems to prevail in this type of employment. On this basis, the report indicates that $12 per week, during the period of employment, is the average wage, and that even the group which supplements its income by non-agricultural work succeeds in raising its pay only to $15.27 per week during the period of employment. The annual income from agricultural work for the group studied was found to be $362.01. Studies made in 1927–1928, upon a somewhat different basis, indicated an average annual income then of

about $513.72. The average family income for the group investigated was
$491.12. As to living conditions, it was found that 98.2 per cent live in
"frame houses," of a type that, in the language of the report, could better
be described as "wooden shacks," only 17.7 per cent having baths. Although the workers studied worked on vegetable farms, only 12.5 per
cent received any kind of discount from their employers on the purchase
of vegetables; 67.1 per cent purchased practically no milk. The report
states that $7.89 is the average weekly food expenditure for the group
and that the average size family is 4.7 persons. The average annual family
expenditure for food alone is $412.36, or 84 per cent of the annual average
gross income, leaving only $78.76 per year, or 16 per cent of the annual
gross income, for housing, medical care, clothing, and other necessities.

Fortunately the report on living conditions was supplemented by a
report submitted by 157 farmers in the area. Of the sample, 94.3 per cent
were Japanese, 2.5 per cent Chinese, 3.2 per cent white. For the year
ending September 1, 1935, the total production for this group was
$1,007,217, or an average gross return for all farms of $6,415.39. Without
exception each class of farm—classified as to acreage—reported a net profit
for the year. For all farms, the average annual expense for paid labor was
33.3 per cent of the gross return, while average overhead expenses accounted for 50.1 per cent, of which rent, 25.7 per cent, water charges,
13.2 per cent, and fertilization, 23.7 per cent, were the chief items (on
the basis of 100 per cent for overhead charges). Most of the farmers involved, being alien Japanese, cannot lawfully own or lease agricultural
land in California. This limitation has, however, been circumvented for
years by various means: The land is owned by American-born children
or leased in the name of a citizen. The growers' report does not indicate
the facts in reference to ownership, but it is common knowledge that most
of the land in question is owned by banking interests and leased, by
various indirections, to Japanese growers. Even accepting the growers'
figures, the survey concludes with the statement that a higher rate of
wages could be paid. The report also makes an interesting statement about
the manipulation of races:

> Most of the friction generated in Southern California between the
> Mexican agricultural worker and his employers has occurred with
> the Japanese grower. *No racial animus* is connected with this
> trouble, so far as observation and inquiry will reveal. The issue
> is simply that the average Japanese grower sets a harder pace and
> pays less in proportion than the balance of the growers.

The question is: Who insists that the Japanese growers pay 22½ cents an
hour and no more for agricultural labor—the lowest average agricultural
wage in the State—in the richest county in California? It is apparent that
the interests in question are powerful enough to assure the Japanese complete immunity from the consequences of the Alien Land Law.

While the strike was in progress, Gene Masintier, "chief special
agent," filed suit in the Los Angeles courts against the Venice-Palms
Industrial Association, a group of Japanese growers. Masintier claimed

that he had been employed to take charge of thirty-four heavily armed guards recruited from a local detective agency at seven dollars a day. "I didn't mind helping break the Los Angeles Railway strike in 1934," Masintier said, "but I wouldn't ask anyone to live like those employees of the Japanese have to. When I left it had cost the Japanese about $7,000 to keep from raising wages of their field hands. The bill for saki and beer at the headquarters while I was there amounted to approximately $600." The strike lasted for about a month, and resulted in some slight gains for the workers and the execution of an agreement which has twice been renewed. The strike was led by the Mexican Federation of Agricultural and Industrial Workers, a loosely organized union of Mexican, Japanese, and Filipino workers under the leadership of William Velarde.

GUNKIST ORANGES

The wave of violence, launched by the Associated Farmers in 1934, swept on into 1935 and 1936, with organized vigilante groups crushing one strike after another.

On June 15, 1936, 2,500 Mexican orange pickers (organized as the Federation of Agricultural Workers Industrial Union—the same organization and the same leadership involved in the celery workers' strike) struck in Southern California, tying up, for several weeks, a $20,000,000 citrus crop. Vigilantism immediately began to flourish. Workers were evicted from their homes; Orange County was virtually in a state of siege, with highway traffic under police surveillance; 400 special armed guards, under the command of former "football heroes" of the University of Southern California masquerading as amateur storm troopers, were recruited; over 200 workers were arrested at the outset of the strike and herded in a stockade, or bull pen, in which the court proceedings, such as their arraignment, were conducted; bail was fixed at a prohibitive figure; and, when attorneys entered the county to defend the workers, they were arrested on petty traffic charges, followed about by armed thugs, and threatened in open court. State-highway patrolmen moved in and established a portable radio station, KAPA, by means of which armed patrols were directed throughout the region. Guards with rifles and shotguns patrolled the fields and "protected" strikebreakers, and the sheriff instructed these guards, mostly high-school and college youngsters, "to shoot to kill," his orders being enthusiastically headlined and warmly italicized in the *Los Angeles Times* and *Examiner*. Workers' camps were bombed and raided. When arrested strikers were brought into court (I was an eye witness to these proceedings), submachine guns, shotguns, rifles and revolvers were openly displayed in the courtroom. The *Los Angeles Examiner* spoke touchingly of the "quieting effect of the drastic wholesale arrests," while the *Times* gave a graphic account of one raid:

> Suddenly, late in the night, three or four automobiles, loaded with grim-faced men, appeared out of the darkness surrounding the little settlement [a workers' camp]. In a few seconds, tear gas bombs

hissed into the small building where the *asserted* strikers were in
conclave, the conferees with smarting eyes broke, and ran out
under cover of darkness and the meeting was at an end. Witnesses
said they heard the mysterious automobiles and the nightriders
whirring away without leaving a trace of their identity.

On July seventh, in a front-page story, the *Times* joyously announced
that "old vigilante days were revived in the orchards of Orange County
yesterday as one man lay near death and scores nursed injuries." The
Examiner[4] proclaimed the fact that the growers had, in addition to
State-highway patrolmen and special deputies, commissioned "bands
of men, armed with tear gas and shotguns," to conduct "open private
warfare against citrus strikers." No one who has visited a rural county
in California under these circumstances will deny the reality of the
terror that exists. It is no exaggeration to describe this state of affairs
as Fascism in practice. Judges blandly deny Constitutional rights to
defendants and hand out vagrancy sentences which approximate the
period of the harvest season. It is useless to appeal, for, by the time
the appeal is heard, the crop will be harvested. The workers are trapped,
beaten, terrorized, yet they still manage to hold out. In the Orange
County strike food trucks, sent by striker sympathizers in Los Angeles,
were hijacked and dumped on the highways.

The provocation for this vicious assault, which was carefully
directed by the local shipper-growers and the Associated Farmers, was
a union demand for forty cents an hour, together with payment of
transportation to and from work, and the correction of certain minor
grievances (the prevailing wage rate at the time was twenty cents
an hour). It should be remembered, moreover, as the growers themselves have repeatedly conceded, that orange picking involves a variety
of skilled labor. At the time of this particular strike, the growers had
just received a reduction in freight rates which resulted in an annual
saving of over $2,000,000 a year. The mass violence in Orange County
was successful in its aim, however, and the strike was broken. At the
end of the third week, the strikers began to go back to work, with
slight wage increases in some instances.

At the conclusion of the strike, one citrus grower, incensed at
the attitude of his fellow growers, published a revealing statement.[5]
Mr. Stokes pointed out that the growers, opposing the organization
of workers, were themselves the beneficiaries of many types of organized
action. In California, the owners of 309,000 citrus-growing acres, valued
at close to $618,000,000, sell their crops through the California Fruit
Growers' Exchange. This exchange picks, packs, pools, grades, ships,
and sells the orange crop. All the grower has to do is to grow the crop.
Through the Fruit Growers' Supply Company, members of the exchange
buy automobile tires, radios, fertilizer, and other types of equipment
and supplies at cost, and can obtain credit until the end of the season.

[4] July 11, 1936.
[5] "Let the Mexicans Organize!" by Frank Stokes, *The Nation*, December 19, 1936.

The Fruit Growers' Supply Company, an agency of the exchange, owns vast tracts of timber and a lumber mill, and thus buys boxes and crates at cost (over a hundred million feet of lumber are required each year for the making of exchange-box shook). As Mr. Stokes pointed out: "I irrigate my orchard with water delivered by a non-profit combination of growers. My trees are sprayed or fumigated by a non-profit partnership." The exchange even notifies the grower when he is supposed to start the smudge pots burning to protect his crop from frost. Every detail of this elaborate industrial setup has been achieved by organized action. On December 4, 1935, the winter before the Orange County strike, the fruit-exchange officials had voted themselves substantial salary increases: The general manager's salary was increased from $18,000 to $22,000 a year; the sales manager's salary was boosted from $16,200 to $18,000. Mr. Stokes made several excursions through the county during the strike:

> I found scab pickers, often high-school boys, "gloming" the "golden fruit" in the beautiful California sunshine, while mocking birds sang on the house-tops, snow-covered Mount Baldy glistened in the distance—and armed guards patrolled the groves behind long rows of "no trespassing" signs. Trucks came to the groves with empty boxes and went away with full ones—trucks with rifle barrels protruding from their cabs. Men in uniforms, mounted on motorcycles, dashed back and forth. Sirens screaming, everybody jittery, everybody damning the reds.

The Mexicans, who, according to Mr. Stokes, are as talented with "clippers" as Kreisler is with a violin, are not only exploited as workers, but as buyers. "They are looked upon as legitimate prey—for old washing machines that will not clean clothes, for old automobiles that wheeze and let down, for woolen blankets made of cotton, for last season's shop-worn wearing apparel." These are the facts, and they are stated by a grower.

SALINAS

The first major test of the organized strength of the Associated Farmers came in September, 1936, with a strike of lettuce packers in Salinas. The union involved in this strike was the Vegetable Packers Association, holding a "floating" Federal Charter from the American Federation of Labor which had been issued in 1928. Membership in the organization was restricted to white workers employed in the packing sheds. The practice in California has long been to restrict shed work to white workers; and, as far as possible, to force the Mexicans and Filipinos to work in the fields. The Vegetable Packers Union migrated: six months of the year in Imperial Valley; six months of the year in Salinas. Although the union had been involved in two serious strikes—at Salinas in 1934 (settled by arbitration) and in Imperial

Valley in February, 1935 (in connection with which two union members were killed)—it had come through the disastrous 1934 anti-union campaign in good shape. In fact, it was about the only organized group active in 1936. In September, 1936, when the agreement which had been won by arbitration in 1934 came up for renewal, the union was, in effect, locked out. It is quite apparent that the Associated Farmers, elated by the victories over the field groups, had determined to crush this one remaining organization. As a consequence of the lockout, the workers organized a strike and the $12,000,000 lettuce crop was paralyzed. The Salinas lettuce crop—"ice house lettuce" it is called—supplies about 90 per cent of the lettuce consumed in the United States. During the season, 35,000 carloads of lettuce, at the rate of 200 carloads a day, leave Salinas for shipment throughout the United States and Canada. Of 70,000 acres devoted to lettuce cultivation, two thirds of the acreage is controlled by a small group of powerful shipper-growers, who spend most of their time driving about Monterey County and gambling for stakes of ten and fifteen thousand dollars.

In the Salinas strike the battle lines were quickly formed: on the one side, the large shipper-growers directed by the Associated Farmers and most of the townspeople; and, on the other side, 3,000 white workers, some small shopkeepers and city laborers, and about 500 Filipino field workers who joined the strike. To the amazement of local residents of Salinas, the Chief of Police and the County Sheriff seemed to abdicate their respective offices, i.e., they were conspicuous by their inactivity. For the period of the strike they were supplanted by a "general staff" especially recruited for the occasion by the Associated Farmers, acting through the local shipper-grower association. The Associated Farmers rented the entire sixth floor of a local hotel where Colonel Henry Sanborn, army reserve officer and publisher of a notorious Red-baiting journal, *The American Citizen,* was given command. Colonel Sanborn, who held no official position whatever, ordered the local officers about and organized raids and directed arrests. The expense of this particular union-smashing campaign totaled about $225,000, which had been raised by an assessment of $3.00 a car on lettuce shipped from Salinas. Colonel Sanborn was carried on the payroll at $300 a month. Strikebreaking agencies in Los Angeles and San Francisco were employed and strikebreakers were shipped into Salinas from points outside the State. The meeting at which Colonel Sanborn had been designated as "co-ordinator" was attended by the Chief of the State Highway Patrol, six local sheriffs, and a representative of the office of the Attorney-General of California, all of whom had sanctioned the extra-legal employment of Colonel Sanborn. A large supply of tear gas was purchased from Federal Laboratories and consigned to Colonel Sanborn, and his staff. Over 200 rounds of tear-gas bombs were fired at strikers.

Extraordinary as were the activities of Colonel Sanborn, still more surprising tactics were to be used. On September nineteenth, the Sheriff emerged from his temporary retirement, and ordered a general mobilization of all male residents of Salinas between the ages of eighteen and forty-five, and threatened with arrest any resident who failed to respond. In this manner the celebrated "Citizens' Army" of Salinas was recruited. In the graphic description of the *Los Angeles Times:* "Three short blasts of the fire whistle repeated four times—the signal for immediate mobilization of the Salinas civilian army to put down riots—electrified the city. In automobiles and on foot, dragging shot-guns, rifles, and clubs, the men, all of whom have been sworn in as special deputy guards, began converging upon the National Guard Armory." At the armory, those of the volunteers who were not armed were given clubs which had been previously manufactured in the manual-arts department of the local high school. Two thousand five hundred men were mobilized, armed, and deputized in this manner.

The usual wholesale arrests followed; and the usual provoked violence ensued. As convoys of "hot lettuce"—the "green gold" of seventy thousand acres—began to move toward the packing houses, which were barricaded with barbed-wire entanglements and with special guards on the roofs with machine guns, picket lines were broken with tear gas. Automobiles with loudspeakers raced through the streets; one section of the town, on Babilan Street, was in a shambles after a police raid; faked "dynamite" and "arson" plots were hatched by the police, and the arrests continued. The *San Francisco Chronicle*, which, under the editorship of Mr. Paul Smith, was fairly and accurately reporting the strike, was virtually told to keep its men out of Salinas. Mr. Smith visited Salinas himself on September 24, 1936, and wrote an excellent story on the situation entitled "It DID Happen in Salinas." He found that the barricaded areas of the town resembled a military zone, and that vigilantes had marched to the Central Labor Council in Salinas and bombed it with tear gas, and that the same mob had threatened to lynch the *Chronicle's* photographer and reporter if they "didn't get the hell out of Salinas." But the strike continued. Strikebreakers were brought in from the neighboring communities and housed in stockades and military barracks. At the height of the excitement, Colonel Sanborn induced Colonel Homer Oldfield of the Ninth Army Corps, and Major Thomas J. Betts, Chief of the Intelligence Division of the Ninth Corps Area, to visit Salinas, and the Hearst press screamed: "Army Officers Rush to Salinas!" On October 16, with the strike still in effect, the press reported that the local jails were literally "filled to capacity" with strikers. But, at a staggering cost to the growers, the crop was harvested. Lettuce was shipped to Los Angeles, and there, through the low connivance of local American Federation of Labor officials, was unloaded, packed, and reloaded for shipment—by members of the American Federation of Labor. After a month, the strike was crushed, the union smashed. But though they had won the strike, the growers continued their intimidation and began to "blacklist" strikers, until they were enjoined from doing so by Federal Judge A. F. St. Sure.[6] The once powerful, compact, and militant Vegetable Packers Association was no more.

At the time of the strike, the attorney for the union sent a telegram

[6] December 21, 1936.

which warrants quotation, as it summarizes the situation in Salinas with apt brevity:

> Sinclair Lewis should be informed that it did happen in Salinas. It was directed from outside the affected zone of Monterey County. It embraces all civil governments, including courts. The State Militia and State Highway Patrol are directed by a civilian local committee acting as the head of a provisional dictatorship. It indicates long preparation, prior rehearsal and the work of men who know law and understand public psychology, as the average citizen is not conscious that it has happened. The plan would not be effective in large urban centers unless modified in certain respects. In semi-agricultural and semi-industrial communities it could crush any strike, however peaceful. Significant that the army of this provisional government tore Roosevelt campaign buttons off the lapels of citizens and trampled them under foot on the streets of Salinas, freely expressing their unexpurgated opinion of the present administration. Hearst's stooge, Colonel Sanborn, admits he is in command. Organized labor will do well to investigate.

Unfortunately the telegram was addressed to Mr. William Green of the American Federation of Labor, and, of course, no investigation was ordered.

STOCKTON

Following up their costly victory at Salinas, the Associated Farmers moved into action with renewed vigor at Stockton, California, on April 24, 1937. On February twenty-seventh and twenty-eighth, a conference of agricultural workers had been called in San Francisco, which represented the first concerted effort to map out a program and plan of action for agricultural labor. Following this conference, the Cannery Workers Union, an affiliate of the American Federation of Labor, struck the plant of the Stockton Food Products Company. Instantly the call went forth for the usual "citizens' army" and about 1,500 men were quickly mobilized for action. Colonel Walter E. Garrison, President of the Associated Farmers, arrived to take personal charge of the offensive. Sheriff Harvey Odell, of Stockton, obligingly abdicated and turned over the reins of power to Colonel Garrison. Mr. Ignatius McCarthy, tear-gas salesman, was imported to provoke trouble, and, on April twenty-fourth, a bloody riot occurred. As trucks attempted to drive through picket lines, tear-gas bombs began to explode and rifles cracked. For over an hour, 300 pickets continued to fight "coughing and choking," as "vigilantes" and "special deputies" poured round after round of tear-gas bombs at them. Fifty workers were injured; the body of one striker was "riddled with buckshot from his mouth to his abdomen." More than a hundred tear-gas bombs were hurled at the picket line by State-highway patrolmen alone, and the list of injured (all strikers) assumed the proportions of a wartime casualty list. When the Governor attempted to mediate, the head of the California Processors and Growers Association told him to mind his own business; which he did. National Guard units were mobilized at Stockton, with four companies "standing by" for service. Although the Associated Farmers conducted the offensive in this strike, who were the parties at interest? Represented on the board of directors of the California Processors and Growers are: California Packing Company; Libby, McNeil & Libby; Barron-Gray Packing Company; Santa Cruz Packing Company; H. J. Heinz Corporation; Kings County Packing Company; and Bercut-Richards Packing Co. These are the "farmers" who, "embittered" by union invasion, elected to "defend their homes." The assault, on this occasion, was so vicious that it broke all attempts to form picket lines and the strikers were soon forced to go back to work, only to be promptly sold out, in the ensuing negotiations, by Mr. Edward Vandeleur of the State Federation of Labor. Stockton, like Salinas, was a milepost in the march of the Associated Farmers to crush union labor in the fields and packing plants.

THE UNITED FARMERS OF THE PACIFIC COAST

A marked change has recently taken place in the activities of the Associated Farmers. In the fall of 1936, the maritime unions struck and tied up the Pacific Coast ports for ninety days. At the beginning of the strike, the farmers were not immediately affected, and, consequently, remained silent. But, toward the end of the strike, when farm products began to arrive in the port of San Francisco for shipment, the farmers moved into action. On January 15, 1937, the Associated Farmers announced that they had mobilized an army of 10,000 "farmers" to march on San Francisco and open the port. Promised police protection by Mayor Rossi and Governor Merriam, it is possible that the "march on San Francisco" was planned in all seriousness and, but for the termination of the strike, would have been executed. The threat was highly significant as an indication of the close co-operation that now exists between the Industrial Association of San Francisco and the Associated Farmers, the two groups functioning now as a single unit. Similar evidence of this unofficial merger has been brought to light recently in the form of recent joint conferences and united-action programs.

On December 7, 1937, the Associated Farmers held an annual convention at San Jose. At this convention it was decided to enlarge the organization and, to this end, the United Farmers of the Pacific Coast was formed. The new organization boasts a large membership in Oregon, Washington, and Arizona. Representatives have been sent to organize similar groups in the Middle West and a Minnesota "Associated Farmers" unit announces a membership of one thousand. Another significant development at the San Jose convention was the concern which the growers evidenced over the problem of transportation. More and more, industrial farming is becoming dependent upon trucking; and, as this dependence increases, the interests of the "farmers" tend to merge with those of the city industrialist. The distinction between farm and city is practically meaningless in California today, and, as I have tried to show, the farms are factories. Inevitably, the Associated Farmers are being drawn into conflict with two powerful labor groups: the teamsters and the maritime workers. At the San Jose convention, a special organization, Producers Protective League, was organized for the express purpose of "controlling transportation" and keeping the "life lines" open from farm factory to city market. Today it is merely a question of time until the Associated Farmers come into headlong conflict with the teamsters' union and with the maritime unions. Eventually, the maritime unions will refuse to handle farm products as "hot cargo" and when this time comes, Californians may prepare to witness a struggle of the first magnitude.

The annual report of the Associated Farmers for 1937 contains several significant statements. The organization was formed, according to the president, to fight Communism, but today, by force of national developments, it is necessarily "opposing unionization of farm labor on any basis." Continuing, he states that the program of the organization is being converted from a defensive to an aggressive plan of action. "We cannot wait until racketeers begin organizing the packing houses and the pickers in the fields. We must oppose them now, before it is too late." The organization, he said, no longer regards itself as a temporary group formed to meet an emergency, but as a permanent organization dedicated to prevent the unionization of farm labor. "If the fight wipes out our entire crop, it would be cheap." The new offensive program could not be explained to the members for "strategic reasons" but they were asked to accept it implicitly on the "good faith" of the leaders.

Significantly, fiery crosses began to burn on the hilltops of Central California, in March, 1938.

Suggestions for Further Reading

For a survey of the Depression, see Dixon Wecter, *The Age of the Great Depression, 1929–1941* (Macmillan, 1949), and Frederick Lewis Allen, *Since Yesterday** (Harper and Row, 1940). Several excellent documentary collections dealing with the Depression years are available, including David A. Shannon (ed.), *The Great Depression** (Prentice-Hall, 1960); Daniel Aaron and Robert Bendiner (eds.), *The Strenuous Decade: A Social and Intellectual Record of the Nineteen-Thirties** (Doubleday, 1970); and Louis Filler (ed.), *The Anxious Years: America in the 1930's** (Putnam's, 1963). Bernard Sternsher has edited two volumes of studies related to specific aspects of the Depression: *The Negro in Depression and War: Prelude to Revolution** (Quadrangle, 1969) and *Hitting Home: The Great Depression in Town and Country** (Quadrangle, 1970). An interesting oral approach to the history of the era is taken in Studs Terkel (ed.), *Hard Times: An Oral History of the Great Depression* (Pantheon, 1970).

For the history of the labor movement during the Depression, see Irving Bernstein, *Turbulent Years: A History of the American Worker, 1933–1941* (Houghton-Mifflin, 1970). An important labor dispute of the period is described in Sidney Fine, *Sit-Down: The General Motors Strike of 1936–1937* (University of Michigan Press, 1969). In *Middletown in Transition** (Harcourt Brace Jovanovich, 1937), Robert and Helen Lynd describe the impact of the Depression on Muncie, Indiana.

The position of blacks in the rural South during the Depression is the subject of Charles S. Johnson, *Shadow of the Plantation** (University of Chicago Press, 1934). On the general economic condition of American blacks in this period, see Raymond Wolters, *Negroes and the Great Depression: The Problem of Economic Recovery** (Greenwood, 1970). For the condition of tenant farmers during the same period, see Arthur F. Raper, *Preface to Peasantry** (University of North Carolina Press, 1934). David Conrad is concerned with the small farmer and the New Deal in *The Forgotten Farmer: The Story of Share Croppers and the New Deal* (University of Illinois Press, 1965). In *Scottsboro: A Tragedy of the American South* (Louisiana State University Press, 1969), Dan T. Carter examines the complex events that surrounded the most famous race trial of the 1930's. For a first-hand view of the same case, see the autobiographical *Scottsboro Boy** (Doubleday, 1950), by Haywood Patterson and Earl Conrad. Agrarian socialism is described in Jerold Auerbach, "Southern Tenant Farmers: Socialist Critics of the New Deal," *Labor History*, Vol. 7 (Winter, 1966), 3–18.

* Available in paperback edition.

Carey McWilliams treats the problems of migrant labor in *Ill Fares the Land: Migrants and Migratory Labor in the United States* (Little, Brown, 1942). A powerful fictional treatment of attempts to organize farm workers in California is John Steinbeck's *In Dubious Battle** (Viking, 1938). The classic statement on the westward movement of poor migrants is John Steinbeck's monumental novel *Grapes of Wrath** (Viking, 1939). For a general study of the homeless wanderers who proliferated during the Depression, see Henry Hill Collins, *America's Own Refugees: Our 4,000,000 Homeless Migrants* (Princeton University Press, 1941). The continuing problems of migrant workers are considered in Dale Wright, *They Harvest Despair: The Migrant Farm Worker* (Beacon, 1965), and in T. E. Moore, *The Slaves We Rent* (Random House, 1965).

The Second World War and After

Pearl Harbor and the Activation of Anti-Japanese Sentiment in California

JACOBUS tenBROEK, EDWARD N. BARNHART, and FLOYD W. MATSON

In 1882, when Congress passed the Chinese Exclusion Act which virtually ended Chinese immigration to the United States, there were fewer than two hundred Japanese in this country. The exclusion of the Chinese, however, produced a drastic shortage of labor on the West Coast, thus stimulating immigration from Japan. Although the rulers of Japan had long been opposed to emigration (in fact, prior to 1854 it was a crime punishable by death), in the late nineteenth century they were persuaded to change their policy, and there was a large movement of Japanese citizens into the Western Hemisphere. In the first ten years of the twentieth century, over ninety thousand Japanese entered the United States.

The immigrants were at first welcomed because they filled necessary slots in the expanding economy, but antagonisms quickly began to mount. Since the turn of the century, Japan had been rising to prominence as a world power, and many Californians saw the influx of Japanese laborers as a prelude to invasion by the Japanese state. Workingmen's groups, fearing competition from foreign labor, worked with an inflammatory press and opportunistic politicians to have the Japanese excluded from the United States along with the Chinese under the act of 1882. In 1900, the Japanese government consented to curb the emigration of labor to the United States by denying passports to would-be emigrants. Then, in 1907, when the Japanese government protested the increasing racial discrimination faced by the Japanese in California, President Theodore Roosevelt arrived at what was called the "Gentlemen's Agreement" with the rulers of Japan, under which both the United States and Japan were to take measures to stop immigration between the two countries. Finally, virtually all immigration from East Asia was permanently halted by the Immigration Act of 1924.

Because the Naturalization Act of 1790 had limited the privilege of naturalization to "free white persons," East Asian migrants to this country legally remained "aliens." This condition was used against them when California passed the Alien Land Act of 1913 barring "aliens ineligible for citizenship" from owning land in the state. Meanwhile, other discriminatory practices were spreading in the West. Many of the stereotypes that white Americans had developed with regard to the Chinese were transferred to the Japanese. They were accused of being devious, unreliable, and dishonest. They were seen as a threat to Christian civilization, to the democratic way of life, to the virtue of white women. Because of the fear of "moral contamination," the San Francisco School Board barred Japanese children from public schools in 1906. The racism inherent in the attitudes of the dominant whites of the West was demonstrated in increased agitation against the "yellow peril."

In the 1930's, Japanese incursions into China built up increasing hostility toward the Japanese-Americans living on the West Coast. Then, on December 7, 1941, when the Japanese bombed Pearl Harbor, shock and outrage swept over the American people—much of which was to be vented on the West Coast Japanese. On the eve of the war, there were 126,947 persons of Japanese ancestry living in the United States, 112,935 of whom were concentrated in the states of California, Oregon, Washington, and Arizona. Of the latter group, 41,089 were foreign born, or Issei; the remainder were Nisei, citizens of the United States who were born in this country to foreign-born parents.

In the early months of 1942, the war went well for the Japanese army and navy in the Pacific but badly for the Japanese residents of the United States. Racist feelings were intensified by wild rumors of sabotage and espionage, and a variety of groups demanded the expulsion of Japanese-Americans from the West Coast. Then, under the direction of the United States Army and the War Relocation Authority set up by President Franklin Roosevelt, the Japanese living along the coast were urged to move from their homes to "resettlement centers" in the nation's interior. When voluntary relocation failed, the army forcibly moved over one hundred thousand persons to the centers and held them there under armed guard. Gradually, the "security" of the camps relaxed, and many of the prisoners—none of whom had been proven guilty of disloyalty—were allowed to work and to move around outside the so-called critical areas. In 1944, some Japanese-Americans were allowed to return to the coast; and in 1946, the last of the shameful internment camps was closed.

In their book entitled **Prejudice, War and the Constitution,** three scholars from the University of California at Berkeley, the late Jacobus tenBroek, Edward N. Barnhart, and Floyd W. Matson, examine the forced evacuation of the Japanese-Americans during the Second World War. The following selection from this book describes the process by which existing hostilities toward the Japanese were activated by the attack on Pearl Harbor. It was the anti-Japanese hysteria generated in the early months of the war that led ultimately to the unconstitutional imprisonment of tens of thousands of Americans.

Half a century of agitation and antipathy directed against Japanese Americans, following almost fifty years of anti-Chinese and antiforeign activity, had by 1941 diffused among the West Coast population a rigidly stereotyped set of attitudes toward Orientals which centered on suspicion and distrust. This hostility reached maturity in the early twenties with the passage of the Alien Land Law and the Oriental Exclusion Act, and although thereafter it became relatively inactive it was kept alive during the thirties by the stimuli of Japanese aggression and economic depression. In the weeks and months following the attack upon Pearl Harbor the traditional charges were widely revived and the stereotype recalled in detail; public attitudes toward the Japanese minority soon crystallized around the well-worn themes of treachery and disloyalty, and expressions of opinion came more and more to be characterized by suspicion, fear, and anger.

The Japanese stereotype was not created at Pearl Harbor; the basic ingredients had been mixed years before. But the enemy bombs of December 7 exploded the mixture on a vaster scale and with more far-reaching consequences than ever in the past. The rumors that emerged from Pearl Harbor gave new sustenance to racist belief in the yellow peril, to romantic movie-fed ideas of the treacherous and inscrutable Asiatic, to undefined feelings of hostility and distrust compounded of the xenophobia of superpatriots and the rationalizations of competitors. Once revitalized by enemy bombs, however, the Japanese stereotype had no need to depend upon the myth of sabotage at Pearl Harbor. Long after the rumors had been disproved, by repeated refutations from the highest authorities, the stereotype remained and Americans along the Western slope and far inland were more suspicious, fearful, and angry than ever before. The very absence of anything resembling subversive activity by resident Japanese was seized upon as "disturbing and confirming" evidence that an "invisible deadline" of disaster was approaching. As weeks passed, the superstructure of rationalizations and defenses built upon this foundation grew more insensibly elaborate.

"Pearl Harbor and the Activation of Anti-Japanese Sentiment in California." From Jacobus tenBroek, Edward N. Barnhart, and Floyd W. Matson, *Prejudice, War and the Constitution: Causes and Consequences of the Evacuation of the Japanese Americans in World War II* (Berkeley: University of California Press, 1954), pp. 68–96. Reprinted by permission of The Regents of the University of California.

DECEMBER: WAR AND RUMORS OF WAR

The Japanese attack on Pearl Harbor came as a profound shock, if not a complete surprise, to residents of the Pacific Coast states. Although for many years most citizens had been aware that war was a possibility, many refused to believe the first reports from Honolulu and were convinced only by repeated broadcasts and ubiquitous black headlines. But the full import of the news soon became apparent as all service personnel was ordered to report to stations, as jeeps and convoys in war regalia appeared on the streets, and military aircraft began to roar overhead. By midafternoon of December 7, 1941, thousands of citizens were rushing to recruiting stations to enlist or offering their services in any capacity.

Before they could recover from the initial shock, West Coast residents were confronted with more bad news. Coincident with the Pearl Harbor attack enemy forces had struck with disastrous effect at Hong Kong, Manila, Thailand, Singapore, Midway, Wake, and Guam. Japanese bombers had at a single blow destroyed the air defenses of Hong Kong, and within a few days occupied Kowloon peninsula and placed the British crown colony in jeopardy. On December 10 the "impregnable" British warships *Repulse* and *Prince of Wales* were sunk by Japanese planes, thus upsetting the balance of naval power in the far Pacific. The little kingdom of Thailand had surrendered on December 8, and the enemy began a swift southward movement through the British Malay states toward Singapore. Other Japanese troops landed in the Philippines on December 10 and were converging on Manila. Guam was captured on December 11, the fate of Wake Island appeared sealed (it fell on December 23), and Midway was imperiled by an enemy task force. Meanwhile, dispatches which had filtered through censorship suggested that American losses at Pearl Harbor were far worse than at first indicated. It was freely predicted that Alaska and the Pacific Coast itself were next in line for Japanese attack and even attempted invasion.

People everywhere were frightened, and their fear was heightened by a feeling of helplessness. The threat of bombings and invasion, plus the absence of precise information as to events in Hawaii, quickly bred rumors of total disaster. It was whispered that the entire Pacific fleet had been destroyed; that every reinforcing ship sent out from the mainland had been sunk off the coast by Japanese submarines.

Almost at once rumors about the resident Japanese began. Japanese gardeners were said to be equipped with short-wave transmitters hidden in garden hose; Japanese servants and laborers who failed to appear for work on December 7 (a Sunday) were accused of prior knowledge of the Hawaii attack. Japanese farmers were charged with smuggling poison into vegetables bound for market, and cans of seafood imported from Japan were said to contain particles of ground glass. Signaling devices similar to those reported found in Hawaii were alleged to have been set up in coastal areas. A number of anxious Californians, according to one report, went so far as to plow up "a beautiful field of flowers on the property of a Japanese farmer," because "it seems the Jap was a fifth columnist and had grown his flowers in a way that when viewed from a plane formed an arrow pointing the direction to the airport."[1]

These rumors and accusations arose largely as a result of the stories of fifth-column activity at Pearl Harbor which were rapidly accumulating in the press. After an inspection of the Pacific base, Secretary of the Navy Knox was quoted as saying that sabotage at Pearl Harbor constituted "the most effective fifth-column work that's come out of this war, except in Norway." Newspaper headlines on the Knox report generally stressed this aspect: "Secretary of Navy Blames Fifth Columnists for the Raid," "Fifth Column Prepared Attack," "Fifth Column Treachery Told." Other stories told of secret signalling and faked air-raid alerts by Hawaiian Japanese at the time of the attack, of arrows cut in the cane fields to aid enemy pilots, and roadblocks improvised to tie up military traffic.[2]

In opposition to the rumors and scare stories was a succession of official assurances that all dangerous enemy aliens had been apprehended, that necessary precautions had already been taken, and that Japanese Americans as a whole were loyal to the United States. This viewpoint was, moreover, echoed in the editorials of most California newspapers during the first days of war. Despite these assurances, however, Americans became increasingly restive as the prospect of Japanese attack or invasion grew more plausible. For half a century they had heard of the treachery and deceitfulness of resident Japanese—of how the "Japs" were concentrated in strategic areas of the state; of how by "peaceful invasion" they hoped to take over first California and ultimately the nation; of how they formed a network of spies and soldiers in disguise, patiently awaiting the Imperial signal to rise against the white man.[3]

The news from the battle-fronts, recording new Allied losses almost daily, made the most alarmist forebodings seem realistic. Charges of fifth-column plots multiplied rapidly and broadened in scope, soon including the mainland as well as Hawaii, and possible future actions as well as past events. It was reported, for example, that a Los Angeles naval sentry had seen signal lights in a Japanese waterfront colony; that the suicide of a Japanese doctor had uncovered a spy ring in the same area; that members of the notorious Black Dragon Society had been planted in cities and fishing communities; that the fifth-column character of Japanese schools in America had been exposed. The halls of Congress echoed with such exposures; Senator Guy Gillette of Iowa warned that "Japanese groups in this coun-

---

[1] Los Angeles *Herald,* December 9, 1941; Sacramento *Bee,* December 17, 1941; San Francisco *Examiner,* December 29, 1941.

[2] Los Angeles *Times,* December 10, 13, 16, 1941; Los Angeles *Examiner,* December 13, 1941; San Francisco *Chronicle,* December 16, 1941; San Francisco *Examiner,* December 16, 1941. Cf. *Wartime Exile: The Exclusion of the Japanese Americans from the West Coast,* U.S. Department of Interior, War Relocation Authority (Processed; Washington, 1946), pp. 102–03.

[3] A secondary cause of apprehension among Americans was the memory of Nazi fifth-column successes in Norway and France, which made more plausible the stories of Japanese fifth-columnism at Pearl Harbor. See *Impounded People: Japanese Americans in the Relocation Centers,* U.S. Department of Interior, War Relocation Authority (Processed; Washington, 1946), p. 3.

try planned sabotage and subversive moves," and Congressman Martin Dies of Texas announced the discovery of a book revealing Japanese plans to attack the United States.[4]

Meanwhile the war was being brought steadily closer to home. On December 20 it was announced that Japanese submarines were attacking West Coast shipping; and on the same day two tankers were reportedly torpedoed off California. Two days later newspapers told of the shelling of a freighter by an enemy sub near Santa Barbara; the next day two more tankers were said to have been attacked off the California coast. Residents of the coastal states began to feel that their shores were under virtual blockade by enemy submarines.

The refugees from Hawaii, arriving in late December, brought new rumors of sabotage by island Japanese on December 7. It was said that Japanese had placed obstructions on the road to Pearl Harbor to keep reinforcements from getting through; that they had sabotaged the planes on the landing fields; that one group had entered Hickam Field in a milk truck, let down the sides, and turned machine guns on American pilots as they ran to their planes.[5]

Impressive "confirmation" of these rumors was contained in a sensational dispatch by a United Press correspondent, Wallace Carroll, who visited Honolulu shortly after the attack. Repeating with an air of authority most of the charges made by Honolulu refugees, the report declared that numbers of Hawaii Japanese had had advance knowledge of the bombing, and that Japanese produce merchants delivering to warships had been able to report on United States fleet movements. Carroll speculated that newspaper advertisements placed by Japanese firms may have been coded messages, and asserted that the enemy raiders had been aided by improvised roadblocks and arrows cut in the cane fields. The hands of Japanese pilots shot down during the assault were, he said, adorned with the rings of Honolulu high schools and of Oregon State University. The dispatch continued:

> Japanese of American nationality infiltrated into the Police Departments and obtained jobs as road supervisors, sanitary inspectors or minor government officials. Many went to work in the postoffice and telephone service, ideal posts for spies. . . .
> An American resident, who had studied Japanese methods in Manchuria and North China, told me that the Japanese fifth column and espionage organizations in the islands were similar to those which had been used to undermine the Chinese.[6]

Accounts such as this, together with reports of new Allied reverses and tales of atrocities in the Philippines, goaded some Filipino Americans

---

[4] Sacramento *Bee*, December 17, 1941; Los Angeles *Times*, December 18, 19, 1941; Fresno *Bee*, December 16, 1941; Los Angeles *Examiner*, December 18, 19, 20, 1941.
[5] *Wartime Exile*, pp. 102–03.
[6] New York *Times*, December 31, 1941. [© 1941 by The New York Times Company. Reprinted by permission.]

into direct retaliation against their Japanese neighbors. On December 23 a Japanese American, honorably discharged from the United States Army, was found stabbed to death on a Los Angeles sidewalk; his assailants were reported to be Filipinos. On Christmas Day in Stockton, windows of numerous Japanese business houses were smashed, assertedly by gangs of Filipinos. The next day in the same city an alien Japanese garage attendant was shot to death by a Filipino; newspapers prominently featured the incident, under such headlines as "Jap, Filipino District Under Guard; 1 Slain," "Stockton Jap Killed by Filipino; Riots Feared; Area Under Guard." By the end of December similar incidents were publicized almost daily. On December 29, a Japanese waiter was shot to death by a Filipino in Chicago. On December 30 an alien Japanese was shot and wounded in Sacramento; on New Year's Day a Japanese and his wife were murdered in the Imperial Valley. Other cases were reported from Gilroy and Livermore, and even from Utah.[7]

Thus, within the first three weeks of war, the familiar Japanese stereotype was again visible on the Pacific Coast, and aroused individuals and groups were militantly reacting to it. The surprise attack of December 7, occurring in the midst of peace negotiations, seemed a definite confirmation of the old remembered tales of Japanese deceitfulness. Although for a time many citizens were reluctant to blame resident Japanese for the actions of Japan, and newspaper comment frequently was on the side of tolerance, the accumulating "evidence" of sabotage and espionage gradually put an end to toleration. Popular anger and apprehension rose in proportion to the continuing successes of the enemy, and by the end of 1941 suspicion and animosity were the most frequently expressed attitudes toward the Japanese Americans.

JANUARY: THE GATHERING STORM

January was another month of disasters for the Allies and frustrations for the people at home, Manila fell to the Japanese on January 2, and an outnumbered American garrison began its struggle at Bataan and on Corregidor, with little hope of reinforcement. Japanese troops were advancing through Malay jungles to the crucial port of Singapore. Borneo was invaded and the entire East Indies came under attack. The scattered islands of the far Pacific were falling before the enemy with incredible rapidity; there were landings in New Guinea, and Australia was directly menaced. At home, reports continued of West Coast shipping attacked by enemy submarines; and off the Eastern coast the Germans were rapidly intensifying their U-boat warfare and had torpedoed several Allied vessels.

In this atmosphere of frustration, fear, and anger, popular sentiment on the West Coast in the first month of 1942 was concentrated more and more against resident Japanese. Although the official restrictions on

[7] Oakland *Tribune*, December 23, 27, 1941; San Francisco *Examiner*, December 27, 1941, January 2, 1942; Los Angeles *News*, December 30, 1941; *Nichi Bei*, December 31, 1941; Stockton *Record*, January 3, 1942.

enemy-alien activity had been directed impartially at Germans, Italians, and Japanese, in the popular mind the Japanese were special targets of suspicion. Their Oriental appearance marked them inescapably in an area whose greatest danger was from the Far Eastern end of the Axis. Acts of violence against Japanese Americans continued to be reported in the press from such widely separate areas as Seattle, Fresno, Sacramento, and Santa Maria. Front-page attention was given FBI raids and arrests of Japanese allegedly possessing contraband. Popular tensions were increased by the charge in the Roberts Committee report that espionage in Hawaii had centered in the Japanese consulate, and that through its intelligence service the Japanese had obtained complete information on Pearl Harbor. The principal effect of such disclosures, however they were intended, was strongly to support the rumors of disloyalty among Japanese in Hawaii and to cast further doubt upon the loyalty of Japanese along the coast.[8]

Early in January prominent voices began to call for more vigorous steps to control the resident Japanese, including their mass removal from the West Coast.[9] News commentators, editorial writers, and public officials expressed displeasure at the "indecision and inaction" of the Department of Justice and urged drastic measures. John B. Hughes, a Los Angeles commentator for the Mutual Broadcasting Company, gained prominence as the first widely heard newsman to press the subject of evacuation. In the first of a month-long series of anti-Japanese broadcasts, Hughes compared the treatment of local Japanese with that of Americans captured by Japanese armies and warned that the failure to adopt strong measures would result in "disaster to the Pacific Coast." In subsequent commentaries he lent his support to rumors of espionage and fifth-column activities, charging that United States Japanese had contributed funds to Japan's war chest and hinting that the control of California's vegetable output was a part of the over-all Japanese war plan.[10]

Hughes also entered into a correspondence with Attorney General Biddle in which he urged the internment of both aliens and citizens of Japanese ancestry. "Persons who know the Japanese on the west coast," he wrote, "will estimate that ninety percent or more of American-born Japanese are primarily loyal to Japan." The commentator's justification for this indictment was the old yellow peril thesis of race: "Their organization and patient preparation and obedience to unified control could never be possible among the nationals of any Caucasian people. The Japanese are a far greater menace in our midst than any other axis patriots. They will die joyously for the honor of Japan." As a clincher, a justification was offered which was to be frequently advanced by proponents of evacuation: "There was an old law in the West, the law of the Vigilantes.

---

[8] [Report of the Roberts Commission on Pearl Harbor], New York *Times,* January 25, 1942, p. 2.

[9] At least one newspaper had openly urged evacuation early in December. The San Luis Obispo *Independent* recommended mass removal of the Japanese on December 12, but the suggestion was not then supported by other journals.

[10] "News and Views by John B. Hughes" (Transcript of broadcasts), January 5, 6, 7, 9, 19, 20, 1942 (Study files).

Its whole code was: Shoot first and argue later. That code will be invoked, I'm afraid, unless authorities formulate a policy, an adequate policy, and put it into effect."[11]

The calculated purpose of the Hughes campaign, like others which followed it in the press and on the air, was to persuade the public to demand a policy of action toward the local Japanese: specifically, that of rounding them up and removing them from the coast. This policy of exclusion, frequently urged in conjunction with demands for internment, had a threefold appeal: first, in the light of what the public feared from the Japanese (espionage and sabotage) it seemed a perfect remedy; second, it offered an outlet for the public's antipathy toward the resident Japanese by urging forceful action against them; and finally, it offered an opportunity for action, a chance to "do something," to a population fretting to strike back against Japan but so far offered no chance for direct action.

Hughes was not long in finding company among newspapermen. By the end of January a radical shift had taken place in the editorial position of California newspapers. During the first month of war these journals had for the most part been tolerant if not sympathetic toward the Japanese in America; but in the following three weeks unfavorable comment gradually increased to the point where it equaled expressions of tolerance. In the last days of January the trend suddenly accelerated and pro-Japanese utterances were lost in a barrage of denunciation—which centered on charges of Japanese disloyalty, demands for strict control measures, and growing sentiment for mass evacuation.[12]

The keynote of the evacuation demands was sounded by the San Diego *Union*, one of the first major journals to press the issue, which opened a sustained editorial campaign on January 20 with arguments drawn largely from fifth-column rumors:

> In Hawaii and in the Philippines treachery by residents, who although of Japanese ancestry had been regarded as loyal, has played an important part in the success of Japanese attacks. . . .
>
> Every Japanese—for the protection of those who are loyal to us and for our protection against those who are not—should be moved out of the coastal area and to a point of safety far enough inland to nullify any inclinations they may have to tamper with our safety here.

In subsequent editorials the *Union* dwelt on the evils of Japanese citizenship, maintained that there was no way of determining the loyalty of "our so-called American citizens of Japanese ancestry," and exclaimed: "We are confronted on both sides by enemies who have devoted their entire careers to development of treachery, deceit, and sabotage. We can

[11] Letter, Hughes to Biddle, January 19, 1942 (Study files).
[12] From a quantitative analysis of newspaper comment undertaken by the University of California Evacuation and Resettlement Study (Study files).

afford to be neither soft-headed nor soft-hearted in dealing with them or their agents."[13]

The Hearst newspapers on the Pacific Coast, which in earlier years had led in the agitation against resident Japanese, did not conspicuously join the editorial clamor for evacuation—although news articles frequently were slanted against the Japanese.[14] But it was in the Hearst press that the first of numerous syndicated columns condemning the Japanese minority was published. On January 29, Henry McLemore, a former sports reporter, wrote from Los Angeles:

> The only Japanese apprehended have been the ones the FBI actually had something on. The rest of them, so help me, are free as birds. There isn't an airport in California that isn't flanked by Japanese farms. There is hardly an air field where the same situation doesn't exist. . . .
>
> I know this is the melting pot of the world and all men are created equal and there must be no such thing as race or creed hatred, but do those things go when a country is fighting for its life? Not in my book. No country has ever won a war because of courtesy and I trust and pray we won't be the first because of the lovely, gracious spirit. . . .
>
> I am for immediate removal of every Japanese on the West Coast to a point deep in the interior. I don't mean a nice part of the interior either. Herd 'em up, pack 'em off and give 'em the inside room in the badlands. Let 'em be pinched, hurt, hungry and dead up against it. . . .
>
> Personally, I hate the Japanese. And that goes for all of them.[15]

The mood of the McLemore attack was not widely evident in editorial comment prior to February. But the "Letters to the Editor" columns of many newspapers in the last weeks of January showed a rising tide of anti-Japanese feeling along the coast. In these informal communications, more graphically than elsewhere, the myths and slanders of bygone years were dusted off and put on display. The Sacramento *Bee* printed a letter from one of its readers who invoked the ancient battle-cry "America for Americans," and complained that Japanese were "forcing other races off the land, including whites from pioneer families." A letter in the Santa Rosa *Press Democrat* asked: "Biologically and economically, is the Jap fitted to mingle in American life?" and asserted that "when our trouble is over they must be returned to their rising sun." Another Sacramento reader declared that Japanese American citizens would "betray the land

---

[13] January 22, 31, February 3, 1942.

[14] A few newspapers were more explicit than the Hearst chain in avoiding the anti-Japanese agitation. Among these was the San Francisco *Chronicle*, which on February 1 published a front-page editorial pleading for nondiscrimination against Japanese Americans and directly opposing the idea of mass evacuation.

[15] San Francisco *Examiner*, January 20, 1942.

of their birth . . . simply because they are treacherous and barbarous by nature." A Native Daughter of the Golden West asked: "Did God make the Jap as He did the snake, did you hear the hiss before the words left his mouth? Were his eyes made slanting and the hiss put between his lips to warn us to be on our guard?" A San Francisco reader urged the authorities to "put all the Japs in camps. . . . First thing you know they will be pulling another surprise on us."[16]

The rapid increase of anti-Japanese sentiment during January had its effect in political circles. The first official body to make an issue of Japanese loyalty was the California legislature, which had earlier maintained a tolerant and even sympathetic attitude toward Japanese residents.

In December the legislature had approved a joint resolution urging federal officials "to prevent any and all racial discrimination in the National Defense Program" and declaring that "racial discrimination has no place . . . in our concept of American Democracy." But on January 14 two resolutions reflecting an altered sentiment were introduced in the state senate, one calling for an investigation of the Alien Land Law and the other creating a committee to study employment of Japanese American citizens by the state. Three days later the senate unanimously adopted a resolution to "investigate any and all possible evasions of the Alien Land Laws and to prosecute to the utmost . . . any violations that may be discovered." Resurrecting the anti-Oriental arguments of earlier generations, the resolution asserted that the land laws of 1913 and 1920 had been passed because of "the clash of two races and two civilizations, socially and economically incompatible." It was stated that the acts had been circumvented "by subterfuge" until they were "a virtual nullity"; moreover, Japanese aliens were said to be in control of large areas of land near vital installations, constituting "a menace to National defense, to the citizens of this State and Nation, and to the American grower and dealer."[17]

On January 17, the California senate also passed without dissent a measure aimed at Japanese employees of the state. Claiming that numbers of state workers appeared to "possess dual citizenship," the bill called upon the State Personnel Board to prevent the employment of anyone "who is not loyal to the United States and to . . . provide for the dismissal from the [state civil] service of such persons as may be proved to be disloyal to the United States."[18] Although Japanese were not directly named in the bill, all the lawmakers who spoke on the proposal referred openly to the need for examining the loyalty of Japanese American employees. Senators Jack Metzger and John Harold Swan, coauthors of the bill, produced a photostatic copy of a payroll sheet of the State Motor Vehicle Department which contained only Japanese names, and Senator

[16] Sacramento *Bee*, January 20, February 2, 1942; Santa Rosa *Press Democrat*, January 18, 25, 1942; San Francisco *Examiner*, January 30, 1942.

[17] Assembly Joint Resolution 3, California Legislature, 54th (First Extraordinary) Session, 1941; *Senate Daily Journal*, pp. 133, 141, 190, *passim*.

[18] Senate Concurrent Resolution 15, California Legislature, 54th (First Extraordinary) Session, 1942.

Swan purported to see in this "a systematic plot to get Japanese on the state payroll and allow them to bore from within." Senator Metzger contributed to the fifth-column rumors by charging that "Japanese fifth columnists in milk wagons drew machine guns instead of milk bottles out of twenty-one wagons in Honolulu the morning of December 7 and turned them on Pearl Harbor barracks." Later the same senator was reported as saying: "I don't believe there is a single Japanese in the world who is not pulling for Japan. They will spy, commit sabotage, or die if necessary."[19]

In the national capital, outcries against the Japanese Americans began to be heard from West Coast congressmen late in January. As in other circles, congressional discussion during the first six weeks of war had generally shown confidence in the loyalty and integrity of resident Japanese.[20] An early harbinger of changing attitudes among West Coast congressmen was the insertion into the *Congressional Record* by Congressman Leland Ford of Los Angeles of an anti-Japanese telegram from movie actor Leo Carillo, which read in part: "Why wait until [the Japanese] pull something before we act. . . . Let's get them off the coast into the interior. . . . May I urge you in behalf of the safety of the people of California to start action at once."[21]

Ford was also the first congressman to urge the cause of evacuation from the floor. On January 20 he called attention to alleged fifth-column activities among California Japanese and asserted that "a patriotic native-born Japanese, if he wants to make his contribution, will submit himself to a concentration camp." In the following thirty days bitter charges against the Japanese were voiced in Congress at least ten times, the assertion of Congressman Homer Angell of Oregon being typical: "We must wake up, and if we do not wake up and protect ourselves from this menace something infinitely worse than Pearl Harbor will be enacted on our very shores."[22]

During January, meanwhile, as military reverses in the Pacific intensified the fear of invasion and sabotage, as fifth-column rumors gained an ever-widening audience and prominent public figures wavered in their initial tolerance, those private organizations on the Pacific Coast which

---

[19] Oakland *Tribune*, February 3, 1942; *Wartime Exile*, p. 104. Following the activity of Senators Swan and Metzger, the State Personnel Board voted to bar "citizens, naturalized citizens, or native-born citizens who are descendants of nationals with whom the United States is at war" pending a loyalty investigation. See California, State Personnel Board, *Minutes of Meeting*, January 28, 1942 (Processed; Sacramento, 1942). Questionnaires were later sent to all employed or eligible personnel with names that "sounded Japanese" (San Francisco *Call-Bulletin*, February 18, 1942); dismissals were underway even before the questionnaires could be returned.

[20] See speech by Congressman John Coffee of Washington one day after Pearl Harbor, in *Congressional Record*, December 8, 1941, p. A55584. See also *ibid.*, December 10, 1941, p. 9630; December 16, 1941, p. A5706.

[21] Letter, Carillo to Ford, January 6, 1942 (Study files).

[22] Letter, Ford to Hoover and Knox, January 16, 1942 (Study files); *Congressional Record*, February 18, 1942, p. 1457.

had traditionally prospered on the issue of anti-Orientalism were quick to seize the new advantage and exploit public fears. The composition of the pressure groups which became most active in the new anti-Japanese movement was not, however, identical with that of earlier crusades. Although most of the well-known names were again in evidence (the American Legion, the Native Sons, the Farm Bureau, the Joint Immigration Committee), to these were added the names of other organizations either recently formed or newly converted to the movement. As in previous years, the particular motives of the wartime pressure groups were varied and complex, but they were alike in resorting readily and monotonously to the familiar stereotypes—racial, social, and economic—which in the past had proved so successful in enlisting public support.

The common attitude of these bodies in the first weeks after Pearl Harbor was expressed in the words of a Joint Immigration Committee official: "This is our time to get things done that we have been trying to get done for a quarter of a century."[23] The JIC, still acting with the support of the Native Sons and the California Department of the Legion, singled out for primary emphasis the evil of Japanese American "dual citizenship." In addition, the committee summarized twenty years of anti-Japanese activity in a public manifesto dispatched to California newspapers on January 2. The release observed that "reported fifth column activities by Japanese residents of Hawaii and the Philippine Islands . . . [have] brought to the fore California's effort over the years to find a solution to the Japanese immigration question." The JIC, it said, had "for years struggled to educate the American public" to its views on the Japanese problem: "Now, the problem is not alone California's. It belongs to the nation." Repeating the familiar charge that Japanese are "totally unassimilable," the proclamation declared that "those born in this country are American citizens by right of birth, but they are also Japanese citizens, liable . . . to be called to bear arms for their Emperor, either in front of, or behind, enemy lines." Japanese-language schools were attacked as "a blind to cover instruction similar to that received by a young student in Japan—that his is a superior race, the divinity of the Japanese Emperor, the loyalty that every Japanese, wherever born, or residing, owes his Emperor and Japan." Congress was scored for failing to take action on dual citizenship, and the committee voiced the hope that "perhaps the savage blow inflicted at Hawaii may cause us to awaken. It is time."[24]

In the first wartime meeting of the JIC, the issue of evacuation as well as that of dual citizenship was introduced, primarily on racist grounds. Former State Attorney General U. S. Webb—whose lifetime contributions to the anti-Oriental cause were rivaled only by those of Senator James D. Phelan and Valentine S. McClatchy—was present to urge the evacuation of all Japanese, maintaining that citizen Nisei might be more dangerous than their alien parents. H. J. McClatchy, son of the com-

[23] California Joint Immigration Committee, *Minutes of Meeting*, February 7, 1942, p. 6.
[24] California Joint Immigration Committee, Press Release No. 544, January 2, 1942.

mittee's founder, concurred with the observation that "so far as the individual Nisei is concerned, he has been educated to be a Jap and he is a Jap."[25]

The intimate relationship between the Joint Immigration Committee and the California Department of the Legion (illuminated by the dual role of James K. Fisk as State Legion Adjutant and Chairman of the JIC) was revealed in January in a resolution of the State Legion's War Council which closely followed the pattern set by the committee, notably in its demand that "all Japanese who are known to hold dual citizenship . . . be placed in concentration camps." Similar resolutions soon appeared from a number of local posts in California, Oregon, and Washington.[26]

Even more racist in character were the charges and proclamations issued by the Native Sons and Daughters of the Golden West. Violent denunciations of the Japanese, similar to those of earlier years, appeared in the first three wartime issues of the *Grizzly Bear*. In the January number, Clarence M. Hunt, Deputy Grand President and editor of the journal, recounted the long history of Native Son agitation, summarized the principal grievances and antipathies developed by the Order in thirty years of agitation, and advanced a singular explanation for the war:

> Had the warnings been heeded—had the federal and state authorities been "on the alert," and rigidly enforced the Exclusion Law and the Alien Land Law; had the Jap propaganda agencies in this country been silenced; had legislation been enacted . . . denying citizenship to the offspring of an alien ineligible to citizenship; had the Japs been prohibited from colonizing in strategic locations; had not Jap-dollars been so eagerly sought by White landowners and businessmen; had a deaf ear been turned to the honeyed words of the Japs and the pro-Japs; had the yellow-Jap and the white-Jap "fifth columnists" been disposed of within the law; had Japan been denied the privilege of using California as a breeding-grounds for dual citizens (Nisei);—the treacherous Japs probably would not have attacked Pearl Harbor December 7, 1941, and this country would not today be at war with Japan.

The motives of the farming groups which joined the new anti-Japanese movement were not, on the surface at least, the same as those of the patriots who composed the Legion and the Native Sons. The Western Growers Protective Association and the Grower-Shipper Vegetable Association, for example, repeated the familiar allegations of cheap labor, unfair competition, and land "bleeding" which had been advanced against the Japanese in previous decades by the State Grange and the California

---

[25] California Joint Immigration Committee, *Minutes of Meeting*, February 7, 1942, pp. 25–30, 18–19.

[26] American Legion, Department of California, Resolution of January 5, 1942 (Mimeographed). One of the most dramatic of local actions was a circular issued in February by a Portland, Oregon, post, which declared: "Jap and Alien War Sneaks are Proving Thick in our Coast Area. It is serious. Help us Remove the Danger!!"

Farm Bureau.[27] Other classic features of the stereotype were not ignored. According to an official of the Western Growers, it was "not far-fetched or beyond the realm of possibility that at least 25,000 Japanese, in the event of invasion, by exchanging civilian clothing for uniforms are full-fledged members of the Japanese armed forces."[28] The underlying griev-ances of the Grower-Shippers were plainly revealed in a magazine article a few months later, in which the managing secretary of the organization was quoted as saying:

> We're charged with wanting to get rid of the Japs for selfish reasons. We might as well be honest. We do. It's a question of whether the white man lives on the Pacific Coast or the brown man. They came into this valley to work, and they stayed to take over. . . . If all the Japs were removed tomorrow, we'd never miss them in two weeks, because the white farmers can take over and produce everything the Jap grows. And we don't want them back when the war ends, either.[29]

Thus, during January, the storm clouds gathered over the heads of the Japanese Americans. The voices which had been heard earlier in their defense were by the end of the month either silenced or lost in a swelling chorus of hatred and suspicion. Popular hostility mounted steadily with the continuing successes of the enemy in the Pacific, and numbers of newspaper writers and radio commentators, public officials, and spokes-men for private interests abandoned whatever hesitation they may once have felt and hastened to add their voices to the clamor for action. The charges they hurled against the resident Japanese were an echo of the grievances of years past; the caricature they drew was soon observed to be the familiar hateful figure, at once comic and threatening—the be-spectacled and bowing Asiatic whose excessive politeness disguised a treacherous heart and a conspiratorial design.

FEBRUARY: THE TIME OF DECISION

By the end of January, 1942, the prospects for tolerant or even moderate treatment of Japanese Americans had all but disappeared. The ultimate fate of alien Japanese was foreshadowed by the announcement of the Justice Department that along with alien Germans and Italians they were to be removed from various prohibited zones, and that their freedom of movement in still other areas would be curtailed. The position of American citizens of Japanese descent, theoretically more secure, was almost equally precarious. Regarded generally as "descendants of the

[27] See *Western Grower and Shipper*, vol. 13 (June, 1942), pp. 8–9.
[28] Letter to Congressman John Z. Anderson, January 22, 1942 (Study files).
[29] Frank J. Taylor, "The People Nobody Wants," *The Saturday Evening Post*, May 9, 1942, p. 66.

Japanese enemy," they found their status as citizens more and more in jeopardy. The confusion of alien ancestry with alien status was compounded in the public mind as newspapers referred indiscriminately to all Japanese—whether citizens or aliens, enemy forces or peaceful residents —as "Japs." An increasing number of organizations and prominent individuals were urging the evacuation of citizens as well as aliens, and the cry of "Once a Jap always a Jap" was heard on all sides. A Nisei citizen expressed the bitterness of many:

> There seems to be a movement to make this present conflict a war between races . . . and over here in our country some people are theorizing that this is a war to end the yellow menace . . . thousands of them [Japanese] live in the United States . . . and are wholeheartedly for the U.S. and democracy—yet they are or may be singled out for special attention if this "racial war" movement gathers momentum.[30]

The decision to evacuate all Japanese Americans from the West Coast, which came during February, was reached in a context of gathering fear, suspicion, and anger on the part of the American public—a mood occasioned by the unanticipated disasters in the Pacific. Had the United States fleet not been decimated at Pearl Harbor, but steamed off intact to meet and destroy the Japanese navy, as most Americans had been certain it would; had the Japanese armies been turned back at Singapore by the land and sea defenses which had been thought invincible; in short, had the Allies taken the initiative at the outset and shown promise of checking the Japanese advance, it is doubtful that American opinion—public and private, official and unofficial—could have been mobilized in support of evacuation. Assured of ultimate victory and sustained by a diet of war successes, a secure and confident America might well have fulfilled its democratic ideal of tolerance and hospitality toward the Japanese minority in its midst.

But the war did not go that way, and Americans were given no prospect of security or gleam of optimism. In mid-February, only seventy days after the first attack on Malaya, "impregnable" Singapore surrendered unconditionally to the Japanese, in what Winston Churchill was to call "the greatest disaster to British arms which history records." The capitulation forced an Allied withdrawal to the Dutch East Indies, and the way now lay open for an enemy attack upon Burma and India. The Japanese, in fact, had entered Burma a week before to cut the Burma Road and isolate China. The Indies were sealed off and their fate ordained by the fall of Sumatra, Borneo, and Celebes; and in a series of sea engagements during February the Japanese first split and then methodically destroyed American and Allied naval forces. Enemy penetration of the southwest Pacific was equally rapid and decisive. In January Japanese

30 *Nichi Bei*, February 1, 1942.

forces had leveled the centers of defense in the Solomons; from these positions they now struck west at New Guinea, bombing Salamaua and Port Moresby and even neutralizing Port Darwin on the Australian coast. By the end of February an invasion of Australia seemed imminent; the final fall of the beleaguered Philippine garrison was virtually assured; the surrender of Java and the complete conquest of the rich Indies was only days away; and the great subcontinent of India was threatened with assault. Nothing had occurred to indicate that the bewildering tide of conquest might soon be stemmed, and not a few Americans wondered when their turn would come in the Japanese schedule of invasion.

Early in the month, meanwhile, in conjunction with its program of alien evacuation from prohibited areas, the Justice Department began a series of "spot raids" to uncover contraband and counter anticipated sabotage. FBI agents, together with state and local officers, descended without warning or warrant upon a number of localities and searched the homes of Japanese. Large amounts of "contraband" were found, and numbers of alien Japanese were apprehended. Each of these surprise raids received attention from California newspapers, usually beneath black banner headlines.[31] Particular stress was placed upon the lists of contraband seized. One search, for example, was reported to have uncovered "11 cameras, 14 short wave radio sets, 12 binoculars, a telescope, nine rifles, six revolvers, many thousands of rounds of ammunition, 84 knives, a large searchlight, four floodlights, four telescope gun sights, a box of sulphuric acid, Japanese maps and three sets of maps and charts of the Monterey Bay area." The Japanese operator of a sporting goods store was said to possess "70,000 rounds of rifle and shotgun ammunition, 12 rifles and shotguns, a public address system, cameras and film, books of Japanese propaganda and a radio operator's handbook."[32]

The effect of these accounts in augmenting public suspicions may be glimpsed in a letter to Attorney General Biddle from a San Diego resident: "How much longer are we going to let these traitorous barbarians strut among us seeking every means of destroying us, storing arms and ammunition right under our noses and within stone's throw of our war industries, just because hasty action on our part might be impolite or offend the one out of every hundred Japs who is not conspiring against us?"[33] Editorial writers also were influenced by the apparent findings of

---

[31] A raid on Terminal Island, for example, drew a two-column article on the front page of the Los Angeles *Times*, under a banner proclaiming "Japs Evicted on Terminal Island," and a subhead reading: "FBI, Police and Deputy Sheriffs Round up 336 of Estimated 800 Aliens in Harbor Area with Long-Planned Raids Still Continuing" (February 3, 1942). The arrest of Japanese aliens in Monterey drew scare headlines from the San Francisco *Examiner*, February 11, 1942: "Ex-Police Chief of Tokio Held by FBI in Raid on Salinas," and "Priest in Buddhist Temple Seized." The accompanying story told how a former Japanese police chief had slipped into the country a few months previously, disguised as a Buddhist priest.

[32] San Francisco *News*, February 10, 1942.

[33] Department of Justice files.

the anti-Japanese raids. A typical comment in the Stockton *Record* declared that "in recent days FBI agents have operated in many parts of California and uncovered caches of arms and contraband. . . . The circumstances smack strongly of those who contributed to the tragedy of Pearl Harbor. . . . The Pacific Coast is in danger."[34]

The inevitable effect of the arrests and spot raids, dramatically pointed up by the press, was to confirm the traditional image of the Japanese handed down from earlier generations and revived upon the outbreak of war. The rising tide of popular feeling is shown by the frequent appeals of the Department of Justice—and especially of Attorney General Francis Biddle—asking the public to forego vigilantism and maintain tolerance toward the Japanese Americans. But such appeals did little to check the rise of anti-Japanese sentiment. In fact, the control measures adopted by the Department of Justice seemed to many only a further confirmation of their fears: the creation of prohibited and restricted zones, the establishment of a curfew, the dramatic searches and seizures —all appeared to justify the deepening public suspicions of the Japanese, both citizens and aliens, as actually or potentially disloyal and dangerous.

The aggravated state of public opinion was also reflected during February in the words and actions of prominent politicians and political bodies. The boards of supervisors of eleven California counties joined in a solemn declaration that "during the attack on Pearl Harbor . . . the Japanese were aided and abetted by fifth columnists of the Japanese."[35] State Attorney General Earl Warren had first proclaimed his attitude on January 30, when a press dispatch quoted him as saying that the Japanese situation in the state "may well be the Achilles heel of the entire civilian defense effort. Unless something is done it may bring about a repetition of Pearl Harbor." On February 2, Warren revealed to a private conference of sheriffs and district attorneys his intense suspicion of resident Japanese —which was so profound that the very absence of sabotage seemed to him a sure sign of its future occurrence: "It seems to me that it is quite significant that in this great state of ours we have had no fifth column activities and no sabotage reported. It looks very much to me as though it is a studied effort not to have any until the zero hour arrives." He concluded that "every alien Japanese should be considered in the light of a potential fifth columnist," and urged that the Alien Land Law be enforced to remove all Japanese from areas near vital installations. (It should be emphasized, however, that the public report of the conference called only for removal of enemy aliens—*not* of all Japanese Americans.)[36]

In subsequent days Attorney General Warren produced a variety of

34 February 21, 1942.

35 Following adoption by the Los Angeles County Board of Supervisors of a resolution calling for removal of Japanese aliens (January 27), Ventura County supervisors resolved to exclude "all persons of the Japanese race" from Pacific Coast areas (February 3). Virtually identical resolutions were then passed by ten other California counties.

36 Monterey *Press Herald*, January 30, 1942; Proceedings of a conference of sheriffs and district attorneys called by Attorney General Warren on the subject of Alien Land Law enforcement. February 2, 1942, pp. 3–7 (Typescript in Study files).

arguments purporting to show that resident Japanese were not only dangerous but much more of a threat than resident Germans or Italians. His arguments constitute a résumé of anti-Japanese cliches which had been accumulating for over half a century. There was, he said, no way to determine the loyalty of Japanese Americans. It was impossible for Americans to comprehend Oriental ways; the alien culture was diffused through religion, language schools, and the practice of sending children to Japan for education. In Japan "they are indoctrinated with the idea of Japanese imperialism. They receive their religious instruction which ties up their religion with their Emperor, and they come back here imbued with the ideas and policies of Imperial Japan." Warren alleged that Japanese in America generally approved of Japan's military conquests, implying that they would also favor the conquest of America, and he declared that the Japanese government exerted a broad control over the activities of all Japanese in this country.[37]

Equally vigorous in his opposition to the Japanese, and in his contributions to the stereotype, was Mayor Fletcher Bowron of Los Angeles. In a radio address of February 5, Bowron warned of the danger of leaving the California Japanese at liberty. Among the Nisei there were "a number who are doubtless loyal to Japan, waiting probably, with full instructions as to what to do, to play their part when the time comes." The next day the mayor was quoted as denouncing the "sickly sentimentality" of Americans who feared injustices to the Japanese. The control "measures taken so far are so ineffectual as to be ridiculous." On Lincoln's birthday he again devoted his weekly radio address to the Japanese problem, arguing that if Lincoln were living he would round up "the people born on American soil who have secret loyalty to the Japanese Emperor." On still another occasion he disclaimed "any racial or other prejudice," but declared that "I know of no rule, no way to separate those who say they are patriotic and are, in fact, loyal at heart, and those who say they are patriotic and in fact at heart are loyal to Japan."[38]

The shift in public sentiment, visible in late January, from comparative tolerance to general hostility toward the Japanese minority was accurately mirrored in the Pacific Coast press. The ratio of unfavorable to favorable editorials was nineteen to one in the five days between January 22 and 26; hostile letters to the editor, chiefly demands for mass evacuation, attained their peak between February 1 and 5. By February, also, news stories favorable to the Japanese Americans were reduced from a December high of 22 per cent to less than 3 per cent, and during the thirty-day period from January 12 to February 10, fifteen times more news space was given to unfriendly items than to favorable copy. News stories devoted to evacuation demands reached their peak in the five days from February 6 to 10; these stories alone occupied seven times the space

---

[37] *Hearings*, 77th Congress, 2d sess., House, Select Committee Investigating National Defense Migration (Washington: G.P.O., 1942), part 29, pp. 11015, 11017, 10974–76. This committee will be cited hereinafter as Tolan Committee.

[38] *Congressional Record*, February 9, 1942, pp. A504–05; Los Angeles *Examiner*, February 6, 1942; Los Angeles *Times*, February 13, 1942; Tolan Committee, *Hearings*, part 31, pp. 11643–44.

taken by all favorable news copy in the month from January 12 to February 10.[39]

Editorial pressure in early February centered chiefly on the danger of a West Coast "Pearl Harbor." There was general agreement with the opinion of the Sacramento *Bee* that "the experience with the fifth col-

[39] From quantitative-analysis charts in the Study files, public-opinion samplings taken along the West Coast from late January through February confirmed the rising distrust of Japanese Americans and showed increasing support for stricter control measures. An exploratory survey conducted during the last week of January, based on 192 interviews in four California localities, found almost as many persons believing the Japanese "virtually all loyal" (36 per cent) as "virtually all disloyal" (38 per cent). Significantly, however, the report noted that "a substantial number among those who feel that most Japanese are loyal went on to say that since one could not tell precisely which ones are loyal and which disloyal, a certain amount of suspicion was naturally attached to all Japanese." The majority of the respondents felt that existing control measures were adequate, only about one-third calling for further action against the Japanese Americans. See U.S. Office of Facts and Figures, Bureau of Intelligence, *Exploratory Study of West Coast Reactions to Japanese*, February 4, 1942 (Processed; Washington, 1942). A subsequent study conducted in the second week of February (covering 797 citizens of California, Oregon, and Washington) found that 40 per cent of the total sample thought that there were "many disloyal aliens in their vicinity"; and practically all of these named the Japanese specifically. Three-fourths of the southern Californians interviewed believed that "only a few" or "practically none" of the Japanese aliens were loyal to the United States, and called for their segregation in camps. One-third of the southern Californians also advocated segregating citizen Japanese, but in the other three coastal areas (northern California, Oregon, and Washington) only 14 per cent recommended this action. See U.S. Office of Facts and Figures, Bureau of Intelligence, *Pacific Coast Attitudes Toward the Japanese Problem*, February 28, 1942 (Processed; Washington, 1942). The third opinion sampling, which covered the last three weeks of February, noted "evidence of growing tension," and observed a general rise of dissatisfaction with Department of Justice measures and of suspicion toward the Japanese Americans. Japanese loyalty to the United States was questioned by over half the respondents; and "most people who make such a judgment believe there is no limit to what a Japanese might be expected to do." Dislike and distrust of the Japanese was estimated by 77 per cent of those interviewed as the prevailing sentiment, with racial and national antagonism as the predominant reasons for disfavor. Government measures for the solution of the Japanese problem were judged adequate by 54 per cent of those interviewed in the period before February 20, but by only 40 per cent during the last week of February. Expectation of sabotage was indicated by 60 per cent of the replies. See U.S. Office of Facts and Figures, Bureau of Intelligence, *West Coast Reactions to the Japanese Situation*, March, 1942 (Processed; Washington, 1942).

Evidence that national public opinion by the end of March, 1942, was similar to that of the Pacific Coast is given by a National Opinion Research Council nationwide poll of March 28. Some 93 per cent of those interviewed thought that "we are doing the right thing in moving Japanese aliens" away from the West Coast; only 1 per cent thought it was wrong. Fifty-nine per cent approved the evacuation of citizen Japanese, while 25 per cent disapproved. A total of 65 per cent of the respondents agreed that all Japanese evacuated should be kept "under strict guard as prisoners of war," with 28 per cent holding that "they should be allowed to go about fairly freely." See Hadley Cantril, ed., *Public Opinion 1935–1946* (Princeton: Princeton University Press, 1951), p. 380. For other polls bearing on national opinion, see *ibid.*, pp. 947 ff.

umn in Hawaii is overwhelming evidence that . . . the authorities must take no chances with possible Jap or Axis sympathizers."[40] Newspapers pointed frequently to contraband seized by the FBI as sufficient evidence of Japanese disloyalty, and much attention was given to the growing number of evacuation demands by politicians, officials, and organizations. The activities of the Western congressional bloc were widely featured, often with speculation that federal action approving Japanese removal was soon to be taken.

Editorial writers voiced increasing opposition during February to the nonevacuation policy of the Department of Justice. Equally noteworthy were the exhortations of several widely syndicated columnists who added their voices to the cry for mass removal. Henry McLemore, whose personal campaign had begun late in January, continued to press his attack against the Department of Justice. Observing that aliens had been allowed weeks in which to evacuate the prohibited zones and would have "time to perfect their time bombs, complete their infernal machines," McLemore charged the Attorney General with handling the Japanese threat "with all the severity of Lord Fauntleroy playing squat tag with his maiden aunt."[41]

Walter Lippmann, one of the most influential political columnists, added his name in mid-February to the list of those opposing federal policy and urging stronger measures.[42] Subsequently Westbrook Pegler, then a Scripps-Howard columnist, translated the Lippmann argument into his own idiom, declaring on February 16 that "the Japanese in California should be under guard to the last man and woman right now and to hell with *habeas corpus* until the danger is over." Pegler went on:

> Do you get what [Lippmann] says? . . . The enemy has been scouting our coast. . . . The Japs ashore are communicating with the enemy offshore and . . . on the basis of "what is known to be taking place" there are signs that a well-organized blow is being withheld only until it can do the most damage. . . .
> We are so dumb and considerate of the minute constitutional rights and even of the political feelings and influence of people whom we have every reason to anticipate with preventive action!

Under the prodding of public opinion and the press, members of Congress from the West Coast states intensified their efforts toward the formulation of a severe control program aimed at the Japanese. On February 10 a committee set up by the joint Pacific Coast delegation approved a resolution recommending total evacuation of all Japanese from

[40] February 6, 1942.
[41] Los Angeles *Examiner*, February 5, 1942. See also San Francisco *Examiner*, February 9, 1942.
[42] Lippmann argued that Nisei citizens were as great a danger as aliens, and declared: "The Pacific Coast is officially a combat zone: some part of it may at any moment be a battlefield. Nobody's constitutional rights include the right to reside and do business on a battlefield. . . . There is plenty of room elsewhere for him to exercise his rights." (New York *Herald-Tribune*, February 12, 1942.)

the coastal area. The recommendation was made despite advice from Army and Navy authorities that a sustained Japanese attack on the coast was "impossible" and that even enemy raids, although possible, "would be sporadic and would have little, if any, bearing on the course of the war."[43] The reasons for disregarding this advice, as given in a letter to the President from the joint delegation, were plainly the exploded myth of sabotage at Pearl Harbor and the stereotyped belief in disloyalty and treachery among Japanese Americans. The letter pointed to "the seriousness of the Japanese menace along the entire Pacific Coast," which had evoked "insistent demands for prompt action," and asserted that "the critical nature of the situation and its latent subversive potentialities are so compelling as to justify the taking of extreme and drastic measures."[44]

Before mid-Feburary, not much was said on the floor of the House or the Senate concerning evacuation. Except for the West Coast contingent, congressmen for the most part displayed only slight interest in the Japanese American problem. But at least three Southern members were conspicuous in their support of the California extremists and influential in their contributions to the stereotype of Japanese American disloyalty. They were Congressman John Rankin of Mississippi, Congressman Martin Dies of Texas, and Senator Tom Stewart of Tennessee.

Congressman Rankin, long famous as a champion of "White Supremacy" in his native South, was the most outspoken of the three in condemning all Japanese. As early as December he had declared: "So far as I am concerned, I am in favor of deporting every Jap who claims, or has claimed, Japanese citizenship, or sympathizes with Japan in this war." In mid-February he went still further: "Once a Jap always a Jap. You cannot change him. You cannot make a silk purse out of a sow's ear." Rankin put himself on record

> for catching every Japanese in America, Alaska, and Hawaii now and putting them in concentration camps and shipping them back to Asia as soon as possible. . . . This is a race war, as far as the Pacific side of this conflict is concerned. . . . The white man's civilization has come into conflict with Japanese barbarism. . . . One of them must be destroyed. . . .
>
> I say it is of vital importance that we get rid of every Japanese whether in Hawaii or on the mainland. They violate every sacred

[43] Admiral Ernest Stark, Chief of Naval Operations, as quoted by Senator Holman of Oregon, chairman of the West Coast delegation's committee on defense, in a letter to Senator Hiram Johnson, dated February 9, 1942. The testimony of Brigadier General Mark W. Clark, representing the Army Chief of Staff, was reported by Senator Holman to be substantially similar. Further adverse testimony had been given the committees by the Department of Justice, which held evacuation to be unwise and unnecessary, and the Department of Agriculture, which warned of severe effects on coastal crop production. (Interview with Senator Sheridan Downey, October 13, 1942, notes in Study files.)

[44] The letter to President Roosevelt, dated February 13, 1942, was signed by Senators Holman and Wallgren and by Congressman Lea Englebright, Welch, Costello, and Angell.

promise, every canon of honor and decency. . . . These Japs who had been [in Hawaii] for generations were making signs, if you please, guiding the Japanese planes to the objects of their iniquity in order that they might destroy our naval vessels, murder our soldiers and sailors, and blow to pieces the helpless women and children of Hawaii.

Damn them! Let's get rid of them now![45]

A few days later, on the House floor, Rankin renewed his insistence that the Japanese be placed in concentration camps. Pointing to the FBI raids along the coast, he declared that Japanese militarists were driving "the dagger in our backs . . . at the same time their racial cohorts are undermining and sabotaging us up and down the Pacific Coast and throughout the Hawaiian Islands." The Mississippi congressman asserted that persons of Japanese ancestry born in this country were "not citizens of the United States and never can be." In support of this argument he read into the *Congressional Record* the dissenting opinion in the *Wong Kim Ark* case, and concluded: "There is a racial and religious difference they can never overcome. They are pagan in their philosophy, atheistic in their beliefs, alien in their allegiance, and antagonistic to everything for which we stand."[46]

Senator Tom Stewart, the author of a Senate bill to intern all Americans of Japanese descent, also was concerned with the status of the Nisei. He argued that

a Jap born on our soil is a subject of Japan under Japanese law; therefore, he owes allegiance to Japan. . . . The Japanese are among our worst enemies. They are cowardly and immoral. They are different from Americans in every conceivable way, and no Japanese . . . should have a right to claim American citizenship. A Jap is a Jap anywhere you find him, and his taking the oath of allegiance to this country would not help, even if he should be permitted to do so. They do not believe in God and have no respect for an oath. They have been plotting for years against the Americas and their democracies.[47]

Congressman Dies, as head of the House Committee on Un-American Activities, had for years engaged in sensational "exposés" of allegedly disloyal individuals and organizations. Months before the war the Texas congressman had released press statements threatening an exposure of Japanese espionage and anti-American propaganda. On January 28

[45] *Congressional Record*, December 15, 1941, p. 9808; February 14, 1942, pp. A691–92. Congressmen Bland of Virginia, Norrell of Arkansas, Randolph of West Virginia, and even Coffee of Washington lauded or approved sections of Rankin's address.

[46] *Congressional Record*, February 23, 1942, pp. A768–69. The majority opinion in the *Wong Kim Ark* case held that only children born in the United States of alien enemies in hostile occupation, and those of diplomatic representatives, were not "subject to the jurisdiction" of the United States.

[47] *Ibid.*, February 26, 1942, pp. 1682–83.

Dies delivered a speech in which he charged that "fear of displeasing foreign powers and a maudlin attitude toward fifth columnists was largely responsible for the unparalleled tragedy at Pearl Harbor," and announced that a forthcoming report would "disclose that if our committee had been permitted to reveal the facts last September the tragedy of Pearl Harbor might have been averted." Demanding that "there be an immediate end to this suicidal policy of coddling the tools and dupes of foreign powers," Dies concluded with the warning that "unless this Government adopts an alert attitude towards this whole question there will occur on the west coast a tragedy that will make Pearl Harbor sink into insignificance compared with it."[48]

The heralded report of the Dies Committee was not forthcoming until late in February; but early in the month its contents were partly revealed, when a widely read columnist predicted that the Dies report would show how Japanese consuls had directed espionage activities through the "front" of the Central Japanese Association at Los Angeles. On February 9 the report was quoted as saying in part: "The United States has been and still is lax, tolerant and soft toward the Japanese who have violated American hospitality. Shinto Temples still operate, propaganda outlets still disseminate propaganda material and Japanese, both alien and American citizens, still spy for the Japanese government." The report was said to maintain that Japanese Americans were exploiting their civil rights "to promote systematic espionage such as prepared the way for the attack on Pearl Harbor on December 7."[49]

Meanwhile, on the West Coast, direct evidence of the hostile state of opinion was to be seen in the increasing acts of violence and threats of vigilantism against resident Japanese. Such incidents had begun to be noted shortly after the Pearl Harbor attack; and by February the argument that evacuation was necessary to insure the safety of the Japanese Americans as well as of the entire population had become a stock contention of public officials and spokesmen for private interests. At a conference of California district attorneys and sheriffs on February 2, it was announced that various civic and agricultural groups were actively fostering extra-legal action against the Japanese. Subsequently the sheriff of Merced County reported "rumblings of vigilante activity"; the chief of police of Huntington Beach described anti-Japanese feeling as "at fever heat"; the police chief of Watsonville announced that "racial hatred is mounting higher and higher" and that Filipinos were "arming themselves and going out looking for an argument with Japanese"; and Oxnard's police chief reported that "it has been planned by local Filipinos and some so-called '200 percent Americans' to declare a local 'war' against local Japanese, during the next blackout."[50]

48 *Ibid.*, January 15, 1942, p. 420; January 28, 1942, pp. 828–29.

49 Drew Pearson, "Washington Merry-Go-Round" (Syndicated newspaper column), February 7, 1942; San Francisco *Chronicle*, February 9, 1942.

50 Proceedings of a conference of sheriffs and district attorneys, pp. 52–55, 61–62; letters to Attorney General Warren from N. L. Cornell, D. M. Blossom, J. M. Graves, and G. M. Pryor, all dated February 19, 1942 (Tolan Committee files).

The mounting anger and suspicion of many citizens was expressed during February in the demands of various officials that the government act against the Japanese Americans without regard to legal or constitutional restraints. The mayor of one California city advised Congressman Tolan that "the Constitution can go overboard, if necessary"; should evacuation prove awkward in constitutional terms, "then we must win the war by dictatorship methods." A California congressman put the case more succinctly: "Let's move these Japanese out and talk about it afterwards." And the district attorney of Madera County declared that "we must forget such things as the right of *habeas corpus* and the prohibition against unreasonable searches and seizures. The right of self-defense, self-preservation . . . is higher than the Bill of Rights."[51]

This growing hostility toward the Japanese also became evident during the process of carrying out the early Department of Justice program of limited evacuation from prohibited zones. The intent of the program was to provide for the reestablishment of alien enemies and their families; but the antipathy of residents of inland areas made it impossible for many Japanese to find either housing or employment. "Housing shortage is almost omnipresent in California," wrote the regional director of the Federal Security Agency; ". . . the evacuees seeking new homes are badly handicapped by the psychological attitude of landlords."[52] The inland population was for the most part only vaguely aware of the nature of voluntary resettlement and commonly assumed that if Japanese were a menace to security on the coast they were equally a menace elsewhere; if they could blow up ships in the harbors, they might also burn the forests of central California, wreck the irrigation system of Arizona, or sabotage the railroads running through Utah.

Many residents of interior states also suspected Californians of dumping a difficult minority problem in their laps. With the exception of Governor Ralph Carr of Colorado, the governors of the Western states were unanimously opposed to the resettlement of Japanese within their borders. Thus Governor Sidney Osborn of Arizona announced: "We do not propose to be a dumping ground for enemy aliens from any other state. We not only vigorously protest but will not permit the evacuation of Japanese, German, or Italian aliens to any point in Arizona."[53] Similar protests were heard in virtually all areas to which enemy aliens were permitted to move, and the beginnings of vigilantism were reported at many points. Repeated attempts to clarify the nature of the program and counteract local opposition were, as one official remarked, inadequate to penetrate "through the walls erected by public opinion, based upon natural

---

[51] Letters: C. A. Ricks (Mayor of Martinez) to Tolan, February 20, 1942; Ward Johnson to Biddle, February 19, 1942; G. Mordecai to Earl Warren, February 19, 1942. Printed in Tolan Committee, *Hearings,* part 29, pp. 10997–98.

[52] Richard M. Neustadt, *Report on Alien Enemy Evacuation* [to Paul V. McNutt, Director, Federal Security Administration and Director of Defense, Health, and Welfare Services], February 18, 1942, p. 6. (Processed; n.p., n.d.)

[53] Letter, Osborn to Tolan, February 28, 1942, printed in Tolan Committee, *Preliminary Report . . . on Evacuation of Military Areas,* House Report No. 1911, March 19, 1942, p. 27.

fear of Japanese sabotage and inflamed by those who were envious of or inherently prejudiced against this race, irrespective of the war." The appearance of race prejudice, according to the same source, was especially marked in inland California, in Washington, and in neighboring states. "Unless we develop far better procedures and greater public confidence in the power of the Federal Government than now exist, I have real reason to fear that the spirit of vigilantism might spread in a way completely foreign to real Americanism. This is a carefully worded attempt at understatement."[54]

There were a number of protests from the interior California counties. Some farmers of the San Joaquin Valley protested the use of their area as a "dumping ground," and the San Joaquin County Farm Bureau demanded passage of a law to prevent the settlement of Japanese. The mayors' and councilmen's section of the League of California Cities called for evacuation beyond the borders of the state. The Fresno County Chamber of Commerce condemned the partial evacuation and urged that Japanese be excluded from the entire Pacific Coast. The Kern County Defense Council wired the Western bloc in Congress recommending the same action, on the grounds that the county contained many defense installations, "that the Japs would like very much to blow up, if they are in a blowing up mood."[55]

California's Tulare County was especially alert to the "dangers" presented by (and to) the Japanese evacuees. A mass meeting of county residents in mid-February demanded removal of Japanese from the state "for the public safety and for their own safety." It was feared that unless action were taken immediately the situation would "get out of hand," a spokesman freely predicted trouble if the Japanese remained, and a home guard was formed by Tulare citizens. Meanwhile District Attorney Walter C. Haight reported to the Tulare County Board of Supervisors that the movement of Japanese into the county presented a hazard and a danger "not only to the resources of our country, but to the interests of our national defense." He pointed to "the possibility of sabotage by means of the poisoning of our water supply, destruction of the metropolitan power lines . . . grain fields and . . . forests." Haight charged that Japanese growers of the area had designed a field of vegetables in the form of an arrowhead that "pointed directly to the Visalia Airport." Warning that under emergency conditions "hysterical people" might "take matters into their own hands," he urged the establishment of martial law requiring that "all enemy aliens, including all members of the Japanese race, be removed from the State of California."[56]

54 Neustadt, *Report on Alien Enemy Evacuation*, pp. 12, 15.
55 San Francisco *Call-Bulletin*, February 17, 1942; San Francisco *Chronicle*, February 17, 1942; Fresno County Chamber of Commerce, Resolution of February 20, 1942 (Tolan Committee, *Hearings*, part 29, p. 11239); Kern County Defense Council telegram dated February 21, 1942 (Study files).
56 San Francisco *Examiner*, February 20, 1942; Tolan Committee, *Hearings*, part 29, pp. 11061–62; report by District Attorney Walter C. Haight before Tulare County Board of Supervisors, "Enemy Alien Situation," February 14, 1942 (Notes in Study files).

The opening days of March found the Japanese ordered away from the coast in the so-called "voluntary evacuation" program instituted by General DeWitt and the Western Defense Command. At the end of the month this "voluntary" program gave way to forced evacuation and internment. But public hostility remained; although newspaper columnists and editorialists turned most of their attention to other issues and policies, attacks against the Japanese continued. For the most part the trouble centered in Tulare and Fresno counties,[57] where open vigilante action continued as the weeks passed and local Japanese still remained in residence. During March an attempt was made to burn down a Japanese-owned hotel at Sultana. On April 13 at Del Ray five evacuees were involved in a brawl with the local constable—following which a crowd of white residents, some armed with shotguns, threatened violence to a nearby camp of Japanese Americans. On succeeding nights the windows of four Japanese stores were smashed, and similar incidents occurred in Fresno. In northern Tulare County, a group known as the "Bald Eagles"—described by one observer as "a guerilla army of nearly 1,000 farmers"—armed themselves for the announced purpose of "guarding" the Japanese in case of emergency. A similar organization was formed in the southeast part of the county, where a large number of evacuees were concentrated.[58]

CONCLUSION: THE FACES OF THE STEREOTYPE

The Japanese stereotype, as reconstructed in the early months of war, was a composite image reflecting a diversity of hates and fears on the part of the West Coast population. Frequently inconsistent and even mutually exclusive, the public expressions of these underlying attitudes were alike in their hostility and in the suspicion they revealed concerning the loyalty of resident Japanese. As rumor and opinion, they circulated through public resolutions and private declarations, while coastal residents in the weeks of crisis cast about for arguments to embody their growing anger and frustration. The arguments they found were with few exceptions neither logical nor original, but represented the tarnished banners of long-past campaigns—the yellow-peril charges of the unionists and politicians, the economic rationalizations of the farm groups, the racist outbursts of the patriots—the alarms and excursions of fifty years of agitation which had merged and recombined to form the popular stereotype of the Japanese character.

Sabotage.—Foremost among the traditional beliefs to be revived in the public mind was the myth of the yellow-peril invasion, the identification of America's Japanese as actual or potential spies and saboteurs. Emerging as an explanation of the shocking and calamitous events of December 7, the Pearl Harbor legend described such purported actions as the destruction of airplanes on the ground, the cutting of arrows in

---

[57] *Fresno Bee,* April 21, 1942; San Francisco *Examiner,* April 21, 1942.

[58] George Dean, *Review of Anti-Japanese Incidents and Local Sentiment in Fresno and Tulare Counties* (Mimeographed; San Francisco: War Relocation Authority, April 30, 1942). *Fresno Bee,* April 23, 1942.

cane fields, and the deliberate obstruction of traffic into military installations. The truth of these accounts, which circulated widely with the arrival of refugees from Hawaii, was seldom doubted. The widespread belief in the actuality of sabotage in Hawaii provided the basis for virtually all organized agitation to oust the West Coast Japanese; it stimulated the circulation of anonymous chain letters throughout California in January and February, and was shown regularly in letters to newspapers, to the United States Attorney General, and to congressmen.

The immediate significance of the Pearl Harbor legend to Pacific Coast residents was, of course, its portent of disaster for themselves. The Sacramento *Bee* voiced a common concern in pointing out that "the experience with the fifth column in Hawaii is overwhelming evidence that . . . the authorities must take no chances with possible Jap or Axis sympathizers," and many Californians shared the opinion of their attorney general that "we are just being lulled into a false sense of security. . . . Our day of reckoning is bound to come . . . we are approaching an invisible deadline."[59] This anticipation of disaster was heard with increasing frequency during February and March, as popular fears mounted despite the refusal of Japanese Americans to demonstrate their "disloyalty" through subversive acts. Local, state, and national officials voiced the conviction that the absence of sabotage in the present made it all the more certain in the future,[60] and the same viewpoint was expressed by private spokesmen and popular commentators. It was eventually incorporated into the final report of General DeWitt as a primary factor justifying evacuation: the absence of sabotage was, according to the general, "a disturbing and confirming indication that such action would be taken."[61]

Most of those who expressed fear over the threat of sabotage argued that American citizens of Japanese ancestry were as much suspect as aliens. This racist belief, summarized in the phrase "Once a Jap always a Jap," was publicized by congressmen such as Rankin and Stewart and appears to have made its way into the official reasoning of General DeWitt.[62] Various officials of the three Pacific Coast states conceded that

[59] Sacramento *Bee*, February 6, 1942; Tolan Committee, *Hearings*, part 29, pp. 11011–12.

[60] During the hearings of his committee Congressman Tolan himself suggested, "They would be fools to tip their hand now, wouldn't they?" Seattle's Mayor Millikin maintained that "there hasn't been any sabotage, because it has been ordered withheld by Tokyo"; and Mayor Riley of Portland agreed that "the only reason the fifth columnists haven't struck so far is because their respective governments haven't given them the go-ahead." (Tolan Committee, *Hearings*, part 29, pp. 11012, 11409; San Francisco *Chronicle*, February 21, 1942.)

[61] U.S. Army, Western Defense Command and Fourth Army, *Final Report: Japanese Evacuation from the West Coast, 1942* (Washington: G.P.O., 1943), p. 34.

[62] In testimony before the House Naval Affairs Subcommittee on April 13, 1943, the general was quoted as stating: "A Jap's a Jap. They are a dangerous element, whether loyal or not. There is no way to determine their loyalty. . . . It makes no difference whether he is an American; theoretically he is still a Japanese and you can't change him. . . . You can't change him by giving him a piece of paper." (San Francisco *Chronicle*, April 14, 1943.)

some Japanese Americans might be loyal to the United States but deemed it impossible, because of racial factors, to distinguish between the loyal and disloyal. The governor and attorney general of California and the mayors of Los Angeles, Seattle, and Portland, among others, adopted this viewpoint; minor law-enforcement officers in California endorsed an equivalent line of reasoning in pleas for evacuation. The theory was greatly advanced by the accumulating stories of fifth-column plots on the mainland, and further encouraged by dramatic press descriptions of spot raids by the FBI.

There is no need to recapitulate here the official denials and refutations which established conclusively that there had been no sabotage or other fifth-column activity at Pearl Harbor, either during or after the Japanese attack.[63] On the other hand, it is impossible to disprove objectively the thesis of "latent sabotage," the argument that West Coast Japanese were awaiting an Imperial signal to rise in concerted fifth-column action. The "facts" on which this thesis was based were soon shown to be mythical; the various rumors of poisoned vegetables, undercover signal devices, messages and arrows in the fields, and so on were one by one proved false. Moreover, the total inability of the FBI to uncover saboteurs among the Japanese population was frankly admitted by Attorney General Biddle in a memorandum to President Roosevelt in May, 1942.[64]

Geographical concentration.—Despite their shadowy character and the frequency of denials, both the Pearl Harbor rumors and the accounts of plans for sabotage remained in wide circulation among the West Coast population throughout the war. The general credence given these beliefs provided support for other traditional apprehensions regarding the Japanese Americans, one of the most persistent of which concerned their alleged "concentration" in strategic military and industrial areas. Numerous persons complained in letters to the Attorney General of the presence of Japanese near "Oil Fields, Tank Farms, Air Ports, and other vital defense industries"; "our coast line"; "the foot of our mountains and the entrances to our canyons, which lead to the dams and water reservoirs"; "vantage places in harbor fisheries . . . strange isolated promontories of our unguarded coastline, and . . . our aircraft plants."[65] An extensive statement charging the Japanese with deliberate settlement in strategic areas was presented before the Tolan Committee by Attorney

[63] Perhaps the first authoritative denial of Hawaii sabotage was that of Hawaii's delegate to Congress, Samuel W. King. (San Francisco *Chronicle*, January 26, 1942.) Subsequent refutations of the Pearl Harbor stories were issued by Secretary of War Henry L. Stimson, James Rowe, Jr. (assistant to Attorney General Biddle), Honolulu Chief of Police W. A. Gabrielson, FBI Director J. Edgar Hoover, and various other local and national officials. (Tolan Committee, *Fourth Interim Report*, pp. 48 ff., *passim*. Also Tolan Committee, *House Report No. 1911*, March 19, 1942, pp. 31 ff. See also Baltimore *Sun*, January 17, 1944.)

[64] The available copy of the Biddle memorandum is simply dated May, 1942. For specific corrections of fifth-column rumors, see: Los Angeles *Evening Herald*, December 9, 1941; Oakland *Tribune*, February 11, 1942; Sacramento *Bee*, February 18, 1942; San Francisco *Call-Bulletin*, February 20, 1942.

[65] Letters dated January 13, January 29, March 6, and January 29, 1942.

General Warren of California—a statement with which many California newspapers seemed to agree.[66]

Disloyalty.—Increasingly, under the stress of war, old and half-forgotten suspicions against the Japanese were dusted off and reintroduced as "evidence" of their disloyalty. Once again it was widely proclaimed that they were racially unassimilable. It was charged that their language schools were instruments of Imperial propaganda; that Nisei children educated in Japan had returned as spies or at least as indoctrinated Japanese fanatics; that the dual citizenship of the second generation was a mask for allegiance to the homeland; that community clubs and associations were manipulated from Tokyo; that Buddhism and Shintoism were agencies of Emperor worship; and that the occupation of farmlands by Japanese was a peaceful invasion which would end in domination of the American mainland.

This mélange of legends, distortions, and half-truths subsequently played a prominent role in the official arguments advanced in defense of mass removal of the Japanese—arguments by which both evacuation and detention were initially justified by the military and ultimately confirmed by the courts. One of the most prevalent of the hostile beliefs took its departure from the apparent approval of Japan's victories in China by some resident Japanese before the outbreak of war with the United States. From this the suspicion grew that many had possessed prior knowledge of the December 7 attack, and that plans for future sabotage operations by individual members were foreknown in the Japanese community. Mayor Bowron of Los Angeles, for example, asserted that many resident Japanese "knew what was coming" and "overplayed their hand" in the year before the war by an excessive pretense of loyalty to America.[67]

Cultural lag.—The retention of old-world culture by Japanese Americans was frequently invoked as proof of their disloyalty. In language, education, religion, and family patterns, they were suspected of willfully avoiding Western ways and favoring alien customs. Letter writers declared that "any Japanese child that attends a Japanese school will . . . be . . . a potential enemy," and that "all of them have been back to Japan for certain educational periods."[68] Attorney General Warren sweepingly condemned as anti-American the language schools, religious organizations, and vernacular press of the resident Japanese, and considered the Japanese tongue itself a suspicious bond with the old country. Attendance at a language school, membership in an organization, or even passive acceptance of old-world customs was held to be sufficient cause for barring Japanese Americans from state employment. In a formal notice of discharge sent to all persons of Japanese ancestry employed by

[66] Tolan Committee, *Hearings*, part 29, pp. 11017, 10974. See San Diego *Union*, March 5, 1942.

[67] Tolan Committee, *Hearings*, part 31, p. 11644.

[68] Letters dated January 28, February 16, 1942, from Los Angeles (Department of Justice files).

the state, the California State Personnel Board declared that "the defendant does read and write the Japanese language, and . . . subscribed to a Japanese newspaper . . . the defendant did attend a Japanese school . . . the defendant is a member and officer of certain Japanese organizations."[69]

Coolie labor.—The familiar accusations of cheap labor and unfair competition, which had long underlain the agitation of farm and labor groups, were once again heard as agriculturists and other interested groups joined the clamor against the Japanese. Despite their declarations that Japanese monopolized farmlands and vegetable production, the farmers saw no inconsistency in also maintaining that their removal would not hamper production. Officials of the California Farm Bureau, the Western Growers Protective Association, and the Grower-Shipper Vegetable Association wrote letters demonstrating that mass evacuation of the Japanese would not affect the food supply. California's Governor Culbert L. Olson conceded that some loss of "squat labor" might follow evacuation but did not consider it serious; Attorney General Warren declared that estimates of the importance of Japanese farm labor were based on "fantastic figures."[70]

Less often heard, but still in evidence, was the old yellow-peril warning against the alleged high birth rate of the Japanese. As always, the Native Sons were especially vociferous on this point, declaring that war might have been avoided had Japan been "denied the privilege of using California as a breeding ground for dual citizens." The Joint Immigration Committee likewise declared that the Japanese were "hardy of stock, militant opponents of race suicide, able to labor and thrive under living conditions impossible to an American."[71]

Race hatred.—The threat of riots and acts of violence against the Japanese, assertedly arising from "race hatred," constituted a potent argument for mass evacuation. The traditional Japanese stereotype included a belief in the existence of mutual hostility between the "white" and "yellow" races which it was thought must inevitably culminate in rioting and vigilantism—unless one or the other group should withdraw. This thesis, of course, was not without historical basis. California, and to a lesser extent Washington and Oregon, had a long history of vigilante activity, especially against the dark-skinned and Oriental minorities. Added to this tradition, in the months after Pearl Harbor, were the frustrating reports of Japanese victories and the accompanying tales of atrocities which were sufficient in themselves to stimulate public anger and the desire for revenge.

[69] Tolan Committee, *Hearings*, part 29, pp. 11014–15; California, State Personnel Board, Notice of Dismissal, April 13, 1942 (Study files).

[70] Tolan Committee, *Hearings*, part 30, pp. 11638–39; part 29, p. 11016. Statements of a similar nature were made by the Commissioner of Agriculture for Los Angeles County; a Los Angeles County Supervisor; the agricultural coordinator of the County Defense Council, and a representative of the Los Angeles Chamber of Commerce. (*Ibid.*, part 31, pp. 11675–91.)

[71] California Joint Immigration Committee, Press Release No. 544, January 2, 1942.

From the evidence that has accumulated it is possible to make an approximate appraisal of the extent of violence and vigilantism in the three coastal states during the months before evacuation. At least seven murders of Japanese Americans are known to have occurred, including among the victims a Los Angeles veteran of World War I and a middle-aged couple of Brawley, California. The number of physical assaults was substantially larger. Six Filipinos attacked a Japanese in Seattle; another Filipino shot and wounded a Japanese in Sacramento. Gunfire from moving automobiles wounded several persons (including a ten-year-old boy) in Gilroy. Similar events occurred at Costa Mesa, at Mount Eden, and at various points in Alameda County. Stockton Filipinos reportedly attacked Japanese with knives on three occasions. Robbery and assault were combined at least twice, in Seattle and in Rio Vista, California. Rape or attempted rape was recorded twice (in one case by men posing as FBI agents who were later identified as state prison guards). In Seattle a Negro truck driver shot a Nisei drugstore owner because he "wanted to get a Jap," and at Kingsburg, California, a Chinese American shot a Japanese American and then committed suicide in his jail cell.[72]

Pacific Coast newspapers generally gave much more prominence to these incidents than was customary in ordinary crime coverage. There can be little doubt that the appearance of vigilantism in the press was more substantial than the reality;[73] but there is no less doubt that the lurid news reports both confirmed and influenced public attitudes toward the Japanese minority. Many citizens felt strongly enough to demand that the government sweep away constitutional restraints in acting against the Japanese; to these extremists there seemed no contradiction between combating fascism abroad and embracing its methods at home. The crowning irony of their demand was that it was expressed almost invariably in terms of solicitude for the welfare of the Japanese who were to be its victims.

[72] Brawley *News,* January 2, 1942; *Nichi Bei,* December 31, 1941, January 3, 7, 14, 16, March 17, 1942; San Francisco *Chronicle,* January 1, 1942; Stockton *Record,* January 2, 16, 1942; *North American Times,* December 11, 1941, February 6, 1942; San Francisco *Examiner,* March 17, 1942.

[73] The motives of extralegal actions varied widely; some no doubt were within the normal incidence of crime, without anti-Japanese design. Again, the cumulative coverage of newspapers gave a misleading effect. Once duplications were eliminated, a careful check by the staff of the University of California Evacuation and Resettlement Study showed 36 cases of actual or potential vigilantism between December 8, 1941, and March 31, 1942. Of these 7 were murders (all in California), 2 were attacks on Japanese American girls, 19 were assaults with deadly weapons, and the remaining 8 consisted of robberies, extortion attempts, and property destruction. Of the assailants eighteen were tentatively identified as Filipinos, seven were white, one was a Negro, and one a Chinese; nine were unidentified. The largest incidence of anti-Japanese violence occurred between December 28 and January 1, when 8 cases were reported. In the preceding fifteen days only 5 cases had been noted. Only 6 cases were reported in February, and 4 in March.

The vast assortment of rumors and suspicions, epithets and accusations, directed at Japanese Americans in the first months of war was almost totally fictitious in content and wholly tragic in effect. Its historical importance, however, lies less in the degree of truth or falsity of specific charges than in its revelation of the prevailing state of mind among the population of the Pacific Coast: a deeply rooted and broadly diffused attitude of suspicion and distrust toward all persons of Japanese descent, which demonstrated scant regard for distinctions of birth or citizenship, for "minute constitutional rights," for the record of political loyalty or the facts of social assimilation. The wave of anti-Japanese sentiment which was set in motion by the attack on Pearl Harbor, and subsequently given before it and carried in its wake numbers of responsible public officials more impetus by an unbroken series of war disasters, swept all opposition and organized private groups. By mid-February the tide of hostility reached its crest, and soon thereafter it broke over the heads of the Japanese Americans—engulfing more than 100,000 persons, citizens and aliens alike, in a vortex of popular anger and official acquiescence.

Death in Kentucky

DAVID WELSH

America, as a rule, has kept its poverty out of sight. Traditionally, the poor people in the countryside have been isolated in "pockets of poverty," and in cities and towns they have lived "across the tracks." By formal or informal zoning regulations, most American towns and cities have successfully walled off areas of affluent living, blocking the poor from entering the communities of the rich, except, of course, as domestic workers or service personnel.

One of the most powerful and persistent myths in American life has been that of social and economic mobility. The pattern of economic growth in nineteenth-century America, along with the traditional Puritan emphasis on hard work, sobriety, and thrift, suggested to most Americans that any man who was willing to work hard and to save his money could get ahead in this society. This idea found popular expression in the rags-to-riches tales of Horatio Alger, and it found powerful spokesmen in industrialists such as Andrew Carnegie and clergymen such as Henry Ward Beecher. In the last quarter of the nineteenth century, a veritable "Gospel of Wealth" was elaborated, taking its cues from the laissez faire mood of the times and from the doctrine of social Darwinism. According to the new gospel, economic success would inevitably come to those who worked hard and were blessed by God's favor. Thus the rich were the natural aristocracy of the state and should be its leaders. The poor were lazy, dissolute, and clearly not in God's good graces. Though their plight was unfortunate, the deprivation of some individuals was natural within the total scheme of things and ought not to be meddled with by the state.

The historical evidence on the causes of poverty in America tells quite a different story. Indeed, even in periods of rapid economic growth and general prosperity, there have always been barriers to the achievement of economic success in this country. Ethnic, religious, and sex discrimination have undermined the efforts of large groups of Americans to attain a reasonable degree of economic security. Re-gressive taxation has favored the well-to-do and further oppressed the poor. Government aid and protection for certain industries have prevented masses of workers from gaining economic independence. The rural poor have been consistently neglected by the state. Yet the myth persists, sustained by rich and poor alike.

At the conclusion of the Second World War, the American economy was in relatively good shape. Demobilization took place rapidly and with a minimum of economic displacement. The G.I. Bill of Rights offered the advantage of higher education to many servicemen who would otherwise have returned to a lower- or lower-middle-class workingman's life. The 1950's were years of continued prosperity for the nation as a whole, prompting John Kenneth Galbraith, a leading economist, to describe the United States as "the affluent society." As Galbraith pointed out in his book of the same title, chronic poverty still existed in certain segments of the population; but for all practical purposes, the public failed to take notice.

Then, in the early 1960's, poverty in America was rediscovered, and for the first time Americans registered alarm. In 1962, Michael Harrington, a socialist writer and editor, published a small book entitled **The Other America: Poverty in the United States,** in which he pointed out that an appalling number of Americans lived in poverty— some forty or fifty million people, or about one-fourth of the population. In addition, he pointed out that most of the poor were whites— not blacks, Puerto Ricans, or Mexican-Americans, as had previously been assumed. The white poor were concentrated in rural areas, and huge numbers of them lived in the mountainous region of the Eastern states, known as Appalachia. There, in the hollows and on the hillsides of the mountains that stretch from Pennsylvania to Georgia, tens of thousands of native-born whites of English, Scottish, and Scots-Irish ancestry lived in poverty and despair, passed over and forgotten by the so-called affluent society. The realization of the extent of poverty among whites in this country shocked the mass media of the nation as well as the federal government and led to the Kennedy and Johnson administrations' programs for a concerted war on poverty.

Ironically, the war on poverty has produced a spate of publicity centering on the plight of America's nonwhite poor, once again drawing attention away from poor whites. In the following article, reprinted from **Ramparts** magazine, David Welsh deals with one aspect of the poor whites' continuing struggle in certain regions of Appalachia, as they attempt to wrest even a meager existence from the few resources left to them in the mountains.

ACT ONE
SLAUGHTER ON CLEAR CREEK

Scene One

[*where the land is Laid Waste by the Strip Mines and the Little People are chased from their Modest Homes*]

The people who live along Clear Creek, Knott County, piled into their old cars and pickups and drove to Hazard in the next county one muggy evening last June. They were going there to "get organized," as one man put it, and their talk was full of extravagant threats, complaints and morbid aphorisms. They were schoolteachers, stonecutters, ex-miners, carpenters, small farmers, storekeepers—poor, but better off than most of the mountain people, who have no means of livelihood but public charity.

Something else distinguished the 150 men and women who gathered that night at the meeting hall of the Pet Milk Co. in Hazard: they owned their own land, and had deeds to prove it. Yet there seemed to be nothing they could do to stop a strip mining company from tearing up their land beyond reclamation, except perhaps, to get organized. One after another they stood up and aired their personal grievances against "the company." There was Herman Ritchie, who used to live on Rattlesnake Branch, Clear Creek—until the bulldozers began shaving off the mountain top to get at the coal:

"My wife was in there with the kids when the rocks began to roll. She got out fast and went to the neighbors. Then the landslide started and the dirt and boulders came down on the house. After that some uprooted trees fell down and knocked in the roof." Ritchie said he applied to the company for compensation but was told there would be none for the present. His in-laws, who own the land, still pay the surface taxes. His furniture is trapped inside the house; neighbors insist that dogs slip in there at night and sleep in the beds.

Burley Combs Jr. went away to work at a foundry in Indiana, but he came back home, like a lot of others, and tried to scratch out a living in the hills. He owns a piece of land and an unpainted log house, vacant now. Two days before the meeting, a stump rolled down the mountain and struck the house. Combs and family moved out. The only sign of life there now is a handful of scrawny chickens, pecking diffidently in the

"Death in Kentucky," by David Welsh. From *Ramparts*, IV (December 1965), 52-64. Copyright Ramparts Magazine, Inc. 1965. By Permission of the Editors.

coal dust. Like the others, Burley Combs must continue to pay taxes on his land, and if he has any recourse against the company, he doesn't know what it is.

But if the coal operator, as the immediate, visible enemy, bears the brunt of their anger, they are also aware of his distant and powerful allies; even—one hesitates to say it—His Beneficence, the Federal Government.

"All this coal they're mining, do you know where it is going? To TVA, that's where it's going." It was the next day, and over the noise of a wheezing bulldozer, Andy Tomlin was talking. "TVA money is being used to tear up these hills, and they talk about reforestation. I ask you, how can you reforest that?"

He pointed to a hillside stripped of vegetation, the rocky soil freshly turned and ready to roll at the slightest provocation, uprooted trees stuck like darts at right angles to the mountain. One look at that grotesque relic of a mountain and one could only nod in agreement. How can you reforest that, indeed.

"And the TVA is just as responsible as anyone," he added. "I call this political death, hell and destruction on these hill people."

"It seems like they don't have any pity's sake on anybody," said an old man, leaning on his walking stick. "I don't know, but it all points on that. It seems like all we own here is the air we breathe."

A small group of Clear Creek people stood on the access road and talked, to no one in particular, their gaze magnetized by the bulldozers working at the hilltop.

"We love these hills. We grew up here. We don't want to be pushed out of here. This is our surroundings, our living area."

"The company cut an access road right through our cemetery. They've got no respect for the dead, let alone the living."

"Our officials, you can hear them hollering, 'Let's beautify these hills.' They give you a $300 fine for throwing a paper on the highway, and then they let them strip and strip and strip."

"The sheriff and his gang, and the state people up at Frankfort: they're all in with them. One of those overloaded coal trucks caved in a county bridge a few months ago and the company didn't have to pay a cent for it."

"They keep pushing dirt down . . . ain't nowhere it can go except in the hollows and valleys. And just wait till the rains come next spring."

Or Venyard Breeding: "They think they have a right to come in and move your house, do anything they want to. They stick up signs, 'Private Property—No Trespassing,' like they own the place. You can't even walk on your own land, and the state police are out there to make sure you don't."

Or the youngest member of the group, between his teeth: "I wonder if someone shouldn't turn a good rifle loose on them." Then he let out a good laugh, the passivity of his situation momentarily exorcised by the violent thought.

This, certainly, is not a comedy of manners of America in the mid-twentieth century. It is an old Western, one would think, perhaps a pre-war soap opera, or a melodrama of the 1890's. A big corporation, with a government contract, with friends in the State house and friends in court, vs. the "little people," with access to none of the levers of power. Only it is not the nice, nonviolent kind of political struggle most Americans are familiar with. In our Appalachian colony, where power is used in its most naked form, people get killed playing politics every year.

Scene Two

[*where the Mellons and other Prominent Magnates count their Gold, thanking the Good Lord for the Boundless Charity of the President-of-All-the-People*]

It all started around the turn of the century, when speculators from New York began buying up mineral rights in the Appalachian hills for 25 and 50 cents an acre. Deeds to the land gave them the right, with stipulations, to extract all minerals below the ground. These "land companies," as they were called, would in turn lease portions of a coal seam to the operators, receiving a royalty on each ton of coal mined. Today their holdings in the area are worth an estimated $7,200 an acre in coal royalties alone. One land company, the Virginia Iron & Coal Co., with offices in Philadelphia and extensive holdings in the Appalachian coalfields, is the most profitable large corporation in the United States according to Dun's Review of Modern Industry (April 1965). Its net profit is 61 cents on the dollar, compared with 10 cents for General Motors.

Land companies, which because of depletion allowances, operate virtually tax-free (they are taxed at roughly the same rate as an auto worker), have built up reservoirs of capital enabling them to acquire huge interests in industry, railroads and power companies. Pittsburgh-Consolidation Coal Corp., the nation's largest bituminous coal producer and a land company in its own right, recently became a major stockholder in both Chrysler and U.S. Steel. Controlled by the Mellon family of Pittsburgh, through the Mellon National Bank and Trust, it also acquired more than 100,000 shares of American Electric Power, a holding company for six Appalachian utilities. The president of American Electric is Donald Cook, a close friend of President Johnson. Through Pittsburgh-Consolidation, the Mellons are major stockholders in the merged Norfolk & Western—Virginian railways, which recently carried 76 per cent of total domestic bituminous coal shipped from the mines. Moreover, they benefit from a tax break tantamount to a government subsidy.

Coal, rails, utilities—the biggest defenders of the status quo in Appalachia, and those incorrigible Mellons, have their fingers in them all. But the Mellons are not the whole story. Within 50 miles of Clear Creek are holdings of U.S. Steel, Midland Steel, Bethlehem Steel, International Harvester, Virginia Iron & Coal: some of the most prosperous companies and some of the poorest people, statistically, in the nation.

Most residents of Clear Creek own strips of land running from their houses in the valley to the hill crest. But the coal beneath is owned by the Kentucky River Coal Co., a land company that recently declared dividends of 45 cents on each dollar of sales volume (Dun's Review). It leases the coal rights to Kentucky Oak Mining Co., a nonunion strip and auger operation and the creation of the biggest operators in the Hazard coalfield, William B. Sturgill and Dick Kelly.

In strip mining, bulldozers literally lop off the top of a mountain, trees and all, to get at the coal seam. Machines then strip off the coal and load it into trucks. In auger mining, a huge drill, or auger, bores into the side of a seam and sends the coal shooting back out for loading. Stripping and augering are much cheaper ways of extracting coal than deep mining, and a sharp drop in the price of coal in recent years did much to encourage their spread. The work is almost invariably nonunion, paying $1.25 an hour or less. Markets, too, have stimulated company growth: Detroit Edison, Consumers Power and other utilities in Michigan, Indiana, Ohio and Illinois are the Hazard strippers' best customers.

But much of their coal goes South, where the Tennessee Valley Authority is in continual quest of cheaper sources of power. When the Sturgill-Kelly combine puts to work its $1 million worth of equipment to despoil the mountain, poison the stream and throw a family out of its meager cabin, it is to fulfill a more than $50 million coal contract with TVA. The price per ton paid by TVA is so low that in general, only a strip or auger mine (and a scab one at that) could fulfill the contract and still make the healthy profit to which the operators are accustomed. The Tennessee Valley, once itself an exploited region, has indeed joined Detroit, Cincinnati and Cleveland in the ranks of the exploiters. With their ready supply of cheap electric power, the prosperous cities of the Tennessee Valley grow even more prosperous while the Kentucky mountain poor get poorer. One can hardly escape the conclusion that TVA, that great government agency, has become an accomplice in the destruction of eastern Kentucky.

Scene Three

[where we learn of a Noble Project to reclaim the land Laid Waste by the Strip Mines]

William Caperton, a husky man in his 30's, runs the Caperton Coal Co., one of the small "dummy" operations set up by the parent company, Kentucky Oak Mining, to avoid paying union wages to the miners.

"How would you like to see our land reclamation project?" he asked, and led us cheerfully to the site, as MacIntosh, taking no pains to conceal his bitterness, grumbled.

"For every acre we tear up, there's $100 bond we put up with the state for land reclaiming," said Caperton.

"$100! Are you kidding?" It was Donald MacIntosh, a gaunt Clear Creek resident. "After what you've done to this mountain you couldn't reclaim ten square feet for that price."

"My friend, you know that's not true. Now just look at these apple trees we've planted. They didn't cost $100, and once they take hold, this part of the mountain will be as good as new."

He pointed to a row of twelve seedlings, already wilting, twelve spindly signs of life on a wasteland of red dirt, and here and there a sprig of new grass.

MacIntosh: "What about that sawdust you've put around your apple trees? You threw all the good topsoil and trees on top of our houses and now nothing grows up here, isn't that right? So you put sawdust around the trees and you still can't make them grow."

Caperton: "Well now, as to that sawdust, I'm not sure but what some truck driver didn't dump it here by mistake. And you see those young apple trees, they're doing all right. And we have been planting elderberry bushes. . . ."

MacIntosh: "I'd like to know how a man can pick apples from a landslide."

Caperton: "We are seeding whole areas with fescue and lespedeza. Those are special varieties of grass. In five years' time we hope to have it all grassed in. We seeded this area two years ago."

MacIntosh: "You need a magnifying glass to find a blade of grass around here."

Caperton: "Why, just last year the governor himself was up here, and they had a big ceremony, planting pine trees and all. I think it was during Conservation Week."

MacIntosh: "You know damn well those pine trees the governor planted didn't live over a week. It's like trying to put makeup on a cadaver and making believe it's alive."

Caperton: "Come on now, you know they lived longer than that. The thing is, they used the wrong fertilizer. . . ."

MacIntosh: "Look at that pool, that red, old, acid mine water. That's what's killed every fish and tadpole on Clear Creek."

Caperton: "There's minnows in that pool."

MacIntosh: "How'd they get there: fall from the sky? Swim upstream? Or did somebody bring them in here yesterday?"

Caperton: "Well now, I was told there was minnows in there. But they might have been talking about some other place. . . ."

Scene Four

[where Deeds mean more than Words]

In Hindman, the Knott County Seat, a group of 19 Clear Creek homeowners trooped up to the mine site with the intention of stopping the work there, if necessary by force. State policemen with shotguns headed them off. Almost immediately, Kentucky Oak Mining sought, and got, an injunction against them. The Knott County Circuit Court issued an order enjoining the 19 from interfering with operations at the strip mine. State police and sheriff's men doubled their guard at the mine.

County Judge Morgan Slone, who was not involved in the incident, says the original deeds signed by Clear Creek residents authorized deep mining of the coal beneath their land, and deep mining only. Slone contends the deeds were altered, in the Knott County Courthouse, to authorize the companies to surface mine as well.

"The companies come in to Hindman from all over this country and get things fixed up the way they want it," he said. "Suddenly they are waving a new deed, and you don't know where they got it from. The companies claim they have on record the right to strip and auger. I don't think they have any right to change the deed from the way it was originally signed. But they just go ahead and run over the people. This day and time, a poor man's just like a frog down a forty-foot well and no way to get out."

Scene Five

[where a Humble Mountain Man speaks with the President-of-All-the-People]

Dan Gibson is a man everyone around here looks up to, a kind of elder statesman of the people. White-haired, with the face of a college professor and two fingers missing from a mining accident, he is not about to take anything lying down.

"In 1960," he recalls, "the coal company was bulldozing on Frank Fugate's property, and ten of us went and put them out. They tried to come on these children's land and we were standing back of the fence. I had a shotgun and I told them bulldozer operators, 'You break that fence and you'll get what's in it.' We run them out, all right, and they got a warrant and arrested Frank Fugate. Then the company sued Frank in Circuit Court at Hindman and got a judgment for the company. Well you know, that always happens. But Frank took it to Federal Court, and he won. That's unusual. But the main thing is, they don't mess with Frank any more because he went to the clerk and got a copy of his deed, which says he deeded them mineral rights for deep mining only. The rest of our deeds is tampered with to suit the coal operators."

But if the Clear Creek landowners made sporadic attempts to stop the strippers, as a group they remained inchoate. Not until last April did they begin really to organize. They had gathered to draw up a "community action program," in the hope of obtaining a federal anti-poverty grant for recreation facilities, when it occurred to them: how can we sit here and talk about recreation when they are tearing up our land? Curious, but in an indirect way a federal program had given birth to the first serious movement to halt the strip mining on Clear Creek.

The mere fact of organization widens people's horizons. Matt Holiday even thought to call President Johnson: "Why can't I speak to the President? I help to pay his salary." State Representative Carl Perkins set it up for him and before he knew it, Holiday was on the line to LBJ.

"He said, 'This is the President, what can I do for you?' I told him how the strip mines were ruining our land. He said, 'I am with you, friend, but I am going to put you onto someone who can do you a lot more good than I can,' and the next thing I knew I was talking with Udall, the Secretary of the Interior. He said we may have to fight it all the way to the Supreme Court, but if the companies are destroying property then they'll have to pay for it."

The people here have little faith in courts which habitually decide in the company's favor, and few have the money to appeal. Nor are they impressed with schemes of compensation for damages. In the past, any compensation has been too little and too late to save the land and has provided no guarantees against future abuses. Recently a coal company was found guilty of polluting a stream and fined $800. The next day "that red, old, acid mine water" was pouring into the stream the same as ever. The mountain people will believe in Washington's good intentions the day the Federal Government says "no" to the pressure groups, the day Washington curbs the power of the coal companies, and their allies, to buy the legislatures, buy the courts, buy the freedom to do exactly as they please.

ACT TWO
STATE OF THE UNION

Scene One

[*where the Little People live on the Charity of the President-of-All-the-People*]

"Look at the muskrat," hooted the driver, peering from his coal truck at the man cleaning paper and debris from a creek bed.

The man straightened up and shook his fist. "I'd sooner be a muskrat than a damn scab."

The "muskrat" was beautifying the countryside for $1.25 an hour under the federal-state "Jobless Fathers" program. He collects $175 a month and puts in 140 hours work for it. The "scab" was trucking coal from a nonunion mine for the same hourly wage. Both are noteworthy in that they have jobs at all in this area of southeastern Kentucky where the official unemployment figure is more than 10 per cent and unofficial estimates go as high as 50 per cent. Their shouting-match is symptomatic of the diseases of their part of the country, and of the conflicts that divide the impoverished and enable a privileged few to prosper.

Estill Amburgey, 40, started work in the pits when he was 11. Today he supports his family of four on $60 worth of federal food stamps a month—one of nearly 2,000 families on the program in a county of 35,000 people. Occasionally he finds an odd job to perform with his truck. He could find work in one of a hundred small truck mines, which, because of their size, are not subject to the federal mine safety code. But he refuses on principle to work for a "scab" operator. And since low-paying, non-union jobs are about the only ones available and recommended by the State Employment Service, his refusal to accept them costs him unemployment compensation.

He lives in Perry County (Hazard), where only 15 per cent of persons over 25 have finished high school, and where the average adult has left school before the ninth grade. The median family income is $2,600; but if one excluded the incomes of coal operators, officials and businessmen, average family income would be closer to $1,600.

Amburgey belongs to the Appalachian Committee for Full Employment, formed here in January, 1964, to represent the interests of the unemployed. Its members are ex-miners in an area where coal is the only industry and, for most of them, their sole source of income is either food stamps or a government check—retirement or disability, unemployment, "Aid to Families with Dependent Children" or "Jobless Fathers." A few have miners' pensions.

"The dole is a way of life around here," says Everette Tharp, secretary of the Committee. "The politicians put us on the dole to avoid interfering with the corporate monopolies that are responsible for the pitiful condition of our people."

Not all the needy benefit from the largesse of our government. Tharp charges that federal and state welfare programs are used politically to reward "friends" of the coal companies and punish their enemies. "Workers in the scab mines have an easier time getting food stamps," he contends. "It's a kind of subsidy to keep them satisfied with low wages and no benefits. The Federal Government really thinks their money is helping the poor, the sick and disabled, and all the time their agents are denying these benefits to people in need. In any case the red tape is so thick many people give up."

Amburgey says they have threatened to cut off his food stamps if he fails to furnish proof of having applied for at least three (nonunion) jobs each week, "willingness to work" being one requirement for obtaining stamps in Kentucky. From the living room of their ramshackle house in the hollows near Kodak, his wife, Eunice, vows: "They can take our food stamps. They can take our furniture and all we have. We've still got our pride."

But this kind of defiance of the welfare bureaucracy is not usual. Thomas E. Gish, editor of the muckraking Mountain Eagle in nearby Whitesburg, says the typical welfare recipient here is "a political slave who knows his welfare payments can be withdrawn tomorrow if he steps out of line. This is the simple fact of life that has destroyed pride in the mountains, not because of welfare payments, but because of the price exacted to qualify for them—one's traditional independence and freedom."

Scene Two

[*where the Forces-of-Law-and-Order preserve the Values-of-Our-Civilization from the Forces-of-Anarchy*]

It was against this background of desperation that the Appalachian Committee was born, out of the remnants of the Roving Picket movement that ran its own stormy gamut in the last months of 1962. Berman Gibson, the Committee's founder and president, had emerged as leader of the Roving Pickets, a miners' group formed more or less spontaneously to protest low pay and dangerous working conditions in the nonunion mines.

Mine after mine had terminated contracts with the United Mine Workers of America (UMW) in preceding years, and many men had settled for less than union scale. Then, in September 1962, the union withdrew the miners' welfare cards entitling them to free medical care at miners' hospitals because coal operators were no longer contributing into the UMW welfare fund. It was the last straw.

Several thousand men converged on nonunion mining sites and coal tipples in seven counties. They picketed. They threatened. They threw rocks. The opposition—hirelings of the coal operators and "the law" itself —fought back. Beatings and shootings were attributed to both sides. A Hazard police lieutenant, Ira Kilburn, testified in court that the dynamiting of a rail tipple, blamed on the Roving Pickets, was in fact the work of other policemen in civilian clothes. Kilburn is no longer on the force.

The Roving Pickets, in the tradition of Kentucky mountaineers when their rights are threatened, were not exactly angels. But to them, it seemed the enemy had all the weapons, including the full force of the law. Gibson and seven other picket leaders were arrested in 1963 by FBI agents and state police and charged with conspiracy to blow up a rail bridge the previous year. Charges against Gibson were dismissed for lack of evidence. But four of his co-defendants were found guilty, on the basis of jailhouse confessions they later repudiated, and sentenced to six-year terms, pending appeal. Berman Gibson called it a frame-up.

On Election Day, 1963, Gibson was arrested again, along with six others, on a charge of assault with intent to kill. The arrests came as they were driving men to the polls to help reelect a circuit judge they considered fair. The judge lost, by 300 votes, to a man who has since handed down a nearly unbroken string of anti-labor decisions. The accused miners were later acquitted. Everette Tharp, a retired miner who once took a correspondence course in law and serves as the movement's intellectual and theorist, put it succinctly: "After the Election Day arrests, for a crime that allegedly took place over a year previous, we figured we were dead right: this was a political conspiracy to get rid of the movement."

Meanwhile, state mediation between the pickets and the Mine Operators' Association had resulted in an agreement to reestablish union pay and conditions in the mines, in return for a halt to picketing. Of the picket leaders, only Berman Gibson noticed there was no enforcement clause and refused to sign. The agreement has yet to be enforced. The UMW, which lost some 75 per cent of its members in the area since 1952 and all its members in Perry County, was weaker than ever, and the Roving Picket movement was dead. About half the pickets went back to the pits.

In picking up the pieces, Tharp and Gibson decided to change tack, and transform what had been an industrial movement with industrial demands—union scale wages, safety rules, clean towels in the washroom—into a political movement, with political demands. They saw their constituency no longer as one of underpaid industrial workers, but of unemployed men, and felt their duty was to demand that federal and state governments provide jobs and more relief for the unemployed. They further called on the UMW to join and lead them in pressing their demands.

In January 1964, a delegation of 27 miners went to Washington and talked things over with Interior Secretary Udall and George Reedy, later the President's press secretary. Reedy told them their demands would carry more weight if they represented a formal organization. The miners thought it over and, shortly afterward, established the Appalachian Committee.

Instrumental in setting up the new organization was the Committee for Miners, a group formed in New York in July 1963 to provide legal defense for Gibson and the Roving Pickets. It soon had two full-time organizers in Hazard and an office in New York. The Committee for Miners' man in Hazard was Hamish Sinclair, 33, a former radio reporter who became concerned with the miners' plight after hearing a speech by Gibson in New York. Scottish-born, he has a simple explanation for his interest in the movement: "I'm from a working-class family and a trade-unionist from birth."

Sinclair was to be a formative influence in the growth of the Appalachian Committee, and among Hazard townspeople, a controversial figure. For Main Street, the quiet, conservatively dressed Sinclair was a "wild-eyed Bolshevik" come to town with his foreign accent and "alien" ideas. His approach was straightforward: "The unemployed miners are literally disenfranchised: their voice isn't heard. Their union used to be their voice. But now it has all but disappeared in the mines here, and only the Appalachian Committee has set out to articulate their demands."

Scene Three

[where the Little People tell the President-of-All-the-People it is not his Charity that they want]

The status quo is dear to all power structures, but in few places is the attempt to preserve it more blatant than in parts of eastern Kentucky. The practice in some counties of "kept" police and sheriffs departments, "kept" judges, welfare officials and social security doctors is often difficult to prove. But almost every poor person you meet in these parts will tell you about it; their repertoire of corruption stories is as long as you have time to sit and listen. But "corruption" is a vague word; "interest" is perhaps more apt. The high sheriff of Perry County, Charlie Combs, is also a nonunion truck mine operator, who boasted recently of making $60,000 in 60 days, and who spent more than $10,000 of his own money equipping the sheriffs department with marked cars, guns and two-way radios. It is small wonder that the unemployed, thwarted by the authorities in their efforts to organize, see a connection.

During the summer and fall of 1964, as the miners' movement grew in strength, the opposition began to retaliate openly. Two student volunteers said they were ordered by County Judge Babe Noplis to "leave town in 24 hours or the hunting season will be open on you." Welfare recipients accused the judge of threatening to cut off their payments if they associated themselves with the movement. The judge denied the allegations.

An unemployed miner was arrested for littering while passing out copies of Jobs and Justice. Five committee workers were called before the county grand jury and questioned about the movement and their political affiliations. George Goss, 22, a student worker, was sentenced to 30 days in jail and fined $300 for "driving without a license." Nightriders fired shots into the home of committee vice-president Jason Combs, narrowly missing him and his wife, and on two occasions fired into the committee's office in Hazard. I. Philip Sipser, a Committee for Miners attorney, charged that the lives of workers were in serious danger, "and the danger emanates from those who are supposed to protect them—the local law enforcement agencies."

Harassment failed to stunt the growth of the Appalachian Committee. If it was still largely an old man's movement—ex-union men conditioned to the idea of organizing to improve specific conditions—it had succeeded in adapting this idea from the working place to the community. For a while the Committee was a real thorn in the side of Hazard officialdom. It held meetings in the hollows to develop local community organizations, and campaigned (successfully) for a raise for the "Jobless Fathers" from $1 to $1.25 an hour. As a direct result of its agitation, the federal school lunch program was extended to some mountain schools that had not previously benefited from it.

If its action was grievance-oriented, it was slowly coming to see the "enemy" as a combination of interests that would remain impregnable without action on a national scale. Hamish Sinclair observes that for the unemployed, the "boss" is no longer a private coal operator but the supervisor in the welfare office. For a while the miners talked of picketing the welfare office if grievances were not resolved. Then came the "war on poverty" and the Committee's first real opportunity to swing political power.

Tharp & Co. drew up a detailed "community action program" and submitted it to the federal Office of Economic Opportunity (OEO), which provides grants to self-help organizations in needy communities. Their proposal called for a six-month preliminary program covering four counties at a cost of $346,000. This would pay for the hiring of 20 local residents as community organizers, a 23-man professional planning staff and the establishment of 20 community centers in the creeks and hollows, where the poor could begin, as the federal bill directs, to shape their own programs. The Appalachian Committee proposed to concentrate its long-range effort in five areas: community organizing, technical assistance, education, medical care and "development of jobs and industry, to begin to do away with both the causes and effects of poverty." The old miners, naive enough to take the OEO at its word, had submitted a program with guts in it—serious, in short—and the politicians in Washington must have had a good laugh at such pretensions.

A few months later an OEO man, Ralph Caprio, showed up at the Committee office and explained why its application could not be granted. It seemed that, contrary to the wording of the legislation, an organization composed exclusively of poor people did not qualify for federal funds. Local elected officials and a welfare administrator would have to be represented—"the very same people," said Tharp, "who have thwarted every move for social progress in Perry County." The Appalachian Committee was further disqualified, Caprio said, because it was not legally incorporated prior to the passage of the Economic Opportunity Act in August 1964. The Mountain Eagle shrieked its indignation:

> What group of our poor people has been legally incorporated since before August 1964? Why can't Washington understand that our county officials, for the most part, are not going to permit the poor to become powerful enough to have a voice of their own? The war on poverty is supposed to be non-political. Yet the OEO insists that a state welfare official have a say in guiding our community action programs—and there is nothing more political than the welfare office in these counties.

Bill Bailey, afflicted with arthritis and silicosis after 35 years in the mines (and typically unable to collect compensation), had limped up and down the hollows getting 100 signatures to back up the Committee's proposal. "You'll see, those Hazard politicians will try to get this money so us people in the hills won't see any of it," said Bailey, a father of 14. "And they'll most likely get it. They always do."

It was not long before the prominent citizens, led by County Judge Noplis, saw the way the wind was blowing and qualified for federal funds. Their modest proposal emphasized "preparatory studies," and promised to include people from "all walks of life" on their advisory board. Hamish Sinclair thinks it is no accident that the courthouse gang's anti-poverty unit got the nod from Washington. He feels the national Democratic Party wants the Democratic governments of Kentucky and Perry County to sponsor OEO programs "to enhance the Party's reputation as the number one 'poverty warrior' and keep this thing from getting out of their control."

The old miners, who started it all, got neither the grant nor the credit, but they had established themselves as a potent political force. The proof came when the boys uptown invited the Committee's representative to sit on the board of the Perry County Development Association, and on the advisory board of the judge's anti-poverty corporation. Not that they approved of the miners' movement any more than in the past; they were merely acknowledging its power. Courtney Wells, a Hazard lawyer and former circuit judge, is one of those rare Main Streeters who does not hold the Appalachian Committee in contempt. "If they have done nothing more," he said, "they have called the attention of the outside world to conditions here. They are more responsible than any other single organization for what help this region is getting and probably will get from Washington."

The Reverend Phil Young, serving in Hazard with the Presbyterian Board of National Missions, sees the Committee's role in power terms: "The powers in this county discovered there are people they can't get to, people who might revolt some day and knock them off the catbird seat, and this scares hell out of them."

Scene Four

[*where there is Violence and Bloodshed, and a Victory for the Forces-of-Law-and-Order*]

To the average miner, whose working life is short, free hospital care, retirement benefits and some assurance of safe working conditions are almost more important than the size of his paycheck. If he works non-union he has no such guarantees. Safety in the nonunion mines is a regional scandal, and whenever there is a new fatality, which is almost every day nationally, the local papers drily include the running totals for the year. Accurate figures are difficult to obtain, however. The Federal Bureau of Mines is prohibited by its code from investigating accidents in small-payroll mines, the most dangerous of them all. One can only surmise what pressure group pushed through that proviso.

It is too easy to blame the miners' plight on the "irresistible forces" unleashed by mechanization. With the exception of a few small operators in genuine financial difficulty, it is a matter of bigger and bigger profits taken literally from the miners' pockets. Into the bargain goes the complicity, cowardice and unconcern of the Federal Government, local officials and the miners' own union. The process is called deunionizing, and the Blue Diamond Coal Co., operator of two deep mines in Perry County, is a master at it.

Blue Diamond Mine No. 2 was the first to go. Late in 1962, the company gave notice to the UMW that it was terminating the contract and the men were told to evacuate their houses in the mining camp and pay up their debts at the commissary. First the Roving Pickets struck. The UMW followed with an official strike, but gave up without a whimper soon afterward. The mine shut down briefly, then reopened with a new crew hired by the Southern Labor Union (SLU).

The SLU is a company union, organized in Birmingham (Ala.) during the '50's as an alternative to the United Steelworkers of America. Old union-busting, head-busting George C. Wallace, afraid the United Steelworkers would integrate the Birmingham locals, helped to set it up. Before long, the SLU had spread to other industries throughout the South, including Kentucky coal. Their method is simple. The SLU hires a crew of men from out-of-state or from historically nonunion counties and delivers them to the company. An election is called, supervised by the National Labor Relations Board, to determine which union will represent the workers at the mine. Since SLU members outnumber those of the UMW, and since the majority owe their jobs to the SLU, the outcome is pre-determined.

Blue Diamond No. 2 reincorporated as the Blair Fork Coal Co. and signed a sweetheart contract with the SLU. Daily wages were from $5 to $10 less than the then prevailing UMW scale of $24. Welfare and hospital benefits were pitifully low.

Blue Diamond No. 1 executed a similar maneuver. It terminated its UMW contract, evicted the men from their homes and shut down for six months—long enough for the miners' state unemployment benefits to expire. Last fall it reopened nonunion with a new work force, and before long the UMW had a picket line at No. 1. The potentates of the union, con-ventioneering in Miami, had just voted to launch a million-dollar or-ganizing drive, and they were anxious to prove their sincerity.

The company, certainly, was preparing for war, and it looked as if the drama of the Roving Pickets was about to be reenacted. Armed com-pany guards went up around the mine, fetching sullen stares from the hundred-odd milling pickets. Trucks were dynamited and cars shot into. State police turned out in force and the "scab" miners continued to pass the picket line. A company official declared: "We are prepared to add to our guard force enough men to station in the hills around our operation, night and day. Anybody who looks like a thief or a dynamiter will get it."

One coal operator said that if there was a mass movement to unionize the mines the independent coal truckers would be the first to resist. "These men number in the hundreds," he said, "and each one is an in-dividual businessman. He knows the mines must stay open if his business is to survive. A fast trucker can clear $10,000 a year. If mass picketing starts again, you will see two riders in every truck, one driving and the other 'riding shotgun.' They are not about to be stopped and beaten like they were in 1962."

Then, in the winter, a man was killed. A high-powered rifle got him in a truck cab as he was on his way home from his job at Blue Diamond No. 1. Who knows who killed him? There were the usual mutual accusa-tions. Twelve men, including the union local president, were arrested ini-tially and charged with the crime.

They called Earnest Creech a scab for working in that mine. But he was father to nine children, and his wife was expecting another child soon. His death is the tragedy of a working class divided against itself, of Big Money's callous disregard for human life. It is the tragedy of a government that faithfully fulfills its dual promise of more relief for the poor and more profits for the rich.

Earnest Creech died early, like everything else of value in eastern Kentucky. His death brought home to many an awareness of how little has changed for the mountain poor since the Roving Pickets first stormed up to the scab mines three years ago. And few in these mountains really believe there will be any changes for a long time to come. The conditions that breed this desperate kind of political murder don't change overnight. In many ways, the region is still back in the heyday of the labor wars, which raged for 35 years up and down the soft coal country, claiming hundreds of lives—thousands if you count deaths from starvation and bad medical care. Only now they don't die so often; because Appalachia, the "Sick Man of America," is now in the care of a modern social doctor, skilled in the techniques of keeping people barely alive.

ACT THREE
PRINCES AND PAUPERS

Scene One

[*where the Cruelties of the Industrial Age are killing the Culture of the Little People*]

The respectable citizens of Hazard deeply resent the reputation their city has acquired as the hub of a poverty culture. "To read the press you would think everyone in Hazard is a starving illiterate living in a tinroof shack with an outdoor toilet and has to go down to the well to fetch his water. We're pretty tired of hearing about it."

Some Hazard residents are, in fact, well below the poverty line, including a good many of the approximately 900 black people who live here. For a Negro this could be almost any town in the upper South, or at least not very much better or worse. Schools are integrated, and the Negro stars of Hazard's basketball team are local heroes to a population whose number one sportive passion is high school athletics. There are at least three Negro schoolteachers. Most churches are integrated in principle. But otherwise, life for the Hazard black community goes on almost as if the last tempestuous decade had never happened. "We're nice to them," said a white townsman, "and they're nice to us. Race relations couldn't be better. You won't find anybody getting uppity around here." Many Negroes live in small wooden dwellings on a hillside "back of the yards," accessible from Hazard by crossing the river on a swinging footbridge, with a picturesque view of the Louisville and Nashville railway yards below. Biracial barbers are difficult to find. La Citadelle, high on a hilltop on the edge of town, is about the only hostelry that dares not refuse a Negro guest, and except for the Combs Drive-in, no restaurant in town will serve them sitting down. One prominent café-owner has vowed publicly to "kill the next nigger that walks through that door." There are no black officials or law officers, and it is difficult for a Hazard person to recall when there last was a Negro on a jury or a grand jury. Even in the Appalachian Committee, which, for many Negroes, was their first active political experience, they were relegated to second-class status.

Mayor Dawahare has done a lot for his town. He is also one of the few city people with an activist kind of concern about the county. He is the first to admit that the real problem does not lie in bustling little

Hazard, where practically everyone has work; the problem is in the county, where unemployment, by the mayor's count, runs to 72 per cent. Gurney Norman, writer of fiction and reporter for the twice-weekly Hazard Herald, says most of the townsfolk "live a comfortable, middle-class existence, seemingly unaware of the suffering that goes on a few miles away from them. They don't realize that it is a false economy here in town, based on the people in the county, who are destitute. Hazard is like a fish, and the county like the water. Our prosperity depends on the money spent here by the hill people; it depends, too, on aid from the outside. I'd hate to say how much of our revenue derives from food stamps and government checks."

Hazard has always been a trading town, especially since it is "wet" and mountaineers can have a few while they do their shopping. It used to be that every Saturday was trading day. Now it is only the first Saturday of the month that Main Street is really crowded—the Saturday after the federal checks arrive. On that day the floor of the People's Bank is strewn with hundreds of those little brown envelopes, familiar to anyone who has ever been in the Army or on the dole.

But one must not hastily conclude that all of Main Street is indifferent to the paupers in the hills. Youth everywhere is a force for social progress, and the Hazard chapter of the Junior Chamber of Commerce is no exception. Concerned, like all Jaycees, that islands of poverty should still exist in our affluent society, those rising young civic leaders organized a Christmas drive and raised $1,000 to buy baskets of food for the poor. The Jaycees sent postcards to families in the mountains, saying they had qualified as poor people and should come to Hazard to pick up their baskets. When the long-awaited distribution day arrived, some 350 families trooped into town from as far away as 30 miles, and lined up silently for the handout. One by one they collected their little Christmas baskets of fruit and tinned food, their faces expressionless, their heads bowed in mute gratitude. And all the while our young princes, the Jaycees—the future judges, merchants and coal operators of Perry County —looked on with paper cups of bourbon in their hands, and giggled.

"The county has the real worthwhile culture here," says Gurney Norman, who was born in these parts. "The city is trying so hard to be like everybody else in America." He points to the unique aspects of mountain life: the bearded chairmaker who spends 100 hours hand-carving a single chair; the country churches, with their emotional prayers and hearty hymn-singing; the mountaineers' songs and stories; their dry, aphoristic sense of humor; even the summer tent-healings, of which the townsfolk are so disdainful. But the country culture is slowly dying out. An industrial complex—coal mining—has been imposed anarchically, on top of this rural setting, leaving a population of urbanized country folk with all the problems of modern adjustment and none of the services or amenities of a city; a people caught between two ways of life, with no more place in the coal mines, the only work they know, and no taste for farming on scraps of land long since rendered useless by coal poisoning and neglect. "Their fathers and grandfathers," says Norman, "worked too hard in the mines to raise gardens."

Scene Two

[*where the President-of-All-the-People has an All-Purpose-Plan to save the Poor and preserve the Profits of his friends the Giant Corporations*]

Now into this "vast wasteland" of charity cases marches the federal administrator, spurred on by a burning new idealism, protesting: "Wait, I'm really a good guy. It's not true that I want to put you people on the perpetual dole. Look at my bold new programs to attack the *causes* of poverty. I'm on your side. Vote Democratic."

The bold new programs stem mainly from two pieces of legislation: the $947 million Economic Opportunity ("anti-poverty") Act of 1964 and the $1.1 billion Appalachian Regional Development Act of 1965.

For eastern Kentucky, the Economic Opportunity Act has meant the OEO community action programs (taken over by courthouse gangs and rendered harmless); the Job Corps (the initial quota for Perry and three adjoining counties combined was 14 youths); and an appropriation to continue and expand the unemployed fathers program through 1966. "Jobless Fathers" has become the primary source of relief in this area, giving work at an average wage of $1.25 an hour to more than 1,200 men in Perry and Knott Counties. Even if most of them earn considerably less than the $250 a month allowed maximum, the program has unquestionably been a boon. To the grim satisfaction of the Appalachian Committee, it even caused a big walkout from low-paying nonunion mines. But the Hazard Herald, in an editorial last December, saw the program right away for what it was:

> $10 million is a lot of money, and of course we in Kentucky are glad to have it. The only thing wrong with it is that it isn't anti-poverty money at all. It's only more welfare money to perpetuate the poverty-level existence of several families for another year. Apparently Washington thinks the unemployed fathers are learning new trades and skills on the public works crews, acquiring what the bureaucrats call the "work experience" to make them more employable. . . . When a man is "repairing roads" the government assumes he is learning highway construction. When his crew is "reclaiming strip-mined areas," the government assumes someone is teaching him soil and forestry conservation. But the fact is, no job training at all is involved in the unemployed fathers program. . . . All it does is help a man and his family survive temporarily, which is welfare. That's why the new federal appropriation is not going to fight poverty, any more than food stamps do.

"I don't think anti-poverty is for us," said Mayor Dawahare. "It's all cut out for the urban areas. You hear all this ballyhoo about the job program for our youth. I go to Washington to ask for help for our four counties and they tell me, 'There's only 90,000 people in your four counties; if you had 100,000 we could help you.' I told them that in our 90,000 we might have 70,000 on poverty. But it's all geared on population. You hear old Hubert Humphrey saying, 'I am my brother's keeper' and 'You can't put a price on a human life.' But it's all numbers, just a political gimmick to get votes, and the votes are in the bigger cities, not here."

So much for anti-poverty. What about the Appalachian aid bill? This long-awaited legislation was signed into law in the White House flower garden with such elaborate ceremony one would have thought Lyndon Johnson was promulgating the Magna Charta. A dozen grinning governors and perhaps a fifth of Congress stood around performing curious court rituals, until the President coughed and a hush fell over the gathering.

"The dole is dead," proclaimed our leader, and the governors nodded solemnly. "The pork barrel is gone. Federal and state, liberal and conservative, Democratic and Republican, Americans of these times are concerned with the outcome of the next generation, not the next election. This legislation marks the end of partisan cynicism toward want and misery." Along with his proven abilities in defending the interests of the big utilities and oil companies over the years, our President is a master at keeping a straight face.

Of the $1.1 billion authorization, $840 million is to be spent over a five-year period to build highways in the 11-state area, with the aim of opening the region to industry and tourism. The remainder, a whopping $230 million split 11 ways over a two-year period, is for hospitals, timber development, "restoration of strip-mined land," vocational education and other projects. The "land reclamation" provision specifies that only public lands shall be reclaimed, whereas most stripped land, in Kentucky at least, is privately owned or "abandoned" and of uncertain ownership. Once again, Lyndon Johnson and his cronies have taken excruciating care not to step on any powerful toes.

Only the roadbuilding program is of any consequence. Even there, Kentucky is not expected to get more than 250 miles of major roads, and these will bypass some of her poorest counties. It was calculated that if a billion dollars in highway funds were distributed evenly throughout the 11 states, there would be "enough money to build about half a mile of highway in each county." One of the premises of the Appalachia Act is that capital investment creates jobs in road construction, and that good roads in turn brighten the prospects of bringing tourism and new industry into the region. But Hamish Sinclair feels there will be precious few new jobs available for eastern Kentuckians. Highway contractors, he contends, have made a practice of bringing skilled labor with them from out-of-state. Jobs in the tourist industry are seasonal and low-paying. And how many companies are going to roar down that brand new highway to settle in an area where the schools are bad, the labor force undereducated and skilled only in mining, where the floods come every spring in the eroded, strip-mined hills, where there is labor unrest and where it is difficult to find a sizeable piece of level land? Only small industry, most folks agree, could be enticed.

"If we get much new industry out of this, I'll be surprised," says Attorney Caudill. "The people who benefit most from the roadbuilding plan are the absentee landlords who own our coal and limestone, our oil and gas and our timber. Now it will be easier than ever for them to ship our riches off to faraway cities, and not leave behind a cent in local taxes to support our schools. The wealth flows out; the misery accumulates at home. And the politicians in Washington haven't the guts to break the steel grip of these corporations on our territory. The Appalachia Act is a grim hoax."

This billion dollar boondoggle is not only faulty in concept, but in structure as well. The Act creates no federal planning authority like TVA. A regional commission, composed of one federal man and the 11 state governors, must pass on all development plans. This leaves the program in the effective control of statehouses that are dominated, for the most part, by the coal-utilities-railroads coalition. With this kind of control, any serious changes in Appalachia will be purely coincidental, and the dream of Franklin D. Roosevelt Jr., the President's Appalachia attaché, to reclaim those "700 miles of sprawling urban slums" will remain a dream indeed.

"It's politics again," said Mayor Dawahare. "All we'll get out of it is maybe a few roads. But we don't need more handouts. We need jobs for people with empty hands, permanent jobs so they can buy food for their children. If Washington wants to do something, why don't they outlaw strip mining and force those ruthless profiteers to make the land as good or better than they found it? How can we develop our enormous tourist potential when the strip mines are despoiling our greatest asset, our mountains?"

"One billion dollars over five years? A billion a year would be more like it," said Gurney Norman. "Washington is spending millions every year on welfare checks. If they only had the foresight to anticipate welfare spending for the next 100 years, they could make this region almost self-sufficient. But they won't do that. The Federal Government is a fantastic contradiction, isn't it?" Washington journalist, I. F. Stone, was explaining that fantastic contradiction when he called the bill "so innocuous that the U.S. Chamber of Commerce did not bother to testify against it." Noting the conspicuous absence of the public utility lobby during the Appalachia Act hearings of the Senate Public Works Committee, Stone added, "Little wonder when the government does their lobbying for them."

The bill was drafted on the basis of a report made in 1964 by the President's Appalachian Regional Commission (PARC), which also set guidelines for future federal aid to the region. Ask Tom Gish what he thinks of the PARC report and he begins to smoulder. Here are some of his criticisms:

It would do nothing to break the pattern of absentee ownership in Appalachia, by firms that take out everything and put nothing back. There is no provision for returning the area to the people who live here.

It proposes nothing to exploit the vast coal reserves, or the area's potential as a producer of cheap electric power.

It proposes no massive housing program. Yet in Letcher County, typically, the Census Bureau reports that 63 per cent of housing is substandard (80 per cent outside incorporated areas).

The Commission, afraid to ask Congress for special aid to education, would instead fritter away more millions on retraining, to treat the effects of an unbelievably bad public school system in eastern Kentucky. Instead of taking the high school graduate with a sixth grade education and trying to rehabilitate him, we should put the money where the problem is—in public school classrooms. The present "massive" retraining program in eastern Kentucky involves about 4,000 trainees. Even if retraining were the answer, the need would extend to tens of thousands.

Projects are to be controlled by the governor and his political structure; yet the only successful federal programs here have been handled directly between the local community and the Federal Government.

It is a myth that eastern Kentuckians had a hand in shaping the program through Area Redevelopment Councils. The councils consist of resident representatives of state and federal agencies who went along with the PARC program out of fear of losing their jobs if they disagreed.

Hamish Sinclair questions the sincerity of two of the stated aims of the President's commission: to encourage private enterprise and diversify the area's industry. "There is nothing wrong with private enterprise in eastern Kentucky," he says. "The land companies and coal operators are thriving; so are the power companies and railroads. And there is a traditional alliance between coal operators and utilities to deliberately discourage diversification and keep a ready supply of cheap mine labor at their disposal. The Appalachia Act makes no attempt to undermine that alliance."

Scene Three

[where the spokesmen of the Little People display their Anger and their Good Ideas]

Hopeless? —Not entirely. Everette Tharp likes to speak of Appalachia as having a potential "equal to the industrial Ruhr Valley of Germany," a rather sweeping assertion substantiated in part by a recent report of the U.S. Geological Survey that only 5 per cent of the eastern Kentucky coalfields have been mined. As a retired miner with little to show for his 30 years in the pits but rock dust in his lungs, Tharp asks why our industrial power developed elsewhere, leaving his part of Kentucky a mere raw material producer, a "colony" of the steel and financial interests to the North. He rejects the conclusions of the PARC report that this is a "region apart," because of natural barriers, and therefore permits of a regional solution. Tharp argues that Appalachian coal, a key to Northern industrial growth, has placed the region in the middle of the nation's economy, and that it should not be isolated as a "black sheep."

"Automation," he says, "is creating the same unemployment throughout America, and without jobs and a wage structure that will permit the unemployed to consume the goods and services produced by automation, the problems of Appalachia will go unsolved."

Harry Caudill, too, gets angry with people who say Appalachia has nothing to offer the nation. He thinks the Federal Government can save Appalachia—and strengthen the national economy—by setting up an agency patterned after TVA to develop the area's electric power potential and to undertake its social and economic rehabilitation. In 1963, the Eastern Kentucky Redevelopment Administration sent resolutions to this effect to the President's commission. Last year Caudill testified before the public works committees of both houses; only the Senate committee gave any encouragement to the plan. Said Caudill to the lawmakers:

"The Edison Electric Institute has estimated that the colossal sum of $175 billion will have to be invested in new electric power generating facilities in the next 20 years. Steps must be taken to insure that the huge coal resources of Appalachia are utilized in meeting this goal. Dams at strategic locations in the Kentucky highlands could provide storage for cooling water to be used by huge mine-mouth generating plants. Extra-high-voltage transmission lines and the expanding grid system would make it possible to send low-cost power into New England, a region of high power costs. . . . The hydro and thermal power potential of eastern Kentucky could be developed for a billion dollars. And this could be made entirely self-liquidating within 35 years. However, such a self-financing corporation should be given a stern mandate to plow back into the impoverished counties in which it would operate a substantial portion of the money from power sales. At least one mill per kilowatt-hour should be added to the price and invested in schools, roads, airports, flood-control, reforestation and reclamation and perhaps the building of entirely new towns. Sustained capital investment over a generation would bring this deprived corner of the American hinterland abreast of the rest of the nation." Caudill feels there is "nothing radical or visionary" about his plan: the mechanics have been tested and proved in the Tennessee Valley. And once Appalachia tapped into the huge electric power market, he says, her sagging coal industry would boom again. Cheap power would attract light manufacturing plants—especially those using wood and coal derivatives—"and begin a cycle of economic diversification."

But the lobbies, quick to detect the smell of public power, snuffed out the proposal long before the Appalachia Act was drafted. Instead, the Act contains a specific prohibition against the use of funds "to finance the generation, transmission or distribution of electric energy"; which was, after all, true to form.

Suggestions for Further Reading

Few good surveys of the period during and after the Second World War are available. For the postwar years, see Eric F. Goldman, *The Crucial Decade—and After: America, 1945-1960** (Knopf, 1960). Richard R. Rovere deals with the fervent anti-Communism of the Korean War years in *Senator Joe McCarthy** (Harcourt Brace Jovanovich, 1959), and Earl Latham is concerned with the same theme in *The Communist Conspiracy in Washington** (Harvard University Press, 1966). Two books that helped to bring about a new understanding of ethnic consciousness in the 1960's are Nathan Glazer and Daniel Patrick Moynihan, *Beyond the Melting Pot: The Negroes, Puerto Ricans, Jews, Italians and Irish of New York City** (Massachusetts Institute of Technology Press, 1963; 2d enl. ed., 1970), and Oscar Handlin, *The Newcomers: Negroes and Puerto Ricans in a Changing Metropolis** (Harvard University Press, 1959).

For the background to anti-Japanese sentiment at the outbreak of the Second World War, see Roger Daniels, *The Politics of Prejudice: The Anti-Japanese Movement in California and the Struggle for Japanese Exclusion** (University of California Press, 1962), and Carey McWilliams, *Prejudice: Japanese Americans, Symbol of Racial Intolerance* (Little, Brown, 1944). Two pertinent works published under the auspices of the University of California Education and Resettlement Study are Dorothy Swaine Thomas and Richard Nishimoto, *The Spoilage: Japanese American Evacuation and Resettlement** (University of California Press, 1946), and Dorothy Swaine Thomas, Charles Kikuchi, and James Sakoda, *The Salvage* (University of California Press, 1952). Eugene V. Rostow published two articles that were harshly critical of the Japanese-American evacuation: "The Japanese-American Cases—A Disaster," *Yale Law Journal*, Vol. 54 (June, 1945), 489-533, and "Our Worst Wartime Mistake," *Harper's*, Vol. 191 (September, 1945), 193-201. The political aspects of the Japanese-American internment are analyzed by Morton Grodzins in *Americans Betrayed: Politics and the Japanese Evacuation* (University of Chicago Press, 1949). Recent studies of the events surrounding the evacuation include Bill Hosokawa, *Nisei: The Quiet Americans* (Morrow, 1969), and Andrie Girdner and Anne Loftis, *The Great Betrayal* (Macmillan, 1969).

Two basic studies of poverty and wealth in postwar America are Michael Harrington, *The Other America: Poverty in the United States** (Macmillan, 1963), and John Kenneth Galbraith, *The Affluent Society** (Houghton-Mifflin, 1958). On the distribu-

* Available in paperback edition.

tion of wealth in the United States, see Gabriel Kolko, *Wealth and Power in America: An Analysis of Social Class and Income Distribution** (Praeger, 1962). Dwight Macdonald helped bring the issue of poverty into the public eye with his article "Our Invisible Poor," *The New Yorker*, Vol. 38 (January 19, 1963), 82–132. Moving descriptions of life in Appalachia are found in Harry W. Caudill, *Night Comes to the Cumberlands** (Little Press, 1963), and Jack E. Weller, *Yesterday's People: Life in Contemporary Appalachia** (University of Kentucky Press, 1965). In *Culture and Poverty** (University of Chicago Press, 1968), Charles Valentine challenges various common assumptions about the nature of poverty and its impact on culture.

5

Revolt of
the Victims

Summary of
the Kerner Report
on Civil Disorders

THE KERNER COMMISSION

In the years since the Second World War, black Americans have developed a variety of programs aimed at freeing themselves from white oppression and discrimination. They scored a major legal victory with the Supreme Court ruling of May 1954, which declared laws requiring racially segregated schools unconstitutional and set a precedent that led to the abolition of almost all legally enforced segregation in this country. The lawyers of the NAACP's Legal Defense and Education Fund were responsible for the preparation of this court case, and it was argued before the Supreme Court by Thurgood Marshall, who later became the first black man appointed to that court. Also during the 1950's, several changes in the customary racial patterns of life in the South were brought about as a result of the nonviolent direct-action campaigns organized by followers of Martin Luther King, Jr., and by the young members of the Student Nonviolent Coordinating Committee (since renamed the Student National Coordinating Committee). Using sit-ins, freedom rides, and boycotts, the nonviolent civil rights movement successfully drew the nation's attention to the South's continued denial of basic rights to its black citizens.

It was clear even in the early years of the civil rights movement that neither legal action nor nonviolent protest could be of much service to blacks in the North and the West, where discriminatory laws rarely existed and where the patterns of racial discrimination were far more subtle and erratic. Yet Northern society was almost as segregated as Southern, and the frustrations of Northern blacks—particularly in the urban ghettos—were rapidly mounting. By the mid-1960's, Northern ghetto-dwellers had found their own form of protest. Variously termed "riots," "revolts," and "civil disorders," literally hundreds of violent protests erupted in both Northern and Southern cities between 1964 and 1967. These outbursts were spontaneous, unorganized expressions of hostility aimed at the symbols of authority and oppression. Because of their clearly political nature, they are perhaps best described as "uprisings."

Unlike the race riots of the past, the new outbreaks of racial violence did not involve aggressive action by opposing groups of whites and blacks. Rather, the whites involved in the disturbances were usually only those who represented white authority and oppression to the ghetto-dwellers—policemen, firemen, and national guardsmen. In the great majority of the uprisings, the violence of the blacks was directed only against property—typically, against slum buildings and exploitative ghetto stores and shops. In fact, looting was the most widely noted activity of the protesters, leading one study to characterize the uprisings as "consumer revolts." Only when police and guardsmen invaded the ghettos—presumably to restore order— did violence against people break out.

Anxious to quiet an alarmed public, President Lyndon Johnson appointed a commission under the chairmanship of Governor Otto Kerner of Illinois to study the background and the causes of the disorders in the cities and to recommend policies to prevent their recurrence. This commission came to the unexpected yet obvious conclusion that "white racism is essentially responsible for the explosive mixture which has been accumulating in our cities since the end of World War II."

The summary of the Kerner Commission's report is reprinted in the following pages. Certainly, the commission's analysis of the conditions of ghetto life was serious and thorough. However, it may have proceeded from a mistaken assumption: that "the major goal is the creation of a true union—a single society and a single American identity." In reality, the creation of a truly plural society and a truly plural American identity may be the only solution to the race problems of America today.

INTRODUCTION

The summer of 1967 again brought racial disorders to American cities, and with them shock, fear and bewilderment to the nation.

The worst came during a two-week period in July, first in Newark and then in Detroit. Each set off a chain reaction in neighboring communities.

"Summary of the Kerner Report on Civil Disorders." From the Kerner Commission, *The Report of the National Advisory Commission on Civil Disorders* (Washington, D.C.: U.S. Government Printing Office, 1968), pp. 1–13.

On July 28, 1967, the President of the United States established this Commission and directed us to answer three basic questions:

What happened?

Why did it happen?

What can be done to prevent it from happening again?

To respond to these questions, we have undertaken a broad range of studies and investigations. We have visited the riot cities; we have heard many witnesses; we have sought the counsel of experts across the country.

This is our basic conclusion: Our nation is moving toward two societies, one black, one white—separate and unequal.

Reaction to last summer's disorders has quickened the movement and deepened the division. Discrimination and segregation have long permeated much of American life; they now threaten the future of every American.

This deepening racial division is not inevitable. The movement apart can be reversed. Choice is still possible. Our principal task is to define that choice and to press for a national resolution.

To pursue our present course will involve the continuing polarization of the American community and, ultimately, the destruction of basic democratic values.

The alternative is not blind repression or capitulation to lawlessness. It is the realization of common opportunities for all within a single society.

This alternative will require a commitment to national action—compassionate, massive and sustained, backed by the resources of the most powerful and the richest nation on this earth. From every American it will require new attitudes, new understanding and, above all, new will.

The vital needs of the nation must be met; hard choices must be made, and, if necessary, new taxes enacted.

Violence cannot build a better society. Disruption and disorder nourish repression, not justice. They strike at the freedom of every citizen. The community cannot—it will not—tolerate coercion and mob rule.

Violence and destruction must be ended—in the streets of the ghetto and in the lives of people.

Segregation and poverty have created in the racial ghetto a destructive environment totally unknown to most white Americans.

What white Americans have never fully understood—but what the Negro can never forget—is that white society is deeply implicated in the ghetto. White institutions created it, white institutions maintain it, and white society condones it.

It is time now to turn with all the purpose at our command to the major unfinished business of this nation. It is time to adopt strategies for action that will produce quick and visible progress. It is time to make good the promises of American democracy to all citizens—urban and rural, white and black, Spanish-surname, American Indian, and every minority group.

Our recommendations embrace three basic principles:

To mount programs on a scale equal to the dimension of the problems.

To aim these programs for high impact in the immediate future in order to close the gap between promise and performance.

To undertake new initiatives and experiments that can change the system of failure and frustration that now dominates the ghetto and weakens our society.

These programs will require unprecedented levels of funding and performance, but they neither probe deeper nor demand more than the problems which called them forth. There can be no higher priority for national action and no higher claim on the nation's conscience.

We issue this Report now, four months before the date called for by the President. Much remains that can be learned. Continued study is essential.

As Commissioners we have worked together with a sense of the greatest urgency and have sought to compose whatever differences exist among us. Some differences remain. But the gravity of the problem and the pressing need for action are too clear to allow further delay in the issuance of this Report.

PART I
WHAT HAPPENED?

Chapter 1
Profiles of Disorder

The Report contains profiles of a selection of the disorders that took place during the summer of 1967. These profiles are designed to indicate how the disorders happened, who participated in them, and how local officials, police forces, and the National Guard responded. Illustrative excerpts follow:

NEWARK

It was decided to attempt to channel the energies of the people into a nonviolent protest. While Lofton promised the crowd that a full investigation would be made of the Smith incident, the other Negro leaders began urging those on the scene to form a line of march toward the city hall.

Some persons joined the line of march. Others milled about in the narrow street. From the dark grounds of the housing project came a barrage of rocks. Some of them fell among the crowd. Others hit persons in the line of march. Many smashed the windows of the police station. The rock throwing, it was believed, was the work of youngsters; approximately 2,500 children lived in the housing project.

Almost at the same time, an old car was set afire in a parking lot. The line of march began to disintegrate. The police, their heads protected by World War I–type helmets, sallied forth to disperse the crowd. A fire engine, arriving on the scene, was pelted with rocks. As police drove people away from the station, they scattered in all directions.

A few minutes later a nearby liquor store was broken into. Some persons, seeing a caravan of cabs appear at city hall to protest Smith's arrest, interpreted this as evidence that the disturbance had been organized, and generated rumors to that effect.

However, only a few stores were looted. Within a short period of time, the disorder appeared to have run its course.

.   .   .

On Saturday, July 15, [Director of Police Dominick] Spina received a report of snipers in a housing project. When he arrived he saw approximately 100 National Guardsmen and police officers crouching behind vehicles, hiding in corners and lying on the ground around the edge of the courtyard.

Since everything appeared quiet and it was broad daylight, Spina walked directly down the middle of the street. Nothing happened. As he came to the last building of the complex, he heard a shot. All around him the troopers jumped, believing themselves to be under sniper fire. A moment later a young Guardsman ran from behind a building.

The Director of Police went over and asked him if he had fired the shot. The soldier said yes, he had fired to scare a man away from a window; that his orders were to keep everyone away from windows.

Spina said he told the soldier: "Do you know what you just did? You have now created a state of hysteria. Every Guardsman up and down this street and every state policeman and every city policeman that is present thinks that somebody just fired a shot and that it is probably a sniper."

A short time later more "gunshots" were heard. Investigating, Spina came upon a Puerto Rican sitting on a wall. In reply to a question as to whether he knew "where the firing is coming from?" the man said:

"That's no firing. That's fireworks. If you look up to the fourth floor, you will see the people who are throwing down these cherry bombs."

By this time four truckloads of National Guardsmen had arrived and troopers and policemen were again crouched everywhere looking for a sniper. The Director of Police remained at the scene for three hours, and the only shot fired was the one by the Guardsman.

Nevertheless, at six o'clock that evening two columns of National Guardsmen and state troopers were directing mass fire at the Hayes Housing Project in response to what they believed were snipers. . . .

DETROIT

A spirit of carefree nihilism was taking hold. To riot and destroy appeared more and more to become ends in themselves. Late Sunday afternoon it appeared to one observer that the young people were "dancing amidst the flames."

A Negro plainclothes officer was standing at an intersection when a man threw a Molotov cocktail into a business establishment at the corner. In the heat of the afternoon, fanned by the 20 to 25 m.p.h. winds of both Sunday and Monday, the fire reached the home next door within minutes. As residents uselessly sprayed the flames with garden hoses, the fire jumped from roof to roof of adjacent two- and three-story buildings. Within the hour the entire block was in flames. The ninth house in the burning row belonged to the arsonist who had thrown the Molotov cocktail. . . .

.   .   .

Employed as a private guard, 55-year-old Julius L. Dorsey, a Negro, was standing in front of a market when accosted by two Negro men and a woman. They demanded he permit them to loot the market. He ignored their demands. They began to berate him. He asked a neighbor to call the police. As the argument grew more heated, Dorsey fired three shots from his pistol into the air.

The police radio reported: "Looters, they have rifles." A patrol car driven by a police officer and carrying three National Guardsmen arrived. As the looters fled, the law enforcement personnel opened fire. When the firing ceased, one person lay dead.

He was Julius L. Dorsey. . . .

.   .   .

As the riot alternately waxed and waned, one area of the ghetto remained insulated. On the northeast side the residents of some 150 square blocks inhabited by 21,000 persons had, in 1966, banded together in the Positive Neighborhood Action Committee (PNAC). With professional help from the Institute of Urban Dynamics, they had organized block clubs and made plans for the improvement of the neighborhood. . . .

When the riot broke out, the residents, through the block clubs, were able to organize quickly. Youngsters, agreeing to stay in the neighborhood, participated in detouring traffic. While many persons reportedly sympathized with the idea of a rebellion against the "system," only two small fires were set—one in an empty building.

.   .   .

According to Lt. Gen. Throckmorton and Col. Bolling, the city, at this time, was saturated with fear. The National Guardsmen were afraid, the residents were afraid, and the police were afraid. Numerous persons, the majority of them Negroes, were being injured by gunshots of undetermined origin. The general and his staff felt that the major task of the troops was to reduce the fear and restore an air of normalcy.

In order to accomplish this, every effort was made to establish contact and rapport between the troops and the residents. The soldiers—20 percent of whom were Negro—began helping to clean up the streets, collect garbage, and trace persons who had disappeared in the confusion. Residents in the neighborhoods responded with soup and sandwiches for the troops. In areas where the National Guard tried to establish rapport with the citizens, there was a smaller response.

NEW BRUNSWICK

A short time later, elements of the crowd—an older and rougher one than the night before—appeared in front of the police station. The participants wanted to see the mayor.

Mayor [Patricia] Sheehan went out onto the steps of the station. Using a bullhorn, she talked to the people and asked that she be given an opportunity to correct conditions. The crowd was boisterous. Some persons challenged the mayor. But, finally, the opinion, "She's new! Give her a chance!" prevailed.

A demand was issued by people in the crowd that all persons arrested the previous night be released. Told that this already had been done, the people were suspicious. They asked to be allowed to inspect the jail cells.

It was agreed to permit representatives of the people to look in the cells to satisfy themselves that everyone had been released.

The crowd dispersed. The New Brunswick riot had failed to materialize.

Chapter 2
Patterns of Disorder

The "typical" riot did not take place. The disorders of 1967 were unusual, irregular, complex and unpredictable social processes. Like most human events, they did not unfold in an orderly sequence. However, an analysis of our survey information leads to some conclusions about the riot process.

In general:

> The civil disorders of 1967 involved Negroes acting against local symbols of white American society, authority and property in Negro neighborhoods—rather than against white persons.

Of 164 disorders reported during the first nine months of 1967, eight (5 percent) were major in terms of violence and damage; 33 (20 percent) were serious but not major; 123 (75 percent) were minor and undoubtedly would not have received national attention as "riots" had the nation not been sensitized by the more serious outbreaks.

In the 75 disorders studied by a Senate subcommittee, 83 deaths were reported. Eighty-two percent of the deaths and more than half the injuries occurred in Newark and Detroit. About 10 percent of the dead and 38 percent of the injured were public employees, primarily law officers and firemen. The overwhelming majority of the persons killed or injured in all the disorders were Negro civilians.

Initial damage estimates were greatly exaggerated. In Detroit, newspaper damage estimates at first ranged from $200 million to $500 million; the highest recent estimate is $45 million. In Newark, early estimates ranged from $15 to $25 million. A month later damage was estimated at $10.2 million, over 80 percent in inventory losses.

In the 24 disorders in 23 cities which we surveyed:

The final incident before the outbreak of disorder, and the initial violence itself, generally took place in the evening or at night at a place in which it was normal for many people to be on the streets.

Violence usually occurred almost immediately following the occurrence of the final precipitating incident, and then escalated rapidly. With but few exceptions, violence subsided during the day, and flared rapidly again at night. The night-day cycles continued through the early period of the major disorders.

Disorder generally began with rock and bottle throwing and window breaking. Once store windows were broken, looting usually followed.

Disorder did not erupt as a result of a single "triggering" or "precipitating" incident. Instead, it was generated out of an increasingly disturbed social atmosphere, in which typically a series of tension-heightening incidents over a period of weeks or months became linked in the minds of many in the Negro community with a reservoir of underlying grievances. At some point in the mounting tension, a further incident—in itself often routine or trivial —became the breaking point and the tension spilled over into violence.

"Prior" incidents, which increased tensions and ultimately led to violence, were police actions in almost half the cases; police actions were "final" incidents before the outbreak of violence in 12 of the 24 surveyed disorders.

No particular control tactic was successful in every situation.

The varied effectiveness of control techniques emphasizes the need for advance training, planning, adequate intelligence systems and knowledge of the ghetto community.

Negotiations between Negroes—including your militants as well as older Negro leaders—and white officials concerning "terms of peace" occurred during virtually all the disorders surveyed. In many cases, these negotiations involved discussion of underlying grievances as well as the handling of the disorder by control authorities.

The typical rioter was a teenager or young adult, a lifelong resident of the city in which he rioted, a high school dropout; he was, nevertheless, somewhat better educated than his nonrioting Negro neighbor, and was usually underemployed or employed in a menial job. He was proud of his race, extremely hostile to both whites and middle-class Negroes and, although informed about politics, highly distrustful of the political system.

A Detroit survey revealed that approximately 11 percent of the total residents of two riot areas admitted participation in the rioting, 20 to 25 percent identified themselves as "bystanders," over 16 percent identified themselves as "counter-rioters" who urged rioters to "cool it" and the remaining 48 to 53 percent said they were at home or elsewhere and did not participate. In a survey of Negro males between the ages of 15 and 35 residing in the disturbance area in Newark, about 45 percent identified themselves as rioters, and about 55 percent as "noninvolved."

Most rioters were young Negro males. Nearly 53 percent of arrestees were between 15 and 24 years of age; nearly 81 percent between 15 and 35.

In Detroit and Newark about 74 percent of the rioters were brought up in the North. In contrast, of the noninvolved, 36 percent in Detroit and 52 percent in Newark were brought up in the North.

What the rioters appeared to be seeking was fuller participation in the social order and the material benefits enjoyed by the majority of American citizens. Rather than rejecting the American system, they were anxious to obtain a place for themselves in it.

Numerous Negro counter-rioters walked the streets urging rioters to "cool it." The typical counter-rioter was better educated and had higher income than either the rioter or the noninvolved.

The proportion of Negroes in local government was substantially smaller than the Negro proportion of population. Only three of the 20 cities studied had more than one Negro legislator; none had ever had a Negro mayor or city manager. In only four cities did Negroes hold other important policy-making positions or serve as heads of municipal departments.

Although almost all cities had some sort of formal grievance mechanism for handling citizen complaints, this typically was regarded by Negroes as ineffective and was generally ignored.

Although specific grievances varied from city to city, at least 12 deeply held grievances can be identified and ranked into three levels of relative intensity:

First Level of Intensity

1. Police practices
2. Unemployment and underemployment
3. Inadequate housing

Second Level of Intensity

4. Inadequate education
5. Poor recreation facilities and programs
6. Ineffectiveness of the political structure and grievance mechanisms

Third Level of Intensity

7. Disrespectful white attitudes
8. Discriminatory administration of justice
9. Inadequacy of federal programs
10. Inadequacy of municipal services
11. Discriminatory consumer and credit practices
12. Inadequate welfare programs

The results of a three-city survey of various federal programs —manpower, education, housing, welfare and community action— indicate that, despite substantial expenditures, the number of persons assisted constituted only a fraction of those in need.

The background of disorder is often as complex and difficult to analyze as the disorder itself. But we find that certain general conclusions can be drawn:

Social and economic conditions in the riot cities constituted a clear pattern of severe disadvantage for Negroes compared with whites, whether the Negroes lived in the area where the riot took place or outside it. Negroes had completed fewer years of education and fewer had attended high school. Negroes were twice as likely to be unemployed and three times as likely to be in unskilled and service jobs. Negroes averaged 70 percent of the income earned by whites and were more than twice as likely to be living in poverty. Although housing cost Negroes relatively more, they had worse housing—three times as likely to be overcrowded and substandard. When compared to white suburbs, the relative disadvantage is even more pronounced.

A study of the aftermath of disorder leads to disturbing conclusions. We find that, despite the institution of some postriot programs:

Little basic change in the conditions underlying the outbreak of disorder has taken place. Actions to ameliorate Negro grievances have been limited and sporadic; with but few exceptions, they have not significantly reduced tensions.

In several cities, the principal official response has been to train and equip the police with more sophisticated weapons.

In several cities, increasing polarization is evident, with continuing breakdown of inter-racial communication, and growth of white segregationist or black separatist groups.

Chapter 3
Organized Activity

The President directed the Commission to investigate "to what extent, if any, there has been planning or organization in any of the riots."

To carry out this part of the President's charge, the Commission established a special investigative staff supplementing the field teams that made the general examination of the riots in 23 cities. The unit examined data collected by federal agencies and congressional committees, including thousands of documents supplied by the Federal Bureau of Investigation, gathered and evaluated information from local and state law enforcement agencies and officials, and conducted its own field investigation in selected cities.

On the basis of all the information collected, the Commission concludes that:

The urban disorders of the summer of 1967 were not caused by, nor were they the consequence of, any organized plan or "conspiracy."

Specifically, the Commission has found no evidence that all or any of the disorders or the incidents that led to them were planned or directed by any organization or group, international, national or local.

Militant organizations, local and national, and individual agitators, who repeatedly forecast and called for violence, were active in the spring and summer of 1967. We believe that they sought to encourage violence, and that they helped to create an atmosphere that contributed to the outbreak of disorder.

We recognize that the continuation of disorders and the polarization of the races would provide fertile ground for organized exploitation in the future.

Investigations of organized activity are continuing at all levels of government, including committees of Congress. These investigations relate not only to the disorders of 1967 but also to the actions of groups and individuals, particularly in schools and colleges, during this last fall and winter. The Commission has cooperated in these investigations. They should continue.

PART II
WHY DID IT HAPPEN?

Chapter 4
The Basic Causes

In addressing the question "Why did it happen?" we shift our focus from the local to the national scene, from the particular events of the summer of 1967 to the factors within the society at large that created a mood of violence among many urban Negroes.

These factors are complex and interacting; they vary significantly in their effect from city to city and from year to year; and the consequences of one disorder, generating new grievances and new demands, become the causes of the next. Thus was created the "thicket of tension, conflicting evidence and extreme opinions" cited by the President.

Despite these complexities, certain fundamental matters are clear. Of these, the most fundamental is the racial attitude and behavior of white Americans toward black Americans.

Race prejudice has shaped our history decisively; it now threatens to affect our future.

White racism is essentially responsible for the explosive mixture which has been accumulating in our cities since the end of World War II. Among the ingredients of this mixture are:

> *Pervasive discrimination and segregation* in employment, education and housing, which have resulted in the continuing exclusion of great numbers of Negroes from the benefits of economic progress.
>
> *Black in-migration and white exodus,* which have produced the massive and growing concentrations of impoverished Negroes in our major cities, creating a growing crisis of deteriorating facilities and services and unmet human needs.
>
> *The black ghettos,* where segregation and poverty converge on the young to destroy opportunity and enforce failure. Crime, drug addiction, dependency on welfare, and bitterness and resentment against society in general and white society in particular are the result.

At the same time, most whites and some Negroes outside the ghetto have prospered to a degree unparalleled in the history of civilization. Through television and other media, this affluence has been flaunted before the eyes of the Negro poor and the jobless ghetto youth.

Yet these facts alone cannot be said to have caused the disorders. Recently, other powerful ingredients have begun to catalyze the mixture:

> *Frustrated hopes* are the residue of the unfulfilled expectations

aroused by the great judicial and legislative victories of the Civil Rights Movement and the dramatic struggle for equal rights in the South.

A climate that tends toward approval and encouragement of violence as a form of protest has been created by white terrorism directed against nonviolent protest; by the open defiance of law and federal authority by state and local officials resisting desegregation; and by some protest groups engaging in civil disobedience who turn their backs on nonviolence, go beyond the constitutionally protected rights of petition and free assembly, and resort to violence to attempt to compel alteration of laws and policies with which they disagree.

The frustrations of powerlessness have led some Negroes to the conviction that there is no effective alternative to violence as a means of achieving redress of grievances, and of "moving the system." These frustrations are reflected in alienation and hostility toward the institutions of law and government and the white society which controls them, and in the reach toward racial consciousness and solidarity reflected in the slogan "Black Power."

A new mood has sprung up among Negroes, particularly among the young, in which self-esteem and enhanced racial pride are replacing apathy and submission to "the system."

The police are not merely a "spark" factor. To some Negroes police have come to symbolize white power, white racism and white repression. And the fact is that many police do reflect and express these white attitudes. The atmosphere of hostility and cynicism is reinforced by a widespread belief among Negroes in the existence of police brutality and in a "double standard" of justice and protection—one for Negroes and one for whites.

To this point, we have attempted to identify the prime components of the "explosive mixture." In the chapters that follow we seek to analyze them in the perspective of history. Their meaning, however, is clear:

In the summer of 1967, we have seen in our cities a chain reaction of racial violence. If we are heedless, none of us shall escape the consequences.

Chapter 5
Rejection and Protest: An Historical Sketch

The causes of recent racial disorders are embedded in a tangle of issues and circumstances—social, economic, political and psychological—which arise out of the historic pattern of Negro-white relations in America.

In this chapter we trace the pattern, identify the recurrent themes of Negro protest and, most importantly, provide a perspective on the protest activities of the present era.

We describe the Negro's experience in America and the development of slavery as an institution. We show his persistent striving for equality in the face of rigidly maintained social, economic and educational barriers, and repeated mob violence. We portray the ebb and flow of the doctrinal tides—accommodation, separatism, and self-help—and their relationship to the current theme of Black Power. We conclude:

> The Black Power advocates of today consciously feel that they are the most militant group in the Negro protest movement. Yet they have retreated from a direct confrontation with American society on the issue of integration and, by preaching separatism, unconsciously function as an accommodation to white racism. Much of their economic program, as well as their interest in Negro history, self-help, racial solidarity and separation, is reminiscent of Booker T. Washington. The rhetoric is different, but the ideas are remarkably similar.

Chapter 6
The Formation of the Racial Ghettos[1]

Throughout the twentieth century the Negro population of the United States has been moving steadily from rural areas to urban and from South to North and West. In 1910, 91 percent of the nation's 9.8 million Negroes lived in the South and only 27 percent of American Negroes lived in cities of 2,500 persons or more. Between 1910 and 1966 the total Negro population more than doubled, reaching 21.5 million, and the number living in metropolitan areas rose more that five-fold (from 2.6 million to 14.8 million). The number outside the South rose elevenfold (from 880,000 to 9.7 million).

Negro migration from the South has resulted from the expectation of thousands of new and highly paid jobs for unskilled workers in the North and the shift to mechanized farming in the South. However, the Negro migration is small when compared to earlier waves of European immigrants. Even between 1960 and 1966, there were 1.8 million immigrants from abroad compared to the 613,000 Negroes who arrived in the North and West from the South.

As a result of the growing number of Negroes in urban areas, natural increase has replaced migration as the primary source of Negro population increase in the cities. Nevertheless, Negro migration from the South will continue unless economic conditions there change dramatically.

Basic data concerning Negro urbanization trends indicate that:

Almost all Negro population growth (98 percent from 1950 to

[1] The term "ghetto" as used in this report refers to an area within a city characterized by poverty and acute social disorganization, and inhabited by members of a racial or ethnic group under conditions of involuntary segregation.

1966) is occurring within metropolitan areas, primarily within central cities.[2]

The vast majority of white population growth (78 percent from 1960 to 1966) is occurring in suburban portions of metropolitan areas. Since 1960, white central-city population has declined by 1.3 million.

As a result, central cities are becoming more heavily Negro while the suburban fringes around them remain almost entirely white.

The twelve largest central cities now contain over two-thirds of the Negro population outside the South, and one-third of the Negro total in the United States.

Within the cities, Negroes have been excluded from white residential areas through discriminatory practices. Just as significant is the withdrawal of white families from, or their refusal to enter, neighborhoods where Negroes are moving or already residing. About 20 percent of the urban population of the United States changes residence every year. The refusal of whites to move into "changing" areas when vacancies occur means that most vacancies eventually are occupied by Negroes.

The result, according to a recent study, is that in 1960 the average segregation index for 207 of the largest United States cities was 86.2. In other words, to create an unsegregated population distribution, an average of over 86 percent of all Negroes would have to change their place of residence within the city.

Chapter 7
Unemployment, Family Structure, and Social Disorganization

Although there have been gains in Negro income nationally, and a decline in the number of Negroes below the "poverty level," the condition of Negroes in the central city remains in a state of crisis. Between 2 and 2.5 million Negroes—16 to 20 percent of the total Negro population of all central cities—live in squalor and deprivation in ghetto neighborhoods.

Employment is a key problem. It not only controls the present for the Negro American but, in a most profound way, it is creating the future as well. Yet, despite continuing economic growth and declining national unemployment rates, the unemployment rate for Negroes in 1967 was more than double that for whites.

Equally important is the undesirable nature of many jobs open to Negroes and other minorities. Negro men are more than three times as likely as white men to be in low-paying, unskilled or service jobs. This concentration of male Negro employment at the lowest end of the oc-

[2] A "central city" is the largest city of a standard metropolitan statistical area, that is, a metropolitan area containing at least one city of 50,000 or more inhabitants.

cupational scale is the single most important cause of poverty among Negroes.

In one study of low-income neighborhoods, the "subemployment rate," including both unemployment and underemployment, was about 33 percent, or 8.8 times greater than the overall unemployment rate for all United States workers.

Employment problems, aggravated by the constant arrival of new unemployed migrants, many of them from depressed rural areas, create persistent poverty in the ghetto. In 1966, about 11.9 percent of the nation's whites and 40.6 percent of its nonwhites were below the "poverty level" defined by the Social Security Administration (currently $3,335 per year for an urban family of four). Over 40 percent of the nonwhites below the poverty level live in the central cities.

Employment problems have drastic social impact in the ghetto. Men who are chronically unemployed or employed in the lowest status jobs are often unable or unwilling to remain with their families. The handicap imposed on children growing up without fathers in an atmosphere of poverty and deprivation is increased as mothers are forced to work to provide support.

The culture of poverty that results from unemployment and family breakup generates a system of ruthless, exploitative relationships within the ghetto. Prostitution, dope addiction and crime create an environmental "jungle" characterized by personal insecurity and tension. Children growing up under such conditions are likely participants in civil disorder.

Chapter 8
Conditions of Life in the Racial Ghetto

A striking difference in environment from that of white, middle-class Americans profoundly influences the lives of residents of the ghetto.

Crime rates, consistently higher than in other areas, create a pronounced sense of insecurity. For example, in one city one low-income Negro district had 35 times as many serious crimes against persons as a high-income white district. Unless drastic steps are taken, the crime problems in poverty areas are likely to continue to multiply as the growing youth and rapid urbanization of the population outstrip police resources.

Poor health and sanitation conditions in the ghetto result in higher mortality rates, a higher incidence of major diseases, and lower availability and utilization of medical services. The infant mortality rate for nonwhite babies under the age of one month is 58 percent higher than for whites; for one to 12 months it is almost three times as high. The level of sanitation in the ghetto is far below that in high-income areas. Garbage collection is often inadequate. Of an estimated 14,000 cases of rat bite in the United States in 1965, most were in ghetto neighborhoods.

Ghetto residents believe they are "exploited" by local merchants; and evidence substantiates some of these beliefs. A study conducted in one city by the Federal Trade Commission showed that distinctly higher prices were charged for goods sold in ghetto stores than in other areas.

Lack of knowledge regarding credit purchasing creates special pit-falls for the disadvantaged. In many states garnishment practices com-pound these difficulties by allowing creditors to deprive individuals of their wages without hearing or trial.

Chapter 9
Comparing the Immigrant and Negro Experience

In this chapter, we address ourselves to a fundamental question that many white Americans are asking: Why have so many Negroes, unlike the European immigrants, been unable to escape from the ghetto and from poverty. We believe the following factors play a part:

The Maturing Economy: When the European immigrants ar-rived, they gained an economic foothold by providing the unskilled labor needed by industry. Unlike the immigrant, the Negro mi-grant found little opportunity in the city. The economy, by then matured, had little use for the unskilled labor he had to offer.

The Disability of Race: The structure of discrimination has stringently narrowed opportunities for the Negro and restricted his prospects. European immigrants suffered from discrimination, but never so pervasively.

Entry into the Political System: The immigrants usually settled in rapidly growing cities with powerful and expanding po-litical machines, which traded economic advantages for political support. Ward-level grievance machinery, as well as personal representation, enabled the immigrant to make his voice heard and his power felt.

By the time the Negro arrived, these political machines were no longer so powerful or so well equipped to provide jobs or other favors, and in many cases were unwilling to share their influence with Negroes.

Cultural Factors: Coming from societies with a low standard of living and at a time when job aspirations were low, the immigrants sensed little deprivation in being forced to take the less desirable and poorer-paying jobs. Their large and cohesive families con-tributed to total income. Their vision of the future—one that led to a life outside of the ghetto—provided the incentive necessary to endure the present.

Although Negro men worked as hard as the immigrants, they were unable to support their families. The entrepreneurial oppor-tunities had vanished. As a result of slavery and long periods of un-employment, the Negro family structure had become matriarchal; the males played a secondary and marginal family role—one which offered little compensation for their hard and unrewarding labor. Above all, segregation denied Negroes access to good jobs and the opportunity to leave the ghetto. For them, the future seemed to lead only to a dead end.

Today, whites tend to exaggerate how well and quickly they escaped from poverty. The fact is that immigrants who came from rural backgrounds, as many Negroes do, are only now, after three generations, finally beginning to move into the middle class.

By contrast, Negroes began concentrating in the city less than two generations ago, and under much less favorable conditions. Although some Negroes have escaped poverty, few have been able to escape the urban ghetto.

PART III
WHAT CAN BE DONE?

Chapter 10
The Community Response

Our investigation of the 1967 riot cities establishes that virtually every major episode of violence was foreshadowed by an accumulation of unresolved grievances and by widespread dissatisfaction among Negroes with the unwillingness or inability of local government to respond.

Overcoming these conditions is essential for community support of law enforcement and civil order. City governments need new and more vital channels of communication to the residents of the ghetto; they need to improve their capacity to respond effectively to community needs before they become community grievances; and they need to provide opportunity for meaningful involvement of ghetto residents in shaping policies and programs which affect the community.

The Commission recommends that local governments:

Develop Neighborhood Action Task Forces as joint community-government efforts through which more effective communication can be achieved, and the delivery of city services to ghetto residents improved.

Establish comprehensive grievance-response mechanisms in order to bring all public agencies under public scrutiny.

Bring the institutions of local government closer to the people they serve by establishing neighborhood outlets for local, state and federal administrative and public service agencies.

Expand opportunities for ghetto residents to participate in the formulation of public policy and the implementation of programs affecting them through improved political representation, creation of institutional channels for community action, expansion of legal services, and legislative hearings on ghetto problems.

In this effort, city governments will require state and federal support. The Commission recommends:

State and federal financial assistance for mayors and city councils to support the research, consultants, staff and other resources needed to respond effectively to federal program initiatives.

State cooperation in providing municipalities with the jurisdictional tools needed to deal with their problems; a fuller measure of financial aid to urban areas; and the focusing of the interests of suburban communities on the physical, social and cultural environment of the central city.

Chapter 11
Police and the Community

The abrasive relationship between the police and the minority communities has been a major—and explosive—source of grievance, tension and disorder. The blame must be shared by the total society.

The police are faced with demands for increased protection and service in the ghetto. Yet the aggressive patrol practices thought necessary to meet these demands themselves create tension and hostility. The resulting grievances have been further aggravated by the lack of effective mechanisms for handling complaints against the police. Special programs for bettering police-community relations have been instituted, but these alone are not enough. Police administrators, with the guidance of public officials, and the support of the entire community, must take vigorous action to improve law enforcement and to decrease the potential for disorder.

The Commission recommends that city government and police authorities:

Review police operations in the ghetto to ensure proper conduct by police officers, and eliminate abrasive practices.

Provide more adequate police protection to ghetto residents to eliminate their high sense of insecurity, and the belief of many Negro citizens in the existence of a dual standard of law enforcement.

Establish fair and effective mechanisms for the redress of grievances against the police, and other municipal employees.

Develop and adopt policy guidelines to assist officers in making critical decisions in areas where police conduct can create tension.

Develop and use innovative programs to ensure widespread community support for law enforcement.

Recruit more Negroes into the regular police force, and review promotion policies to ensure fair promotion for Negro officers.

Establish a "Community Service Officer" program to attract

ghetto youths between the ages of 17 and 21 to police work. These junior officers would perform duties in ghetto neighborhoods, but would not have full police authority. The federal government should provide support equal to 90 percent of the costs of employing CSO's on the basis of one for every ten regular officers.

Chapter 12
Control of Disorder

Preserving civil peace is the first responsibility of government. Unless the rule of law prevails, our society will lack not only order but also the environment essential to social and economic progress.

The maintenance of civil order cannot be left to the police alone. The police need guidance, as well as support, from mayors and other public officials. It is the responsibility of public officials to determine proper police policies, support adequate police standards for personnel and performance, and participate in planning for the control of disorders.

To maintain control of incidents which could lead to disorders, the Commission recommends that local officials:

Assign seasoned, well-trained policemen and supervisory officers to patrol ghetto areas, and to respond to disturbances.

Develop plans which will quickly muster maximum police manpower and highly qualified senior commanders at the outbreak of disorders.

Provide special training in the prevention of disorders, and prepare police for riot control and for operation in units, with adequate command and control and field communication for proper discipline and effectiveness.

Develop guidelines governing the use of control equipment and provide alternatives to the use of lethal weapons. Federal support for research in this area is needed.

Establish an intelligence system to provide police and other public officials with reliable information that may help to prevent the outbreak of a disorder and to institute effective control measures in the event a riot erupts.

Develop continuing contacts with ghetto residents to make use of the forces for order which exist within the community.

Establish machinery for neutralizing rumors, and enabling Negro leaders and residents to obtain the facts. Create special rumor details to collect, evaluate and dispel rumors that may lead to a civil disorder.

The Commission believes there is a grave danger that some communities may resort to the indiscriminate and excessive use of force. The harmful effects of overreaction are incalculable. The Commission condemns moves to equip police departments with mass destruction weapons, such as automatic rifles, machine guns and tanks. Weapons which are designed to destroy, not to control, have no place in densely populated urban communities.

The Commission recognizes the sound principle of local authority and responsibility in law enforcement, but recommends that the federal government share in financing of programs for improvement of police forces, both in their normal law enforcement activities as well as in their response to civil disorders.

To assist government authorities in planning their response to civil disorder, this report contains a Supplement on Control of Disorder. It deals with specific problems encountered during riot-control operations, and includes:

>Assessment of the present capabilities of police, National Guard and Army forces to control major riots, and recommendations for improvement.
>
>Recommended means by which the control operations of those forces may be coordinated with the response of other agencies, such as fire departments, and with the community at large.
>
>Recommendations for review and revision of federal, state and local laws needed to provide the framework for control efforts and for the call-up and interrelated action of public safety forces.

Chapter 13
The Administration of Justice Under Emergency Conditions

In many of the cities which experienced disorders last summer, there were recurring breakdowns in the mechanisms for processing, prosecuting and protecting arrested persons. These resulted mainly from long-standing structural deficiencies in criminal court systems, and from the failure of communities to anticipate and plan for the emergency demands of civil disorders.

In part because of this, there were few successful prosecutions for serious crimes committed during the riots. In those cities where mass arrests occurred many arrestees were deprived of basic legal rights.

The Commission recommends that the cities and states:

>Undertake reform of the lower courts so as to improve the quality of justice rendered under normal conditions.
>
>Plan comprehensive measures by which the criminal justice system may be supplemented during civil disorders so that its deliberative functions are protected, and the quality of justice is maintained.

Such emergency plans require broad community participation and dedicated leadership by the bench and bar. They should include:

>Laws sufficient to deter and punish riot conduct.

Additional judges, bail and probation officers, and clerical staff.

Arrangements for volunteer lawyers to help prosecutors and to represent riot defendants at every stage of proceedings.

Policies to ensure proper and individual bail, arraignment, pre-trial, trial and sentencing proceedings.

Procedures for processing arrested persons, such as summons and release, and release on personal recognizance, which permit separation of minor offenders from those dangerous to the community, in order that serious offenders may be detained and prosecuted effectively.

Adequate emergency processing and detention facilities.

Chapter 14
Damages: Repair and Compensation

The Commission recommends that the federal government:

Amend the Federal Disaster Act—which now applies only to natural disasters—to permit federal emergency food and medical assistance to cities during major civil disorders, and provide long-term economic assistance afterwards.

With the cooperation of the states, create incentives for the private insurance industry to provide more adequate property-insurance coverage in inner-city areas.

The Commission endorses the report of the National Advisory Panel on Insurance in Riot-Affected Areas: "Meeting the Insurance Crisis of Our Cities."

Chapter 15
The News Media and the Riots

In his charge to the Commission, the President asked: "What effect do the mass media have on the riots?"

The Commission determined that the answer to the President's question did not lie solely in the performance of the press and broadcasters in reporting the riots. Our analysis had to consider also the overall treatment by the media of the Negro ghettos, community relations, racial attitudes and poverty—day by day and month by month, year in and year out.

A wide range of interviews with government officials, law enforcement authorities, media personnel and other citizens, including ghetto residents, as well as a quantitative analysis of riot coverage and a special conference with industry representatives, leads us to conclude that:

Despite instances of sensationalism, inaccuracy and distortion, newspapers, radio and television tried on the whole to give a balanced, factual account of the 1967 disorders.

Elements of the news media failed to portray accurately the scale and character of the violence that occurred last summer. The overall effect was, we believe, an exaggeration of both mood and event.

Important segments of the media failed to report adequately on the causes and consequences of civil disorders and on the underlying problems of race relations. They have not communicated to the majority of their audience—which is white—a sense of the degradation, misery and hopelessness of life in the ghetto.

These failings must be corrected, and the improvement must come from within the industry. Freedom of the press is not the issue. Any effort to impose governmental restrictions would be inconsistent with fundamental constitutional precepts.

We have seen evidence that the news media are becoming aware of and concerned about their performance in this field. As that concern grows, coverage will improve. But much more must be done, and it must be done soon.

The Commission recommends that the media:

Expand coverage of the Negro community and of race problems through permanent assignment of reporters familiar with urban and racial affairs, and through establishment of more and better links with the Negro community.

Integrate Negroes and Negro activities into all aspects of coverage and content, including newspaper articles and television programming. The news media must publish newspapers and produce programs that recognize the existence and activities of Negroes as a group within the community and as a part of the larger community.

Recruit more Negroes into journalism and broadcasting and promote those who are qualified to positions of significant responsibility. Recruitment should begin in high schools and continue through college; where necessary, aid for training should be provided.

Improve coordination with police in reporting riot news through advance planning, and cooperate with the police in the designation of police information officers, establishment of information centers, and development of mutually acceptable guidelines for riot reporting and the conduct of media personnel.

Accelerate efforts to ensure accurate and responsible reporting of riot and racial news, through adoption by all news-gathering organizations of stringent internal staff guidelines.

Cooperate in the establishment of a privately organized and funded Institute of Urban Communications to train and educate journalists in urban affairs, recruit and train more Negro journalists, develop methods for improving police-press relations, review coverage of riots and racial issues, and support continuing research in the urban field.

Chapter 16
The Future of the Cities

By 1985, the Negro population in central cities is expected to increase by 72 percent to approximately 20.8 million. Coupled with the continued exodus of white families to the suburbs, this growth will produce majority Negro populations in many of the nation's largest cities.

The future of these cities, and of their burgeoning Negro populations, is grim. Most new employment opportunities are being created in suburbs and outlying areas. This trend will continue unless important changes in public policy are made.

In prospect, therefore, is further deterioration of already inadequate municipal tax bases in the face of increasing demands for public services, and continuing unemployment and poverty among the urban Negro population.

Three choices are open to the nation:

> We can maintain present policies, continuing both the proportion of the nation's resources now allocated to programs for the unemployed and the disadvantaged, and the inadequate and failing effort to achieve an integrated society.

> We can adopt a policy of "enrichment" aimed at improving dramatically the quality of ghetto life while abandoning integration as a goal.

> We can pursue integration by combining ghetto "enrichment" with policies which will encourage Negro movement out of central city areas.

The first choice, continuance of present policies, has ominous consequences for our society. The share of the nation's resources now allocated to programs for the disadvantaged is insufficient to arrest the deterioration of life in central-city ghettos. Under such conditions, a rising proportion of Negroes may come to see, in the deprivation and segregation they experience, a justification for violent protest, or for extending support to now isolated extremists who advocate civil disruption. Large-scale and continuing violence could result, followed by white retaliation and, ultimately, the separation of the two communities in a garrison state.

Even if violence does not occur, the consequences are unacceptable. Development of a racially integrated society, extraordinarily difficult today, will be virtually impossible when the present black ghetto population of 12.5 million has grown to almost 21 million.

To continue present policies is to make permanent the division of our country into two societies; one, largely Negro and poor, located in the central cities; the other, predominantly white and affluent, located in the suburbs and in outlying areas.

The second choice, ghetto enrichment coupled with abandonment of integration, is also unacceptable. It is another way of choosing a permanently divided country. Moreover, equality cannot be achieved under conditions of nearly complete separation. In a country where the economy, and particularly the resources of employment, are predominantly white, a policy of separation can only relegate Negroes to a permanently inferior economic status.

We believe that the only possible choice for America is the third— a policy which combines ghetto enrichment with programs designed to encourage integration of substantial numbers of Negroes into the society outside the ghetto.

Enrichment must be an important adjunct to integration, for no matter how ambitious or energetic the program, few Negroes now living in central cities can be quickly integrated. In the meantime, large-scale improvement in the quality of ghetto life is essential.

But this can be no more than an interim strategy. Programs must be developed which will permit substantial Negro movement out of the ghettos. The primary goal must be a single society, in which every citizen will be free to live and work according to his capabilities and desires, not his color.

Chapter 17
Recommendations for National Action

INTRODUCTION

No American—white or black—can escape the consequences of the continuing social and economic decay of our major cities.

Only a commitment to national action on an unprecedented scale can shape a future compatible with the historic ideals of American society.

The great productivity of our economy, and a federal revenue system which is highly responsive to economic growth, can provide the resources.

The major need is to generate new will—the will to tax ourselves to the extent necessary to meet the vital needs of the nation.

We have set forth goals and proposed strategies to reach those goals. We discuss and recommend programs not to commit each of us to specific parts of such programs but to illustrate the type and dimension of action needed.

The major goal is the creation of a true union—a single society and a single American identity. Toward that goal, we propose the following objectives for national action:

> Opening up opportunities to those who are restricted by racial segregation and discrimination, and eliminating all barriers to their choice of jobs, education and housing.
>
> Removing the frustration of powerlessness among the disadvantaged by providing the means for them to deal with the prob-

lems that affect their own lives and by increasing the capacity of our public and private institutions to respond to these problems.

Increasing communication across racial lines to destroy stereotypes, to halt polarization, end distrust and hostility, and create common ground for efforts toward public order and social justice.

We propose these aims to fulfill our pledge of equality and to meet the fundamental needs of a democratic and civilized society—domestic peace and social justice.

EMPLOYMENT

Pervasive unemployment and underemployment are the most persistent and serious grievances in minority areas. They are inextricably linked to the problem of civil disorder.

Despite growing federal expenditures for manpower development and training programs, and sustained general economic prosperity and increasing demands for skilled workers, about two million—white and non-white—are permanently unemployed. About ten million are underemployed, of whom 6.5 million work full time for wages below the poverty line.

The 500,000 "hard-core" unemployed in the central cities who lack a basic education and are unable to hold a steady job are made up in large part of Negro males between the ages of 18 and 25. In the riot cities which we surveyed. Negroes were three times as likely as whites to hold unskilled jobs, which are often part time, seasonal, low-paying and "dead end."

Negro males between the ages of 15 and 25 predominated among the rioters. More than 20 percent of the rioters were unemployed, and many who were employed held intermittent, low-status, unskilled jobs which they regarded as below their education and ability.

The Commission recommends that the federal government:

Undertake joint efforts with cities and states to consolidate existing manpower programs to avoid fragmentation and duplication.

Take immediate action to create 2,000,000 new jobs over the next three years—one million in the public sector and one million in the private sector—to absorb the hard-core unemployed and materially reduce the level of underemployment for all workers, black and white. We propose 250,000 public sector and 300,000 private sector jobs in the first year.

Provide on-the-job training by both public and private employers with reimbursement to private employers for the extra costs of training the hard-core unemployed, by contract or by tax credits.

Provide tax and other incentives to investment in rural as well as urban poverty areas in order to offer to the rural poor an alternative to migration to urban centers.

Take new and vigorous action to remove artificial barriers to employment and promotion, including not only racial discrimination but, in certain cases, arrest records or lack of a high school diploma. Strengthen those agencies such as the Equal Employment Opportunity Commission, charged with eliminating discriminatory practices, and provide full support for Title VI of the 1964 Civil Rights Act allowing federal grant-in-aid funds to be withheld from activities which discriminate on grounds of color or race.

The Commission commends the recent public commitment of the National Council of the Building and Construction Trades Unions, AFL-CIO, to encourage and recruit Negro membership in apprenticeship programs. This commitment should be intensified and implemented.

EDUCATION

Education in a democratic society must equip children to develop their potential and to participate fully in American life. For the community at large, the schools have discharged this responsibility well. But for many minorities, and particularly for the children of the ghetto, the schools have failed to provide the educational experience which could overcome the effects of discrimination and deprivation.

This failure is one of the persistent sources of grievance and resentment within the Negro community. The hostility of Negro parents and students toward the school system is generating increasing conflict and causing disruption within many city school districts. But the most dramatic evidence of the relationship between educational practices and civil disorders lies in the high incidence of riot participation by ghetto youth who have not completed hgh school.

The bleak record of public education for ghetto children is growing worse. In the critical skills—verbal and reading ability—Negro students are falling further behind whites with each year of school completed. The high unemployment and underemployment rate for Negro youth is evidence, in part, of the growing educational crisis.

We support integration as the priority education strategy; it is essential to the future of American society. In this last summer's disorders we have seen the consequences of racial isolation at all levels, and of attitudes toward race, on both sides, produced by three centuries of myth, ignorance and bias. It is indispensable that opportunities for interaction between the races be expanded.

We recognize that the growing dominance of pupils from disadvantaged minorities in city school populations will not soon be reversed. No matter how great the effort toward desegregation, many children of the ghetto will not, within their school careers, attend integrated schools.

If existing disadvantages are not to be perpetuated, we must drastically improve the quality of ghetto education. Equality of results with all-white schools must be the goal.

To implement these strategies, the Commission recommends:

> Sharply increased efforts to eliminate de facto segregation in our schools through substantial federal aid to school systems seeking to desegregate either within the system or in cooperation with neighboring school systems.
>
> Elimination of racial discrimination in Northern as well as Southern schools by vigorous application of Title VI of the Civil Rights Act of 1964.
>
> Extension of quality early childhood education to every disadvantaged child in the country.
>
> Efforts to improve dramatically schools serving disadvantaged children through substantial federal funding of year-round compensatory education programs, improved teaching, and expanded experimentation and research.
>
> Elimination of illiteracy through greater federal support for adult basic education.
>
> Enlarged opportunities for parent and community participation in the public schools.
>
> Reoriented vocational education emphasizing work-experience training and the involvement of business and industry.
>
> Expanded opportunities for higher education through increased federal assistance to disadvantaged students.
>
> Revision of state aid formulas to assure more per student aid to districts having a high proportion of disadvantaged school-age children.

THE WELFARE SYSTEM

Our present system of public welfare is designed to save money instead of people, and tragically ends up doing neither. This system has two critical deficiencies:

First: It excludes large numbers of persons who are in great need, and who, if provided a decent level of support, might be able to become more productive and self-sufficient. No federal funds are available for millions of men and women who are needy but neither aged, handicapped nor the parents of minor children.

Second: For those included, the system provides assistance well below the minimum necessary for a decent level of existence, and imposes restrictions that encourage continued dependency on welfare and undermine self-respect.

A welter of statutory requirements and administrative practices and regulations operate to remind recipients that they are considered untrustworthy, promiscuous and lazy. Residence requirements prevent assistance to people in need who are newly arrived in the state. Regular searches of recipients' homes violate privacy. Inadequate social services compound the problems.

The Commission recommends that the federal government, acting with state and local governments where necessary, reform the existing welfare system to:

> Establish uniform national standards of assistance at least as high as the annual "poverty level" of income, now set by the Social Security Administration at $3,335 per year for an urban family of four.
>
> Require that all states receiving federal welfare contributions participate in the Aid to Families with Dependent Children–Unemployed Parents program (AFDC-UP) that permits assistance to families with both father and mother in the home, thus aiding the family while it is still intact.
>
> Bear a substantially greater portion of all welfare costs—at least 90 percent of total payments.
>
> Increase incentives for seeking employment and job training, but remove restrictions recently enacted by the Congress that would compel mothers of young children to work.
>
> Provide more adequate social services through neighborhood centers and family-planning programs.
>
> Remove the freeze placed by the 1967 welfare amendments on the percentage of children in a state that can be covered by federal assistance.
>
> Eliminate residence requirements.

As a long-range goal, the Commission recommends that the federal government seek to develop a national system of income supplementation based strictly on need with two broad and basic purposes:

> To provide, for those who can work or who do work, any necessary supplements in such a way as to develop incentives for fuller employment.
>
> To provide, for those who cannot work and for mothers who decide to remain with their children, a minimum standard of decent living, and to aid in the saving of children from the prison of poverty that has held their parents.

A broad system of supplementation would involve substantially greater federal expenditures than anything now contemplated. The cost will range widely depending on the standard of need accepted as the "basic allowance" in individuals and families, and on the rate at which additional income above this level is taxed. Yet if the deepening cycle of poverty and dependence on welfare can be broken, if the children of the poor can be given the opportunity to scale the wall that now separates them from the rest of society, the return on this investment will be great indeed.

HOUSING

After more than three decades of fragmented and grossly under-funded federal housing programs, nearly six million substandard housing units remain occupied in the United States.

The housing problem is particularly acute in the minority ghettos. Nearly two-thirds of all nonwhite families living in the central cities today live in neighborhoods marked with substandard housing and general urban blight. Two major factors are responsible.

First: Many ghetto residents simply cannot pay the rent necessary to support decent housing. In Detroit, for example, over 40 percent of the nonwhite-occupied units in 1960 required rent of over 35 percent of the tenants' income.

Second: Discrimination prevents access to many nonslum areas, particularly the suburbs, where good housing exists. In addition, by creating a "back pressure" in the racial ghettos, it makes it possible for landlords to break up apartments for denser occupancy, and keeps prices and rents of deteriorated ghetto housing higher than they would be in a truly free market.

To date, federal programs have been able to do comparatively little to provide housing for the disadvantaged. In the 31-year history of subsidized federal housing, only about 800,000 units have been constructed, with recent production averaging about 50,000 units a year. By comparison, over a period only three years longer, FHA insurance guarantees have made possible the construction of over ten million middle- and upper-income units.

Two points are fundamental to the Commission's recommendations:

First: Federal housing programs must be given a new thrust aimed at overcoming the prevailing patterns of racial segregation. If this is not done, those programs will continue to concentrate the most impoverished and dependent segments of the population into the central-city ghettos where there is already a critical gap between the needs of the population and the public resources to deal with them.

Second: The private sector must be brought into the production and financing of low- and moderate-rental housing to supply the capabilities and capital necessary to meet the housing needs of the nation.

The Commission recommends that the federal government:

Enact a comprehensive and enforceable federal open housing law to cover the sale or rental of all housing, including single family homes.

Reorient federal housing programs to place more low- and moderate-income housing outside of ghetto areas.

Bring within the reach of low- and moderate-income families within the next five years six million new and existing units of decent housing, beginning with 600,000 units in the next year.

To reach this goal we recommend:

> Expansion and modification of the rent supplement program to permit use of supplements for existing housing, thus greatly increasing the reach of the program.
>
> Expansion and modification of the below-market interest rate program to enlarge the interest subsidy to all sponsors and provide interest-free loans to nonprofit sponsors to cover pre-construction costs, and permit sale of projects to nonprofit corporations, cooperatives or condominiums.
>
> Creation of an ownership supplement program similar to present rent supplements, to make home ownership possible for low-income families.
>
> Federal writedown of interest rates on loans to private builders constructing moderate-rent housing.
>
> Expansion of the public housing program, with emphasis on small units on scattered sites, and leasing and "turnkey" programs.
>
> Expansion of the Model Cities program.
>
> Expansion and reorientation of the urban renewal program to give priority to projects directly assisting low-income households to obtain adequate housing.

CONCLUSION

One of the first witnesses to be invited to appear before this Commission was Dr. Kenneth B. Clark, a distinguished and perceptive scholar. Referring to the reports of earlier riot commissions, he said:

> I read that report . . . of the 1919 riot in Chicago, and it is as if I were reading the report of the investigating committee on the Harlem riot of '35, the report of the investigating committee on the Harlem riot of '43, the report of the McCone Commission on the Watts riot.
>
> I must again in candor say to you members of this Commission —it is a kind of Alice in Wonderland—with the same moving picture re-shown over and over again, the same analysis, the same recommendations, and the same inaction.

These words come to our minds as we conclude this Report.

We have provided an honest beginning. We have learned much. But we have uncovered no startling truths, no unique insights, no simple solutions. The destruction and the bitterness of racial disorder, the harsh polemics of black revolt and white repression, have been seen and heard before in this country.

It is time now to end the destruction and the violence, not only in the streets of the ghetto but in the lives of people.

The Alianza Movement
of New Mexico

FRANCES L. SWADESH

In 1848, when the Treaty of Guadalupe Hidalgo was signed ending the Mexican War, about half the territory of Mexico was incorporated into the United States. With the land came its inhabitants, of whom many were Mexican citizens of Spanish or Spanish-Indian descent but the majority were Indians. Under the terms of the treaty, former Mexican citizens were granted American citizenship. But the Indians were treated in the traditional American fashion, and the subsequent history of the Mexican-American has been one of dispossession and discrimination.

In the 1960's, however, a widespread revolt began among the Spanish-speaking citizens of the United States. This segment of the American population is divided into three major groups: the **chicanos,** or Mexican-Americans; the **latinos,** immigrants from other Latin American countries; and Puerto Ricans. In the past there has been little cooperation among these various groups, who have different historical and cultural backgrounds and are concentrated in different areas of the country. Under chicano leadership, however, a movement to unify the Spanish-speaking people of the country is now taking place, and a Denver-based organization known as the "Crusade for Justice" has held several national meetings for the express purpose of binding together the various elements of **La Raza** (the race), a term used in reference to all Spanish-speaking Americans.

Among the issues that concern the leaders of La Raza are the use of Spanish as the primary language of instruction in schools in Spanish-speaking communities; land reform, including the restoration to chicanos of land taken from them after the Mexican War; economic protection for migrant farm workers, many of whom are chicano, latino, or Puerto Rican; and the development of cooperative economic institutions that will allow the communities themselves to benefit from their labor.

One of the most dramatic episodes in the growing chicano

revolt has been the successful organization, led by Cesar Chavez and the United Farm Workers Organizing Committee, of the migrant workers in California. This campaign has been conducted largely in the Spanish language, and its rallying cries of **huelga** (strike) and **la causa** (the cause) have echoed through the vineyards of California, doing much to unify members of La Raza. Fittingly, the union's symbol is the Mexican eagle, and organizers have made frequent use of appeals to the Mexican heritage and religious tradition.

On the local level, one of the most effective attempts at chicano organization took place in Crystal City, Texas—the "Spinach Capital of the World." Here, 85 percent of the population is chicano, but only 5 percent of the farms are chicano-owned. For decades, the town has been run by the Anglos, largely for their own benefit. But recently, as a result of political organization, the chicanos were able to take over the town government, an event that promises in the future to focus attention on the needs of the majority of the town's inhabitants.

The most startling program of land reform to emerge from the revolt of the 1960's is that proposed by Reies Lopez Tijerina in New Mexico. His movement, known as the **Alianza**, is attempting to make the United States government honor the terms of the Treaty of Guadalupe Hidalgo and restore to the chicanos of the state the land guaranteed to them in perpetuity by the treaty. The story of Tijerina's campaign and the background of his claims is told in the following selection by Frances L. Swadesh, an anthropologist who has written widely about the American Southwest.

The most controversial of all the organizations representing Spanish-speaking people in the United States is the "Alianza" (Alliance of Free City-States) with headquarters in Albuquerque, New Mexico. The Alianza has been variously described as a nativistic cult movement (Gonzalez, 1967:71), a criminal conspiracy (Stang, 1967, 1968) and a movement for social and political change whose leader, Reies Lopez Tijerina, is its major catalytic agent: "Whatever happens in the courts to Reies Tijerina, 41, leader of thousands of poverty-worn Spanish-Americans in northern New Mexico, he may have been the instrument of social and political change in the state and he himself may become a legendary figure" (Ed Meagher, *Los Angeles Times*, 2/5/1968).

The Alianza made front-page headlines in newspapers around the

"The Alianza Movement of New Mexico," by Frances L. Swadesh. Reprinted from *Minorities and Politics*, edited by H. J. Tobias and C. E. Woodhouse, pp. 53–84. Copyright 1969, The University of New Mexico Press. Reprinted by permission.

world on June 5, 1967, when about twenty of its members raided the Rio Arriba County Courthouse at Tierra Amarilla in northern New Mexico. They supposedly had intended to make a "citizen's arrest" of the district attorney, Alfonso Sanchez, on the grounds that he had illegally arrested some of their fellow Alianza members and had forcibly prevented the holding of a public meeting on land-grant demands.

BACKGROUND OF THE LAND-GRANT CONTROVERSY

Alianza members are descendants of grantees of lands in New Mexico, Colorado, Arizona, Texas, Utah and California, donated in the seventeenth and eighteenth centuries by the kings of Spain and, from 1822 to 1846, by the Mexican government.

These lands were granted under Castilian laws, exported and adapted to the settlement policies of the New World. In the vast arid lands of what is now the Southwestern United States, volunteer settlers were moved onto lands not occupied by the sparse indigenous population, to live as independent yeomen growing irrigated crops and raising livestock, chiefly sheep.

Under the body of law defining Spanish and Mexican land grants, donations of land could be made to individuals but were more characteristically made to towns or to groups of families desiring to found new communities. Part of each grant was composed of house lots and irrigable lands specifically assigned to individual families. These could be sold by the recipient family or its heirs after the conditions of settlement had been met: building a house, clearing a field, digging an irrigation ditch, growing crops and defending the area from the attacks of nomadic Indians for a period of several years.

By far the largest portion of most grants, however, was the "ejido" (common holding) of the community, which was inalienable and not subject to individual appropriation. Within this category were included irrigated town pastures, usually enclosed, plus the surrounding, unenclosed range and forest lands which, in New Mexico and some other areas, were mountainous and not suitable for agriculture.

Ejido lands throughout Hispanic America have been lost, especially as a market economy began to break down the economic self-sufficiency of subsistence-oriented, traditional, rural communities. The older system of bartering persisted in some underpopulated areas, including northern New Mexico. With the entry of cash transactions, some people inevitably became indebted to others and were forced to pay their debts with their land.

In the United States, however, the loss of the ejido lands on grants was primarily owing to the failure of United States authorities to recognize the ejido principle of land ownership, even though the 1848 Treaty of Guadalupe Hidalgo guaranteed protection of the personal, cultural and property rights of those Mexican citizens who remained north of the newly extended United States border. As a result of this lack of recognition, the grant heirs lost their subsistence base as well as access to such vital resources as timber for fuel and construction and the mineral wealth beneath their former ejido lands. These losses account partially for the fact that more than one-third of all Spanish-speaking families in the Southwest—41% in New Mexico and over 50% in Texas—have incomes below $3,000 per year, a figure which falls well within the designated poverty levels (Samora, 1966: 195).

The central programmatic demand of the Alianza is for a thorough investigation of wholesale violations of the guarantees of the Treaty of Guadalupe Hidalgo. The Alianza claims that these violations have denied personal and cultural rights as well as property rights. This demand has been interpreted in some quarters as a "con game" designed to enrich Reies Tijerina and his associates. In other quarters the Alianza is seen as a standing threat to law and order; and only some observers see the Alianza demands as reasonable premises for negotiations patterned on the Indian claims cases.

Such contradictory interpretations have affected public opinion on the purposes and leadership of the Alianza. This instability of opinion, in turn, has affected the very pattern of development of the Alianza.

VIEW FROM THE SOUTH

The views expressed in the press of Mexico, which have potential influence upon future developments, are well exemplified by a series of six articles, published in November, 1967, by Manuel Mejida, a reporter for the Mexico City daily, *Excelsior*. Mejida had toured the Hispano villages of New Mexico and had interviewed many villagers, seeking to enlighten his Mexico City readers on the precipitating causes of the Tierra Amarilla raid.

As a Mexican citizen, Mejida evaluated the land problems of New Mexico from the standpoint of the ejido lands in Mexico. These lands, in substantial areas, had been monopolized by "latifundistas" (plantation owners) who reduced the small farmers to peonage. In the 1930's, a sweeping movement of agrarian reform restored and developed the ejidos in the hands of the communities to which they originally belonged.

Mejida, on the predecent of Mexican experience, considered the grievances of the New Mexicans to be justified. He was impressed by the fact that the land-grant heirs, young and old alike, could state with fair precision the boundaries of their original grants and the acreage which had been appropriated for the public domain, to become, eventually, part of National Forest or state lands, or else to be sold to wealthy Anglo ranchers. Each villager knew the details of who, when, for what purpose and with which consequences areas of their lands had been lost, and each felt the community's loss as a "wound to his own self-esteem" (*Excelsior*, 11/24/67).

Mejida found virtual idolatry among the poverty-stricken villagers for Reies Tijerina, whom they saw as the "incarnation of the justice denied them for one hundred years." Although well-to-do Hispanos tended to see Tijerina and his followers as a "bunch of agitators and bandits," the poor were touchingly confident that, through the Alianza, they could recover their lost subsistence base in the forest and range of their ancestral grants. Some who had been forced to leave the home village to seek livelihood elsewhere expressed hope that their situation was "temporary" and that soon they could return to their traditional life as small independent agriculturalists and stockmen (*Excelsior,* 11/23/67, 11/24/67, 11/25/67).

In view of the violent events of the Tierra Amarilla raid, Mejida found the villagers surprisingly mild-mannered and free of hatred. Many expressed reluctance to take a stand against their own government for, as Mejida had to remind his Mexico City readers, these were people who valued their United States citizenship, had paid taxes, and served in the armed forces without complaint. But they were determined: "We are waiting for the hour of justice . . . never mind how many years our battle for justice takes, we shall win" (*Excelsior,* 11/25/1967).

Women as well as men had devoted vast amounts of time and effort, as well as what little money they had, to the Alianza's cause and they were prepared for more sacrifices in the future. Conversing as individuals or groups, the villagers displayed optimism and determination.

Mejida felt, nonetheless, that he was witnessing "the twilight of Hispanoamerican life in New Mexico." The villages had become so severely depopulated that the Hispano population of New Mexico, long the majority, had sunk below thirty percent in the 1960's. Forced by lack of training (in fields other than farming and livestock) into the ranks of migrant farm labor, many Hispanos had experienced the disruption of community and family life in the process of moving from one state to another in search of jobs. Despite their stubborn loyalty to kin- and community-based values of Hispanic rural culture, the culture was in the grip of disintegrating forces.

Mejida doubted that this poverty-stricken minority group, contemptuously accorded the treatment of a "Beggar's Army," could prevail against the forces of Anglo-dominated wealth and vested interest in confronting their federal government.

Interviewing Governor David Cargo of New Mexico, Mejida found him cautious about gambling his political future on sustained support of the land issues whose validity he acknowledged. Reluctantly, Mejida came to the conclusion that the realities and expediencies of contemporary life in the United States dictate the final extinction of the Hispano way of life in New Mexico (*Excelsior,* 11/27/1967).

DOMINANCE AND THE ETHNOCENTRIC VIEW

Manuel Mejida's melancholy prediction has been voiced for years by people who eagerly anticipate the extinction of the Hispano way of life in New Mexico. Crudely stated, their widespread belief is that the Hispanic culture of the Southwest is incurably inferior to the dominant Anglo culture; its language is a broken patois which must be rapidly forgotten in favor of English; besides, they maintain, the normal fate of all ethnic minority groups in the United States is to plunge headfirst into the Melting Pot and come out "Real Americans"—even if you wouldn't want your daughter to marry one.

This belief, often operating at deeply unconscious levels of otherwise informed minds, has tragically affected dominant-group views of the problems of three groups—the Negro, Indian and Spanish-speaking people of the United States.

Negroes, in the overwhelming majority, did not voluntarily come to the United States seeking a better life, but were brought in chains and subjected to centuries of enslavement followed by social discrimination and exclusion from the economic opportunities others enjoyed. Indians and Hispanos lived in territories which were seized by the United States, since which time they have lived as second-class citizens. Puerto Ricans too became United States citizens by force of arms. The ideology of the Melting Pot, therefore, has no basis in reality for these groups.

Dominant-group ethnocentrism has profoundly affected the political functioning of the above three groups. In the case of the New Mexicans, this ideology provided the rationale for keeping New Mexico in the status of a territory long after statehood should have been granted, with the result that certain semi-colonial characteristics were strengthened and perpetuated to the disadvantage of the Hispano and Indian populations.

Here is how the editor of the *Harper's Weekly* reacted in 1876 to Senate passage of a statehood bill for New Mexico:

> Of the present population, which is variously estimated, and at the last census was 111,000, nine-tenths are Mexicans, Indians, "greasers," and other non–English-speaking people. About one-tenth or one-eleventh part of the population speak the English language, the nine-tenths are under the strictest Roman Catholic supervision. . . . The proposition of the admission of New Mexico as a State is, that such a population, in such a condition of civilization, of industries, and intelligence, and with such forbidding prospects of speedy improvement or increase—a community almost without the characteristic and indispensable qualities of an American State—shall have a representation in the national Senate as large as New York, and in the House shall be equal to Delaware. It is virtually an ignorant foreign community under the influence of the Roman Church, and neither for the advantage of the Union nor for its own benefit can such an addition to the family of American States be urged. There are objections to a Territorial government, but in this case the Territorial supervision supplies encouragement to the spirit of intelligent progress by making the national authority finally supreme (*Harper's Weekly*, 4/1/1876).

When this diatribe was published, Colorado had already been granted statehood, although its population in 1870 only totaled 39,864 and its mining camps were hardly known for the refinement of their "civilization." By 1910, New Mexico's population had more than tripled, but statehood was delayed another two years. In the interim, the ruling circles of the Anglo minority had formed a partnership with a selected few of the Hispano majority, who were rewarded with material benefits and positions of nominal leadership in exchange for keeping their people under control.

The heritage of this partnership was the characteristic political patronage system of New Mexico, which is often represented as a traditional Hispanic form. In fact, this system overthrew the established democratic forms of Hispanic municipal government, in which the principle of seniority was dominant within a framework of full manhood suffrage, and replaced it with the "paid election," reinforced by threats and promises. By the time New Mexico achieved statehood, the Hispano majority was reduced in ratio and in its capacity to function in its own interest. It had been effectively saddled with a "leadership" that owed its first loyalty to the dominant clique of Anglos.

The Hispano majority managed to impose its will on occasion, for instance, by including in the New Mexico State Constitution a pledge to abide by the terms of the Treaty of Guadalupe Hidalgo. This pledge, however, has been so little honored that it is now widely believed by Anglos that the Treaty and its terms are irrelevant to discussions of the current status of Hispanos.

The descendants of the Spanish-speaking people who became United States citizens under the Treaty, however, believe that its terms are the "supreme law of the land," taking precedence over other laws. They consider the Treaty permanently binding upon *both* signatories. For this reason, the Alianza has, from the beginning, sought to win the active support of the Mexican government to its demand for an investigation into the charges of Treaty violations. The Mexican government, thus far, has avoided taking a position on the matter; on the other hand, the issues involved have stirred widespread popular sympathy when discussed in such press reports as the Mejida series. In Mexico, the New Mexican Hispanos are seen as "the brothers outside."

Such public support might persuade the Mexican government or another government with representation in the United Nations to instruct its delegates to lodge an official request for investigation of possible violation of the Universal Declaration of Human Rights, as the Alianza has been requesting for several years. What is most surprising, in fact, is that New Mexicans have not previously sought a remedy through international channels. Previous failure to utilize means that are nominally available is the result of the lack of political experience and of a genuine political leadership among the Hispanos. Functioning within the existing political structure of New Mexico, Hispanos can only perpetuate their own subordination.

RELATIVE DEPRIVATION AND THE TACTICS OF DESPAIR

A common line of questioning the intentions and methods of the Alianza begins with the query: Why does the Alianza focus its efforts so sharply on the land question? When it is pointed out that traditional Hispano family and community life depend on a land base, the further questions are raised: Why did the Hispanos wait so long to protest the loss of their lands, and why don't they now seek a remedy through the courts instead of resorting to violence?

Such questions can only be answered by examining the direction of Hispano changes over periods of time, with particular attention to those periods when rapid changes entailing social dislocations have forced groups of Hispanos to action.

The following paragraphs draw upon the author's previous researches (Swadesh, 1964, 1966, 1968) amplified by a series of scholarly articles published in *El Dia*, a Mexico City daily newspaper, by Agustin Cue Canovas and entitled "The Forgotten People" (Canovas, 1963).

The Canovas articles reviewed the provisions of the Treaty of Guadalupe Hidalgo from the standpoint of maneuvers by the Mexican leadership to protect the rights of its former citizens now incorporated in the United States. Articles 8, 9 and 10 of the Treaty specified the civil and property rights of the transferred citizens, and were ratified by the Mexican government. Article 9 was modified by the United States Senate, but the United States envoys who negotiated the final draft signed a protocol saying that the new wording had the same protective coverage as the earlier draft (Canovas, 5/23/63). Article 10 made provision that all land grants in the territories in question would be "respected as valid and of the stated extension," and that grants whose confirmation had not been completed prior to the United States invasion would be completed or forfeited within a period of two years. The Senate suppressed Article 10 and Canovas surmised that failure to provide for the speedy and automatic confirmation of all valid land grants, as previously pledged, was a prelude to the wholesale and violent expropriations which followed. By failing to specify a procedure and a time period for the confirmation of the grants, Congress set the stage for interminable delays in processing claims, while the Colonial and Mexican Archives were seized and systematically pillaged by the enemies of the grantees (Canovas, 5/23/63, 6/12/63).

The grantees were forced to hire lawyers at their own expense and produce what title papers they could; to go through a lengthy and complex procedure before the Land Commissioner, District Court and Supreme Court; and then seek confirmation by the Surveyor General and, once again, in the Supreme Court. In California, the influx of gold prospectors in 1849 brought about immediate and wholesale violations of the terms of the Treaty; in Texas the picture was even worse.

Mexican authorities protested illegal expropriations, evictions and assassinations, continuing to do so along the Texas border until well into this century, but to no avail (Canovas, 6/12/63). Ironically, President Manuel Peña y Peña, the Mexican president who signed the Treaty of Guadalupe Hidalgo, would have been willing to make even greater territorial concessions to the United States in order to secure the rights of his former fellow-citizens, but he was assured that their freedom was guaranteed and their rights and interests would be protected (Canovas, 10/25/63).

Contrary to the rapid and violent expropriation of grant lands in California and Texas, the same process was more delayed and more veiled in New Mexico. From the time of the arrival of the first New Mexico Surveyor General in 1854 until well after the Civil War, the land-grant heirs presented their claims with little apparent evidence that they would fail to be confirmed. The fact that the overwhelming majority of the population continued to be Hispano masked their growing loss of property and civil rights, for the ejido lands which the Surveyor General immediately began to assign to the public domain continued to be unfenced and available for grazing, and the Anglo population was nowhere large enough to present a real threat.

By 1888, however, Antonio Joseph protested to the House of Representatives the situation provoked by denial of statehood to New Mexico. He pointed out that of more than one thousand land-grant claims submitted only 71 had so far been confirmed. Land-grant heirs, despite the Treaty promise to protect them from depredations by nomadic Indian tribesmen, had suffered more than five million dollars' worth of uncompensated damages in the hostilities between the United States and the Navahos and Apaches. Joseph made pointed reference to the distinguished Civil War service rendered by the new citizens from New Mexico (Canovas, 6/24/63).

The protests of Antonio Joseph had little effect. A Court of Private Land Claims was established in 1891 to expedite matters and, when it closed its deliberations in 1904, less than two million acres of land out of thirty-five million acres claimed by the heirs had been confirmed (Read, 1912: 596). Of this acreage, a large portion had remained in the hands of lawyers representing the heirs; for instance, one half the acreage of the Cañon de San Diego Grant (U.S.D.A., 1937: 5–8).

Even so, until grazing lands were fenced off, and the heirs were reduced to their limited agricultural lands, the Hispanos never seem to have recognized the existence of a policy designed systematically to deprive them of their property rights. Each local group, as access was lost, reacted sharply, often with violence, to what they considered an outrage. Starting in the 1880's and continuing to the present, these local groups resorted to vigilante action—cutting fences, burning barns and haystacks and slashing livestock. This was the beginning of the tactics of despair.

During a brief period of years, the ever-deepening impoverishment of the New Mexican Hispano population was relieved by federal and state programs to restore their economy and meet their educational needs. In the 1930's, community studies conducted under the Soil Conservation Service of the U.S. Department of Agriculture focused on the relationship between loss of the subsistence base, land, and social dislocation. In a few communities, direct measures were taken to restore some of the lost ejido lands to the community. The development of a few stockmen's cooperatives promised to modernize grazing practices for general community benefit (Loomis and Grisham, 1943). The Taylor Grazing Act of the 1930's was intended to increase the grazing lands available to the poverty-stricken communities of northern New Mexico, but its actual long-term effect has been to strengthen the domination of corporate live-stock interests (see partial listing of U.S.D.A. publications and Harper et al., 1943: 65).

After this brief respite, the condition of the Hispano villages took a rapid plunge into deeper impoverishment, as a result of the wholesale loss of most of their young men to military service in World War II. When the local population temporarily could not maintain the livestock industry to the required levels of meat production for the armed forces, a sharp increase in leasing of the National Forest range by corporate out-of-state interests took place, and the villagers have never recovered access to substantial segments of their traditional range.

Forced emigration from the villages in search of wage work, which for many years had been a seasonal or temporary means of meeting sub-sistence needs for the younger men, now took entire families away and increased the number of ghost towns in New Mexico. Between 1950 and 1960, the percentage of New Mexico Hispanos living in rural communities dropped from nearly 60% to less than 43% (Samora, 164, Table 2).

While urbanization is a worldwide trend, the cultural shock for people of a traditional culture, as that involved in such a forced move-ment, brings social disaster in its wake. The majority of former villagers who are now obliged to live in the slums of New Mexico's towns and cities constantly express the desire to return to the country, even if they could not hope for better than a marginal subsistence. In large measure, even this thin hope is barred by existing welfare regulations, which deny aid to families owning even the tiniest plot of land which might produce a supplement to their benefits. People forced to go on the welfare rolls, therefore, can only do so after they have sold their land and spent the proceeds.

Comparing life as it is today with what it used to be, forcibly urbanized Hispanos express a keen sense of loss. It is this sense of relative deprivation which is the main motivating force of the Alianza. Even those who have managed to make a livelihood in the city feel that only as small village landholders can they maintain the core values of their culture: the cooperative unity of the enlarged kin group, the firm rules of "respect and honor" handed down from one generation to the next and the proud sense of their hereditary status, bestowed on them by Philip II, of "hijosdalgo de solar conocido"—landed gentlemen (Canovas, 7/3/23).

FIRST NOTICE OF THE ALIANZA

Although the Alianza was formally founded on February 2, 1963, Reies Tijerina and his brother Cristobal were in Mexico City early in April, 1962, and the press of the capital ran interviews with the brothers in which they explained their mission.

The Tijerina brothers said that they had come to Mexico City to seek a hearing with the Secretary of Foreign Relations, to request his intervention with United States authorities concerning compliance with the terms of the Treaty of Guadalupe Hidalgo. They explained that for fifty years land-grant heirs had been vainly trying to get recognition of their rights and their lands according to the guarantees of the Treaty. No remedy could be anticipated through the federal district courts because, whenever claims cases had been brought before them, the outcome was predetermined by those who run the courts—relatives and cronies of the very millionaires who monopolized the lands.

The descendants of land grantees, said the Tijerinas, had asked for United Nations intervention on the grounds of violation of Articles I, III, IV, VII, IX, XV, XXIII and XXV of the Universal Declaration of Human Rights. When Milton Eisenhower, then a delegate to the United Nations, visited Mexico in August, 1959, he had been asked by Dr. Benjamin Laureano Luna, President of the International Front for Human Rights, to intervene on behalf of the petitioners. Despite promises, little had been done because the United States opposed such intervention.

The Tijerinas cited from published works and from recent incidents to illustrate the hardships and discrimination suffered by native New Mexicans who had been penalized by land seizures. Both Hispanos and Indians were included among the examples, for the Pueblo Indian titles to their lands are validated by colonial Spanish documents and the nomadic Indians of the area had a recognized range which was never subjected to permanent settlement prior to the United States occupation. As a matter of fact, Indian claims cases in the Southwest and Rocky Mountain areas have relied on background evidence from the Spanish and Mexican Archives.

One of the cases cited by the Tijerinas as an example of exploitation was the plight of 350 families of heirs to the Sangre de Cristo Grant in southwestern Colorado. In November, 1961, a judge had ruled in favor of the claims of a North Carolinian, John Taylor, and had barred the heirs from access to the range and timber of this grant, a right which they had continuously enjoyed until this time. This grant was within the area formerly embraced by New Mexico.

Much emphasis was given in the Mexico City press to the Tijerinas' allegations of denials of cultural rights, in direct violation of the Treaty. The many schools in which children were forbidden to speak Spanish, the constant treatment by Anglos as inferior "foreigners," the reduction of former landowners and independent stockmen to the woeful status of exploited farm laborers toiling in the cotton, tomato and beet fields of the Southwest, were all given as reasons why Hispanos felt robbed and outraged.

The Tijerinas characterized the land-grant heirs as living on the cultural islands of what remained of their land grants in hostile enclavement against the encroaching dominance of the Anglos. Community members who assimilated to Anglo ways were despised as "pochos" (depigmented ones).

Hate, the Tijerinas announced, was growing on both sides. New Mexico papers were announcing with increasing frequency the activities of night riders who attacked Anglo ranches, burned their barns and haystacks and damaged their livestock. In many instances, this was a long-delayed vengeance against the Anglo vigilantes of the 1880's and 1890's who had lynched ancestors of the present heirs.

The Tijerinas expressed their concern that, because no attention had ever been paid to their repeated efforts to gain justice, the Hispanos of New Mexico were becoming so desperate that great violence might suddenly erupt. They urged the Mexican government to intervene on behalf of the descendants of former Mexicans, in order to resolve the crisis.[1]

These reports, which aroused intense interest in Mexico, did not go altogether unnoticed in New Mexico. The *Albuquerque Tribune*, 9/9/1959, reported the Laureano Luna–Eisenhower interview and commented that the century-old struggle for Southwestern lands whose titles derived from the governments of Spain and Mexico had now been reopened as a historic international issue.

EMERGENCE OF THE ALIANZA

Shortly after the founding meeting of the Alianza, on February 2, 1963, Reies Tijerina wrote a letter to the Mexico City daily, *El Dia*, outlining the current situation as he saw it. He wrote that as many as ten million heirs might have a stake in the drive that was about to reopen all 1,715 land-grant claims in the Southwest.[2]

In his letter, Tijerina compared the lot of dispossessed land-grant heirs to that of people in underdeveloped countries. Forced into the migrant labor stream, many were precluded from earning an adequate family livelihood and, as an alternative to starvation, became permanently dependent upon surplus commodities handed out by the government.

Tijerina reiterated the appeal of land-grant heirs to the Mexican government to investigate the Treaty violations in the light of complaints

[1] The above paragraphs on the April, 1962, Tijerinas' interviews are a summary of articles in *El Tiempo*, 4/4/62, 4/11/62 and 4/12/62, and in *La Prensa*, 4/11/62 and 4/13/62. A more detailed account of the Arizona case was carried in *La Prensa Libre*, another Mexico City daily, on 4/7/63. In this account, it is stated that hundreds of women had appealed to Attorney General Robert Kennedy asking his help to obtain observance of the Treaty of Guadalupe Hidalgo. In none of these accounts was the name of the community mentioned—"City of Peace"—nor the fact that the Tijerinas had been among the victims of depredations.

[2] The 1960 "Spanish-surname" population for the five states of New Mexico, Colorado, Arizona, Texas and California has been given as about four million, of whom some half million are of Mexican parentage. Such estimates are admitted to be subject to correction, and, for the country at large, estimating the Hispanic population becomes largely guesswork. This is because the children of non–Spanish-surname fathers and the wives of non–Spanish-surname husbands, regardless of their own Hispanic descent and affiliation, are placed in other categories. Some people anglicize their surnames in order to "pass." Some Mexican nationals slip across the border each year without registering. Finally, if we include among Tijerina's ten million potential claimants those Mexican nationals whose ancestors fled New Mexico after 1846, a group of large but undetermined numbers in the northern states of Mexico, it is possible that his estimate is reasonably accurate.

and historical documents which had been assembled: "For five years, we have been telling the Mexican people and the whole world about our pressing problems, which are really based on the drive to take away all our grants." Tijerina expressed confidence in the genuine concern Mexican people felt for this issue, and added for their information that U.S. Secretary of the Interior Stewart Udall had recently voiced objections to widespread land frauds and robbery (*El Dia*, 4/21/1963).

Within a month, *El Dia* responded to the Tijerina letter by running the Agustin Cue Canovas series. This entire series was reprinted in the original Spanish by the alert editor of the *Albuquerque News-Chieftain*, starting on September 7, 1963. Nigel Hey, editor of the *News-Chieftain* at that time, early recognized the public interest and potential significance of the Alianza cause. For more than two years, he provided space for a weekly column by Reies Tijerina, written in Spanish and widely discussed among Spanish-speaking people. The Spanish-broadcast radio station KABQ also provided time for daily talks by Tijerina. As a result, a high level of awareness concerning land-grant issues grew among the Hispanos of Albuquerque, while the information remained largely unknown to the monolingual Anglo population.

Nigel Hey also covered the first annual convention of the Alianza. It was held on September 1, 1963, in the Rio Grande High School gymnasium. Representatives of about fifty land grants attended. The main discussion concerned the building of a central mutual-aid group for all land-grant heirs in the Southwest. They would pool their efforts, employ the best attorneys and bring political pressure to bear in Washington in order to obtain redress. Another highlight of the convention was a report on Reies Tijerina's recent trip to Washington to enlist the aid of the Attorney General on the land-grant issue. On the same trip, Tijerina had attended the American Emancipation Centennial in Chicago and had invited its Negro president, Dr. Alton Davis, to be keynote speaker at the Alianza convention. Mexico's former president, Miguel Alemán, had been a speaker at the centennial and had expressed interest in the land-grant struggle (*Albuquerque News-Chieftain*, 9/7/63).

The 1962 interviews in the Mexico City press had touched on the parallels which Tijerina saw between the Negro struggle for liberation and equality and that of New Mexico's Hispanos as well as the entire "raza" (all New World, Spanish-speaking peoples, regardless of racial antecedents). Tijerina had also expressed his view that a special relationship of long duration and much intimacy existed between Indians and Spanish-speaking people of the Southwest. Although he held that each group had its special problems and methods of struggle, he actively sought understandings with Indian leadership and urged his members to learn from the Negro struggle.

Tijerina's inter-ethnic outlook and strategy was as much of an innovation at the first annual convention of the Alianza as was his proposal to link the fortunes of all grants into one major drive in which property rights and civil and cultural rights were seen as indivisible. It is remarkable that both the outlook and the proposal were so readily adopted by the bulk of the Alianza membership, considering their lack of previous exposure to broadly based, politically oriented movements and also considering the frequently voiced condemnation by middle-class Hispanos of this adoption of "Negro tactics" and "loss of traditional Spanish dignity" (see the Spanish-language "Poco a Poco" column in the *Española New Mexican,* 7/21/66, for a characteristic statement along these lines).

As reported in the press of both Mexico and New Mexico, 1964 was a year of intensive organizing activities for the Alianza, spurred by an April delegation to Washington to lay their problems before congressmen. According to the *Albuquerque Tribune,* "Rep. Montoya said he has given his assurance that he will support any legal means that might be found within the existing legal framework to resolve title conflicts" (7/30/1964). Montoya was asked to introduce a bill for a congressional investigation into the heirs' complaints and claims, which Representatives Roybal of California and Gonzales of Texas promised to support once it was initiated.

In 1964, tensions were mounting on the Tierra Amarilla Grant. The grant heirs were posting signs ordering all people lacking an heirship claim to the grant land to vacate. A plaintive letter from a Tierra Amarilla resident indicated the state of mind of the heirs. "Some of us are pretty desperate. We have tried to be good citizens and our reward has been no justice in the courts and powdered milk from the Welfare. We don't want Welfare, we want enough of our land to graze a milk cow." The same writer asked how it was possible for the United States to enforce to the hilt the treaties that gave it the Canal Zone and Guantanamo Base, yet to ignore its own obligations in the Treaty of Guadalupe Hidalgo (*Albuquerque Journal,* 7/1964).

ATTENTION FROM LAWMEN

On February 13, 1964, *El Mexicano,* a Ciudad Juarez daily, published an interview with Reies Tijerina concerning a proposed motorcade of land-grant heirs from Albuquerque to Mexico City. They wanted to bring their demands to the attention of the people and governments on both sides of the border. Tijerina cited the Laws of the Indies and the 1493 Papal Bull "Noverunt Universi," establishing a policy for colonization of the New World. These laws had set the basis of land ownership which the United States had pledged to respect in the Treaty of Guadalupe Hidalgo and Tijerina pointed out that it was the duty of both signatories to the Treaty to see that it was upheld.

When Tijerina went to map the route of the caravan, however, he was arrested by agents of the Judicial Police and held in the Chihuahua State Prison, pending a decision on his status by the Secretariat of Gobernacion (which controls travel and immigration in Mexico). The shock and anger which this abrupt and unexplained action aroused throughout Mexico, where festivities for the New Mexico pilgrims were being planned, was reflected in the news report of the Chihuahua City publication *Accion* (7/15/1964).

Secretary Diaz Ordaz of the Gobernacion, who has since become the president of Mexico, allowed Tijerina to be released from prison and to proceed to Mexico City, where he was suddenly rounded up and deported. Ironically, while all this was going on, Governor Campbell of New Mexico announced that he would provide a police escort for the motorcade to the Texas border (*Albuquerque Tribune*, 7/30/1964). News of the arrest had not yet come to New Mexico. In 1967, Mexican journalist Eduardo Septrien reminisced that New Mexico Hispanos had been thunderstruck by the arrest and deportation of their leader, since they had never dreamed that the country of their forefathers might one day reject them (n.d.).

THE ALIANZA GROWS

When the second annual convention of the Alianza took place in Seth Hall, Santa Fe, on August 28–29, 1964, its membership was claimed to be 6,000 (*Albuquerque North Valley News*, 8/27/1964); by 1966 the number had risen to 20,000 (*Denver Post*, 4/25/1966). The early growth of the Alianza was no doubt spurred by hopes that Joseph Montoya, now a senator, would sponsor a bill for an investigation of land-grant grievances. In mid-1965, however, Reies Tijerina announced in his weekly *News-Chieftain* column that neither Montoya nor the President, who had received many appeals, appeared to be concerned about the problems of the land-grant heirs. Tijerina began to discuss the possibility of bringing the issue of the Treaty directly before the Supreme Court (*Albuquerque News-Chieftain*, 8/6/1965).

The third annual convention of the Alianza, held on September 4–5, 1965, voted to assess each member family $100 in order to create a legal action fund. A New Mexico attorney and one from Texas were retained to study procedures aimed at opening up the question of vacant lands taken from the grants by either the state or federal government. By January, 1966, the heirs had managed to raise $5,000 but it became increasingly apparent that vastly larger sums would be needed to launch such a case (*Albuquerque Journal*, 1/1/1966).

At this time, Tijerina began to consider laying the groundwork for a litigation in which the Alianza would be the defendant and would thereby be spared the high cost of going to court as plaintiff. By acts of civil disobedience on grant lands which had been taken by the federal government, the Alianza could challenge the government to prove that these lands were, indeed, its rightful property.

Other kinds of acts of civil disobedience had already been committed by land-grant heirs. For example, members of the "Abiquiu Corporation" of the Tierra Amarilla Grant were accused by District Attorney Alfonso Sanchez of violating a 1964 court injunction forbidding them to issue hunting, grazing and fishing permits to people who were not grant heirs. In the citation, Sanchez stated: "The Alianza Federal de Mercedes and Reies Lopez Tijerina are the primary instigators and advisors to the remaining defendants in the unlawful acts herein complained of" (*New Mexican*, 1/5/1966). Mr. Sanchez gave no factual basis for this allegation.

Another case of civil disobedience which became linked in the popular mind with the Alianza led to the filing of criminal charges by District Attorney Sanchez in the fall of 1966 against the parents of twenty-five primary-school children of the town of Cañones, a remote hamlet of northern New Mexico. The parents had refused to send their children to school in Coyote, over twenty miles away, on the grounds that the road out of Cañones became too dangerous in rainy or snowy weather. It was generally felt that the parents were also protesting the closing of the Cañones school, which caused the transfer to Coyote. The parents disavowed ties with the Alianza (*Albuquerque Journal*, 10/6/1966).

While it is quite possible that the parents were acting on their own, it is equally possible that issues raised by the Alianza served as a stimulus to their actions. But the Alianza was beginning to launch a different kind of struggle as its central educational demand: to assert the right of Hispano children to use their own language in school. Tijerina told reporter Peter Kelly that recovery of lands was simply a part and, to an extent, a symbol of the full purpose of the Alianza, which was to mold an effective, influential organization of Hispanos, united in culture, language and pride of identity. In his vivid, nonidiomatic English, Tijerina pictured the suffering and alienation experienced by Hispano children in school: "Culture is a live part of people. All language of ours has been deprived from public schools. Our children feel there's no future in education. They have no zeal. Cultural ties become our chains" (*Denver Post*, 4/25/1966).

While pondering the implementation of acts of civil disobedience, the Alianza made one last effort to secure justice through congressional action. A march to Santa Fe was undertaken during the Fourth of July holiday to ask Governor Campbell's assistance in pushing for a congressional bill. This was the Alianza's first mass, direct action, and for many Alianza members it was the first demonstrative public action of their lives. Reaction to the demonstration was vocal, some highly critical. Dr. Nancie Gonzalez of the University of New Mexico Department of Anthropology probably expressed the dominant reaction, however, when she predicted to an *Albuquerque Journal* reporter that there would be "more ferment as this American discovers and raises his Spanish-speaking voice" (7/3/1966).

The fourth annual convention of the Alianza, held September 3–4, 1966, demonstrated the growth of interests among the members in topics ranging far beyond the Laws of the Indies and the Treaty of Guadalupe Hidalgo, which some observers tended to view as obsessional concerns. Much interest was registered in such topics as language discrimination and de facto segregation in the schools, the virtues and defects of poverty programs, and the war in Vietnam, with its high death toll among Spanish-surname soldiers (*Albuquerque Journal*, 9/3/1966).

In October, 1966, the Alianza members occupied the Echo Amphitheater Campground in the Carson National Forest, a site in northern New Mexico which was on the 500,000 acre San Joaquin del Cañon de Chama Grant. The purpose of the occupation, as stated by Mrs. Isabel Garcia at the trial which resulted one year later, was to get the land-grant issue into the courts: "The purpose was that we would go to the Echo Amphitheater and if we were arrested, we would get our case in court and maybe go to the Supreme Court." Deliberate mass exposure to arrest had been voted by the membership and was approved by the Supreme Council of the Alianza, a group of twelve "older, more experienced men," according to Mrs. Garcia (*Alamogordo Daily News,* 11/9/1967).

PROS AND CONS

During the occupation of the Echo Amphitheater Campground, the Santa Fe *New Mexican* (10/27/1966) ran an editorial entitled "Not a Laughing Matter," which reflected the rising tide of public support for a thorough study of the land-grant question. It said in part:

> We can't laugh because our conscience is pricked . . . morally the case is far less clear . . . behind the legal technicalities we are confronted with the shameful fact that the United States of America made a solemn promise and failed, in many instances, to honor the obligations of that promise. People who were guaranteed the perpetual (and often tax-free) right to the use of ancestral lands have lost that right and the United States, which assumed an obligation to protect them, did nothing to honor its pledge. . . . Land Grant heirs are asking that a federal commission investigate this situation and right the old injustice. Whatever the technicalities of the law, we think the national conscience would rest easier if this were done.

The Forest Service attempted to dampen support by alleging that a Chama Cañon Grant of the size claimed by the heirs had never existed. In 1894, the Rio Grande Land and Cattle Company, headed by Thomas Burns, had indeed laid claim to a grant of this name, alleging that it consisted of some 500,000 acres. Upon investigation, the Court of Private Land Claims found the grant consisted of only 1,422 acres. This finding was confirmed by the Supreme Court in 1897. The grant was confirmed to legal heirs, and still exists as a small enclave within the Carson National Forest (*New Mexican*, 10/30/1966).

The Forest Service neglected to mention later litigation on the Chama Cañon Grant which tends to vindicate the Alianza claim. A fresh suit for the full half-million acres was entered by attorney Thomas B. Catron on behalf of the Rio Arriba Land and Cattle Company in 1898, and Thomas Burns received patent on the entire grant minus the 1,422 acres in 1905. Mr. Burns did not hold this grant for long because it lay within the area which soon became the central section of the Carson National Forest (Cañon de Chama Grant, Reel 20, New Mexico Land Grant Microfilm Series).

SHOCK WAVES

The June 5, 1967, raid on the Tierra Amarilla courthouse alienated some Anglo opinion but obviously aroused enthusiasm and downright pride among wide sections of the Hispano population. A number of research-oriented articles appeared in the press, probing into the under-lying causes of the raid. Few of these articles were as sympathetic toward Alianza members as the aforementioned Mejida articles in *Excelsior;* on the other hand, emphasis was laid on the existence of justified grievances.

The Las Cruces trial, held in early November, 1967, received fair and restrained press coverage in all parts of the country. Although the prosecution made much of holding the two forest rangers for an informal "trial" during the occupation of the Echo Amphitheater Campground, and described the temporary confiscation of their trucks and radios as "seizure of government property," a number of the reporters paid more attention to the implications of social change among the New Mexico Hispanos which were revealed through the trial.

On November 9, 1967, the *Sun-News* of Las Cruces summed up the testimony of Reies Tijerina as follows:

> While explaining his aims, Tijerina claimed that the U.S. Supreme Court and Court of Appeals have consistently ruled that the courts do not have jurisdiction over political matters or entities such as the pueblos his groups claim. He explained that his group is striv-ing to "build up moral strength" to give its case validity in the courts. . . . "The law means only what people behind it mean," Tijerina declared. He explained that judges follow an established pattern in court and that his group is working to adjust that estab-lished way of looking at the law.

Ed Meagher of the *Los Angeles Times* summarized an account of the Tijerina testimony in which the drive for civil and cultural rights was stressed: "The economic, political and social rights questions raised by the Spanish-American movement have New Mexico in a turmoil" (11/20/1967).

ATTACK FROM THE RIGHT

In October, 1967, a pamphlet was issued by *American Opinion*, a publication of the John Birch Society, entitled "Reies Tijerina—the Com-munist Plan to Grab the Southwest." The pamphlet came out in time to be widely circulated just before the trial in Las Cruces, and rumor has it that some 50,000 free copies were distributed within the area from which the jury was soon to be drawn. However this may be, the pamphlet's author, Alan Stang, made a number of speeches along the lines of the pamphlet in various communities in New Mexico, both before and during the trial.

Defense attorneys for the five defendants in the Echo Amphitheater Campground case considered the pamphlet so prejudicial to their clients that they asked that the trial be moved out of New Mexico altogether. "The John Birch Society is now attempting to smear the land grant movement as a Marxist revolutionary cabal," stated the attorneys, as they deposited along with their motion sixteen exhibits, consisting of newspaper clippings and comment by radio stations (Santa Fe *New Mexican,* 10/21/1967).

In March, 1968, *American Opinion* published a second Stang pamphlet entitled "Terror Grows—'War on Poverty' Supports Castroite Terrorists." This was Stang's "exposé" of the "links" between the Alianza and employees of the New Mexico State Office of Economic Opportunity.

The speedy effect of the Stang pamphlets and the investigation into "possible Tijerina-Red links" which the State Attorney General ordered in the fall of 1967 (*Albuquerque Tribune,* 9/12/1967) was to cool the interest of those individuals who had hoped to reap political advantage by basking in the reflected glow of the Alianza's growing popularity. Another effect was to usher in a period of increasingly harsh treatment of Alianza members, which was justified in newspaper editorials.

On the night of January 2, 1968, the Tierra Amarilla jailor, Eulogio Salazar, who was to have been a key witness in the raid case, was brutally bludgeoned to death. Cristobal Tijerina and another Alianza member, Felix Martinez, were arrested the following day. Although it rapidly became apparent that they could not have been guilty of the crime, and no guilt could be attached to any Alianza member, Governor Cargo recommended cancellation of bond for seventeen other defendants in the raid case. Many were forced to spend more than a month in prison, yet to this day the Salazar case remains unsolved.

A January 6, 1968, editorial in the *Albuquerque Journal,* signed by editor John McMillion, stated: "If not directly involved the Alianza is indirectly involved because it has nurtured such hate as never before existed in Rio Arriba County." McMillion warned the citizens of the area that "while they may have been shortchanged in the past they certainly will be denied even more in the future if the community, and the area, becomes a fiefdom run by hoodlums."

When the preliminary hearing on the Tierra Amarilla raid took place in early February, 1968, signs stating "Tierra o Muerte" (Land or Death) appeared on fenceposts of the Tierra Amarilla Grant. Without pausing to learn that this was the traditional slogan of the followers of Emiliano Zapata during the Mexican Revolution, one paper termed it an "ominous warning" (*Clovis Journal,* 2/11/1968) and another described a "drawing of a Pancho Villa–type Mexican bandit with a bandolier of ammunition across his chest" (*Rio Grande Sun,* 2/8/1968).

The most hostile editorial attack occurred when the preliminary hearing on the raid ended with charges against nine of the defendants dismissed and those against the remaining eleven defendants greatly reduced. The editor of the *Albuquerque Tribune*, George Carmack, wrote an open letter to his readers on February 10. He demanded that preliminary court hearings in criminal cases be replaced by the Grand Jury system. District Attorney Alfonso Sanchez, who was bitterly critical of the judge's rulings, promptly called a meeting of the Rio Arriba County Grand Jury. The consequent Grand Jury indictment restored all the charges eliminated or reduced by the judge (*Albuquerque Journal*, 4/28/1968).

Nothing further was mentioned about the social-change role of the Alianza, the grievances it sought to redress and the success of its organizing efforts. Then on February 14, 1968, Santa Fe *New Mexican* reporter Peter Nabokov managed to interview Reies Tijerina between his release from prison and his departure on a fund-raising tour of California. Tijerina was hoping for help in this campaign from César Chavez, leader of the farm workers; from Bert Corona, head of the Mexican-American Political Association; and from a number of other well-known West Coast leaders. He also discussed the preparation of the Alianza's claims for presentation before the United Nations.

POOR PEOPLE'S MARCH

The New Mexico public, saturated with the bloody details of the Salazar slaying and the preliminary hearing on the Tierra Amarilla raid, was startled to learn in April, 1968, that Reies Tijerina had been the personal choice of Dr. Martin Luther King to coordinate the New Mexico section of the Poor People's March. King also chose him to be a principal leader of the entire Southwest contingent. Under the title "Tijerina: the Wrong Choice," the *Albuquerque Journal* editorialized concerning "Tijerina's record . . . marked by violence." Itemizing every instance in which the Alianza had been involved in violent episodes, including the Salazar murder and the dynamiting of the Alianza headquarters by a saboteur who clumsily blew off his own hand, the editorial concluded: "Tijerina's presence seems almost certain to lessen the prospects that the march will be a non-violent one" (3/2/1968).

Expressions of this sort brought forth abundant anti-Tijerina statements, all of which were duly relayed to the organizing staff of the Southern Christian Leadership Conference. Despite ensuing misunderstandings, blunders, harsh words and harsher feelings, the New Mexico contingent did leave with Tijerina at its helm.

ASSESSMENT AND PROGNOSIS

With the Poor People's Campaign, the Alianza entered a new and complex phase of its development. Assessments of its promise vary. Paul Wieck of the *Albuquerque Journal* was negatively impressed by

Tijerina's disagreements with the SCLC leadership and felt that they largely arose because he "didn't get his cut of the cash." Wieck also objected to Tijerina's statement that the SCLC leadership had betrayed the land-reform goals of the campaign. Wieck concluded that "Tijerina, as a spokesman for a land-based movement, has little to offer the more sophisticated men in SCLC and other civil rights organizations" (*Albuquerque Journal*, 7/15/1968).

Paul Wieck apparently forgot that Dr. King had emphasized his intention to link land demands of the former sharecroppers of the Deep South, who have in recent years been displaced by machine operations and who represent the most critically dislocated element forced into the urban ghettoes, with the Hispano and Indian demands. Whereas the Hispano and Indian claims derive from treaties, the Negro claim is based on the post–Civil War promise of "forty acres and a mule" for every freedman.

Faith Berry, a Negro free-lance writer who spent a good deal of time at both the Washington, D.C., Resurrection City and the Hawthorne School, where the Spanish-speaking delegation had its headquarters in Washington, gave a different picture from that presented by Paul Wieck. She found that rifts between the SCLC leadership and the leaders of the Indian and Hispano ethnic groups occurred because the latter objected to "being handed final decisions on policy by the Southern Christian Leadership Conference," instead of being directly represented in policy making.

Miss Berry was greatly impressed by the growth of inter-ethnic dialogue, which had become a feature of life at the Hawthorne School and which involved youths from all groups, including the whites from Appalachia. She felt that Hispano initiative had launched this significant development, which might well turn out to be the most enduring achievement of the entire campaign.

Miss Berry quoted Tijerina as follows:

> We need unity. This is the first opportunity the poor and deprived of this country have had to come together. But some of our goals and demands are different. We Spanish-Americans put emphasis on our treaty because for us the treaty would settle the issue for many of us for jobs, food, discrimination, education and the improvement of our rural areas. In the cities of the Southwest, we are discriminated against just like the black man, but like the black man we are learning to fight back (*New York Times Magazine*, 7/7/1968). [© 1968 by The New York Times Company. Reprinted by permission.]

Retracing the development of the Alianza from a small, isolated group of tradition-oriented Hispanos through its brief and stormy years, one hesitates to predict the future dimensions of this organization and the areas of its emphasis. From the start, it has disregarded all the rules for developing an organization, and has never thrived more than when apparently on the brink of failure. In the absence of any other effective

Hispano organization in New Mexico devoted to social change, the Alianza has taken on an unwieldy program that puts it in the position of having to learn many things very fast, both in the field of practical politics and in statesmanlike advancement of proposals for economic betterment, education and the like.

Yet, in these formidable tasks, the Alianza can now draw upon a wide reserve of interested allies, who are learning as much from rural Hispanos as they are teaching them. The author is convinced that the Alianza movement is developing in accordance with the classic form of innovative movements in conflict situations with revolutionary overtones:

> While a great deal of doctrine in every moment (and, indeed, in every person's mazeway) is extremely unrealistic in that predictions of events made on the basis of its assumptions will prove to be more or less in error, there is only one sphere of behavior in which such error is fatal to the success of the revitalization movement: prediction of the outcome of conflict situations. If the organization cannot predict successfully the consequences of its own moves and of its opponents' moves in a power struggle, its demise is very likely. If, on the other hand, it is canny about conflict, or if the amount of resistance is low, it can be extremely "unrealistic" or extremely unconventional in other matters without running much risk of early collapse (Wallace, 1956:279).

Today, with great emphasis, the minority groups are joining together to demand that the majority group speedily shed itself of racism, ethnocentrism and the propensity to control "lesser" peoples by means of violence. Representatives of the majority group cannot agree whether to meet those demands with tactics of repression and terror, with token concessions, or with full compliance. Considering the fears, guilty consciences and indecisions that plague so many majority group Americans and the growing experience, self-confidence and unity which increasingly unites the discriminated and dispossessed, the larger movement of which the Alianza is an integral part can hardly fail.

NOTES

Canovas, Agustin Cue
1963 El Pueblo Ovidado, series in *El Dia*, a daily newspaper of Mexico City, 5/23/1963, 5/29/1963, 6/12/1963, 7/3/1963, 6/no date/1963, 6/20/1963, 6/24/1963, 7/10/1963, 10/4/1963, 10/10/1963, 8/1/1963, 8/29/1963, 10/25/1963, 10/30/1963

Gonzalez, Nancie L.
1967 The Spanish American of New Mexico: A Distinctive Heritage, Advance Report #9 Mexican-American Study Project, Los Angeles: University of California Graduate School of Business Administration

Harper, Allen G., Cordova, Andrew, and Oberg, Kalervo
1943 Man and Resources in the Middle Rio Grande Valley, Inter-American Studies, II, Albuquerque: University of New Mexico Press

Loomis, C. P., and Grisham, Glen
1943 "Spanish Americans: The New Mexico Experiment in Village Rehabilitation," *Applied Anthropology*, 2(3): 13–37

Meagher, Ed
1967 "Tijerina Forays Seen as Civil Rights Struggle," *Los Angeles Times*, 11/20/1967
1968 "Tijerina Raid May Bring Social Change," *Los Angeles Times*, 2/5/1968

Mejida, Manuel
1967 Series in *Excelsior*, a daily newspaper of Mexico City: El Problema Moreno, 11/23/1967, Fantasmas Junto al Rio Bravo, 11/24/1967, Ejercito de los Desarrapados, 11/25/1967, Ocaso de los Hispanoamericanos, 11/27/1967

Read, Benjamin
1912 *Illustrated History of New Mexico*, Santa Fe: Santa Fe New Mexico Printing Company

Samora, Julian, ed.
1966 *La Raza: Forgotten Americans*, Notre Dame: University of Notre Dame Press

Septrien, Eduardo
1967 n.p.d., *¿Guerrillas en los Estados Unidos?*

Stang, Alan
1967 "Reies Tijerina—The Communist Plan to Grab the Southwest," Belmont, Massachusetts: *American Opinion*
1968 "Terror Grows—'War on Poverty' Supports Castroite Terrorists," Belmont, Massachusetts: *American Opinion*

Swadesh, Frances L.
1965 "Property and Kinship in Northern New Mexico," *Rocky Mountain Social Science Journal*, 2/1: 209–14
1966 "Hispanic Americans of the Ute Frontier," Unpublished Ph.D. Dissertation, University of Colorado (Research Report #50, Tri-Ethnic Project)
1968 "The Alianza Movement: Catalyst for Social Change," Text of a Report Delivered at the Annual Meeting of the American Ethnological Society, Detroit, Michigan, May 5, 1968. To be published in Proceedings of the Annual 1968 Spring Meeting of the American Ethnological Society (Fall, 1968)

United States Department of Agriculture, Soil Conservation Service, Regional Studies
1936 Reconnaissance Survey of Human Dependency on Resources in the Rio Grande Watershed, Regional Bulletin #33
1937 Notes on Community-Owned Land Grants in New Mexico, Regional Bulletin #48

1939 Tewa Basin Study, Vol. 2. The Spanish-American Villages, Office of Indian Affairs Land Research Unit, 1935. Released by United States Soil Conservation Service, Region 8, Albuquerque, New Mexico

Wallace, Anthony F. C.
1956 "Revitalization Movements," *American Anthropologist*, 58: 264–83

N.B. I am indebted to leaders of the Alianza for lending me their press file. Unfortunately, some of the clippings are without dates, name of publication or even title of article. Particularly for some of the Mexican press clippings, these deficiencies cannot be remedied.

Why Women's Liberation

MARLENE DIXON

In an age of revolt and general questioning of traditional authority, it comes as no surprise that the largest oppressed segment of society should try to free itself from the restraints that have bound it over the years. Thus, in the 1960's, a new women's liberation movement was born.

The current movement can be traced to a variety of sources. For many women, the issues behind the women's revolt were defined in 1963 by Betty Friedan in **The Feminine Mystique,** a book in which she discusses the profound discontent of the middle-class, college-educated housewife who finds herself tied to a house in the suburbs and expected to find personal fulfillment through her husband and her children. Other women joined the movement as a result of disillusioning experiences in the radical student movement of the middle 1960's. Many young women activists working in the civil rights drive and in a variety of college-based organizations found themselves relegated by male associates to the stereotyped female roles, such as typing, cooking, housekeeping, and providing sexual companionship. In recent years, still another source of support for the movement has been a group composed predominantly of poor black women, the increasingly militant National Welfare Rights Organization, which is fighting to improve national welfare programs.

On occasion, the different strands of the new women's rights movement have cooperated to bring their case against male supremacy dramatically before the public eye. For instance, a broad-based coalition of groups participated in the Women's Strike for Equality on August 26, 1970, the fiftieth anniversary of the ratification of the Nineteenth Amendment giving women the right to vote. As a rule, however, the various women's groups function independently, seeking different, specific goals related to the liberation of women.

The middle-class, professional associates of Betty Friedan, who founded the National Organization of Women (NOW) in 1966, have been primarily interested in securing equal opportunity in education and employment for women. Although there are federal laws designed to protect women in these respects, they are frequently neglected or ignored. Thus the women of NOW are urging the enactment of the equal rights amendment to the Constitution first proposed to Congress by Alice Paul of the Women's Rights Party in 1923. This amendment, which would forbid any sex-based discrimination by state or federal governments, has been opposed by some women's labor organizations on the grounds that it would abolish certain protective legislation that works to the advantage of women in commerce and industry. Aspects of the NOW program that have more general support from the nation's women include the establishment of free twenty-four-hour day-care centers for the children of working mothers and the provision of free abortion on demand.

Another segment of the women's liberation movement stresses what it calls "consciousness raising"—the formation of small groups of women who come together regularly to discuss their common problems and ways in which society might be changed to permit more freedom for women. According to this group, it is necessary for women to reach a heightened awareness of the discrimination inherent in the traditional sex roles before they can realize the possibilities of true liberation. In an effort to raise the general consciousness, the radical women's groups are now publishing several new journals with titles such as **Up from Under** and **No More Fun and Games,** which contain intensely personal and probing analyses of sex roles in the present society and of continued male attempts to keep women in inferior and submissive positions. For the most part, the women of the liberation movement are seeking neither female supremacy nor isolation from men. Rather, they are seeking to define their social roles for themselves. If they are successful, their struggle may free men also from the burden of a stereotyped sex role.

In the following article, Marlene Dixon, a sociologist at McGill University, outlines the character and the underlying causes of the new women's movement and analyzes the cultural factors that have permitted inequality of the sexes to persist in this country.

The 1960's has been a decade of liberation; women have been swept up by that ferment along with blacks, Latins, American Indians and poor whites—the whole soft underbelly of this society. As each oppressed group in turn discovered the nature of its oppression in American society, so women have discovered that they too thirst for free and fully human lives. The result has been the growth of a new women's movement, whose base encompasses poor black and poor white women on relief, working women exploited in the labor force, middle class women incarcerated in the split level dream house, college girls awakening to the fact that sexiness is not the crowning achievement in life, and movement women who have discovered that in a freedom movement they themselves are not free. In less than four years women have created a variety of organizations, from the nationally based middle class National Organization of Women (NOW) to local radical and radical feminist groups in every major city in North America. The new movement includes caucuses within nearly every New Left group and within most professional associations in the social sciences. Ranging in politics from reform to revolution, it has produced critiques of almost every segment of American society and constructed an ideology that rejects every hallowed cultural assumption about the nature and role of women.

As is typical of a young movement, much of its growth has been underground. The papers and manifestos written and circulated would surely comprise two very large volumes if published, but this literature is almost unknown outside of women's liberation. Nevertheless, where even a year ago organizing was slow and painful, with small cells of six or ten women, high turnover, and an uphill struggle against fear and resistance, in 1969 all that has changed. Groups are growing up everywhere with women eager to hear a hard line, to articulate and express their own rage and bitterness. Moving about the country, I have found an electric atmosphere of excitement and responsiveness. Everywhere there are doubts, stirrings, a desire to listen, to find out what it's all about. The extent to which groups have become politically radical is astounding. A year ago the movement stressed male chauvinism and psychological oppression; now the emphasis is on understanding the economic and social roots of women's oppression, and the analyses range from social democracy to Marxism. But the most striking change of all in the last year has been the loss of fear. Women are no longer afraid that their rebellion will threaten their very identity as women. They are not frightened by their own militancy, but liberated by it. Women's Liberation is an idea whose time has come.

The old women's movement burned itself out in the frantic decade of the 1920's. After a hundred years of struggle, women won a battle, only to lose the campaign: the vote was obtained, but the new millennium did not arrive. Women got the vote and achieved a measure of legal emancipation, but the real social and cultural barriers to full equality for women remained untouched.

For over 30 years the movement remained buried in its own ashes. Women were born and grew to maturity virtually ignorant of their own history of rebellion, aware only of a caricature of blue stockings and suffragettes. Even as increasing numbers of women were being driven into the labor force by the brutal conditions of the 1930's and by the massive drain of men into the military in the 1940's, the old ideal remained: a woman's place was in the home and behind her man. As the war ended and men returned to resume their jobs in factories and offices, women were forced back to the kitchen and nursery with a vengeance. This story has been repeated after each war and the reason is clear: women form a flexible, cheap labor pool which is essential to a capitalist system. When labor is scarce, they are forced onto the labor market. When labor is plentiful, they are forced out. Women and blacks have provided a reserve army of unemployed workers, benefiting capitalists and the stable male white working class alike. Yet the system imposes untold suffering on the victims, blacks and women, through low wages and chronic unemployment.

With the end of the war the average age at marriage declined, the average size of families went up, and the suburban migration began in earnest. The political conservatism of the '50's was echoed in a social conservatism which stressed a Victorian ideal of the woman's life: a full womb and selfless devotion to husband and children.

As the bleak decade played itself out, however, three important social developments emerged which were to make a rebirth of the women's struggle inevitable. First, women came to make up more than a third of the labor force, the number of working women being twice the prewar figure. Yet the marked increase in female employment did nothing to better the position of women, who were more occupationally disadvantaged in the 1960's than they had been 25 years earlier. Rather than moving equally into all sectors of the occupational structure, they were being forced into the low-paying service, clerical and semi-skilled categories. In 1940, women had held 45 per cent of all professional and technical positions; in 1967, they held only 37 per cent. The proportion of women in service jobs meanwhile rose from 50 to 55 per cent.

Second, the intoxicating wine of marriage and suburban life was turning sour; a generation of women woke up to find their children grown and a life (roughly 30 more productive years) of housework and bridge parties stretching out before them like a wasteland. For many younger women, the empty drudgery they saw in the suburban life was a sobering contradiction to adolescent dreams of romantic love and the fulfilling role of woman as wife and mother.

Third, a growing civil rights movement was sweeping thousands of young men and women into a moral crusade—a crusade which harsh

political experience was to transmute into the New Left. The American
Dream was riven and tattered in Mississippi and finally napalmed in Viet-
Nam. Young Americans were drawn not to Levittown, but to Berkeley,
the Haight-Ashbury and the East Village. Traditional political ideologies
and cultural myths, sexual mores and sex roles with them, began to disintegrate in an explosion of rebellion and protest.

The three major groups which make up the new women's movement
—working women, middle class married women and students—bring very
different kinds of interests and objectives to women's liberation. Working
women are most concerned with the economic issues of guaranteed employment, fair wages, job discrimination and child care. Their most immediate oppression is rooted in industrial capitalism and felt directly
through the vicissitudes of an exploitative labor market.

Middle class women, oppressed by the psychological mutilation and
injustice of institutionalized segregation, discrimination and imposed inferiority, are most sensitive to the dehumanizing consequences of severely
limited lives. Usually well educated and capable, these women are re-
belling against being forced to trivialize their lives, to live vicariously
through husbands and children.

Students, as unmarried middle class girls, have been most sensitized
to the sexual exploitation of women. They have experienced the frustration of one-way relationships in which the girl is forced into a "wife"
and companion role with none of the supposed benefits of marriage.
Young women have increasingly rebelled not only against passivity and
dependency in their relationships but also against the notion that they
must function as sexual objects, being defined in purely sexual rather than
human terms, and being forced to package and sell themselves as commodities on the sex market.

Each group represents an independent aspect of the total institutionalized oppression of women. Their differences are those of emphasis and
immediate interest rather than of fundamental goals. All women suffer
from economic exploitation, from psychological deprivation, and from
exploitive sexuality. Within women's liberation there is a growing understanding that the common oppression of women provides the basis for
uniting across class and race lines to form a powerful and radical movement.

RACISM AND MALE SUPREMACY

Clearly, for the liberation of women to become a reality it is necessary to destroy the ideology of male supremacy, which asserts the biological and social inferiority of women in order to justify massive institutionalized oppression. Yet we all know that many women are as loud in
their disavowal of this oppression as are the men who chant the litany of
"a woman's place is in the home and behind her man." In fact, women are
as trapped in their false consciousness as were the mass of blacks 20 years
ago, and for much the same reason.

As blacks were defined and limited socially by their color, so women are defined and limited by their sex. While blacks, it was argued, were preordained by God or nature, or both, to be hewers of wood and drawers of water, so women are destined to bear and rear children, and to sustain their husbands with obedience and compassion. The Sky-God tramples through the heavens and the Earth Mother–Goddess is always flat on her back with her legs spread, putting out for one and all.

Indeed, the phenomenon of male chauvinism can only be understood when it is perceived as a form of racism, based on stereotypes drawn from a deep belief in the biological inferiority of women. The so-called "black analogy" is no analogy at all; it is the same social process that is at work, a process which both justifies and helps perpetuate the exploitation of one group of human beings by another.

The very stereotypes that express the society's belief in the biological inferiority of women recall the images used to justify the oppression of blacks. The nature of women, like that of slaves, is depicted as dependent, incapable of reasoned thought, childlike in its simplicity and warmth, martyred in the role of mother, and mystical in the role of sexual partner. In its benevolent form, the inferior position of women results in paternalism; in its malevolent form, a domestic tyranny which can be unbelievably brutal.

It has taken over 50 years to discredit the scientific and social "proof" which once gave legitimacy to the myths of black racial inferiority. Today most people can see that the theory of the genetic inferiority of blacks is absurd. Yet few are shocked by the fact that scientists are still busy "proving" the biological inferiority of women.

In recent years, in which blacks have led the struggle for liberation, the emphasis on racism has focused only upon racism against blacks. The fact that "racism" has been practiced against many groups other than Today most people can see that the theory of the genetic inferiority of more accurate term for the phenomenon would be "social Darwinism." It was the opinion of the social Darwinists that in the natural course of things the "fit" succeed (i.e., oppress) and the "unfit" (i.e., the biologically inferior) sink to the bottom. According to this view, the very fact of a group's oppression proves its inferiority and the inevitable correctness of its low position. In this way each successive immigrant group coming to America was decked out in the garments of "racial" or biological inferiority until the group was sufficiently assimilated, whereupon Anglo-Saxon venom would turn on a new group filling up the space at the bottom. Now two groups remain, neither of which has been assimilated according to the classic American pattern: the "visibles"—blacks and women. It is equally true for both: "it won't wear off."

Yet the greatest obstacle facing those who would organize women remains women's belief in their own inferiority. Just as all subject populations are controlled by their acceptance of the rightness of their own status, so women remain subject because they believe in the rightness of their own oppression. This dilemma is not a fortuitous one, for the entire society is geared to socialize women to believe in and adopt as immutable necessity their traditional and inferior role. From earliest training to the grave, women are constrained and propagandized. Spend an evening at the movies or watching television, and you will see a grotesque figure called woman presented in a hundred variations upon the themes of "children, church, kitchen" or "the chick sex-pot."

For those who believe in the "rights of mankind," the "dignity of man," consider that to make a woman a person, a human being in her own right, you would have to change her sex: imagine Stokely Carmichael "prone and silent"; imagine Mark Rudd as a Laugh-In girl; picture Rennie Davis as Miss America. Such contradictions as these show how pervasive and deep-rooted is the cultural contempt for women, how difficult it is to imagine a woman as a serious human being, or conversely, how empty and degrading is the image of woman that floods the culture.

Countless studies have shown that black acceptance of white stereotypes leads to mutilated identity, to alienation, to rage and self-hatred. Human beings cannot bear in their own hearts the contradictions of those who hold them in contempt. The ideology of male supremacy and its effect upon women merits as serious study as has been given to the effects of prejudice upon Jews, blacks, and immigrant groups.

It is customary to shame those who would draw the parallel between women and blacks by a great show of concern and chest beating over the suffering of black people. Yet this response itself reveals a refined combination of white middle class guilt and male chauvinism, for it overlooks several essential facts. For example, the most oppressed group within the feminine population is made up of black women, many of whom take a dim view of the black male intellectual's adoption of white male attitudes of sexual superiority (an irony too cruel to require comment). Neither are those who make this pious objection to the racial parallel addressing themselves very adequately to the millions of white working class women living at the poverty level, who are not likely to be moved by this middle class guilt-ridden one-upmanship while having to deal with the boss, the factory, or the welfare worker day after day. They are already dangerously resentful of the gains made by blacks, and much of their "racist backlash" stems from the fact that they have been forgotten in the push for social change. Emphasis on the real mechanisms of oppression—on the commonality of the process—is essential lest groups such as these, which should work in alliance, become divided against one another.

White middle class males already struggling with the acknowledgment of their own racism do not relish an added burden of recognition: that to white guilt must soon be added "male." It is therefore understandable that they should refuse to see the harshness of the lives of most women—to honestly face the facts of massive institutionalized discrimination against women. Witness the performance to date: "Take her down off the platform and give her a good fuck," "Petty Bourgeois Revisionist Running Dogs," or in the classic words of a Berkeley male "leader," "Let them eat cock."

Among whites, women remain the most oppressed—and the most unorganized—group. Although they constitute a potential mass base for the radical movement, in terms of movement priorities they are ignored; indeed they might as well be invisible. Far from being an accident, this omission is a direct outgrowth of the solid male supremist beliefs of white radical and left-liberal men. Even now, faced with both fact and agitation, leftist men find the idea of placing any serious priority upon women so outrageous, such a degrading notion, that they respond with a virulence far out of proportion to the modest requests of movement women. This only shows that women must stop wasting their time worrying about the chauvinism of men in the movement and focus instead on their real priority: organizing women.

MARRIAGE: GENESIS OF WOMEN'S REBELLION

The institution of marriage is the chief vehicle for the perpetuation of the oppression of women; it is through the role of wife that the subjugation of women is maintained. In a very real way the role of wife has been the genesis of women's rebellion throughout history.

Looking at marriage from a detached point of view one may well ask why anyone gets married, much less women. One answer lies in the economics of women's position, for women are so occupationally limited that drudgery in the home is considered to be infinitely superior to drudgery in the factory. Secondly, women themselves have no independent social status. Indeed, there is no clearer index of the social worth of a woman in this society than the fact that she has none in her own right. A woman is first defined by the man to whom she is attached, but more particularly by the man she marries, and secondly by the children she bears and rears—hence the anxiety over sexual attractiveness, the frantic scramble for boyfriends and husbands. Having obtained and married a man the race is then on to have children, in order that their attractiveness and accomplishments may add more social worth. In a woman, not having children is seen as an incapacity somewhat akin to impotence in a man.

Beneath all of the pressures of the sexual marketplace and the marital status game, however, there is a far more sinister organization of economic exploitation and psychological mutilation. The housewife role, usually defined in terms of the biological duty of a woman to reproduce and her "innate" suitability for a nurturant and companionship role, is actually crucial to industrial capitalism in an advanced state of technological development. In fact, the housewife (some 44 million women of all classes, ethnic groups and races) provides, unpaid, absolutely essential services and labor. In turn, her assumption of all household duties makes it possible for the man to spend the majority of his time at the workplace.

It is important to understand the social and economic exploitation of the married woman, since the real productivity of her labor is denied by the commonly held assumption that she is dependent on her husband, exchanging her keep for emotional and nurturant services. Margaret Benston, a radical women's liberation leader, points out:

> In sheer quantity, household labor, including child care, constitutes a huge amount of socially necessary production. Nevertheless, in a society based on commodity production, it is not usually con-

sidered even as "real work" since it is outside of trade and the marketplace. This assignment of household work as the function of a special category "women" means that this group *does* stand in a different relationship to production. . . . The material basis for the inferior status of women is to be found in just this definition of women. In a society in which money determines value, women are a group who work outside the money economy. Their work is not worth money, is therefore valueless, is therefore not even real work. And women themselves, who do this valueless work, can hardly be expected to be worth as much as men, who work for money.

Women are essential to the economy not only as free labor, but also as consumers. The American system of capitalism depends for its survival on the consumption of vast amounts of socially wasteful goods, and a prime target for the unloading of this waste is the housewife. She is the purchasing agent for the family, but beyond that she is eager to buy because her own identity depends on her accomplishments as a consumer and her ability to satisfy the wants of her husband and children. This is not, of course, to say that she has any power in the economy. Although she spends the wealth, she does not own or control it—it simply passes through her hands.

In addition to their role as housewives and consumers, increasing numbers of women are taking outside employment. These women leave the home to join an exploited labor force, only to return at night to assume the double burden of housework on top of wage work—that is, they are forced to work at two full-time jobs. No man is required or expected to take on such a burden. The result: two workers from one household in the labor force with no cutback in essential female functions—three for the price of two, quite a bargain.

Frederick Engels, now widely read in women's liberation, argues that, regardless of her status in the larger society, within the context of the family the woman's relationship to the man is one of proletariat to bourgeoisie. One consequence of this class division in the family is to weaken the capacity of men and women oppressed by the society to struggle together against it.

In all classes and groups, the institution of marriage functions to a greater or lesser degree to oppress women; the unity of women of different classes hinges upon our understanding of that common oppression. The nineteenth century women's movement refused to deal with marriage and sexuality, and chose instead to fight for the vote and elevate the feminine mystique to a political ideology. That decision retarded the movement for decades. But 1969 is not 1889. For one thing, there now exist alternatives to marriage. The most original and creative politics of the women's movement has come from a direct confrontation with the issue of marriage and sexuality. The cultural revolution—experimentation with life-styles, communal living, collective child-rearing—have all come from the rebellion against dehumanized sexual relationships, against the notion of women as sexual commodities, against the constriction and spiritual strangulation inherent in the role of wife.

Lessons have been learned from the failures of the earlier movement as well. The feminine mystique is no longer mistaken for politics, nor gaining the vote for winning human rights. Women are now all together at the bottom of the work world, and the basis exists for a common focus of struggle for all women in American society. It remains for the movement to understand this, to avoid the mistakes of the past, to respond creatively to the possibilities of the present.

Women's oppression, although rooted in the institution of marriage, does not stop at the kitchen or the bedroom door. Indeed, the economic exploitation of women in the workplace is the most commonly recognized aspect of the oppression of women.

Most women who enter the labor force do not work for "pin money" or "self-fulfillment." Sixty-two per cent of all women working in 1967 were doing so out of economic need (i.e., were either alone or with husbands earning less than $5,000 a year). In 1963, 36 per cent of American families had an income of less than $5,000 a year. Women from these families work because they must; they contribute 35 to 40 per cent of the family's total income when working full-time, and 15 to 20 per cent when working part-time.

Despite their need, however, women have always represented the most exploited sector of the industrial labor force. Child and female labor were introduced during the early stages of industrial capitalism, at a time when most men were gainfully employed in crafts. As industrialization developed and craft jobs were eliminated, men entered the industrial labor force, driving women and children into the lowest categories of work and pay. Indeed, the position of women and children industrial workers was so pitiful, and their wages so small, that the craft unions refused to organize them. Even when women organized themselves and engaged in militant strikes and labor agitation—from the shoemakers of Lynn, Massachusetts, to the International Ladies' Garment Workers and their great strike of 1909—male unionists continued to ignore their needs. As a result of this male supremacy in the unions, women remain essentially unorganized, despite the fact that they are becoming an ever larger part of the labor force.

The trend is clearly toward increasing numbers of women entering the work force: women represented 55 per cent of the growth of the total labor force in 1962, and the number of working women rose from 16.9 million in 1957 to 24 million in 1962. There is every indication that the number of women in the labor force will continue to grow as rapidly in the future.

Job discrimination against women exists in all sectors of work, even in occupations which are predominantly made up of women. This discrimination is reinforced in the field of education, where women are being short-changed at a time when the job market demands higher educational levels. In 1962, for example, while women constituted 53 per cent of the graduating high school class, only 42 per cent of the entering college class were women. Only one in three people who received a B.A. or M.A. in that year was a woman, and only one in ten who received a Ph.D. was a woman. These figures represent a decline in educational achievement for women since the 1930's, when women received two out of five of the B.A. and M.A. degrees given, and one out of seven of the Ph.D's. While there has been a dramatic increase in the number of people, including women, who go to college, women have not kept pace with men in terms of educational achievement. Furthermore, women have lost ground in professional employment. In 1960 only 22 per cent of the faculty and other professional staff at colleges and universities were women—down from 28 per cent in 1949, 27 per cent in 1930, 26 per cent in 1920. 1960 does beat 1919 with only 20 per cent—"you've come a long way, baby"— right back to where you started! In other professional categories: 10 per cent of all scientists are women, 7 per cent of all physicians, 3 per cent of all lawyers, and 1 per cent of all engineers.

Chart A

Comparative Statistics for Men and Women in the Labor Force, 1960

OCCUPATION	Percentage of Working Women in Each Occupational Category	Income of Year-Round Full-Time Workers		Numbers of Workers in Millions	
		WOMEN	MEN	WOMEN	MEN
Professional	13%	$4,358	$7,115	3	5
Managers, Officials and Proprietors	5	3,514	7,241	1	5
Clerical	31	3,586	5,247	7	3
Operatives	15	2,970	4,977	4	9
Sales	7	2,389	5,842	2	3
Service	15	2,340	4,089	3	3
Private Household	10	1,156	—	2	—

SOURCES U.S. Department of Commerce, Bureau of the Census: "Current Population Reports," P-60, No. 37, and U.S. Department of Labor, Bureau of Labor Statistics, and U.S. Department of Commerce, Bureau of the Census.

Even when women do obtain an education, in many cases it does them little good. Women, whatever their educational level, are concentrated in the lower paying occupations. The figures in Chart A tell a story that most women know and few men will admit: most women are forced to work at clerical jobs, for which they are paid, on the average, $1,600 less per year than men doing the same work. Working class women in the service and operative (semi-skilled) categories, making up 30 per cent of working women, are paid $1,900 less per year on the average than are men. Of all working women, only 13 per cent are professionals (including low-pay and low-status work such as teaching, nursing and social work), and they earn $2,600 less per year than do professional men. Household workers, the lowest category of all, are predominantly women (over 2 million) and predominantly black and third world, earning for their labor barely over $1,000 per year.

Not only are women forced onto the lowest rungs of the occupational ladder, they are in the lowest income levels as well. The most constant and bitter injustice experienced by all women is the income differential. While women might passively accept low-status jobs, limited opportunities for advancement, and discrimination in the factory, office and university, they choke finally on the daily fact that the male worker next to them earns more, and usually does less. In 1965 the median wage or salary income of year-round full-time women workers was only 60 per cent that of man, a 4 per cent loss since 1955. Twenty-nine per cent of working women earned less than $3,000 a year as compared with 11 per cent of the men; 43 per cent of the women earned from $3,000 to $5,000 a year as compared with 19 per cent of the men; and 9 per cent of the women earned $7,000 or more as compared with 43 per cent of the men.

What most people do not know is that in certain respects, women suffer more than do non-white men, and that black and third world women suffer most of all.

Chart B

Median Annual Wages for Men and Women by Race, 1960

WORKERS	MEDIAN ANNUAL WAGE
Males, White	$5,137
Males, Non-White	$3,075
Females, White	$2,537
Females, Non-White	$1,276

SOURCE   U.S. Department of Commerce, Bureau of the Census. Also see: President's Commission on the Status of Women, 1963.

Women, regardless of race, are more disadvantaged than are men, including non-white men [Chart B]. White women earn $2,600 less than white men and $500 less than non-white men. The brunt of the inequality is carried by 2.5 million non-white women, 94 per cent of whom are black. They earn $3,800 less than white men, $1,800 less than non-white men, and $1,200 less than white women.

There is no more bitter paradox in the racism of this country than that the white man, articulating the male supremacy of the white male middle class, should provide the rationale for the oppression of black women by black men. Black women constitute the largest minority in the United States, and they are the most disadvantaged group in the labor force. The further oppression of black women will not liberate black men, for black women were never the oppressors of their men—that is a myth of the liberal white man. The oppression of black men comes from institutionalized racism and economic exploitation: from the world of the white man. Consider the following facts and figures.

The percentage of black working women has always been proportionately greater than that of white women. In 1900, 41 per cent of black women were employed, as compared to 17 per cent for white women. In 1963, the proportion of black women employed was still a fourth greater than that of whites. In 1960, 44 per cent of black married women with children under six years were in the labor force, in contrast to 29 per cent for white women. While job competition requires ever higher levels of education, the bulk of illiterate women are black. On the whole, black women—who often have the greatest need for employment—are the most discriminated against in terms of opportunity. Forced by an oppressive and racist society to carry unbelievably heavy economic and social burdens, black women stand at the bottom of that society, doubly marked by the caste signs of color and sex.

The rise of new agitation for the occupational equality of women also coincided with the re-entry of the "lost generation"—the housewives of the 1950's—into the job market. Women from middle class backgrounds, faced with an "empty nest" (children grown or in school) and a widowed or divorced rate of one-fourth to one-third of all marriages, returned to the workplace in large numbers. But once there they discovered that women, middle class or otherwise, are the last hired, the lowest paid, the least often promoted, and the first fired. Furthermore, women are more likely to suffer job discrimination on the basis of age, so the widowed and divorced suffer particularly, even though their economic need to work is often urgent. Age discrimination also means that the option of work after child-rearing is limited. Even highly qualified older women find themselves forced into low-paid, unskilled or semi-skilled work—if they are lucky enough to find a job in the first place.

The realities of the work world for most middle class women—that they become members of the working class, like it or not—are understandably distant to many young men and women in college who have never had to work, and who tend to think of the industrial "proletariat" as a revolutionary force, to the exclusion of "bourgeois" working women. Their image of the "pampered middle class woman" is factually incorrect and politically naive. It is middle class women forced into working class life who are often the first to become conscious of the contradiction between the "American Dream" and their daily experience.

Faced with discrimination on the job—after being forced into the lower levels of the occupational structure—millions of women are inescapably presented with the fundamental contradictions in their unequal treatment and their massive exploitation. The rapid growth of women's liberation as a movement is related in part to the exploitation of working women in all occupational categories.

Male supremacy, marriage, and the structure of wage labor—each of these aspects of women's oppression has been crucial to the resurgence of the women's struggle. It must be abundantly clear that radical social change must occur before there can be significant improvement in the social position of women. Some form of socialism is a minimum requirement, considering the changes that must come in the institutions of marriage and the family alone. The intrinsic radicalism of the struggle for women's liberation necessarily links women with all other oppressed groups.

The heart of the movement, as in all freedom movements, rests in women's knowledge, whether articulated or still only an illness without a name, that they are not inferior—not chicks, nor bunnies, nor quail, nor cows, nor bitches, nor ass, nor meat. Women hear the litany of their own dehumanization each day. Yet all the same, women know that male supremacy is a lie. They know they are not animals or sexual objects or commodities. They know their lives are multilated, because they see within themselves a promise of creativity and personal integration. Feeling the contradiction between the essentially creative and self-actualizing human being within her, and the cruel and degrading less-than-human role she is compelled to play, a woman begins to perceive the falseness of what her society has forced her to be. And once she perceives this, she knows that she must fight.

Women must learn the meaning of rage, the violence that liberates the human spirit. The rhetoric of invective is an equally essential stage, for in discovering and venting their rage against the enemy—and the enemy in everyday life is men—women also experience the justice of their own violence. They learn the first lessons in their own latent strength. Women must learn to know themselves as revolutionaries. They must become hard and strong in their determination, while retaining their humanity and tenderness.

There is a rage that impels women into a total commitment to women's liberation. That ferocity stems from a denial of mutilation; it is a cry for life, a cry for the liberation of the spirit. Roxanne Dunbar, surely one of the most impressive women in the movement, conveys the feelings of many:

> We are damaged—we women, we oppressed, we disinherited. There are very few who are not damaged, and they rule. . . . The oppressed trust those who rule more than they trust themselves, because self-contempt emerges from powerlessness. Anyway, few oppressed people believe that life could be much different. . . . We are damaged and we have the right to hate and have contempt and to kill and to scream. But for what? . . . Do we want the oppressor to admit he is wrong, to withdraw his misuse of us? He is only too happy to admit guilt—then do nothing but try to absorb and exorcize the new thought. . . . That does not make up for what I have lost, what I never had, and what all those others who are worse off than I never had. . . . Nothing will compensate for the irreparable harm it has done to my sisters. . . . How could we possibly settle for anything remotely less, even take a crumb in the meantime less, than total annihilation of a system which systematically destroys half its people. . . .

The Red Man's Burden

PETER COLLIER

After the defeat and subjugation of the Plains Indians late in the nineteenth century, the United States government undertook a program of breaking up the Indian reservations that remained in out-of-the-way corners of the West and thus forcing the nation's Indians to disperse and to adapt to white ways of life. For the purpose of dismantling the reservations, the government revived the policy of land allotment developed during the presidency of Andrew Jackson to remove the Five Civilized Tribes from the Southeast. Under the Jacksonian removal program, land that had been granted by treaty to the entire Indian nation was divided among individual Indians, who were subsequently persuaded—often fraudulently—to sell to white speculators. Theoretically, individual land holdings would lead the Indians to work harder and would thus help them to conform to the white American ideal of individual achievement. But economic individualism is foreign to Indian culture, and the land-allotment program only worked to divest the Indians of the little land that still belonged to them.

In the late nineteenth century, government policies struck hard at the Indian way of life, forbidding the practice of Indian religions and seeking to undermine tribal organization. Typical of the Indian legislation passed during this period was the Dawes Severalty Act of 1887, which empowered the President to allot one hundred and sixty acres of reservation land to individual Indian families and lesser amounts to single Indians. The leftover reservation land—often the choice portions—was then sold by the government. Under this program, the Indians lost about 86,000,000 acres from a total of 138,000,000 between 1887 and 1934.

With the New Deal and President Roosevelt's appointment of John Collier as Commissioner of Indian Affairs, the government's devastating Indian policy was temporarily reversed. Collier was a scholarly and sensitive friend of the Indians and recognized the destruction wrought by the severalty process. He recommended not only that the allotment program be ended but also that previously distributed lands be returned to the Indian nations for communal use. At Collier's urging, Congress passed the Wheeler-Howard Act (known as the Indian Reorganization Act) in 1934, which ended the allotment process and called for the use of public funds to purchase new lands for certain Indian nations victimized by the old policy. Under Collier's leadership, the New Deal government also gave a boost to Indian culture. The constitutional right of the Indians to practice their own religions was asserted despite complaints from various missionary organizations, and Indian crafts were revived even though the Indians had forgotten many of the traditional skills. Government relief policies and public health measures contributed to a slight improvement in the standard of living and a decrease in the death rate among Indians. For the first time since their conquest by white America, the Indian population began to increase.

Unfortunately, the beneficial effects of the Indian Reorganization Act began to be undone in the 1950's when the Eisenhower administration adopted the policy of "terminating" all Indian reservations in order to "get the government out of the Indian business." Currently, however, the outlook for the Indian is somewhat brighter. Various Indian groups are working hard to develop a viable movement for the preservation of a distinctive Indian life and culture, and the Nixon administration has gone on record as opposing the policy of termination and advocating Indian control of Indian affairs.

In the following article, Peter Collier, of **Ramparts** magazine, discusses the plight of the Indians today as a result of past and present federal action. In particular, he is concerned with the problems of health, employment, and education and with the adverse cultural effects of the policies pursued in recent years by the United States Bureau of Indian Affairs.

When fourteen Indian college students invaded Alcatraz on a cold, foggy morning in the first part of November—claiming ownership "by right of discovery," and citing an 1868 treaty allowing the Sioux possession of unused federal lands—they seemed in a light-hearted mood. After establishing their beachhead, they told the press that they had come there because Alcatraz already had all the necessary features of a reservation: dangerously uninhabitable buildings; no fresh water; inadequate sanita-

"The Red Man's Burden," by Peter Collier. From *Ramparts*, VIII (February 1970), 27–38. Copyright Ramparts Magazine, Inc. 1970. By Permission of the Editors.

tion; and the certainty of total unemployment. They said they were planning to make the five full-time caretakers wards of a Bureau of Caucasian Affairs, and offered to take this troublesome real estate off the white man's hands for $24, payment to be made in glass beads. The newspapers played it up big, calling the Indians a "raiding party." When, after a 19-hour stay, the Indians were persuaded to leave the island, everyone agreed that it had been a good publicity stunt.

If the Indians had ever been joking about Alcatraz, however, it was with the bitter irony that fills colonial subjects' discourse with the mother-country. When they returned to the mainland, they didn't fall back into the cigar-store stoicism that is supposedly the red man's prime virtue. In fact, their first invasion ignited a series of meetings and strategy-sessions; two weeks later they returned to the Rock, this time with a force of nearly 100 persons, a supply network, and the clear intention of staying. What had begun as a way of drawing attention to the position of the contemporary Indian developed into a plan for doing something about it. And when the government, acting through the General Services Administration, gave them a deadline for leaving, the Indians replied with demands of their own: Alcatraz was theirs, they said, and it would take U.S. Marshals to remove them and their families; they planned to turn the island into a major cultural center and research facility; they would negotiate only the mechanics of deeding over the land, and that only with Interior Secretary Walter Hickel during a face to face meeting. The Secretary never showed up, but the government's deadlines were withdrawn.

On this island, I saw not whether the people had personal property, for it seemed to me that whatever one had, they all took share of, especially of eatable things.

CHRISTOPHER COLUMBUS

Alcatraz is Indian territory: The old warning to "Keep Off U.S. Property" now reads "Keep off Indian Property"; security guards with red armbands stand near the docks to make sure it is obeyed. Women tend fires beneath huge iron cauldrons filled with food, while their kids play frisbee in what was once a convicts' exercise yard. Some of the men work on the prison's wiring system or try to get more cellblocks cleared out for the Indian people who are arriving daily from all over the country; others sit fishing on the wharf with hand-lines, watching quietly as the rip-tides churn in the Bay. During the day, rock music plays over portable radios and a series of soap operas flit across a TV; at night, the prison is filled with the soft sounds of ceremonial drums and eerie songs in Sioux, Kiowa and Navajo.

In the few weeks of its occupation, Alcatraz has become a mecca, a sort of red man's Selma. Indian people come, stay a few days, and then leave, taking with them a sense of wonderment that it has happened. Middle-aged "establishment" Indians are there. They mix with younger insurgents like Lehman Brightman (the militant Sioux who heads a red power organization called the United Native Americans), Mad-Bear Anderson (the Iroquois traditionalist from upstate New York who fought to get the United Nations to stop the U.S. Army Corps of Engineers' flooding of precious Seneca Indian lands), Sid Mills (the young Yakima who demanded a discharge from the Army after returning from Viet-Nam so that he could fight his real war—against the state of Washington's denial of his people's fishing rights), and Al Bridges (one of the leaders of the first Washington fish-ins in 1964, who now faces a possible ten-year prison sentence for defying the state Fish and Game Commission). The composition of the ad hoc Indian community changes constantly, but the purpose remains the same: to make Alcatraz a powerful symbol of liberation springing out of the long American imprisonment.

The people enjoy themselves, spending a lot of time sitting around the campfire talking and gossiping. But there is a sense of urgency beneath the apparent lassitude. Richard Oakes, a 27-year-old Mohawk who worked in high steel construction before coming West to go to college, is one of the elected spokesmen. Sitting at a desk in the old Warden's Office, he talks about the hope of beginning a new organization, the Confederacy of American Indian Nations, to weld Indian groups all over the country into one body capable of taking power away from the white bureaucracy. He acknowledges that the pan-Indian movements which have sprung up before have always been crushed. "But time is running out for us," he says. "We have everything at stake. And if we don't make it now, then we'll get trapped at the bottom of that white world out there, and wind up as some kind of Jack Jones with a social security number and that's all. Not just on Alcatraz, but every place else, the Indian is in his last stand for cultural survival."

This sentiment is reflected in the slogans lettered on walls all over the prison, the red paint bleeding down onto the concrete. One of them declares: "Better Red than Dead."

> *I also heard of numerous instances in which our men had cut out the private parts of females and wore them in their hats while riding in the ranks.*
>
> A U.S. ARMY LIEUTENANT, TESTIFYING
> ABOUT THE SAND CREEK MASSACRE OF 1864

The Alcatraz occupation is still popularly regarded as the engaging fun and games of Indian college kids. In its news coverage of the U.S. Coast Guard's feeble attempt to blockade ships running supplies to the island, one local television station found amusement in showing their films to the musical accompaniment of U.S. cavalry bugle calls. It was not so amusing to the occupiers, however. The California Indians now on the Rock know that their people were decimated from a population of 100,000 in 1850 when the gold rush settlers arrived, to about 15,000 thirty years later, and that whole tribes, languages and cultures were erased from the face of the earth. There are South Dakota Indians there whose grandparents were alive in 1890 when several hundred Sioux, mostly women and children leaving the reservation to find food, were caught at Wounded Knee, killed, and buried in a common grave—the old daguerreotypes still showing heavily-mustachioed soldiers standing stiffly over the frozen bodies like hunters with their trophies. Cowboys and Indians is not a pleasant game for the Alcatraz Indians and some must wonder whether, in another 150 years, German children will be gaily playing Nazis and Jews.

But the past is not really at issue. What is at stake today, as Richard Oakes says, is cultural survival. Some of the occupiers have known Indian culture all their lives; some have been partially assimilated away from it and are now trying to return. All understand that it is in jeopardy, and they want some assurance that Indian-ness will be available to their children. It sounds like a fair request, but fairness has never ruled the destiny of the Indian in America. In fighting for survival, the Indians of Alcatraz are challenging the lies perpetuated by anthropologists and bureaucrats alike, who insist that the red man is two things: an incompetent "ward" addicted to the paternalism of government, and an anachronism whose past is imprisoned in white history and whose only future is as an invisible swimmer in the American mainstream. The people on Alcatraz have entered a struggle on a large scale that parallels the smaller, individual struggles for survival that many of them have known themselves; it is the will to exist as individuals that brought them together in determination to exist as a people.

When Robert Kennedy came, that was the only day they ever showed any respect for the Indian, just on that one day, and after that, they could care less.

A FRESHMAN STUDENT AT BLACKFOOT, IDAHO, HIGH SCHOOL

One of the original 14 on Alcatraz was a pretty 22-year-old Shoshone-Bannock girl named La Nada Means. Her hair is long and reddish-black; her nose arches slightly and prominent cheekbones square out her face. Her walk is slightly pigeon-toed, the result of a childhood disease for which she never received treatment. If you tell her that she looks very Indian, she will thank you, but with a searching look that suggests she has heard the same comment before, and not as a compliment.

"When I was little," she says, "I remember my family as being very poor. There were 12 of us kids, and we were always hungry. I remember sometimes getting to the point where I'd eat anything I could get my hands on—leaves, small pieces of wood, anything. The other thing I remember is the meanness of the small towns around the reservation. Blackfoot, Pocatello—they all had signs in the store windows to keep Indians out. One of them I'll never forget; it said, 'No Indians or Dogs Allowed.' There were Indian stalls in the public bathrooms; Indians weren't served in a lot of the restaurants; and we just naturally all sat in the balcony of the theaters. You learn early what all that means. It becomes part of the way you look at yourself."

She grew up on the Fort Hall reservation in Southern Idaho. The

Jim Crow atmosphere of the surrounding small towns has lessened somewhat with the passage of time and the coming of the civil-rights bills, but it is still very much present in the attitude of white townsfolk towards Indians. And while there are no longer the small outbreaks of famine that occurred on the reservation when La Nada was growing up in the '50's, Fort Hall is still one of the bleakest areas in the country, and the people there are among the poorest.

Like most Indian children of her generation (and like a great many today), La Nada Means was sent away to school. Her youth became a series of separations from home and family, each more traumatic than the one before. The first school she attended was St. Mary's School for Indian Girls in Springfield, South Dakota. "I took a lot of classes in subjects like 'Laundry,'" she remembers, "where the classwork was washing the headmaster's clothes. All Indian people are supposed to be good with their hands, you know, and also hard workers, so we didn't do too much regular schoolwork at St. Mary's. They also had what they called a Summer Home Program where you're sent out during the summer break to live with a white family. It was supposed to teach you white etiquette and things like that, and make you forget your savage Indian ways. When I was 13, I was sent up to Minnesota, where I became a sort of housekeeper for the summer. I don't remember too much about it, except that the wages I got, about $5 a week, were sent back to St. Mary's and I never saw them. After being at that school a little while, I got all upset. They said I was 'too outspoken,' and expelled me. After I got back to Fort Hall, I had my first breakdown."

For awhile she attended public school in Blackfoot, the small town bordering the reservation. She was suspended because she objected to the racial slurs against Indians which were built into the curriculum. She was 15 when the Bureau of Indian Affairs (BIA) sent her to its boarding school in Chilocco, Oklahoma. On her first day there, the matrons ordered her to lower the hems on the two dresses she owned. She refused and was immediately classified as a troublemaker. "At Chilocco, you're either a 'good girl' or a 'bad girl,'" she says. "They put me in the bad girls' dormitory right away with Indians mainly from the Northwest. The Oklahoma Indians were in the good girls' dorm, and the matrons constantly tried to keep us agitated by setting the tribes to fighting with each other. Everything was like the Army. There were bells, drills and set hours for everything. The food was called 'GI Chow.' There was a lot of brutality, but it was used mainly on the boys, who lived in another wing. Occasionally they'd let the boys and girls get together. You all stood in this big square; you could hold hands, but if the matrons saw you getting too close, they'd blow a whistle and then you'd have to march back to the dorm."

La Nada made the honor roll, but was expelled from Chilocco after a two-month stay for being involved in a fight. "The matrons just had it in for me, I guess. They got about 100 other Indian girls against me and a few other 'bad girls.' They put us in a small room and when the fight was ready to begin, they turned out the lights and walked out, locking the doors behind them. We had a 'riot,' and I got beat up. The next day, the head of the school called me into his office and said that I didn't fit in."

She was sent off with one dollar, a sack lunch, and a one-way bus ticket from Chilocco back to Idaho. She lived with her family for a few months, helping her father collect data about conditions at Fort Hall, and then was sent by the BIA to another of its boarding schools, Stewart Institute, in Carson City, Nevada. Her reputation as a "difficult Indian" followed her, and she was again sent home after being at Stewart for less than a day. The BIA threatened to send her to "reform" school; then it forgot about her. "I stayed around the reservation for awhile," she says, "and when I got to be 17, I took GED [high school equivalent] exams. I only had about nine real years of schooling, but I scored pretty well and got into Idaho State College. I lasted there for a semester, and then quit. I didn't really know what to do. At Fort Hall, you either work in some kind of menial job with the BIA agency there, or you go off the reservation to find a job in one of the towns. If you choose the BIA, you know that they'll try to drill a subservient mentality into you; and in the towns, the discrimination is pretty bad."

La Nada again spent time working with her father, a former tribal chairman. They sent out letters to congressmen and senators describing conditions on the reservations, and tried to get the Bureau of Indian Affairs office to respond. As a result, her father was harassed by local law enforcement officials. La Nada drifted for a time and then asked the BIA for "relocation" off the reservation. Many of the Fort Hall Indians have taken this route and 80 per cent of them return to the reservation, because as La Nada says, "things in the slums where you wind up are even worse than on the reservation, and you don't have your people to support you."

The BIA gave her a one-way ticket to San Francisco, one of eight major relocation centers in the country. When she first arrived, she sat in the local BIA office from 8 to 5 for a few days, waiting for them to help her find a job. They didn't, and she found a series of temporary clerk jobs by herself. As soon as she found work, the BIA cut off her $140 a month relocation payment. She wound up spending a lot of time in the "Indian bars" which are found in San Francisco and every other relocation town. She worked as a housekeeper in the private home for Indian girls where the BIA had first sent her, and as a barmaid in a beer parlor. She was "drunk most of the time," and she became pregnant. She was 17 years old.

"After I had the baby," she says, "my mother came out from the reservation and got him. She said they'd take care of him back home until I got on my feet. I really didn't know what to do. The only programs the BIA has are vocational training for menial jobs, and I didn't especially want to be a beautician. Actually, I wanted to try college again, but when I told this to a BIA counselor, he said they didn't have any money for that and told me I was being 'irrational and unrealistic.'

"All types of problems develop when you're on relocation. The Indian who has come to the city is like a man without a country. Whose jurisdiction are you under, the BIA's or the state's? You go to a county hospital when you're sick and they say, 'Aren't you taken care of by the Indian Affairs people?' It's very confusing. You hang around with other Indians, but they are as bad off as you are. Anyway, I started sinking lower and lower. I married this Sioux and lived with his family awhile. I got pregnant again. But things didn't work out in the marriage, and I left. After I had the baby, I ended up in the San Francisco General psychiatric ward for a few weeks. I was at the bottom, really at the bottom. Indian people get to this point all the time, especially when they're relocated into the big city and are living in the slums. At that point, you've got two choices: either kill yourself and get it all over with —a lot of Indians do this—or try to go all the way up, and this is almost impossible."

As she looks at it now, La Nada feels she was "lucky." She tried to get admitted to the local colleges, but was refused because of her school record. Finally, because the University of California "needed a token Indian in its Economic Opportunity Program for minority students," she was admitted in the fall of 1968. She did well in her classes and became increasingly active, helping to found the United Native Americans organization and working to get more Indian students admitted into the EOP program. "After my first year there," she says, "everything was going along all right. I liked school and everything, and I felt I was doing some good. But I felt myself getting swallowed up by something that was bigger than me. The thing was that I didn't want to stop being an Indian, and there were all these pressures, very hidden ones, that were trying to make me white." At the summer break she went back to the reservation and spent some time with her family. The next quarter she became involved in the Third World Liberation Front strike at Berkeley, fighting for a School of Ethnic Studies, including a Native American program. She was suspended by the University.

La Nada's experiences, far from being extreme cases, are like those of most young Indians. If she is unique at all, it is because she learned the value of fighting back.

We need fewer and fewer "experts" on Indians. What we need is a cultural leave-us-alone agreement, in spirit and in fact.

VINE DELORIA, JR.

Each generation of Americans rediscovers for itself what is fashionably called the "plight" of the Indian. The American Indian today has a life expectancy of approximately 44 years, more than 25 years below the national average. He has the highest infant mortality rate in the country (among the more than 50,000 Alaskan natives, one of every four babies dies before reaching his first birthday). He suffers from epidemics of diseases which were supposed to have disappeared from America long ago.

A recent Department of Public Health report states that among California Indians, "water from contaminated sources is used in 38 to 42 per cent of the homes, and water must be hauled under unsanitary conditions by 40 to 50 per cent of all Indian families." Conditions are similar in other states. A high proportion of reservation housing throughout the country is officially classified as "substandard," an antiseptic term which fails to conjure up a tiny, two-room log cabin holding a family of 13 at Fort Hall; a crumbling Navajo hogan surrounded by broken plumbing fixtures hauled in to serve as woodbins; or a gutted automobile body in which a Pine Ridge Sioux family huddles against the South Dakota winter.

On most reservations, a 50 per cent unemployment rate is not considered high. Income per family among Indian people is just over $1,500 per year—the lowest of any group in the country. But this, like the other figures, is deceptive. It does not suggest, for instance, the quality of the daily life of families on the Navajo reservation who live on $600 per year (exchanging sheep's wool and hand-woven rugs with white traders for beans and flour), who never have real money and who are perpetually sinking a little further into credit debt.

To most Americans, the conditions under which the Indian is forced to live are a perennial revelation. On one level, the symptoms are always being tinkered with half-heartedly and the causes ignored; on another level, the whole thrust of the government's Indian policy appears calculated to perpetuate the Indians' "plight." This is why La Nada Means and the other Indians have joined what Janet McCloud, a leader of the Washington fishing protests, calls "the last, continuing Indian War." The enemies are legion, and they press in from every side: the studiously ignorant politicians, the continuously negligent Department of the Interior, and the white business interests who are allowed to prey upon the reservations' manpower and resources. But as the Indian has struggled to free himself from the suffocating embrace of white history, no enemy has held the death grip more tightly than has his supposed guardian, in effect his "keeper": the Bureau of Indian Affairs.

The Bureau came into being in 1834 as a division of the War Department. Fifteen years later it was shifted to the Department of the Interior, the transition symbolizing the fact that the Indian was beginning to be seen not as a member of a sovereign, independent nation, but as a "ward," his land and life requiring constant management. This is the view that has informed the BIA for over a century. With its 16,000 employees and its outposts all over the country, the Bureau has become what Cherokee anthropologist Robert Thomas calls "the most complete colonial system in the world."

It is also a classic bureaucratic miasma. A recent book on Indian Affairs, *Our Brother's Keeper*, notes that on the large Pine Ridge reservation, "$8,040 a year is spent per family to help the Oglala Sioux Indians out of poverty. Yet median income among these Indians is $1,910 per family. At last count there was nearly one bureaucrat for each and every family on the reservation."

The paternalism of the BIA, endless and debilitating, is calculated to keep the Indian in a state of perpetual juvenilization, without rights, dependent upon the meager and capricious beneficence of power. The

Bureau's power over its "wards," whom it defines and treats as children, seems limitless. The BIA takes care of the Indian's money, doling it out to him when it considers his requests worthy; it determines the use of the Indian's land; it is in charge of the development of his natural resources; it relocates him from the reservation to the big city ghetto; it educates his children. It relinquishes its hold over him only reluctantly, even deciding whether or not his will is valid after he dies.

This bureaucratic paternalism hems the Indian in with an incomprehensible maze of procedures and regulations, never allowing him to know quite where he stands or what he can demand and how. Over 5,000 laws, statutes and court decisions apply to the Indians alone. As one Indian student says, "Our people have to go to law school just to live a daily life."

The BIA is the Indian's point of contact with the white world, the concrete expression of this society's attitude towards him. The BIA manifests both stupidity and malice; but it is purely neither. It is guided by something more elusive, a whole world view regarding the Indian and what is good for him. Thus the BIA's overseership of human devastation begins by teaching bright-eyed youngsters the first formative lessons in what it is to be an Indian.

> *It is unnecessary to mention the power which schools would have over the rising generation of Indians. Next to teaching them to work, the most important thing is to teach them the English language. Into their own language there is woven so much mythology and sorcery that a new one is needed in order to aid them in advancing beyond their baneful superstitions.*
>
> JOHN WESLEY POWELL

The Darwinian educational system which La Nada Means endured is not a thing of the past. Last spring, for instance, the BIA's own Educational Division studied Chilocco and came to the following conclusions: "There is evidence of criminal malpractice, not to mention physical and mental perversion, by certain staff members." The report went on to outline the disastrous conditions at the school, noting among other things that "youngsters reported they were handcuffed for as long as 18 hours in the dormitory . . . or chained to a basement pillar or from a suspended pipe. One team member . . . verified a youngster's hurt arms, the deformed hands of another boy, and an obviously broken rib of another. . . ."

The BIA responded to this report by suppressing it and transferring the investigators who submitted it. The principal of Chilocco was fired, but more as punishment for letting such things be discovered than for the conditions themselves. The same story is repeated at other BIA boarding schools. At the Intermountain Indian School in Utah, Indian children suspected of drinking have their heads ducked into filthy toilets by school disciplinarians. At Sherman Institute in Riverside, California, students of high school age are fed on a budget of 76 cents a day.

But there is a far more damaging and subtle kind of violence at work in the school as well. It is, in the jargon of educational psychology, the initiation of a "failure-orientation," and it derives from the fact that the children and their culture are held in such obviously low regard. Twenty-five per cent of all BIA teachers admit that they would rather be teaching whites; up to 70 per cent leave the BIA schools after one year. If a teacher has any knowledge at all of his students' needs and backgrounds, he gets it from a two-week non-compulsory course offered at the beginning of the year. One teacher, a former Peace Corps volunteer who returned to teach at the Navajo reservation, told the Senate Subcommittee on Indian Education that the principal of her BIA school habitually made statements such as "All Navajos are brain-damaged," and "Navajo culture belongs in a museum."

The results of the Indian's education, whether it be supervised by the BIA or by the public school system, indicate how greatly the system fails him. Twenty per cent of all Indian men have less than five years of schooling. According to a recent report to the Carnegie Foundation, there is a 60 per cent drop-out rate among Indian children as a whole, and those who do manage to stay in school fall further behind the longer they attend. A study of the Stewart Institute in Carson City, Nevada, for instance, shows that Indian sixth graders score 5.2 on the California Achievement Test. Six years later, at graduation, their achievement level is 8.4.

In a strange sense, the Indian student's education does prepare him for what lies ahead. What it teaches him is that he is powerless and inferior, and that he was destined to be so when he was born an Indian. Having spent his youth being managed and manhandled, the Indian is accustomed to the notion that his business must be taken care of for him. He is thus ideally equipped to stand by and watch the BIA collect mortgages on his future.

> *We should test our thinking against the thinking of the wisest Indians and their friends, [but] this does not mean that we are going to let, as someone put it, Indian people themselves decide what the policy should be.*
>
> STUART UDALL

The Indians of California have more than their share of troubles—in part because they never received an adequate land base by government treaty. They are scattered up and down the state on reservations which are rarely larger than 10,000 acres and on rancherias as small as one acre. It takes a special determination to find these Indians, for most of them live in backwoods shacks, hidden from view as well as from water and electricity.

They have to struggle for every bit of federal service they get; disservice, however, comes easy. In 1969 the only irrigation money the BIA spent in all of Southern California, where water is an especially precious commodity to the Indians, was not for an Indian at all, but for a white farmer who had bought an Indian's land on the Pala reservation. The BIA spent $2,500—of money appropriated by Congress for the Indians—to run a 900-foot pipeline to this white man's land. The Indians at Pala have been asking for irrigation lines for years, but less than one-half of their lands have them.

At the Resighini rancheria, a 228-acre reservation in Northern California, the Simpson Timber Company had been paying the Indians 25 cents per 1,000 feet for the lumber it transported across their land. The total paid to the Indians in 1964 was $4,725, and the right of way was increasing in value every year. Then the BIA, acting without warning, sold the right of way outright to Simpson Timber Company for $2,500, or something less than one-half its yearly value.

The tiny Agua Caliente band of Indians sits on top of some of the most valuable land in the country: over 600 acres in the heart of Palm Springs. In the late '50's, the BIA, reacting to pressure from developers, obligingly transferred its jurisdiction over the Agua Caliente to a judge of the State Superior Court in the Palm Springs area who appointed "conservators" and "guardians" to make sure that the Indians would not be swindled as development took place. Ten years later, in 1967, a Riverside Press Enterprise reporter wrote a devastating series of articles showing the incredible fees collected for "protecting" the Agua Calientes. One conservator collected a fee of $9,000 from his Indian's $9,170 bank account; an Indian minor wound up with $3,000 out of a $23,000 income, his guardian taking the rest. The "abdication of responsibility" with which the BIA was charged is surely a mild description of what happened to the Agua Calientes, who are supposedly the "richest Indians in the world" living on what is regarded as "an ermine-lined reservation."

The Indian Claims Commission was set up in the 1940's to compensate tribes for the lands stolen during the period of white conquest. In the California claims award of 1964, the Indians were given 47 cents an acre, based on the land's fair market value in 1851. The total sum, $29 million, less "offsets" for the BIA's services over the years, still has not been distributed. When it is, the per capita payout will come to about $600, and the poorest Indians in the state will have to go off welfare to spend it. The BIA opposed an amendment to the Claims Award which would have exempted this money in determining welfare eligibility. The BIA testified that such an amendment constituted preferential treatment, and that it had been struggling for years to get *equal* treatment for the Indian. The amendment failed, and California's Indians will have to pay for a few months' bread and rent with the money they are getting in return for the land that was taken from them.

Cases such as these exist in every state where Indian people live. If the Indian is the Vanishing American, it is the BIA's magic which makes him so. California Indians are fortunate only in one respect: they have an OEO-funded legal rights organization, the California Indian Legal Services, which attempts to minimize the depredations. Most Indians have no one to protect them from the agency which is supposed to be their advocate.

Once we were happy in our own country and we were seldom hungry, for then the two-leggeds and the four-leggeds lived to-

*gether like relatives, and there was plenty for them and for us. But
the Wasichus [white men] came, and they have made little islands
for us . . . and always these islands are becoming smaller, for
around them surges the gnawing flood of the Wasichu; and it is
dirty with lies and greed. . . .*

BLACK ELK, AN OGLALA HOLY MAN

At the entrance to the Fort Hall reservation, where La Nada Means
grew up, there is a plaque which commemorates the appearance in 1834
of the first white traders and indicates that the Hudson Bay Company
later acquired the Fort and made it into an important stopover on the
Oregon Trail. But other aspects of the history of Fort Hall are left un-
mentioned. It is not noted, for instance, that by the time a formal treaty
was signed with the Bannock and Northern Shoshone in 1868, the whites
who settled this part of Southern Idaho were paying between $25 and
$100 for a good Indian scalp.

Today, the approximately 2,800 Shoshone-Bannocks live on the
520,000-acre reservation, all that remains of the 1.8 million acres of their
land which the treaty originally set aside for their ancestors to keep. The
largest single reduction came in 1900, when the government took over
416,000 acres, paying the Indians a little more than $1 an acre for the
land. As late as the beginning of World War II, the government took
over another 3,000 acres to make an airfield. It paid the Indians $10 an
acre; after the war, it deeded the land to the city of Pocatello for $1 an
acre, for use as a municipal airport. Each acre is now worth $500.

But the big problem on the Fort Hall reservation today is not the
loss of large sections of land; rather it is the slow and steady attrition of
Indian holdings and their absolute powerlessness to do anything about it.
In 1887, the Dawes Allotment Act was passed as a major piece of "progressive" Indian legislation, providing for the break-up of community-
held reservation land so that each individual Indian would receive his plot
of irrigable farming land and some grazing land. The federal government
would still hold the land in trust, so it could be sold only with BIA
approval, the assumption being that an individual holding would give the
Indian incentive to be a farmer and thus ease him into American agricultural patterns. Fort Hall shows that the law had quite different effects.

Today, some of these original allotments are owned by anywhere
from two to 40 heirs. Because of the complexity of kinship relationships,
some Indian people own fractional interests in several of these "heirship
lands" but have no ground that is all their own. These lands are one of
the symbols of the ambiguity and inertia that rule at Fort Hall. As
Edward Boyer, a former chairman of the tribal council, says, "Some of
the people, they might want to exchange interests in the land or buy some
of the other heirs out so they can have a piece of ground to build a house
on and do some farming. Also, a lot of us would like the tribe to buy these
lands up and then assign them to the young people who don't have any
place of their own. But the BIA has this policy of leasing out these lands

to the white farmers. A lot of the time the owners don't even know about it."

The BIA at Fort Hall doesn't like the idea of any Indian lands laying idle. And the land is rich, some of the best potato-growing land there is. Its value and its yield are increasing every year. Driving through the reservation, you can't avoid being struck by the green symmetry of the long cultivated rows and by the efficiency of the army of men and machinery working them. The only trouble is that the men are white, and the profits from Fort Hall's rich land all flow out of the Indian community. The BIA is like any technocracy: it is more interested in "efficient" use than in proper use. The most "efficient" way for Fort Hall's lands to be used is by white industrialist-farmers with capital. Thus the pattern has been established: white lessees using Indian land, irrigating with Indian water, and then harvesting with bracero workers.

All leases must be approved by the BIA superintendent's office; they may be and are given without the consent of the Indians who own the land. The BIA has also allowed white lessees to seek "consents" from the Indians, which in effect provide for blank leases, the specific terms to be filled in later on. The BIA authorizes extremely long leases of the land. This leads to what a recent field study of Fort Hall, conducted by the Senate Subcommittee on Indian Education, calls "small fortunes" for white developers:

> One non-Indian in 1964 leased a large tract of Indian land for 13 years at $.30–$.50/acre/year. While the lease did stipulate that once the lessee installed sprinkler irrigation the annual rent would rise to $1.50–$2.00/acre, Indians in 1968 could have demanded $20–$30 for such land. Meanwhile, the independent University Agriculture Extension Service estimates that such potato operations bring the non-Indian lessee an annual *net* profit of $200 per acre.

In addition, these leases are usually given by the BIA on a non-competitive, non-bidding basis to assure "the good will of the surrounding community." Fort Hall has rich and loamy land, but Indian people now work less than 17 per cent of it themselves and the figure is declining.

The power of white farmer-developers and businessmen within the local Bureau of Indian Affairs office is a sore point with most people at Fort Hall. They have rich lands, but theirs is one of the poorest reservations. They are told that much revenue comes both to the tribe and to individuals as a result of the BIA farm and mine leasing program, yet they know that if all the revenues were divided up the yield would be about $300 per capita a year. But for some of them, men like Joseph "Frank" Thorpe, Jr., the question of farming and mining leases is academic. Thorpe was a successful cattleman until BIA policies cut down the herds; now he is in the business of letting other people's cattle graze on his land.

Livestock are something of a fixation with Thorpe. He comes from a people who were proud horsemen, and he owns an Apaloosa mare and a couple of other horses. As he drives over the reservation, he often stops to look at others' cattle. In the basement of his home are several scrap-books filled with documents tracing the destruction of the cattle business at Fort Hall. There is a yellowing clipping from the Salt Lake City *Tribune* of November 4, 1950, which says: "Fort Hall Indians have been more successful in cattle raising than any other activity. Theirs is the oldest Indian Cattleman's Association in the country. Association members raise more than 10,000 head of purebred herefords, and plan gradually to increase the herd. . . ." That was how it was 20 years ago. Thorpe, just back from war-time duty with the Marines, worked his herd and provided jobs for many of his kinsmen; the future was promising. Yet by 1958, there were only 3,000 head of Indian-owned cattle left, and today there are only ten families still involved in full-time cattle operation.

"Around the early '50's," Thorpe says, "the BIA decided that the Indians who'd been using tribal grazing lands without paying a grazing fee were going to be charged. The BIA also made us cattle people set up a sinking fund to pay grazing fees in advance. The bills just got higher and higher, and pretty soon we found we had to start selling off our seed stock to pay them."

Less than 30 per cent of all Fort Hall Indians are permanently em-ployed today. Men like Frank Thorpe once had a going business that harked back to the old times and also provided jobs on the reservation. The BIA had decided that the best use for Fort Hall land was farming; it removed the Indians' cattle from trust status, which meant they could be sold, and began the accelerated program of leasing Indian lands to whites that is still in effect today.

Thorpe spends a good deal of time driving his dust-covered station wagon along the reservation's unpaved roads. A former tribal chairman, he spends much time checking up on the BIA and trying to function as a sort of ombudsman. He drives slowly down the dirt highways where magpies pick at the remains of rabbits slaughtered by cars. He points out where white farmers have begun to crop-dust their leased fields from air-planes. "The game, rabbits and pheasants and all, is disappearing," he says. "Our Indian people here rely on them for food, but the animals are dying out because of the sprays. And sometimes our kids get real sick. These sprays, they drift over and get in the swimming holes. The kids get real bad coughs and sometimes rashes all over their bodies."

Near the BIA agency office on the reservation sits a squat, weathered concrete building. "That's the old blouse factory," he says. "The BIA cooked up this deal where some outfit from Salt Lake City came in here to start a garment plant. The tribe put up the money for the factory, about $30,000, and in return the Salt Lake people were going to hire Indians and train them to sew. It lasted for about a year, and now we've still got the building. The last few years, they've used it to store the government surplus food that a lot of Indians get."

The old blouse factory is one symbol of the despair that has seized Fort Hall. Thorpe points out another one nearby. It is known as a "hold-ing center," and it is a place for Fort Hall Indians who are suspected of being suicidal. The reservation has one of the highest suicide rates in the nation. Last year there were 35 attempts mostly among the 18–25 age group. Many of them occurred in the nearby Blackfoot City Jail.

Blackfoot town authorities, embarrassed by the number of Indian suicides which have occurred in their jail, now use the holding facility at Fort Hall. It is headed by John Bopp, a former Navy man who is the public health officer on the reservation. "I guess kids here just feel that their future is cut off," he says. "A lot of them are dropouts and rejects from schools. They look around and see their elders pretty downtrodden. They get angry, but the only thing they can do is take it out on themselves. From reading some of their suicide notes, I'd say that they see it as an honorable way out of a bad situation."

"The young people," says Thorpe, "they're our only hope. They've got to clean things up here. But a lot of our young guys, they've just given up." The human resources at Fort Hall, like the land, seem to be slipping away. The best interpretation that could be placed on the BIA's role in it all is to use the words of a teacher at nearby Idaho State College who says that they are "guardians of the poorhouse."

There are other reservations that seem to be in better shape. One is the mammoth Navajo reservation, whose 25,000 square miles reach into portions of Arizona, New Mexico, Utah and Colorado. On the one hand, it too is a place of despair: many of the 120,000 Navajos live in shocking poverty, doing a little subsistence farming and sheep-raising, suffering severe discrimination when they go outside the reservation for a job, and being preyed upon by the white traders and the exotic diseases which infest the reservation. But it is also a place of hope: Navajo land is rich in resources—coal, oil, uranium and other minerals—and the tribe gets about $30 million a year from rents and royalties. While this would come to less than $1,000 a year if distributed to each family, the Navajos have tried, and to some extent succeeded, in using it as seed money to begin a small but growing series of tribal industries—a sawmill, a handcrafts center, a tourist motel—which provide valuable jobs and income organized around the tribal community.

Private enterprise has also come onto the reservation, epitomized by the large Fairchild Industries plant. There has been much discussion of giving tax incentives to get industry to locate on reservations all over the country, but in general little has come of it. Of an estimated 10,000 jobs opened up by industries on Indian lands, more than half of them have been filled by whites. On the Navajo reservation, however, the tribe has seen to it that practically all the employees hired are Indian, and it seems like a good beginning. Everything there, in fact, appears to be on the upswing; the Navajos seem to be the one tribe that is beginning to solve its problems. This, however, is an oversimplification.

As far as private enterprise is concerned, the plants are mainly defense-oriented: they use federal money for job training and then work on a cost-plus basis. In effect, the government is underwriting private profit, when the same money could have gone into setting up community businesses. The Navajos do get about 1,000 jobs, but they are generally low-paying and are given to women, thus destroying the ecology of the Indian family.

Roughly the same thing applies to the rapid development of their natural resources. The way in which these resources are exploited —be it strip-mining or otherwise—depends on the desires of the businesses exploiting them, not on what the Navajos want or need. One result is that the Navajos have no way of planning the development of resources for their own future needs as a community. Navajos get royalties, but private concerns off the reservation get the profits (as well as the depletion allowances, though it is Navajo resources which are being depleted). Indian people have often brought up the possibility of joint economic development of their reservation with the help of private firms. This is always rejected by the BIA, which has an age-old bias against "socialistic" tribal enterprise as well as a very contemporary regard for big business.

The Navajos are seemingly doing well, but their environment is in the hands of others who are interested only in revenue, and not in the Indians' future. The Navajos are thankful, however, for short-term gains, which most tribes don't have; and they have no choice but to leave tomorrow up to the BIA. As anthropologist David Aberle has pointed out,

> Let us suppose that we cut a cross-section through the reservation territory . . . and make a rapid-motion picture of the flow of population, money and resources. . . . We would see oil, helium, coal, uranium, and vanadium draining off into the surrounding economy; we would see rents and royalties flowing into the tribal treasury, but, of course, major profits accruing to the corporations exploiting the reservation. We would see the slow development of roads, water for stock and drinking, government facilities, and so forth, and a flow of welfare funds coming in, to go out again via the trader. The net flow of many physical resources would be outward; the flow of profits would be outward; and the only major increases to be seen would be population, with a minor increment in physical facilities and consumer goods. This is the picture of a colony.

The BIA is an easy organization to whip. Its abuses are flagrant, and the Indians it is charged with protecting are in great jeopardy. But if places like the Navajo reservation resemble a colony, the BIA is no more than a corps of colonial officers whose role is not to make policy but rather to carry it out. It is impossible not to feel that the Bureau itself has, over the years, taken on the most outstanding feature of the Indians it administers: their utter lack of power. It could make life on the reservation less complicated and cruel and establish some provisions for the Indians' cultural future, but it could never solve the larger issues that lie behind federal Indian policy. The BIA is only a unit within the Department of Interior, and not a very important one at that—certainly nothing like the powerful Bureaus of Land Management and Reclamation. It is the Department of Interior itself which is involved in the big power moves in Indian affairs. As trustees both for the Indians' private trust lands and for public trust lands, it is involved in an irremediable conflict of interest which it solves by taking from the red man's vanishing domains.

> *It can be said without overstatement that when the Indians were put on these reservations they were not considered to be located in the most desirable area of the Nation. It is impossible to believe that when Congress created the great Colorado River Indian reservation . . . they were unaware that most of the lands were of the desert kind—hot, scorching sands—and that water from the river would be essential to the life of the Indian people. . . .*
>
>   CALIFORNIA VS. ARIZONA

The Navajo reservation is mainly arid, and alkaline deposits gather at the foot of the small hills like snowdrifts. Here, as on other reservations, water is a precious asset, and groundwater is minimal. And when the tribal council recently almost gave away the Navajos' rights to the Colorado River, it didn't do so willingly or with forethought; it was conned.

The population of the Colorado River Basin has exploded during this century, and there has been much feuding among the various states over water. The 1922 Colorado River Compact apportioned the Colorado River water between the Upper Basin states (Colorado, Utah, Wyoming, New Mexico and Arizona) and those of the Lower Basin (California, Nevada and, again, Arizona). After the Supreme Court water decision of 1963, Arizona conceived an ingenious plan to use the water it had been allotted: the annual 50,000 acre-feet of Upper Basin it had been awarded would be used for power to pump its Lower Basin water (2.8 million acre-feet per year) into the gigantic Central Arizona Project, thus irrigating much of the state and providing for its industrial development. The only thing standing in the way of this plan was the Navajos.

Water rights are one of the few Indian prerogatives laid out in clear judicial terms. They are considered an intrinsic part of the reservation the Indians occupy, and the so-called Winters Doctrine, most recently validated in *California vs. Arizona*, specifies that Indians have priority in the use of waters adjacent to, surrounding or underneath their land, and that upstream and downstream non-Indian users can have only that which is left over after Indian needs are fulfilled. These rights are guaranteed, and not subject to some "use it or lose it" free for all.

The Navajos have never yet asserted a claim to the Colorado River because their underdevelopment has not required it. But if and when they do, most water lawyers feel that their award could be very large, especially since a much smaller group of Indian tribes on the lower Colorado was awarded one million annual acre-feet in 1963 in *California vs. Arizona*. The Navajos could, in fact, probably get enough of the Colorado to turn their reservation into an oasis. For this reason, and because their potential rights could destroy Arizona's plan for using the water it had been awarded (not to mention the whole basis for the apportionment of water among the Upper and Lower Basin states), the Navajo tribal council was persuaded, in December 1968, to waive virtually all rights to the river "for the lifetime of the [pumping] plant, or for the next 50 years, whichever occurs first." In return for passing this resolution, the council received some minor considerations, including a $125,000 grant for its new Navajo Community College. The deal was presented casually as an administrative courtesy with adequate compensation, and the tribe was not aware of what lay behind it.

Actually, the Navajos were caught in the middle of some high-level maneuvers. Wayne Aspinal, congressman from Colorado and chairman of the House Subcommittee on Interior and Insular Affairs, had made it clear to the Department of Interior that he would kill legislation funding the Central Arizona Project unless this waiver of the Navajos' Upper Basin Claim—which could affect his own state—was obtained. By the same token, then Secretary of the Interior Stuart Udall was committed to the Central Arizona Project, which, among other things, would benefit his own home state. Thus it was he who had the resolution drafted and sent to the tribal council via the local BIA superintendent's office.

All of this would probably have gone unchallenged, perhaps to be discovered several years later, if it hadn't been for the OEO-funded legal rights organization on the reservation. This group, the DNA (the acronym derived from the Navajo phrase meaning "economic revitalization of the people"), has been a constant irritation to those who are accustomed to raiding Navajo resources, and it has earned both a large grassroots following and the enmity of the BIA-influenced tribal hierarchy. The DNA found out about the politics behind the waiver last spring, documented its implication for the Navajos' future, and by early summer was able to persuade the tribal council to rescind its resolution.

The Fort Mojaves of California are currently involved in another fight related to the Colorado River. They have learned, over the last few months, the truth of the maxim widely quoted in California parapolitics: "Water is the name of the game." The Fort Mojaves woke up one morning to find that the state of California, working in concert with the Interior Department's Bureau of Land Management, had swindled them out of 1,500 acres of invaluable river frontage.

The state had had its eyes on this acreage for many years. It first tried to grab it in 1910, using provisions of the Swamp and Overflow Act of 1850 (which allows swampland created by a river to be placed under state jurisdiction). This initial attempt failed, as did others over the years. Then, early in 1967, the state, supported by the Bureau of Land Management, finally succeeded in obtaining the land, again citing the Swamp and Overflow Act because its regular powers of eminent domain did not apply to tribal land. The Mojaves didn't even know that hearings on the matter were taking place; they found out that their land had been confiscated only several months afterward, and then it was by accident.

The acreage claimed by California is clearly too high to have ever been a swamp. Moreover, in 1850, when the Swamp and Overflow Act applied, the wild Colorado River's course ran nowhere near the 1,500 supposedly swampy acres, having been "channelized" into its present regular course only in the early 1940's. Independent hydrologists' studies have proven conclusively that the contested area was never part of the river bed.

The state is driven to assert fraudulent claims to land in this apparently low-value desert area, just as Interior is bound to back them up, because of their fear that the Mojaves will develop the area. Private developers are eager to come in: they feel that the Colorado River area will become invaluable, especially as Southern California's population spills outward in search of recreation space. Indian water rights are the prime water rights and developers know that even if there is a water shortage, the Indians will get their allotment first because of the Winters Doctrine, spelled out in *California vs. Arizona.*

The state of California and the Bureau of Land Management, reacting to pressure from the powerful Metropolitan Water District of Southern California, do not want this development to take place, even though it is a key to the Indians' future survival. They fear a water shortage and they are fighting it in the easiest way—by confiscating the prior water rights attached to Indian land out of the Indians' hands.

The Earth is our Mother, and we cannot sell our Mother.

IROQUOIS SAYING

Behind the machinations of the BIA and the grander larcenies of the Department of Interior stands the Indians' final enemy, that vague sense of doom called federal policy. It has always been sinister, and no less so today than in the days when Indian tribes were nearly annihilated by the white man's gifts of blankets saturated in smallpox. The current mode of attack began in the 1950's, with by far the most ominous title in the lexicon of Indian affairs: termination. Its objectives were stated innocuously in a 1953 act of Congress:

> It is the policy of Congress, as rapidly as possible to make the Indians within the United States subject to the same privileges and responsibilities as are applicable to other citizens of the United States, to end their status as wards of the United States, and to grant them all of the rights and prerogatives pertaining to American citizenship. . . .

Cultural assassination always comes cloaked in such altruisms, and the crucial phrase, "to end their status as wards of the United States," was neatly circumscribed by florid rhetoric. But that phrase was the heart of the resolution, and its impact was disastrous.

Over the last two decades, the Indian has learned that he must fear most those who want to eliminate the Bureau of Indian Affairs and who make pompous statements about it being time "for this country to get out of the Indian business." A hundred and fifty years ago, perhaps, attaining such equilibrium with the red man would have been laudable; but America got into the Indian business for good when it stole a continent and put its inhabitants in land-locked jails. While the Indian knows that the BIA works against him most of the time, he also realizes its symbolic value as the embodiment of promises made in the treaties which secure his land and culture. Indian people and lands have been, and continue to be, terribly damaged by their relationship to the federal government. But their federal trust status guarantees their Indian-ness. And if it is terminated, they know there will be nothing left to mismanage.

The reservations which were actually terminated as a result of this sudden shift in federal policy in the '50's provide ample warning. The Minominees of Wisconsin, for instance, whose termination began in 1854 and was completed in 1961, had a stable pattern of life which was destroyed. They owned a thriving tribally run sawmill. They had a hospital and other community services; they had a fairly large tribal bank account. Then came termination, which made the Minominees citizens of Wisconsin and nothing more. The hospital had to close down because it didn't meet state standards; the tribal bank account was doled out to the tribesmen in per capita payments, which were quickly dissipated. The sawmill became a corporation and floundered because of mismanagement, thereby no longer providing the Minominees with jobs. The Indians were supposed to become just like everyone else in Wisconsin, but today they still stand apart as among the poorest people in the state. Much of their land, which was not taxable when held in trust, has been sold at forced auctions to make up defaulted state property taxes.

Another classic case of termination is that of the Klamaths of Oregon. As part of the proceedings in 1954, their richly forested reservation was sold off and the receipts distributed equally among enrolled members of the tribe. The payout came to over $40,000 per person, and even before it was made the predators began to descend, offering high-interest loans and a treasure house of consumer goods. A few years after termination was accomplished, many of the Klamaths were destitute and on welfare; they had no land left, no money and no future. As one member of the tribe said, "My grandchildren won't have anything, not even the right to call themselves Indian."

Because of the disasters it caused, termination is now "voluntary," although the Congressional resolution which authorized it has yet to be rescinded. Temporarily, at least, it has taken a backseat to the New Frontierish strategies like luring private enterprise onto the reservation and allocating meager OEO funds. However, today there are still tribes in the process of termination—several small ones in California and the Colvilles of Washington—and no attempt is made to stop the misinformation given Indians about the benefits that will result from such an option. Nor will termination ever disappear for good until Indians hold in their own hands the life and death powers over their communities which others now wield. Every time an Indian is "successfully" relocated in a city far from his people, it is a kind of termination, as it is when a plot of ground or the rights to water slip out of his hands. It is not necessary for Indian people to have Secretary of Interior Hickel tell them that they should "cut the cord" that binds them to their reservation to know that termination exists as the final solution to the Indian Problem.

> *He is dispossessed in life, and unforgiving. He doesn't believe in us and our civilization, and so he is our mystic enemy, for we push him off the face of the earth.*
>
> D. H. LAWRENCE

Strangled in bureaucracy, swindled out of lands, forcibly alienated from his own culture, the Indian continues to be victimized by the white man's symbolism: he has been both loved and hated to death. On the one hand, the white looked out at him from his own constricted universe of acquisition and grasping egocentrism and saw a Noble Savage, an innocent at peace with his world. Here was a relic of a better time, to be protected and preserved. But on the other hand the white saw an uncivilized creature possessing, but not exploiting, great riches; the vision was conjured up of the Murdering Redskin whose bestiality provided the justification for wiping him out and taking his land. The Indian's "plight" has always inspired recurrent orgies of remorse, but never has it forced us to digest the implications of a nation and culture conceived in genocide. We act as if the blood-debt of the past cannot be canceled until the Indian has no future; the guiltier he has made us, the more frantic have been the attempts to make him disappear.

Yet, having paid out almost everything he has, the Indian has survived the long exercise in white schizophrenia. And there are some, like Hopi mystic Thomas Banyaka, who give out prophecies that the red man will still be here long after whites have been destroyed in a holocaust of their own making.

Suggestions for Further Reading

The revolt of the victims of American history reached early milestones with the 1954 Supreme Court decision against the racial segregation of schools, the Montgomery, Alabama, bus boycott of 1955, and the black student sit-ins of 1960. On the Supreme Court decision and the nation's subsequent failure to implement it, see the book by Anthony Lewis and *The New York Times*, entitled *Portrait of a Decade: The Second American Revolution** (Random House, 1964). Martin Luther King, Jr., tells the story of the bus boycott in *Stride Toward Freedom: The Montgomery Story** (Harper and Row, 1958). The sit-ins are described by Howard Zinn in *SNCC: The New Abolitionists** (Beacon, 1964). In *The Negro Revolt** (Harper and Row, 1962), Louis Lomax describes the background of the revolt that broke out in the late 1950's and early 1960's.

An increasingly problematic question in this age of revolt is the place of violence in American history. A valuable collection of essays on violence prepared for the President's Commission on the Causes and Prevention of Violence is Hugh Davis Graham and Ted Robert Gurr (eds.), *Violence in America: Historical and Comparative Perspectives** (2 vols.; U.S. Government Printing Office, 1969), also available in one-volume paperbound editions from New American Library and Bantam. Richard Hofstadter and Michael Wallace are the editors of *American Violence: A Documentary History** (Knopf, 1970), which contains a long and very useful introductory essay by Hofstadter. A good collection of essays on contemporary violence is Shalom Endleman (ed.), *Violence in the Streets** (Quadrangle, 1968).

The changes in the mood of the black revolt as it moved from nonviolence to self-defense are described in two excellent articles: Allen J. Matusow, "From Civil Rights to Black Power: The Case of SNCC, 1960–1966," in Barton J. Bernstein and Allen J. Matusow (eds.), *Twentieth-Century America: Recent Interpretations** (Harcourt Brace Jovanovich, 1969), pp. 531–57, and Vincent Harding, "Black Radicalism: The Road from Montgomery," in Alfred F. Young (ed.), *Dissent: Explorations in the History of American Radicalism** (Northern Illinois University Press, 1968), pp. 321–54. See Julius Lester, *Look Out Whitey! Black Power's Gon' Get Your Mama** (Dial, 1968), for another treatment of the same topic.

Charles E. Silberman, in *Crisis in Black and White** (Random House, 1964), provides an excellent study of the background to the racial explosions that took place in Northern cities in the mid-1960's. In *Dark Ghetto: Dilemmas of Social Power** (Harper and

* Available in paperback edition.

Row, 1965), Kenneth Clark explores the psychological aspects of life in a black ghetto. Claude Brown is concerned with many of the same themes in his autobiographical *Manchild in the Promised Land** (Macmillan, 1965). Novelist and essayist James Baldwin describes the mood of black people on the eve of the urban insurrections in *The Fire Next Time** (Dial, 1963). Robert Conot's excellent *Rivers of Blood, Years of Darkness** (Bantam, 1967) describes the background and the foreground of the Watts rebellion of 1965. The conditions of urban ghetto life that lead to violent outbreaks are explored in Paul Jacobs, *Prelude to Riot: A View of Urban America from the Bottom** (Random House, 1966).

The ideas and impact of Malcolm X, whose legacy inspires several strands of contemporary black protest, are explored in *The Autobiography of Malcolm X** (Grove, 1964); George Breitman (ed.), *Malcolm X Speaks** (Merit, 1965); and John Henrik Clarke (ed.), *Malcolm X: The Man and His Times** (Macmillan, 1969).

Bobby Seale, a founder of the Black Panther party, tells the story of this organization in *Seize the Time: The Story of the Black Panther Party and Huey P. Newton** (Random House, 1970). A useful collection of statements by Panther leaders is Philip F. Foner (ed.), *The Black Panthers Speak** (Lippincott, 1970).

On white racism, see Gary B. Nash and Richard Weiss (eds.), *The Great Fear: Race in the Mind of America** (Holt, Rinehart and Winston, 1970); Thomas F. Gossett, *Race: The History of an Idea in America** (Southern Methodist University Press, 1963); and Joel Kovel, *White Racism: A Psychohistory**(Pantheon, 1970).

For an introduction to various groups discussed in this section, see John R. Howard (ed.), *The Awakening Minorities: American Indians, Mexican-Americans, Black Americans and Puerto Ricans** (Aldine, 1970).

The history of the Mexican-American is told in Carey McWilliams, *North from Mexico** (Lippincott, 1949), and in Manuel P. Servín (ed.), *The Mexican-Americans: An Awakening Minority** (Glencoe, 1970). The contemporary situation of America's chicanos is explored in Julian Samora (ed.), *La Raza: Forgotten Americans** (University of Notre Dame Press, 1966), and in Stan Steiner, *La Raza: The Mexican Americans** (Harper and Row, 1970). Peter Nabokov tells the story of the Alianza in *Tijerina and the Courthouse Raid**(University of New Mexico Press, 1969). The California grape-pickers' strike led by Cesar Chavez is described in John Gregory Dunne, *Delano** (Farrar, Straus and Giroux, 1967), and in Peter Matthiessen, *Sal Si Puedes: Cesar Chavez and the New American Revolution** (Random House, 1969).

On the Puerto Ricans in the United States, see Oscar Handlin, *The Newcomers: Negroes and Puerto Ricans in a Changing*

*Metropolis** (Harvard University Press, 1959); Clarence Senior, *The Puerto Ricans: Strangers—Then Neighbors** (Quadrangle, 1961); and Patricia Cayo Sexton, *Spanish Harlem** (Harper and Row, 1965). A more personal view of Puerto Rican life in this country is presented in Piri Thomas' autobiographical *Down These Mean Streets** (Knopf, 1967) and in Oscar Lewis' *La Vida: A Puerto Rican Family in the Culture of Poverty—San Juan and New York** (Random House, 1967).

The current women's liberation movement began with the publication of *The Feminine Mystique** (Norton, 1963), by Betty Friedan. A study that offers a good deal of insight into the problems of women in America is Robert J. Lifton (ed.), *The Woman in America** (Beacon, 1967), first published in the spring 1964 issue of *Daedalus*. Kate Millett's *Sexual Politics* (Doubleday, 1970) is a provocative analysis of the literary sources of male supremacy. Two important collections of essays on male-female relationships are Robin Morgan (ed.), *Sisterhood Is Powerful: An Anthology of Writings from the Women's Liberation Movement** (Random House, 1970), and Betty Roszak and Theodore Roszak (eds.), *Masculine/Feminine: Readings in Sexual Mythology and the Liberation of Women** (Harper and Row, 1969).

For the history of Indian-white relations in the United States, see William T. Hagan, *American Indians** (University of Chicago Press, 1961). Also useful is the collection of documents edited by Wilcomb E. Washburn, *The Indian and the White Man** (Doubleday, 1964). Two good introductions to Indian life and culture are Alvin M. Josephy, Jr., *The Indian Heritage of America** (Knopf, 1968), and Peter Farb, *Man's Rise to Civilization as Shown by the Indians of North America from Primeval Times to the Coming of the Industrial State** (Dutton, 1968). The story of the white man's conquest of the Western Indians in the late nineteenth century is told by Dee Brown in *Bury My Heart at Wounded Knee: An Indian History of the American West* (Holt, Rinehart and Winston, 1971).

The current revolt among young Indians is described by Stan Steiner in *The New Indians** (Harper and Row, 1968). Vine Deloria, Jr., a Standing Rock Sioux, has challenged American history in *Custer Died for Your Sins: An Indian Manifesto** (Macmillan, 1969). A stimulating symposium on the contemporary Indian is Stuart Levine and Nancy O. Lurie (eds.), *The American Indian Today** (Everett-Edwards, 1968), originally published in the fall 1965 issue of *Mid-Continent American Studies Journal*. Three novels that offer perhaps the best means of understanding the cultural conflict faced by American Indians today are Frank Waters, *The Man Who Killed the Deer** (Holt, Rinehart and Winston, 1942); Hal Borland, *When the Legends Die** (Lippincott, 1963); and N. Scott Momaday, *House Made of Dawn** (Harper and Row, 1968).